Making Japanese Citizens

Making Japanese Citizens

Civil Society and the Mythology of the
Shimin *in Postwar Japan*

Simon Andrew Avenell

UNIVERSITY OF CALIFORNIA PRESS
Berkeley · Los Angeles · London

University of California Press, one of the most
distinguished university presses in the United States,
enriches lives around the world by advancing
scholarship in the humanities, social sciences, and
natural sciences. Its activities are supported by the UC
Press Foundation and by philanthropic contributions
from individuals and institutions. For more
information, visit www.ucpress.edu.

Parts of chapter 1 appeared previously in "From the
'People' to the 'Citizen': Tsurumi Shunsuke and the
Roots of Civic Mythology in Postwar Japan," in
positions: east asia cultures critique 16, no. 3 (Winter
2008): 711–42. Copyright 2008, Duke University
Press. Reprinted by permission of the publisher. Parts
of chapter 5 appeared previously in "Civil Society and
the New Civic Movements in Contemporary Japan:
Convergence, Collaboration, and Transformation,"
Journal of Japanese Studies 35, no. 2 (Summer 2009):
247–83. Copyright 2009, Society for Japanese Studies.
Reprinted by permission of the publisher.

University of California Press
Berkeley and Los Angeles, California

University of California Press, Ltd.
London, England

Library of Congress Cataloging-in-Publication Data

Avenell, Simon Andrew.
    Making Japanese citizens : civil society and the
mythology of the shimin in postwar Japan / Simon
Andrew Avenell.
        p.   cm.
    Includes bibliographical references and index.
    ISBN 978-0-520-26270-6 (cloth : alk. paper)—
    ISBN 978-0-520-26271-3 (pbk. : alk. paper)
        1. Citizenship—Japan.   2. Civil society—Japan.
3. Political activists—Japan.   4. Japan—Politics
and government—1945–   I. Title.
    JQ1681.A94   2010
    323.60952—dc22   2010008308

Manufactured in the United States of America

19   18   17   16   15   14   13   12   11   10
10   9   8   7   6   5   4   3   2   1

This book is printed on Cascades Enviro 100, a 100%
post consumer waste, recycled, de-inked fiber. FSC
recycled certified and processed chlorine free. It is acid
free, Ecologo certified, and manufactured by BioGas
energy.

Contents

Illustrations

Acknowledgments

First and foremost I thank my wife and family for their patience and encouragement as I researched and wrote the book. I am particularly grateful to my wife for supporting my move from the financial world to academia.

Many individuals have facilitated and enriched this research. M. William Steele sparked my interest in Japanese history and directed my attention to grassroots thought and activism while I was at the International Christian University. He also offered generous institutional support as I made numerous research trips back to Japan. Andrew Barshay and Irwin Scheiner were constant pillars of support from the very outset of the project. They provided both intellectual and financial sustenance during my years at the University of California, Berkeley; they read numerous drafts at the dissertation stage; and they generously critiqued various versions of this book. My ideas about Japan have been deeply shaped by both of them. Thanks to Thomas Havens, whose door at the East Asian Library at Berkeley was always open, and who spent countless hours discussing my project and providing advice. I am equally grateful to Steven Vogel and Nobuhiro Hiwatari for introducing me to the political science literature on Japan and to Setsuo Miyazawa for his guidance on the study of Japanese law. Steven Vogel, in particular, provided invaluable feedback on my work, especially with respect to issues of causality and the tension between institutional and ideational approaches. He also offered a thoughtful and extremely valuable critique from a political science perspective. Thanks also to the late Reginald Zelnik, historian of Russia, and to Waldo Martin, historian of the African American experience. Elements of this book (especially chapters 2 and 3) would not have been possible without the knowledge I gained from them about Marxist thought and the civil rights movement, respectively. I am eternally grateful to Japanese sociologist Kurihara Akira, who spent countless Monday afternoons introducing me to theories and case studies on Japanese social movements and civic groups. Professor Kurihara also graciously facilitated meetings with many of the activists and intellectuals discussed in the book. Many thanks also to Fujibayashi Yasushi for guiding me through the wealth of movement newsletters at the Center for Education and Research in Cooperative Human Relations.

Thanks to Reed Malcolm at the University of California Press for his encouragement, support, and optimism from the outset and to Kalicia Pivirotto and Jacqueline Volin for patiently guiding me through the book production process. I am especially grateful to Robin Whitaker for her thoughtful, thorough, and wholly enlightening editing work on the book.

Robert Pekkanen provided unwavering encouragement and constructive critique as I researched and wrote the book. His openness to my approach and his faith in my potential intellectual contribution were constant sources of motivation. His meticulous comments on the penultimate draft, together with those of an anonymous reviewer for the UC Press, were nothing short of intellectual gold. Robert, more than any other, pushed me to clarify and articulate the central thesis of the book, which I hope I've done.

Others who have provided invaluable assistance or intellectual input along the way include Daniel Aldrich, Timothy Amos, Mary Elizabeth Berry, Steve Blom, Luke Franks, Fujita Kazuyoshi, Curtis Anderson Gayle, Mary Alice Haddad, Harima Yasuo, Laura Hein, J. Victor Koschmann, Marilyn Lund, Vera Mackie, Gavan McCormack, Stuart Picken, Sue Pryn, Wesley Sasaki-Uemura, Naoko Shimazu, Patricia Sippel, Patricia Steinhoff, Takami Yūichi, Terada Takashi, Thang Leng Leng, Timothy Tsu, Tsujinaka Yutaka, Paul Waley, Watanabe Gen, Brad Williams, and Yoshikawa Yūichi.

I am indebted to the following institutions for assistance and support: the Center for Japanese Studies and the Department of History at UC Berkeley; the Institute of Asian Cultural Studies at the International Christian University, Japan; the Faculty of Law at the University of

Tokyo; the Japanese Ministry of Education, Culture, Sports, Science, and Technology; the Toyota Foundation; the Hitachi Foundation; the Daiwa-Anglo Japanese Foundation; the Asian Research Institute (ARI) and the Faculty of Arts and Social Sciences (FASS) at the National University of Singapore; and the National Consumer Affairs Center of Japan.

Introduction

Here *citizen* does not mean the resident of an administrative
unit such as prefecture, city, town, or village. Nor does it
refer to a specific stratum such as the petit bourgeoisie.
Citizen means a spontaneous type of human shaped by a
"republican" spirit of freedom and equality. . . . Of course,
citizenship is not a godlike existence. It is nothing more than
we ordinary people with all our joy and anger.

—Matsushita Keiichi, 1971

WHO IS A *SHIMIN*?

Who is a citizen and how is citizenship expressed? Is it all about
qualification, or is citizenship just as much a performance—as much
doing as it is being, to borrow from one of Japan's great thinkers?[1] For
Matsushita Keiichi, a local government reformer and author of the
above observation, democratic citizenship certainly depends on the
robustness of institutions, but he also saw citizenship in a performative
way, as a creation of ordinary people engaging in the public sphere and
making politics their own. Such performative citizenship was especially
important for Matsushita and others because its supposed earlier
absence—or, at least, incompleteness—explained for them much of
what had gone wrong in Japanese history from the mid-nineteenth
century onward. It was at once a commentary on failures of the past
(both individual and national) and a prototype for a new national community to be fashioned by ordinary citizens in the present and beyond.
In fact, so important was this concept of performative citizenship for
reformers that they gave it a name: *shimin* (citizen)—a word that spoke
to some of the central aspirations of the Japanese people as they refashioned their nation into a modern liberal democracy in the wake of war
and national humiliation.

The historian Bronislaw Geremek, though he was speaking of citizenship in Poland and Czechoslovakia, succinctly captured the spirit of this *shimin* idea when he observed, the "magic of the word 'citizen' . . . came from the widespread sense that it referred less to one's subordination to the state and its laws than to one's membership in an authentic community, a community whose essence was summed up in the term 'civil society.' "[2] This was very much the case for postwar Japanese activists and progressives: *shimin* encapsulated a vision of individual autonomy beyond the outright control of the state or the established left and within an idealized sphere of human activity they called civil society *(shimin shakai)*. For them, as well as many others, *shimin* became one of the quintessential symbols of liberal democracy in postwar Japan, taking its place beside other powerful motifs such as peace *(heiwa)* and democracy *(minshushugi)*.

This book is a history of the activists, intellectuals, politicians, bureaucrats, and advocates who invoked and deployed the *shimin* idea and the civic movements and public programs in which it found form. I have two aims. First, by retracing key movements of the postwar era I want to show how ideas have affected civic activism and, more broadly, the development of civil society in the country. Leading activists and their ideas, I will argue, helped shape both the mechanics of civic activism and the meanings participants and others attributed to it. Second, I want to use the *shimin* idea and its manifestations in civic movements to scrutinize the motivations and aspirations fueling grassroots activism and progressive politics throughout the period. As I discuss below, a case can be made for understanding postwar civic movements as a Japanese variety of the new social movements (NSMs) prevalent in many advanced industrial nations. I will argue, however, that the NSM approach often obscures more than it explains and that, to truly comprehend the historical significance of postwar civic activism in Japan, we need to move beyond one-dimensional progressive master narratives and carefully unearth the multifaceted, complex, and sometimes troubling motivations underlying it. Put simply, I am interested in both *how* ideas have mattered and *what* those ideas have symbolized and meant for activists and others—especially the *shimin* idea.

Consider first the *how* of the *shimin* idea. Scholarship to date has given us many important insights into the shaping influence of political and economic institutions on these spheres of activity, and indeed, this work confirms such influence.[3] Nevertheless, each of the case studies I present shows how activists used the *shimin* idea and its related concepts to legitimize, encourage, facilitate, or otherwise make action possible.[4] A relatively obscure term for much of modern Japanese history, it was fashioned in the postwar era by activists, intellectuals, and others into a kind of master frame or paradigm for social action and was employed to mobilize, shape, and legitimize a stunning diversity of grassroots civic movements and public policy initiatives.[5] Within civic movements the *shimin* idea informed patterns of decision making, membership, and participation by endorsing nonhierarchical, ideologically plural, small-scale, voluntary mobilizations. On an individual level, the *shimin* idea legitimized spontaneous political action, encouraged autonomy and self-reliance, and promoted active engagement in the public sphere. As an idea, *shimin* proposed a new relationship between individual and state; it made possible a progressive reimagination of the nation; it legitimized the defense of private interest against corporate and political interference; and, most important of all, it infused individual and social action with significance far beyond the specific issues at stake, linking them to an ideal—if protean—vision of a new civil society for a new Japan.

More concretely, I intend to show how the *shimin* idea has fueled and invigorated key civic movements in Japan since the mid-1950s. In the struggle against the U.S.-Japan Security Treaty of 1959–60 (Anpo *tōsō*, the Anpo struggle), activists set the *shimin* idea in motion, using it to mobilize citizens into street protests and, thereafter, into a plethora of local initiatives. In the anti–Vietnam War movement from 1965, the *shimin* idea inspired a broad-based grassroots protest movement, supporting the movement leaders' antistate, anti-U.S. ideology and their belief in Pan-Asian liberationism. In antipollution and antidevelopment protests of the same era, activists used the *shimin* idea to justify regional autonomy and a strategy of localism, while in progressive local governments it informed policies encouraging citizen participation. And, after a period of intense contention between the state and civic groups, beginning in the mid-1970s a new generation of activists and civil society advocates used the *shimin* idea to fashion a communitarian vision of civil society based on collaboration and so-called constructive activism.

In the hands of activists, intellectuals, and other advocates, I argue, the *shimin* idea was rendered into a mythology—what I call the mythology of the *shimin*—not because it was imaginary or somehow fictitious (although it was a plastic idea), but because of what it represented and the kind of action it made possible in the present. As Claude Lévi-Strauss has explained, mythmaking is very much like bricolage,

exactly what the new left

because it "takes to pieces and reconstruct[s] sets of events (on a psy-chical, socio-historical or technical plane) and use[s] them as so many indestructible pieces for structural patterns in which they serve alterna-tively as ends or means."[6] The French syndicalist Georges Sorel simi-larly suggested that the value of myth is not so much "whether it will actually form part of the history of the future" but whether it has the capacity to move people now.[7] For Sorel myth contained the "strongest inclinations of a people, of a party or of a class," and it gave "an aspect of complete reality to the hopes of immediate action upon which the reform of the will is founded."[8] The key here, it seems to me, is the way leading activists actively constructed the mythology of the *shimin* around ideas of spontaneous action, individual autonomy, and democ-racy, and, more important, how their use of this mythology inspired and mobilized participants in public actions with a stamp of authentic-ity. To borrow an idea from the philosopher-activist Tsurumi Shun-suke, the appellation *shimin* became a kind of "talisman" for activism of all kinds during the postwar era.[9] Mobilizing this symbolism—invok-ing the mythology—gave groups legitimacy, because it connected them directly to everything that postwar Japan and its citizenry were sup-posed to, or could potentially, be. So powerful did the *shimin* idea become that simply invoking the term became, in the words of the *shimin* critic Saeki Keishi, a display of the "magnitude" of a person's "political consciousness," almost as though the *shimin* identity imparted a kind of "magical power" *(majutsuteki na chikara)* on those who adopted it.[10]

I begin, then, by showing how the *shimin* idea became important—so magical—for postwar activists and progressives and, more significantly, how it made civic action and social change possible. Following that, I use the *shimin* idea in a more broadly historiographical way to rethink the historical *meanings* of civic activism and thought in the postwar period; in other words, *what* has the *shimin* idea symbolized and meant? I suggest that in activist discourse and scholarship alike, the *shimin* idea, its politics, and its movements have been all too easily slotted into a master narrative of progressive civic movements versus a powerful bureaucracy, a reactionary conservative government, and a rapacious corporate sector.

As I mentioned above, some have explained *shimin* movements as a kind of Japanese permutation of the so-called new social movements prominent in many industrialized nations in the post-1960s decades.[11] According to the theorist Claus Offe, these NSMs are distinguished by their commitment to individual "autonomy" and "identity," their organizational "decentralization," "self-government," and "self-help," and their "opposition to manipulation, control, dependence, bureaucratization, [and] regulation."[12] Alberto Melucci points to the NSMs' critical perspective, which resists "the intrusion of the state and market into social life, reclaiming the individual's identity, and the right to determine his or her private and affective life, against the omnipresent and comprehensive manipulation of the system."[13] I am quite sympathetic to the NSM characterization of *shimin* movements in Japan, especially the emphasis this perspective gives to identity and autonomous action as independent variables in contemporary social activism.

Nevertheless, in this study I purposely step away from both the "*shimin* versus establishment" master narrative and the NSM paradigm, not because I disagree, but because I want to explore historical aspects of the *shimin* idea not adequately captured by such approaches.[14] As John Hoffman notes, though "the new social movements [from the 1960s] can be presented as a way of developing citizenship capacity and responsibility," their focus on activism beyond the state as evident in the thought of Alain Touraine and Alberto Melucci is "curiously conservative,"[15] because it essentially forgoes the all-important task of making "real inroads" into the actual locus of power: the state.[16] Derek Heater articulates a similar concern with the imagination of citizenship in a "civil society" rather than citizenship in a state. Reflecting on developments in the United Kingdom since the 1980s, he notes how "paradoxically, both Right and Left, discarding and despairing of conventional citizenship respectively, turned to civil society. Thatcherites preached the virtues of 'active citizenship,' interpreted as membership of school governing bodies or neighborhood watch schemes," while the young leftists "turned Green, forming and joining groups to challenge the immobility and insensitivity of politicians and bureaucrats." As Heater notes, supporters of civil society "have even celebrated it as a means of beneficially depoliticizing citizenship."[17]

I am particularly interested in how the *shimin* idea has been utilized as a discursive tool for articulations of nationalism, parochial localism, consumerism, and communitarianism. I want to draw attention to the often-troubling connections between the *shimin* idea and deeply racialized notions of ethnic nationalism, as well as the ways both state and nonstate actors have mobilized the idea in recent years to propagate a communitarian, marketized, and largely apolitical vision of civil society. Thus, while acknowledging the significance of the *shimin* idea and postwar civic mobilizations within broader global trends since the 1960s, I also focus my attention on the more direct historical context in which they emerged: the aftermath of war, the manifestations of leftist nationalism, and the transformations wrought by economic growth and affluence. One of the central historical puzzles I explore is how the *shimin* idea and civic activism evolved from a stance of resolute antiestablishmentism in the late 1950s to symbols for self-responsible, noncontentious, participatory citizenship in the Japanese nation by the 1990s. As others have shown, generational changes, new social issues, and institutional pressures all played a role in pushing activism this way, but here I will show how activists and their ideas about the nation, community, and daily life deeply shaped this process.[18]

Put simply, to appreciate the impact of activists' ideas we need to look at all the ideas they have used and not only those that fit into predetermined progressive *or* conservative master narratives. It is not that the "*shimin* versus establishment" or NSM paradigms are wrong but, to paraphrase Roland Barthes, that they tend to smooth out the complexity of postwar civic thought and activism, affording them "the simplicity of essences." The reality, of course, is an extremely complicated field of thought and action.[19] Incorporating this complexity provides a new—if sometimes troubling—perspective on the way grassroots actors and their advocates have expressed agency in Japan's postwar era.

THEORIZING IDEAS: MOVEMENT INTELLECTUALS AND THE MYTHOLOGY OF THE *SHIMIN*

I will use three concepts from social movement theory to guide my historical approach throughout the study: the theory of ideational *framing processes*, the related concept of *collective action frames*, and the notion of *movement intellectuals*. As Sheri Berman notes, "How an idea rises to political prominence does not necessarily reveal anything about how it might entrench itself as a durable factor in political life." To understand this we need to study not only how ideas change but also how they persist: how they become embedded in "organizations, patterns of discourse, and collective identities," outlasting the "original conditions that gave rise to them."[20] Berman's observation neatly encapsulates my approach herein. I am arguing that intellectuals, activists, and civil society advocates played a key role in articulating a civic mythology summed up in the *shimin* idea. This mythology not only expressed the innermost aspirations of those who propagated it but, more significantly, had the power to motivate participation as well as shape behavior within a wide range of civic initiatives throughout the postwar era.

I see the mythology of the *shimin* as akin to the collective action frames and cognitive framing processes conceptualized by social movement theorists such as David Snow and Robert Benford.[21] Summarizing such approaches, McAdam, McCarthy, and Zald note that, while structural factors can tell us much about the conditions under which social movements mobilize and operate, they cannot adequately explain the decisions that social movement actors make. Political opportunities and material resources afford only a "certain structural potential for action," and "mediating between opportunity, organization, and action are the shared meanings people bring to their situation. At a minimum people need to feel both aggrieved about some aspect of their lives and optimistic that, acting collectively, they can redress the problem. Lacking either one or both of these perspectives, it is highly unlikely that people will mobilize."[22] Crucial for scholars working in this theoretical perspective, then, is the core of ideas produced, debated, contested, and put into practice by movement participants—in other words, the collective action frames. Snow and Benford define such ideational framing processes as "an active processual phenomenon that implies agency and contention at the level of reality construction. It is active in the sense that something is being done, and processual in the sense of a dynamic, evolving process. It entails agency in the sense that what is evolving is the work of social movement organizations and activists. And it is contentious in the sense that it involves the generation of interpretive frames that not only differ from existing ones but may also challenge them. The resultant products of this framing activity are referred to as 'collective action frames.'"[23] Snow and Benford see "collective action frames" as "action-oriented sets of beliefs and meanings that inspire and legitimate the activities and campaigns of a social movement organization (SMO)." They "render events or occurrences meaningful and thereby function to organize experience and guide action."[24] The mythology of the *shimin*, I argue, evolved and has functioned similarly in civic movements throughout the postwar period.

Of course, ideas do not spontaneously materialize; they must be articulated by people or collectivities. Snow and Benford, for example, point to "movement actors" who are "actively engaged in the production and maintenance of meaning for constituents, antagonists, and bystanders or observers." The "productive work" of these actors, they explain, "may involve the amplification and extension of extant meanings, the transformation of old meanings, and the generation of new meanings."[25] Modifying Antonio Gramsci's notion of "organic intellectuals," sociologists Ron Eyerman and Andrew Jamison identify a group they call "movement intellectuals." As they explain, "Many, if not all, social movements initially emerge on the basis of some kind of intellectual activity, usually, but not always, carried out by 'established' intellectuals. Intellectuals as social critics often play a crucial role in articulating the concerns of emergent forms of protest, putting them into broader frameworks, giving specific protest actions a deeper meaning or significance."[26] For Eyerman and Jamison movement intellectuals provide "a larger framework of meaning in which individual and collective actions can be understood."[27] Such individuals assist in the "construction of the Other, the opposition, against which the movement is protesting and struggling."[28] Michiel Baud and Rosanne Rutten concretize this definition by suggesting three central characteristics of movement intellectuals. First, they must be "acknowledged as producers of meaning and as representatives of collective interests by a popular group or local society." Second, they must "possess the explicit ambition to transform society and to put into practice their recipes for change." In other words, they "combine reflexive activity with cultural and political activism." And third, they involve a motley crew, including "traditional intellectuals" educated in formal institutions as well as "members of the popular classes and persons who gained their knowledge outside the realm of formal education."[29]

Movement intellectuals are a crucial element in this study. They support my argument that human agency and personality (i.e., the personal history and identity of distinct individuals) have been important in the development of collective action and civil society in postwar Japan. As I show throughout the study, movement intellectuals—university professors, writers, journalists, former socialist or communist party members, former student radicals, local government reformers, environmental activists, grassroots entrepreneurs, and corporate philanthropists—actively used ideas to mobilize participants. Though they by no means had a monopoly on the imagination of the *shimin* idea, their pronouncements were the most audible, consistent, coherent, and influential of all these proponents. Movement intellectuals' conceptualization and presentation of the *shimin* idea motivated others to act and gave that action meaning.

Focusing on movement intellectuals and their ideas allows me to tackle the thorny question of agency and structure in postwar civic activism. Though I adopt a social constructivist approach, I do not (indeed cannot) divorce ideas and action from the institutional structure in which they emerged. As I show throughout the study, civic movements mobilized in the name of the *shimin* were often thwarted by a conservative establishment with remarkably different priorities. The colossal defeat of the Anpo struggle in 1960 is the most obvious example, but we can also see state impact in the new civic movements since the late 1970s. In both phases the state played a role in shaping civic activism: driving activists from the streets into local mobilizations in the first case and encouraging noncontentious activism in the second. The temptation, of course, is to narrate subsequent shifts in civic activism in absolute terms: a strong state co-opting or destroying a burgeoning realm of contentious activism and, simultaneously, fashioning a sphere of apolitical, socially useful movements. I think such portrayals are only partly correct, because they discount or ignore altogether the role civic activists played in these processes. Faced with institutional roadblocks, movement intellectuals did not retreat. They took action, modifying the *shimin* idea and reconstituting or redirecting civic activism, which, in turn, encouraged new forms of mobilization, stimulated new tactics, and promoted new relationships.

Consider the two examples mentioned above. After the defeat of the Anpo protests one group of intellectuals began to foster local civic activism in the belief that it was the best way to overcome conservative domination. This effort ultimately bore fruit in reformist local governments of the late 1960s and new progressive consumer cooperatives. *Shimin* advocates made a similar intervention starting in the late 1970s. Reacting to the supposedly "failed" radicalism in the student movement and the "accusation" of consumer movements, activists began to embed the *shimin* idea in a praxis of "proposal," "symbiosis," and "constructive" activism. In the late 1980s their interventions opened a space for dialogue among activists, corporate officials, and state bureaucrats, feeding into a successful movement for nonprofit legislation that allowed many civic groups to incorporate and gain social legitimacy. Faced with institutional hurdles, movement intellectuals in both cases used the *shimin* idea to propel civic activism in new directions. Though to do so is somewhat counterintuitive, stepping away from theories such as the NSM paradigm, which privileges specific actors and predetermined modes of action, is the only way we can uncover these complex ways Japanese movement intellectuals have exercised their agency, responding to structural conditions and fostering new forms of social action. This more nuanced comprehension of human agency is what informs this study.

THE CASE STUDIES: THE *SHIMIN* IDEA IN ACTION

Given this theoretical framework, what did the *shimin* idea connote in practice, and how did movement intellectuals use it in concrete mobilizations? To begin with the idea itself, we might best conceptualize the mythology of the *shimin* as a patchwork of ideas that drew on some of the most potent aspirations and symbolism in postwar Japan. Since its creation in the mid-nineteenth century, the term *shimin* has been used variously as the Japanese translation for the French *citoyen*, *burgher, citizen,* and—for Marxists—*bourgeois*. It is also the translation for *civil*, as in civil society *(shimin shakai)* and civil rights *(shimin-ken)*, and for *civic*, as in civic center *(shimin kaikan)*.[30] From the mid-1950s, however, intellectuals began to reformulate the idea beyond its neutral meaning as the inhabitant of a town or city and in distinction to its negative petit bourgeois connotations in Marxist thought. They presented the *shimin* identity as a new and progressive agent of social change, keeping in check the state and the forces of reaction and valiantly defending the now-legitimate realm of private daily life. Over time, the *shimin* idea came to be associated with a form of democratic subjectivity and activism based on spontaneity, autonomy, everydayness, cosmopolitanism, and (for a time) antiestablishmentism. Movement intellectuals' persistent and obsessive desire to distinguish their paradigm from the established left and its arguably hierarchical, rigid, ideological style of activism produced an idealized image of *shimin*-style activism as the exact opposite of the left's: democratically organized, small-scale, voluntary, and nonideological.

Movement intellectuals also gravitated toward the *shimin* idea as much because of what it was not or had not previously been. Until the country's defeat in the Second World War, there were no citizens in Japan, since all Japanese were legally subjects *(shinmin)* of the emperor.[31] With the promulgation of the postwar constitution in late 1946, almost everyone on the archipelago legally became a citizen of the nation, or—to use the Japanese term—part of the *kokumin*. The rights and duties of the people (also referred to as *kokumin* in the constitution) were set out for the first time in Article 3 of this legal instrument, which went a long way toward establishing, though by no means inventing, the idea of a civic nation as the most desirable configuration for the postwar reconstruction of the country (both materially and psychologically). From 1947, then, most people in Japan became citizens of a legitimate sovereign nation, just like those in other liberal democracies. *Kokumin* remains the sole official signifier of Japanese citizenship, and the decision as to who can be part of the *kokumin* or, more prosaically, who can hold a passport endorsing the holder as a Japanese national *(Nihon kokumin)* is entirely in the hands of the state.[32] Being part of the *kokumin*, in other words, is to proclaim one's citizenship in the Japanese nation and, hence, involvement or complicity in the policies of the Japanese state—passive though this might be. Recognizing the association between the Japanese state and *kokumin* citizenship is crucial if we are to fully understand the appeal of the *shimin* idea for many civic activists. In the 1960s, for example, the anti–Vietnam War protester Tsurumi Yoshiyuki made the symbolic gesture of "relinquishing" his citizenship *(kokumin o dannen suru),* turning instead to the *shimin* identity, which represented for him a vision of citizenship independent of the state and based in a nonclass community of rights and mutual responsibility. The appeal of the *shimin* idea for Tsurumi and others was that, unlike *kokumin*, it never had to be reclaimed from the state, since it emanated from, subsided in, and, indeed, drew its life force from civil society.

But the *shimin* idea's appeal to activists also lay in its receptivity to more visceral attachments to the ethnic nation, the locale, or an affluent private life. So long as movement intellectuals avoided overt class rhetoric and directed their message to ordinary people *(futsū no hito-bito),* they could count on the mythology of the *shimin* as a legitimizing armor. As the American researchers Ellis Krauss and Bradford Simcock noted in a landmark 1981 essay, "The *shimin undō* ideal legitimized protest action on behalf of one's actual or potential interests as actions for the *collective* good, and it legitimized political activities through noninstitutionalized channels and by direct action methods as being consonant with the best democratic ideals. . . . The 'citizens' movement idea' [what I am calling the mythology of the *shimin*] helped to decrease the potential 'costs' of participating in a protest movement and being branded as a deviant or a rebel working for selfish ends."[33] So the mythology of the *shimin* had appeal as much for how it could be used as for the ideals it represented; in fact, the one fed off the other: ideas affected action, which affected ideas, and so on. In the chapters that follow I trace this ongoing dialectical process through six phases of civic thought and activism. I stress two aspects of the *shimin* idea: first, its *modularity* or adaptability over time and in the context of different movements, and, second, its *historicality* as a marker of a novel and quintessentially postwar mentality in Japan informed by defeat, democratization, national consciousness, and the institutional realities faced by activists.

Chapter 1 begins in the period before the *shimin* idea became prominent in progressive discourse, roughly from war's end to the mid-1950s. I see this period as a nascent moment for both nonaligned activism (i.e., activism not instigated or directed by political parties or organs of the left) and the imagination of the *shimin* idea, even though the term was hardly used at the time. For individuals such as philosopher Tsurumi Shunsuke, the experience of war, defeat, and occupation brought with it a complex set of messages and challenges for the intellectual and for the Japanese people more generally. Like many of his generation, Tsurumi felt an almost-ceaseless sense of remorse for not lifting a "single finger" in resistance to Japan's war in Asia. Tsurumi and others certainly blamed the Japanese state for what had happened, but they also blamed themselves as progressive intellectuals for not having led or even attempted to lead a proactive resistance. Notably, this remorse unfolded not only in an interrogation of the intellectual but also, more critically, in an intensive search for more authentic sources of identity and possible resistance to the state. This search led Tsurumi and his colleagues away from the intellectual toward the people, a collective imaginary rooted in the ethnic nation *(minzoku)* and the authentic space of daily life *(seikatsu)*. It is in these early imaginations of the people, I argue, that the mythology of the *shimin* began to take form. In other words, one source of the *shimin* idea can be found in intellectuals' war remorse and their commitment—as Japanese patriots—to rebuild Japan as a democratic nation controlled by the people, not the state. Many intellectuals involved in this project (the first postwar generation of movement intellectuals) also began to foster various grassroots initiatives in the early 1950s. These cultural circle groups, which I explore in the second half of chapter 1, became testing grounds for later *shimin* activism, setting some important precedents for movement organization and modes of individual expression.

While such developments can be considered the positive sources of later *shimin* thought and activism, I also use chapter 1 to explore more troubling antecedents. Tsurumi and others' attempt to imagine democratic subjectivity through the lens of ethnicity, while understandable, always ran the risk of replicating earlier essentialisms it was supposed to overcome. Intellectuals' progressive reimagination of the ethnic nation paved the way for its close and often deeply troubling association with the *shimin* idea and numerous civic mobilizations in the years to come. In terms of activism as well, the absolute rejection of Marxist ideas by many cultural circles in favor of a philosophy of self-help and inclusivity, while liberating, also tended to impede the critical faculties of these groups, making them all the more susceptible to the numbing impact of mass society. As I show in chapter 1, the prehistory of the *shimin* idea, then, is a story of intellectual remorse, designs for a new democratic praxis, and a complex set of legacies for later civic thought and activism.

In chapter 2, I turn to the anti–U.S.-Japan Security Treaty struggle of 1959–60 (Anpo *tōsō*), a moment remembered by academics and activists alike as the birth of independent citizen protest in postwar Japan. Rather than rehearse the erstwhile narrative of "the progressive democratic movement versus the reactionary government," however, I search for the roots of *shimin* thought and activism during the Anpo struggle in two sources: first, the impact and intellectual implications of mass society, and, second, the role of intellectuals in Anpo struggle citizens' movements in delineating and shaping models of civic activism. I am particularly interested in the subtle—and sometimes not-so-subtle—intermingling of materialist values and democratic purpose in the civic mobilizations of the Anpo struggle, or, put in crudely schematic terms, the mixing of the conservative and the progressive. As Ueno Chizuko's identification of "daily life conservatism" and Takabatake Michitoshi's description of "conservative sentiment" in the Anpo protest indicate, the desire to defend an affluent daily life from external intrusion adhered quite seamlessly to higher aspirations for democracy and democratic process.[34]

The *shimin* idea, as its most perceptive adherents recognized, was a product of mass society, emerging partly out of a mid-1950s debate about the impact of this social formation on popular political consciousness. Matsushita Keiichi, the leading theorist in the debate, originally focused on the pathological consequences of mass society: the stifling impact on political participation and the supposedly delusional influence of mass nationalism. Unlike other critics of mass society, such as William Kornhauser, Hannah Arendt, and, in Japan, Shimizu Ikutarō, however, Matsushita traced these pathologies more to institutions than to any irreparable degeneration in popular political consciousness. He was thus able to see positive potentialities in mass society, especially within the affluent and urbanized new middle stratum *(shinchūkansō)*. The Anpo struggle experience only confirmed the potential of this group for Matsushita, causing him to abandon altogether the socialist project and the proletariat as historical subject in favor of a new civic vision constructed around public-spirited and self-responsible individuals embodying the qualities of the "civic type of human" *(shiminteki ningengata)*.

During the Anpo struggle, progressive scholars further developed this discourse on an emergent, urbanized political citizenry, trumpeting the "birth of a civic consciousness" and a new form of "civic resistance." More significant, some of them joined with activists to mobilize the earliest citizen protest movements. Tapping into the rhetoric of public intellectuals and scholars, leaders of groups such as the Voices of the Voiceless Association called on unaffiliated individuals to join their marches as *shimin* in the heat of the protests. These movement intellectuals played a key role in transforming theoretical discussions about the *shimin* into a collective-action frame capable of attracting citizens into their movements and, later, of shaping the nature of participation, membership, and activism. Their efforts proved quite successful: during and after the struggle, movement intellectuals used the *shimin* idea to fashion two streams of civic activism: one conscientious, the other pragmatic. The former stream engaged in protest and forms of symbolic dissent, pursuing questions of rights, democracy, and pacifism. Its participants focused on defending Japan's peace constitution, opposing the American military presence in the country, and advocating the rights of peripheral groups. The latter, pragmatic stream of activism connected the Anpo issue to more prosaic questions of daily life, such as sewage, education, and garbage disposal. These movements took activism to the localities where they pursued the project of local democracy and the reform of local government. Of course, the breakthrough of movement intellectuals in both streams during the Anpo struggle was their successful deployment of the *shimin* idea to mobilize unaffiliated people who otherwise might have passively viewed events from the sidelines. The Anpo struggle may have been a "grand defeat" for some critical observers, but in the sphere of citizen politics it heralded the rise of a new and potent symbol for collective action born from the very heart of mass society.

In chapter 3 I trace the conscientious stream of activism into Beheiren, the anti–Vietnam War movement, looking at the ways movement intellectuals such as Oda Makoto and Tsurumi Yoshiyuki attached the *shimin* idea to notions of race, ethnicity, and nation. Leaders blended their war memories with nationalism, anti-Americanism, and Pan-Asianism to produce a vision of the Asian *shimin* actively struggling for the liberation of fellow Asian peoples from Western (read: American) imperialism. Oda, Kaiko Takeshi, and other Beheiren leaders connected their wartime experience as victims of the Japanese state and the United States to the plight of the Vietnamese by tracing a direct line from Hiroshima, Nagasaki, and the Allied firebombing of Osaka to U.S. bombing in Vietnam. As Oda explained in 1965, when he saw images of Vietnam on the television he was transported back to the carnage of 1945 and the "meaningless deaths" of ordinary Japanese citizens. In the faces of the Vietnamese he saw his own face, and this motivated him to act. Identifying a victim-aggressor mechanism at work in Japan, Oda suggested that, to the extent Japanese people did not resist their state—a captive of the United States—they would remain not only victims of that state but also victimizers of the Vietnamese, with whom they shared a common ethnic bond as Asians. The task that movement intellectuals set Beheiren members was thus twofold: first, recognizing the shared historical experience of victimhood with the Vietnamese and, second, exorcising the Western imperialism and pseudouniversalism supposedly driving Japan's postwar national consciousness. Although Beheiren is usually presented as the quintessential postwar peace movement, such ideas clearly propelled it beyond simple humanism and pacifism, connecting it to struggles for third-world revolution and Pan-Asianist liberation. Drawing on his experiences with black activists in the United States and revolutionaries in Cuba, Oda imagined Beheiren as the source of a new openminded nationalism *(hirakareta nashonarizumu)* that would transcend the state, combining with other progressive nationalisms into a form of global pluralism.[35] Oda, Tsurumi Shunsuke, and the latter's cousin Yoshiyuki presented the movement as an opportunity for the Japanese people to remake their nation as a progressive vehicle for peace in the world—what I call Beheiren's peace constitution nationalism. And, as I mentioned above, the *shimin* idea proved extremely useful for Beheiren's leadership in pursuit of these aims, because it was an identity neither implicated in the deeds of the postwar state nor stained by the past of ultranationalism.

While Beheiren attempted to fashion an Asian *shimin* in its antiwar struggle, throughout the 1960s and the early 1970s a wave of antipollution and antidevelopment protest swept across the country. This protest was accompanied by the election of many progressive administrations at the municipal and prefectural levels, prompting some to speak of a "new era of Japanese politics." In chapter 4 I chart the development of pragmatic civic activism in these two spheres, looking closely at practices of self-help in local movements and policies for citizen participation in local administrations. I want to show how both strategies, although born in response to widespread protest, served as precedents and ideational tools for activists and civil society advocates in the conciliatory phase to come.

The logic of self-help emerged from local activists' protracted struggle to defend their localities from pollution and overdevelopment. As I show in chapter 4, though observers often disagreed vehemently about the historical significance of the new movements, most agreed that their success was linked to strategies of active self-help. As observers from all ideological perspectives recognized, successful movements tended to organize locally and used a range of strategies, including not only protest but also negotiation and even collaboration with local officials and conservative politicians. They usually avoided political affiliation or ideology, building instead a nonpartisan alliance of protesters. Most groups had little concern for big political or ideological issues, focusing narrowly on protecting their own backyard and exploiting any useful institutional, financial, and ideological resources. As scientist and environmental activist Ui Jun noted, victory happened only in movements in which activists stopped depending on officials and took matters into their own hands. Such ideas prefigured what has become the central ethos of civic activism in Japan since the mid-1970s: namely, that activists should generate their own constructive strategies for social change in the small universes of daily life while carefully avoiding dependency on others, especially bureaucrats. Antipollution and antidevelopment protesters of the 1960s and early 1970s by no means articulated this approach in full, but in their commitment to autonomy and their pragmatic and instrumental approach to activism we find the intellectual seedbed of such developments.

The implementation of policies for citizen participation in local governments of the 1960s also portended the future of state-civic group relations. Building on widespread resentment of excessive development and pollution, these administrations promised to bring a civic perspective to local governance through direct participation, local government reform, and the implementation of civil minimums. Matsushita Keiichi and his political allies, such as Tokyo governor Minobe Ryōkichi, believed that the energy of local protests—if properly directed into local government—could become the basis for challenging so-called conservative domination. Progressive administrations in Tokyo, Yokohama, and elsewhere genuinely attempted to implement such policies, but outcomes were at best mixed, often deteriorating into tokenism and political opportunism. Matsushita and his political think tank, the Tokyo Municipal Research Association, however, used the idea of citizen participation to propagate a powerful new vision of a civic community in Japan. Through participation, local residents *(jūmin)* would shed their "egoistic" tendencies and develop into fully fledged *shimin*, spontaneously and selflessly working for the construction of a new community. As participants in formal institutions, these *shimin* would supposedly develop into a *kokumin*—a progressive vessel by which Japan could blossom into a citizen of the world. This civic national vision of Matsushita and others certainly invigorated progressive local administrations in the early 1960s, but distinguishing good citizens with civic discipline from bad citizens who clung to egoistic private concerns tended to undermine the institutionalization of pluralistic politics. Moreover, colored as it was with civic nationalism and communitarian ethics, citizen participation could be a useful ideological tool for fostering soft volunteerism in areas of official concern, such as social welfare provision or community building. Just as with the logic of self-help in local protest movements, then, the idea of citizen participation was vulnerable to neoliberal and neocommunitarian programs initiated by and in the interests of bureaucratic elites—an ironic legacy of this period of high protest.

In chapter 5 I retrace civic activism from the so-called ice age of the 1970s through the 1990s. Although claims of a deep freeze in the civic sector are somewhat overstated, civic activism inarguably began to change from this period: movements of protest did decline, and in their wake emerged a generation of new civic movements focused on the creation of concrete alternatives to mainstream society. A number of factors fueled this shift. First, state and corporate officials intervened by preempting and preventing widespread protest and by forging symbiotic and supportive relationships with cooperative groups. In the mid-1970s, for example, stringent legislation remedied many of the protested problems and the establishment of a system for bureaucratic mediation diffused pollution conflicts before they escalated. But, as I argue in this chapter, the changes in civic activism and the rise of new civic movements during this period are not wholly explained by state and corporate intervention or by public disillusionment with radicalism. Some of the changes were the result of the intervention of movement intellectuals, who articulated a new vision of the *shimin* idea and civic activism based on notions of creative, collaborative, and financially sustainable activism. These activists promoted a pervasive logic of alternative proposal-style *(teian-gata)* civic activism, contrasting their approach with protest groups of the 1960s and 1970s, which they claimed adopted "losing" strategies of opposition and bureaucratic dependence. Many civic activists of the 1970s became disenchanted with the extremism of the student movement and concluded that true autonomy *(jiritsu)* would be possible only through concrete activism and pragmatic engagement with the state, the market, and society in general.

From the mid-1970s onward, movement intellectuals injected this approach into a wide range of spheres, including movements for the disabled, the elderly, social welfare, community businesses, organic food and agriculture, ecology, and international cooperation. Their initiatives benefited greatly from state and corporate support. Facing new socioeconomic and demographic challenges in the 1970s, state officials began to promote, fund, and provide logistical support for new civic groups involved in community and social welfare activism. State officials embraced the imagery of such groups, praising their autonomy, their sense of community, and their ethos of self-help. Corporate philanthropic organizations also came onboard in the 1980s in their funding for new civic groups and support for networking initiatives. The Toyota Foundation, for example, promoted new civic groups under the banner of citizens' activities, intentionally disassociating this realm from the unruly citizens' movements of the past. The foundation's financial and logistical support for networking events beginning in the mid-1980s provided proponents of the proposal paradigm with a perfect platform to advocate the formal legal legitimization of their model—something ultimately realized with the Law to Promote Specified Nonprofit Activities of 1998.

As I show in chapter 5, in the space of three decades influential movement intellectuals, supported by state officials and corporate elites, reshaped the *shimin* idea, denigrating a past of so-called failed protest and radicalism and championing a future of creation, symbiosis, proposal, and collaboration. Although they drew liberally on aspects of earlier *shimin* thought, such as self-help, participation, and community, movement intellectuals' employment of these ideas propelled civic activism in bold new directions and into novel areas of activity. Significantly, not only did their approach tend to marginalize those groups that challenged the prerogatives of the state and corporate Japan; it also opened the way for an ironic reengagement and reconciliation among civic groups, bureaucrats, and corporate elites—ironic, I suggest, because the departure point for the new paradigm was activists' self-avowed project to transcend conservative hegemony and unrestrained corporate power.

What connected these activists to those of decades before, however, was their vigorous use of the *shimin* idea to inspire ordinary citizens and to shape the realm of civic activism. In the following chapters I retrace the efforts of movement intellectuals first to conceptualize the *shimin* idea and then deploy it to motivate people into collective action and fashion a sphere of independent civic activism. I will show how the *shimin* idea, confounding and troubling though it often was in practice, became a quintessential symbol of human agency in postwar Japan.

CHAPTER I

Before the *Shimin*

The Dark Energy of the People

THE PEOPLE, DAILY LIFE, AND THE ETHNIC NATION

Conventional treatments of the *shimin* idea and civic activism—especially in Japanese-language scholarship—usually begin with the anti-security-treaty protests of 1960 or just before.[1] This starting point is quite understandable: before this event the term *shimin* was hardly used in political discourse, and when it was the connotation was most often negative or, at best, qualified. For most Marxists, *shimin* and *shimin shakai* (civil society) amounted to no more than the bourgeoisie and bourgeois society and, as such, could—at best—be a step on the pathway to somewhere better. The fact that many of Japan's major cities lay in ruins after the war also made it difficult for people to imagine themselves as part of an urban political citizenry—as *"citoyen"*—when the pressing question for many was how to avoid starvation. Moreover, legally speaking, the Japanese people were not sovereign citizens until the promulgation of the new constitution in 1946, and until 1952 their sovereignty was overseen by the Allied Occupation of the country. The American crackdown on militant labor activism in the late 1940s and state moves against other forms of leftist activity in the 1950s also did nothing to promote a popular sense of the people being in control. In short, the *shimin* idea remained in the shadows until the late 1950s for a whole range of reasons.

But simply because activists and intellectuals were not using or deploying the *shimin* does not mean that ideas and practices that would later become central in *shimin* thought and activism were also absent. On the contrary, the period from the end of the war until the mid-1950s was crucial in laying the intellectual foundations for later civic thought associated with the *shimin* idea, especially its connection to the nation and notions of daily life. For intellectuals, of course, one of the primary projects in the early postwar years was a search for the holy grail of subjectivity *(shutaisei)*, which many felt was sorely absent in the psyche of modern Japan. Marxists, modernization advocates, literary specialists, and others tried their best to forge such subjectivity within the bounds of their own ideologies and disciplinary fields. The civil society theorist Uchida Yoshihiko even identified a group of civil society youth *(shimin shakai seinen)*, populated by a who's who of the postwar intellectual community: Ōkōchi Kazuo, Ōtsuka Hisao, Takashima Zenya, Noma Hiroshi, and Maruyama Masao, for example. Such intellectuals—especially in their commitment to notions of individual autonomy and "ethos"—laid important ideational foundations for later civic thought. Their public activism through essays in widely read progressive journals also contributed to an emergent public sphere in which issues of national import could be debated (if not decided) beyond formal political channels. Indeed, we could begin a study of the *shimin* idea and citizen activism by tracing a line from the ideas of intellectuals such as Maruyama and Ōtsuka to the concrete civic activism of 1960, showing how the people took hold of such ideas and became *shimin*.

In this chapter, however, I approach the prehistory of the *shimin* idea from a slightly different perspective: in the space where intellectuals and ordinary people interacted. This space is important for two reasons. First, progressives who would later mature into influential movement intellectuals cut their teeth in this space. Second, the ideas produced there influenced later *shimin* thought and activism in direct and palpable ways. Specifically, progressives' remorse about the war prompted a self-critique of their status as intellectuals and a search for a new democratic subjectivity within ordinary Japanese people and their daily lives. Intellectuals imagined the Japanese people not only in contradistinction to a delegitimized state and a class of professional thinkers but also as a social formation tightly coupled with the nation and daily life—both of which they felt had been violated by the wartime regime. The people became cathartic vehicles for intellectuals simultaneously to deal with their own remorse and to construct a new form of progressive leftist nationalism. To be sure, intellectuals recognized the need to nurture a renewed democratic consciousness in the country, but they believed this would take root only if ordinary people made this consciousness their own. Universalistic ideas such as democracy had to be connected to aspirations and identities that made sense for ordinary people; otherwise these ideas risked abstraction and ideological manipulation. Hence, such intellectuals not only looked outward for a solution to the recent past; they also saw value in a conceptual and ethical rehabilitation of the Japanese people and their quotidian lifeways. It is in these early imaginations and articulations of the ethnic nation *(minzoku)* and daily life *(seikatsu)* that we discover the intellectual seedbed for later *shimin* discourse and civic activism.

In the first part of the chapter I look closely at the interventions of the philosopher Tsurumi Shunsuke and his intellectual club, the Institute for the Science of Thought (Shisō no Kagaku Kenkyūkai), formed in 1946 by Tsurumi, his sister Kazuko, and a group of like-minded academics. Among the various intellectual groups of the early postwar period, the institute became a key theoretical and organizational hub for the *shimin* idea and citizens' movements. Many institute members were actively involved in postwar civic activism, becoming movement intellectuals in their own right.[2] The institute also became a kind of nursery for citizens' groups: members of the Voices of the Voiceless Association—the quintessential citizens' movement of the Anpo struggle—actually belonged to a group affiliated with the institute and its various cultural circle activities. All the more significant, then, that Tsurumi and institute members spent the years before the Anpo struggle conceptualizing the people *(hitobito)* not as the bearers of a deracinated and universalized democracy but in terms of a progressive ethnic nationalism and an authentic sensibility of the inhabitants of daily life *(seikatsusha)*. Contrary to accusations that the institute's members were American ideologues or *"ninja"* of the communist left, we discover a remarkably rooted— *culturally* rooted—set of aspirations in their search for a people's philosophy *(hitobito no tetsugaku)*.[3]

The institute's early postwar ruminations bequeathed a number of intellectual legacies for later *shimin* thought. First was the idea that the people—as a synthesis of the nation and daily life—were the most qualified to resist the state. Institute members hardly idealized the people and often lamented their limitations, but for Tsurumi Shunsuke, at least, the "mild cunning" of the people born from the yoke of daily life seemed far more legitimate and trustworthy than intellectuals and their sullied Westernized rationality. This belief in the durability and genuineness of daily life is a central thread connecting civic thought and activism throughout the postwar period. Second, despite this belief and even though the institute authenticated a cultural identity and space, members stopped short of providing any concrete definition or conceptualization of what the people should be or how they should act. Replicating the more general disorder of the early postwar moment, the early imaginations of the people contained a degree of interpretive and descriptive plasticity—a core of certainty surrounded by a pliant exterior. The plethora of appellations for the people is instructive: the masses *(taishū),* the common folk *(shomin),* the populace *(minshū),* the civic nation *(kokumin),* the ethnic nation *(minzoku),* the ordinary people *(futsū no hitobito),* the people *(hitobito),* the inhabitants of daily life *(seikatsusha),* the eternal folk *(jōmin),* the Japanese *(Nihonjin),* and, more rarely, citizens *(shimin)* or the people of Marxist discourse *(jinmin).* This plasticity also carried over into the *shimin* idea, affording it a modularity, inclusivity, and receptivity remarkably at odds with the Marxist proletariat, which "belonged" to the established left and its predetermined historical project.

In the second part of the chapter I turn to the independent cultural circle *(sākuru)* activism of the 1950s—the training ground for later citizens' movements. As it developed throughout this period, circle activism challenged leftist initiatives to direct and shape social energies into essentialized class categories. Circles brought into question the idea that people should be organized hierarchically and led from above by farsighted elites. Intellectually, circle activism challenged the privileged position of a vanguard—intellectuals, politicians, bureaucrats—as the only source of socially useful meaning. Organizationally, circle activism presented an alternative to the hierarchical, centrally directed model of the established left, forging instead a more egalitarian form of human organization and interaction—what literary critic Ara Masato referred to as "horizontal connections" *(yoko no tsunagari).*[4] Such intellectual and organizational innovations made the circle movement an ideal model for later, more overtly political civic groups.

But the circle movement passed on ambiguous legacies too. As observers discovered, circles were not always forward or outward looking. They were not always openly progressive and could be remarkably narrow and exclusivist. Although an enthusiastic advocate of the circle movement, Tsurumi Kazuko lamented how participants in cultural groups often failed to connect their individual predicaments to broader social inequities, while her brother Shunsuke had to admit that circles often displayed a passive acceptance of the status quo, and their members a primitive materialism of daily life. Circles' commitment to individual autonomy and self-help also ran the risk of replicating conservative attempts to fashion a self-reliant and self-responsible citizenry imbued with the ethos of "spontaneous service."[5] In short, for all its promise, circle activism also foreshadowed the vulnerabilities of nonaligned civic activism from the earliest years of the postwar era onward.

TSURUMI SHUNSUKE, WAR REMORSE, AND THE DISCOVERY OF THE PEOPLE

Actually, the discovery of the people did not begin as a discussion. It began in the experience of war and defeat by a group of intellectuals who would soon find solace and hope in the Institute for the Science of Thought. Although early postwar discussions about the people certainly provided the intellectual backdrop for the *shimin* idea, we need to step back and consider the impact of the war on institute members if we want to discover the idea's emotional and psychological locus. Among these members none is more important than the institute's founder, Tsurumi Shunsuke, because his war experience was both emblematic and central in shaping the ethos of the institute and its approach to the people.

When hostilities broke out between Japan and the United States, Tsurumi was an undergraduate student at Harvard University. He later recalled how the outbreak of war was one of the rare moments in his life when he felt a real sense of ethnic consciousness and a desire to be in Japan.[6] After being arrested on somewhat dubious charges of anarchism, Tsurumi found himself in an internment camp for Japanese Americans in Maryland. Here he was given the choice of staying on in the United States or returning home. Wanting to be in Japan at the moment of defeat and expecting exemption from active military duty (he had tuberculosis), Tsurumi—together with his sister Kazuko and others—decided to return. After arriving in Japan, Tsurumi received orders to undertake the military physical exam and, to his great surprise, was found fit for military service. His physical condition ruled out active combat duty, so instead he was assigned to the navy as a civilian employee and dispatched to the island of Java in February 1943. He was twenty years old.[7]

It was on Java that Tsurumi faced the realities of war head on, specifically the issue of how he was personally going to deal with his role in a war that he purportedly opposed. Indeed, Tsurumi's failure to oppose the war actively while on Java (or anywhere else) deeply shaped his postwar sense of remorse, his attitude toward the state, his attack on the intellectual, and his ultimate turn to the people. This was an experience Tsurumi shared with many other intellectuals of his generation, and it would bring him to the center of postwar discussions about wartime responsibility. How Tsurumi differed from other intellectuals was that he opened up his wartime activities to public scrutiny in the postwar period.[8] From the very outset his project was as much about personal vilification as it was about detached scientific scrutiny.

Tsurumi's recounting of his interactions with local women on the Indonesian island of Java are among the most revealing and troubling. On his arrival in 1943, the civilian official Tsurumi was charged with monitoring enemy broadcasts, disposing of official documents, and taking care of high-ranking officials. Among other things, this caretaking included the procurement and provision of "comfort women" for officers.[9] At the ring of a bell it was Tsurumi's duty to provide a woman and, if necessary, a condom. From the outset Tsurumi concluded that such tasks were a "far better path than killing others."[10] He decided that if at any time during the war he was put in the position to kill another, he would commit suicide first. Arranging comfort women, then, represented the lesser of two evils—what Tsurumi called a passive ethic *(shōkyokuteki rinri)* of resistance—and it was a task he admitted doing in a "businesslike" and "thorough" way.[11] In between his duties Tsurumi spent time reading religious books and praying to God for his own moral improvement.

Tsurumi vehemently refused sexual relations with comfort women or any other local women while on Java—much to the amusement of his peers, who labeled him *Yokozuna,* or grand champion on their virgin ranking *(dōtei banzuke)*.[12] Tsurumi explained his abstinence quite differently, however. "I clearly felt that my attraction to women was in conflict with the state," he later explained. "Sex vs. State: this was the basic equation for me. I did not want to liberate my [sexual] attraction to women in a medium certified by the state."[13] So nonparticipation in the institutionalized sex of the comfort stations became for Tsurumi a concrete manifestation of his passive ethic of resistance to total control by the state. Similarly, Tsurumi kept his attraction to a "bright-eyed" seventeen-year-old housemaid at the level of desire—unconsummated. In the midst of his daily wrongdoings *(yūgai naru doryoku)* he quietly harbored the fantasy of a liberated relationship *(kaihōtekina kōshō)* with this "girl." According to Tsurumi, confining his sexual desire to the realm of fantasy partly separated him from the system of domination the Japanese exerted over local people.[14] Again, this became a kind of resistance for him—albeit a passive one.

Of course, other questions remained and rightly troubled him: passively resisting by *not doing* was one thing, but why had he worked so conscientiously in this wartime system? As his intellectual peer Maruyama Masao later pointed out, *not doing* constituted one form of wartime responsibility.[15] One reason, Tsurumi explained, was simple cowardice; another was a habit of formalistic effort he had learned from around the age of fifteen or sixteen.[16] But, in the end, he had not been able truly to resist; he had not produced any kind of decisive springboard by which to cut himself off from the state.[17] Here lay the roots of his postwar remorse and his reconceptualization of philosophy.

Too ill to continue his duty, Tsurumi was eventually repatriated to Japan in late 1944, and after a brief stint at the Naval General Staff Division, he spent the remainder of the war recuperating in the resort town of Atami. It was here that he heard the emperor's broadcast of defeat and surrender on August 15, 1945. His reaction, of course, was totally negative, particularly because the emperor focused on Japan's losses, bypassing the pain inflicted by Japan on others—a pain that Tsurumi knew he had not lifted one finger to oppose.[18] "It made me feel absolutely terrible," he recalled. "I thought the emperor was a rogue *(iya na yatsu).*"[19] Unlike other intellectuals such as Shimizu Ikutarō, who supposedly broke down and wept, Tsurumi found in the moment nothing more than indifference *(mukandō)* and self-hatred *(jiko ken'o).*[20]

On an individual level, Tsurumi's involvement in the war produced a deep sense of remorse, which he articulated ceaselessly in his postwar writings. For example, as late as 2004 he was still asking, "Why did I not raise my voice in protest? I was not even arrested during the war. I was shamed by this."[21] But Tsurumi's remorse found form in more than personal expressions of contrition. It also had an important effect on his intellectual activity in the postwar period. We need to understand Tsurumi's remorse as that of a reflexive individual whose intellectual training had proven powerless in the face of the state and the full weight of society.[22] He and other intellectuals had surrendered to militarism in the same way as the supposedly uneducated masses.[23] That book learning had let him—and most other educated people—down led Tsurumi almost by default to an interrogation of intellectuals (including himself) and their problematic abstraction of knowledge from daily life.

Tsurumi's remorse-as-intellectual ultimately fed into his lionization of the people, but this came about only after a relentless critique of academic philosophy, the intellectual, and so-called knowledge. In two essays published just after war's end, Tsurumi mounted an attack on philosophy and language. Contained in the inaugural edition of *Shisō no Kagaku* in May 1946, "Kotoba no Omamoriteki Shiyōhō ni tsuite" (On the Talismanic Use of Words) outlined Tsurumi's critique of wartime ideology in slogans such as "the national polity" *(kokutai)* and "the imperial way" *(kōdō)*. According to Tsurumi, by incorporating such slogans into political speeches and official documents, individuals and groups had protected themselves from criticism with a kind of talismanic effect.[24] The mobilization of slogans was not unique to Japan, but, as the war revealed, the talismanic effect increased diametrically when slogans were monopolized by a particular institution or group.[25] Of crucial significance in the essay was Tsurumi's explanation for the spread of such slogans. He noted the significant gap between the populace *(minshū)* who remained relatively uneducated and the small number of academics *(gakusha)* who approached political and ethical principles through the manipulation of difficult words imported from the West or drawn from ancient Japan and China.[26] The point for Tsurumi was that this disjuncture left the people without any critical cognitive tools to expose the political motives behind the state's mobilization of terms such as *kokutai*. As a solution he suggested the "formalistic" and "functional" reform of linguistic practice: simplifying the Japanese language by eliminating Chinese characters and, functionally, by teaching schoolchildren how to analyze political rhetoric.[27] Such reform, he believed, would be useful in the postwar period with its new talismanic slogans "democracy," "peace," and "freedom."[28]

His longer and far richer essay "Tetsugaku no Hansei" (Reflections on Philosophy), written during the last months of the war and published in 1946, incorporated many similar themes and, as others have noted, anticipated some of the central ideas in Tsurumi's later thought.[29] What is more pertinent is the attempt in this essay to reconceptualize philosophy as a tool for ordinary people negotiating daily life rather than as a purely academic endeavor. For Tsurumi philosophy had become an enterprise for idlers living in a world of leisure. "Most of them won't lift a finger to clarify the truth of their statements through investigation of concrete examples."[30] Instead philosophy had "provided students with a simple set of secrets on how to win a debate. If you master these, then even if you don't convince your opponent, you can draw him into a labyrinth and force a tie."[31] Conversely, Tsurumi wanted to recalibrate philosophy toward three practical tasks for daily life: criticism *(hihan)*, guidance *(shishin)*, and empathy *(dōjō)*.[32]

The key point is that each of these tasks—criticism, guidance, and empathy—refracted Tsurumi's wartime experience into an intellectual methodology emancipated (or potentially emancipated) from the academic realm. Criticism *(hihan)* was necessary because during the war Japanese people had all too easily believed that East Asian liberation *(Tōa no kaihō)*, for example, was a general principle *(ippan genri)*, when it was nothing more than a disguise for a specific goal *(tokushu na mono)*—Japanese expansionism.[33] Similarly, people needed philosophy as a guideline *(shishin)*, because, as the war experience had revealed, in the absence of individual rules, daily life could be manipulated from without. And, finally, the lack of empathy *(dōjō)* for others had freed the Japanese army to commit brutal atrocities, leaving a terrible scar on Japan's relationship with other Asian nations.

As Oguma Eiji notes, Tsurumi's concept of *dōjō* became a central and distinctive element of his thought and also of civic thought more generally. He suggests that Tsurumi's empathy was not about pity or sympathy but represented a kind of solidarity *(rentai)* and a sense of shared emotion *(kyōkan)* based on acceptance of difference.[34] Tsurumi's empathy forced the individual to search for commonality beneath yet *through* difference, for example, in everyday language, which supposedly transcended the diversity of the ethnic languages *(minzokugo)* of the world.[35] Significantly such commonality in Tsurumi's thought was necessarily mediated through the concrete ethnic nation *(minzoku)*, where it found specific voice. Philosophy-as-empathy thus led Tsurumi from the intellectual to the people as the ethnic nation. But this was not the ethnic nation of wartime dogma. It was the aggregation of a people long dominated by their state but now poised to lead a true democratic revolution in the country. In the midst of defeat, occupation, and national humiliation, empathy helped him reimagine the nation positively—a position that would remain central in Tsurumi's understanding of the people even during the 1960s, when he began to use the term *shimin*.[36] Consider Tsurumi's statement toward the end of the essay: "The Japanism of old was a mistake but this does not mean we have to shift our interest suddenly to America or Russia. Now is the time to formulate a new set of guidelines by comprehending the specific circumstances of our own predicament while maintaining empathy with others and those from other nations. Now is the time to

fashion a new national essentialism *(kokusuishugi)* by knowing the self
and knowing the other."[37] Here, of course, we can see the roots of
Tsurumi's later activism on behalf of minorities and peripheralized
groups. But the crucial point is that such empathy emerged through a
rejection of the intellectual and a rehabilitation of the people as the
Japanese *minzoku.* Tsurumi reiterated this sentiment in more abstract
terms in 1962:

> If one descends deeper, beyond the self determined by the state, and beyond
> the self determined by society, school, and home, there is a self produced
> by the ethnic culture from the time of our ancestors, and deeper still, there
> exists a self as living creature *(dōbutsu)*; a nameless self-as-life. Descending
> there one can reconstitute the self in a way different from the fashions of
> contemporary society, and search for a new way to conjoin with the world.
> This is a pathway to universalism through ethnic nationalism *(minzo-
> kushugi).* [It is] that nameless element at the base of the ethnic spirit
> *(minzoku no tamashii).*[38]

Of course, the ethnic nation was but one stimulus leading Tsurumi
to the people in the early postwar years. Just as important, in the same
1946 essay was his conceptualization of philosophy as a practical tool
for guidance *(shishin)* in daily life, and this connected at the deepest
level to his critique of the intellectual. If the war had taught Tsurumi
one thing, it was certainly the cold reality that the educated fared no
better than the uneducated under Japanese militarism. In fact, the war
proved that "educated men were surprisingly like the masses *(tai-
shūteki)*."[39] From this perspective Tsurumi was able to rethink the role
of philosophy in matter-of-fact terms. In what proved to be a prophetic
comparison, he suggested that academic philosophy learn from the
literary tradition of life composition in Japan.[40] Promoted by progressive teachers during the prewar years and again in the 1950s and after,
life composition *(seikatsu tsuzurikata* or *seikatsu kiroku)* encouraged
schoolchildren (and later adults) to write down their everyday experiences in essay or poetic form. As Tsurumi noted, life composition not
only promoted writing skills but, more significantly, involved an "investigation of the human world" and "reflection on one's own daily
life." Unlike state-formulated "moral education" *(shūshin)*, which "inculcated" students in "established morality," life composition forced
the individual to "spontaneously contemplate" *(jihatsuteki shisaku)*
moral issues. It empowered students by forcing them to engage with
"actualities" through the medium of "detailed signs."[41] If philosophy
could similarly adopt this "language of rudimentary experience" *(genshi*

keiken go) and shed its penchant for abstraction, Tsurumi believed, it could become a useful tool for ordinary people negotiating daily life.[42] Professional philosophers would no longer be the sole proprietors of a philosophy redefined; it would belong to the people with their knowledge as inhabitants of daily life *(seikatsusha)*.[43]

This, then, was the other lesson Tsurumi took from the war: intellectuals and academic philosophy had failed, but a philosophy reconstituted on the foundation of everyday sensibility might not. Of course, the concrete nature of this sensibility remained troublingly ambiguous. Moreover, why the ethnic nation and the everyday were more qualified to underwrite postwar democracy than the academic knowledge of the intellectual or the philosophy of academic philosophers was never entirely clear.

AMERICAN PRAGMATISM AND THE PEOPLE

Ambiguities aside, "Reflections on Philosophy" was important because in it we can see the logic leading Tsurumi from wartime remorse to a critique of the intellectual and academic knowledge. Moreover, it was an early expression of his imagination of the people as both the ethnic nation and the inhabitants of daily life, an imagination that belied accusations that he and the institute were merely mouthpieces for the American occupiers. That said, Tsurumi's discovery of the people was more than a product of his remorse over the war; his critique of the intellectual could quite as easily have linked to a self-reflexive investigation into the pathology of those who produce knowledge for a living. And, in fact, it did.[44] But to understand how Tsurumi became fully committed to the people and their everyday philosophy, we need to add another formative element: American pragmatism.

Tsurumi's prewar encounter with this philosophy began in an appropriately matter-of-fact way: he was in the United States and "wanted to study something American." In time, however, he became convinced that pragmatism could be separated from American civilization and contribute as an independent force in world thought.[45] Tsurumi wrote prolifically on pragmatism in the early postwar years, publishing some fourteen essays between 1946 and 1950.[46] Together with his analysis of the thought and lives of Charles Sanders Peirce, William James, Oliver Wendell Holmes, and George Herbert Mead (among others), Tsurumi's early postwar work engaged with the structure, position, and potential of pragmatism as a philosophy in Japan. Tsurumi was by no means the only intellectual interested in American pragmatism at the time. The sociologist Shimizu Ikutarō and the philosopher Kuno Osamu—colleagues in the influential Twentieth Century Research Institute (Nijusseiki Kenkyūjo)—were avid readers of Charles Sanders Peirce in the early postwar years.[47] In 1946, Shimizu published a collection of essays on pragmatism titled *Minshushugi no Shisō* (The Philosophy of Democracy) with a fittingly titled first essay, "Bonjin no Tetsugaku" (The Philosophy of the Ordinary Person).[48]

Tsurumi's engagement with pragmatism was important primarily for its methodological implications within the institute. As Amano Masako has noted, the originality of Tsurumi's thought lay in his understanding of pragmatism as a method *(hōhō)* rather than as an intellectual or ideological thing-in-itself *(jittai)*.[49] This probably oversimplifies Tsurumi's engagement with pragmatism somewhat; after all, his writings evidence more than an instrumental attraction to the philosophy. But Amano's depiction is right on target when we consider how Tsurumi wanted to use pragmatism. In the Japanese context, Tsurumi suggested, pragmatism would be useful in three ways. First, it would be a means to overcome Japanese "spiritualism" *(seishinshugi)*. Pragmatism would allow Japanese to deal with the problems of modernization and science more objectively by refocusing attention from the simplistic question of means to the more important question of ends. Second, pragmatism would be the best way to legitimize existing native thought in Japan. I return to this tension between modernization and nativism in Tsurumi's thought below, but for the moment note the following: what modernist and Marxist ideologies had previously discarded as the instinctive and primitive logic of Japanese daily life could become a potentially democratic force through pragmatism. Third, Tsurumi felt that pragmatism would help create the basis for a new linguistic practice in Japan. It would enable philosophers, journalists, politicians, and ordinary people to communicate and exchange their opinions more freely.[50]

More concretely, pragmatism-as-methodology profoundly influenced Tsurumi and other institute members' ideas vis-à-vis the subject(s) of research and the approach of the researcher. We can see the roots of such an approach in Tsurumi's early postwar writings on pragmatism, for example, particularly in his essay "Otto: The Man and His Thought," originally published in 1947. Max C. Otto (1877–1968) was an obscure and relatively unimportant figure in the American pragmatism movement, developing his thought while a professor in philosophy at the University of Wisconsin.[51] His most important work, published in 1941, was *The Human Enterprise: An Attempt to Relate Philosophy to Daily Life.* Tsurumi argued that Otto's writing on pragmatism had remained relatively obscure simply because scholars in eastern universities (i.e., the East Coast of the United States) did not recommend it to students. Unperturbed, however, Otto had turned his attention away from the scholarly community, writing instead for the young and the masses *(taishū)* in simple language.[52] Otto's personal task, Tsurumi explained, became one of uncovering the "philosophy of the average citizen" *(heikin shimin no tetsugaku)*, which at base was all about living a peaceful life. To be sure, Otto admitted the inelegance and simplicity of common language used to articulate this philosophy, but he rejected this as grounds for its dismissal. On the contrary, the aim of the professional philosopher was to figure out ways to advance such ideas and, moreover, to solve the problems raised by the people's philosophy *(hitobito no tetsugaku)* in a more adroit and correct manner.[53] Unlike other philosophers, Tsurumi argued that Otto did not begin with the history of philosophy but rather by asking what kind of philosophy was required in everyday life *(nichijō seikatsu)*. From this standpoint he could analyze the strengths and weaknesses of idealism and existentialism as pillars of daily life.[54] According to Tsurumi, this thorough commitment to the perspective of the everyday made Otto's thought unique—even within the pragmatist movement. As he explained, even William James and John Dewey had not broken free from the age-old vision of the philosopher's position "over and above" the people.[55] Otto's pragmatism, by contrast, was an organic outgrowth of everyday consciousness, and this aspect of Otto's work led Tsurumi to some important conclusions. A philosophy tied to the consciousness of the average citizen would value a primitiveness *(genshisei)* or ambiguity prior to scientific or cognitive understanding. It would attempt to grasp the totality of life *(zenjinsei)*; it would welcome individuality *(kojinsei)*; it would have a social aspect *(shakaisei)* constructed through mutual understanding (i.e., empathy); and, above all else, it would be profoundly linked to human nature *(ningensei)*.[56] Indeed, Otto's rejection of academic philosophy slotted neatly into Tsurumi's own reconsideration of philosophy in the late 1940s. At the time of writing, Tsurumi was also intimately involved in the Institute for the Science of Thought's project for a people's philosophy, so his praise for Otto was also very much an expression of his broader aspirations for a functional philosophy in the postwar period.

As he declared in the 1950 book *Amerika Tetsugaku,* the "revolution in philosophy" would have no effect until the "overthrow of philosophy" had begun. This implied nothing less than removing the "class of philosophy professionals" and shifting control to "those outside," to the "nonphilosophers" *(hi-tetsugakusha).* More than pursuing a simple hobby, these outsiders *(kyokugaisha)* would genuinely engage with philosophy as their own problem. Instead of engaging in the preciseness of academic philosophy, their approach would embrace ambiguous contemplation in a self-conscious way. The only reliable basis for a philosophy freed of academicism would be the people's self-awareness of their philosophy as a false discipline *(nisegakumon)* imbibed with human bias *(omoikomi),* likes, and dislikes.[57]

Admittedly, these ideas hardly reveal a robust and systematic application of pragmatism in Tsurumi's thought; for this we need to look elsewhere. In the 1946 essay "The Structure of Pragmatism," Tsurumi articulated a detailed nine-point plan for linguistic (Japanese-language) reform through the application of pragmatic thinking.[58] Moreover, in 1948 as part of the institute's project for a people's philosophy, he formulated a detailed questionnaire *(shitsumonsho)* to test popular aspirations, and he provided detailed analysis of the collected data.[59] In other words, there were concrete applications of his pragmatism. I want to stress two more general outcomes of Tsurumi's early postwar engagement with pragmatism, however.

First, as Amano suggests, when Tsurumi's pragmatism was combined with his remorse over the war, it propelled his thought beyond a self-reflexive critique of the intellectual and abstract language and into an engagement with the people and their philosophy. War and pragmatism became two foundations for the institute's project for a people's philosophy. Second, Tsurumi's engagement with pragmatism revealed the complicated yet powerful ideas informing progressives' understanding of the people and, later, the *shimin.* Consider again Tsurumi's claim that pragmatism should not be imported as a complete intellectual system but, rather, used to render indigenous ideas pragmatic without altering their essential indigenousness.[60] Harada Tōru has conceptualized such tendencies in Tsurumi's thought as a wavering *(yure)* or vacillation between Tsurumi the modernizer *(kindaishugisha)* and Tsurumi the nativist *(dochakushugisha).*[61] We might also view this as a tension between Tsurumi's modernity *(kindai)* and his concept of the ethnic nation *(minzoku).* In the face of such tension Tsurumi's intellectual strategy was to focus on his imagined and preferred vision of the people, even at the expense of slightly blurring scientific understanding.

Though Tsurumi by no means ignored the limitations of the people and at times clearly wanted to enlighten them, his ultimate aim was to uncover their potential and use this as a staging ground for their final comeback.[62] But pragmatism not only provided Tsurumi with a methodology for highlighting the progressive aspects of native culture; more interestingly, it also seems to have shaped his later assertion that the apparent backwardness of the people could be reinterpreted (and redirected) positively—what Amano Masako explains as Tsurumi's wager on the "limited potential" *(genteisareta kanōsei)* of the people.[63] In 1953, for example, Tsurumi argued that intellectuals "must foster the ability to see the wisdom *(chie)* in reactionary and backward things."[64]

Tsurumi's wavering did not go unnoticed. In 1959, activist-poet Tanigawa Gan flatly rejected Tsurumi's hesitancy in regard to the dense human relations of the old village community.[65] And, still later, in 1964 the poet Yoshimoto Takaaki took Tsurumi's internationalism to task, arguing instead for autonomy *(jiritsu)* and popular nationalism rooted in the very mundane reality of the everyday—ironically, something close to what Tsurumi was searching for himself.[66] Wavering aside, however, pragmatism provided Tsurumi with yet another intellectual tool to reimagine the people as an entity distinct from the state and the intellectual and through the lens of a rehabilitated ethnic nation and a legitimate sensibility of daily life. As subsequent developments reveal, this vision proved appealing—irresistible, in fact—to many intellectuals frustrated with Marxist dogma yet deeply committed to nurturing some kind of progressive collectivity capable of resisting the state and anchoring democracy. Nowhere was this more pronounced than in the institute's project for a people's philosophy.

A PEOPLE'S PHILOSOPHY

Tsurumi Kazuko, Shunsuke's sister, emerges as a key figure in the formation of the Institute for the Science of Thought in early 1946. Like Shunsuke, Kazuko suspended her studies and returned to Japan when war broke out. During the war years she was employed in the American Annex of the Pacific Association (Taiheiyō Kyōkai), an army-navy research institute established by the siblings' father, politician Tsurumi Yūsuke, to keep track of developments on the enemy's side.[67] This position proved useful, because through it Kazuko connected with intellectuals who would later form the core of the institute's membership, such as Maruyama Masao and physicist Taketani Mitsuo.

Soon after the war Kazuko convinced her father to make his publishing facilities available for printing a new magazine that would eventually be named *Shisō no Kagaku* (The Science of Thought).[68] Kazuko's motivation was more personal than professional: she wanted something to cheer up her depressive younger brother, Shunsuke. As Tsurumi Shunsuke recalled, Kazuko was a devoted Marxist for at least the first five postwar years and would have been quite happy to link up with the Japanese Communist Party.[69] But out of concern for her brother she determined to mobilize her wartime contacts into the magazine. Of course, attributing the institute's inception totally to Kazuko would be a mistake: it was Shunsuke, for example, who encouraged Kazuko to go and visit Maruyama after he had read the Imperial University professor's musings on "nature" and "invention." Maruyama fondly recalled how Tsurumi had avidly read the essay despite being unable to pronounce the character for "So" in "Sorai."[70] As Tsurumi's later activism would reveal, he was the consummate networker.

Among the original seven founding members who met first in February 1946, four had studied in America: Tsurumi Shunsuke and his sociologist sister Kazuko, the economist Tsuru Shigeto, and the intellectual historian Takeda Kiyoko; one in France: the theoretical physicist Watanabe Satoshi; and the other two in Japan: Maruyama Masao and the physicist Taketani Mitsuo. According to Lawrence Olson, institute members were "self-conscious intellectuals who felt a heavy responsibility to set new moral and ethical as well as political goals; moreover they shared a sense of urgency and felt a crying need to promote foreign knowledge after the relative isolation of the previous decades."[71] Though Kazuko was initially hesitant about the new magazine's stance, other founding members quickly decided that it would be neutral vis-à-vis the established left. It was Taketani Mitsuo, a Marxist not affiliated with the JCP, who most vehemently argued for this position, apparently an outcome of his experiences with the antifascist 1930s magazines *Sekai Bunka* (World Culture) and *Doyōbi* (Saturday), established by philosopher Nakai Masakazu in Kyoto.[72] The institute's founding statement spelled out this neutrality in the clearest of terms: "[The institute] is not an organization representing a single political ideology. Rather, we want to develop in Japan the practice of thinking about things clearly and communicating this in language that anyone can understand. Moreover, we want to become a space where people doing different work can come together and compare notes." Echoing the renewed interest in the quotidian perspective, the statement noted, "We are extremely ashamed of the fact that the ideas and language of Japanese intellectuals have to date been out of the reach of the Japanese masses *(taishū)*. Thus, little by little, we want to shed the intellectualism in our ideas and adopt a mode of thought as one of the masses *(taishū no hitori toshite)*. . . . Yet our direction will not be the erstwhile one of treating the masses as a mass *(masu)*; rather, we will be interested in each and every one of the masses *(taishū no hitorihitori)*. Through this interest we want to learn from the masses and improve our own sensibility and contemplative activity."[73]

As Kazuko later recalled, from the very outset there was a tension in the objectives of the institute—much like the tension I highlighted in Tsurumi's thought: on the one hand, to tutor the Japanese people in new ideas and scholarship from England and the United States and, on the other, to conduct research to shed light on the authentic Japanese folk, their values, and their culture. How these two objectives were to be connected was never clarified, of course, and according to Kazuko, as late as 1951 members still tended to treat the people as subjects to be analyzed and explained.[74] At this early stage members were still committed to objective academic analysis, and only through the experience of cultural circle activism and the events of the Anpo struggle would some transform into citizen movement intellectuals, merging with the people in a substantive way. Nevertheless, the idea of connecting with and understanding the people was on the agenda of the institute from very early on and by 1947 had evolved into a formal project to uncover the people's philosophy.

From a historical perspective, the institute's interest in the people was by no means unique in the early postwar, nor was it intellectually immune to trends of the moment. On the broadest level the institute operated side by side with a number of similar groups established during the period. The Twentieth Century Research Institute, for example, brought together academics and public intellectuals such as Shimizu Ikutarō, Ōkōchi Kazuo, Kawashima Takeyoshi, Kuno Osamu, and Maruyama Masao. According to Shimizu Ikutarō, this group was more about dissemination of ideas than research and focused its energies on giving lectures.[75] In a similar vein were the early postwar public lectures on philosophy by Nakai Masakazu in the Hiroshima region. Around the same time the People's University (Shomin Daigaku) was established in Shizuoka and supported by Maruyama Masao and others who lectured to the people. Just south of Tokyo too, the Kamakura Academia, a fascinating yet short-lived attempt to create an alternative to mainstream tertiary education, was established.[76] And still later (1949), the Peace Problems Symposium (Heiwa Mondai Danwakai) brought together an ideologically diverse range of intellectuals concerned with the issue of the postwar peace settlement.[77]

I would also note the so-called Movement for a People's History (Kokuminteki Rekishigaku Undō), led by the Marxist historian Ishimoda Shō during the early 1950s. Though ultimately victim of the mid-1950s turnaround in JCP strategy and its own inability to deal with groups "not scripted into [its] 'discovery' of Japanese 'ethnic culture,'" this movement made some interesting ground in shifting intellectual focus to the lives of ordinary people, not to mention its imagination of a progressive ethnic nationalism.[78] Ishimoda's 1952 book *The Discovery of History and the Nation,* for example, not only engaged with the issue of the ethnic nation *(minzoku)* but also presented the possibility of a people's history *(minshū no rekishi)* from below.[79] Following Ishimoda's lead, during 1952 and 1953 the left-leaning journal *Rekishi Hyōron* (Historical Review) focused on some of Japan's legendary indigenous martyrs *(gimin),* such as the famed Edo-period hero Sakura Sōgorō and the Meiji activist Tanaka Shōzō.[80]

As early as 1946 the Marxist literary critic Ara Masato was beginning to ask questions about the supposed breach between the "petit bourgeois intelligentsia" and the populace.[81] Ara was interested in finding legitimacy for the human ego in a leftist literature dominated by unitary conceptions of class as the sole revolutionary subject. He was an important participant in the debate on subjectivity *(shutaisei),* which was started in the late 1940s by rebellious leftist literary critics but later included philosophers and social scientists of Marxist and non-Marxist leanings.[82] Of primary relevance here, however, is Ara's suspicion of the gap between the intellectual and the people. In a February 1946 essay titled "Minshū to wa Tareka" (Who are the People?), Ara proclaimed, "I alone—the solitary me—am the people. This is neither irony nor paradox. . . . I cannot believe in petit bourgeois intelligentsia who look at reality through the eyes of the workers or the farmers. . . . I state resolutely that, other than my own unaided vision—in other words, the daily life sensibility of a petit bourgeois intelligentsia—all else is false."[83]

The point for Ara, at least in a literary sense, was that the "way to the people" could come about only through a "blood-soaked struggle with the inner self."[84] In other words, discovering the people led one back to the ego. In another similarly interrogatively titled essay of the same year, Ara asked "Minshū wa Doko ni iru" (Where Are the People?), to which he answered, "The people are inside me—the womb of literature is here!"[85] Obviously, Ara's people *(minshū)* were always imagined within his literary project to find legitimacy for the petit bourgeois ego, and this differed fundamentally from the institute's people. But the important point in common must certainly be the way Ara began to imagine a progressive subjectivity beyond Marxist categories and more closely tied to the individual (elitist though this certainly was). And, as a kind of augur of where such thought was heading, Ara was one of the few scholars to use the term *shimin* in a positive sense during these years, for example, in his 1947 essay "Shimin toshite" (As a Citizen).[86]

At the other end of the spectrum of influences on Tsurumi and the institute were various discussions on the ethnic nation *(minzoku)* and the common folk *(shomin)* during the late 1940s and early 1950s. In the writings of Shimizu Ikutarō, for example, we see a fascinating blending of concepts such as the Japanese *(Nihonjin)*, the common folk *(shomin)*, and the masses *(taishū)*. In his 1948 essay "Tokumei no Shisō" (Anonymous Thought), Shimizu called on intellectuals to refocus their inquiry from the narrow thought *(shisō)* of the academy toward the anonymous thought *(tokumei no shisō)* that the great majority of the nation *(kokumin)* followed in the context of daily life *(nichijō seikatsu)*.[87] Mirroring the tension between the modern and the indigenous that we saw in Tsurumi's early postwar thought, Shimizu argued that it was not simply a matter of distinguishing between so-called thought and anonymous thought. Rather, it would be necessary to "dislodge existing anonymous thought" via the "roundabout way of science" and produce instead a "principle for national action" based on the self. In other words, an anonymous thought centered on self-renewal.[88] The great paradox, or "wager," as Shimizu noted toward the end of the essay, was that anonymous thought was to be mobilized to bring itself under control *(nejifuseru)*.[89]

In another darkly ambivalent essay, "Shomin" (Common Folk), first published in early 1950, Shimizu juxtaposed the silent and obscure masses with the public identities of nation *(kokumin)*, people *(jinmin)*, and subjects *(shinmin)*.[90] Not confident enough to posit the potential for a new public ethic in the common folk, all Shimizu could manage was the possibility of intellectuals "climbing to a new level" by finding the common folk "within Japan" and "among ourselves" and by discovering "our values in their desires and our method in their experiences."[91] Important to note in the thought of Shimizu—seemingly more so from the 1950s onward—is the link between the ethnic nation *(minzoku)* and the situation of the common folk. Coinciding with the rise of leftist Asian ethnic nationalism, in the 1950s Shimizu proactively tied his call for improvement in the people's daily lives to an anti-U.S. ethnic nationalism. In his 1951 essay "The Japanese," responding to the question "What is a Japanese?" he said, "A Japanese is an Asian."[92] Even more provocatively, in a 1953 publication, *Kichi no Ko* (Children of the Military Bases), Shimizu and his fellow editors spoke of how the "various ethnic nations of Asia" were beginning to "discard" their "long and stained histories" and walk the "path of beautiful independence." The Japanese people, however, had been drawn into a "new state of colonization."[93]

We can see the influence of ethnic nationalism on the institute even more directly in Tsurumi Shunsuke and others' deep admiration for the sinologist Takeuchi Yoshimi. Tsurumi discovered Takeuchi through the latter's 1948 essay "Shidōsha Ishiki" (Leader Consciousness) and was so impressed that he bought copies for Kazuko and others in the institute. "I rarely write fan letters," Tsurumi recalled, "but on this occasion I was so moved that I sent a letter to Takeuchi." Tsurumi was moved by a number of elements in Takeuchi's work: the portrayal of the Japanese wartime army as aggressor in Asia, the critique of leader consciousness among Japanese intellectuals in the established left, and, finally, Takeuchi's critique of Japanese modernization through the juxtaposition of Chinese novelist Lu Xun. As Tsurumi put it, Takeuchi "clearly hammered out problems that I only vaguely grasped."[94] One of these was that a progressive postwar nationalism could be developed from the ethnic culture of the people and exist outside state and bureaucratic control *(kanryō tōsei).*[95]

The institute's project for a people's philosophy from 1946 to 1955 was deeply shaped by these early postwar intellectual trends and, in particular, the renewed interest in the ethnic nation. Kurata Ichirō, a student of the famed folklorist Yanagita Kunio, published the earliest essays on the people's philosophy in *Shisō no Kagaku* in late 1946 and 1947—much to the confusion of contemporary observer Ronald Dore, who saw these pieces as "strangely out of place among articles dealing with the problems of a modern industrial society."[96] With the benefit of hindsight, of course, we can see how Kurata's discussion of the eternal folk *(jōmin)* and their *hare* (festive) and *ke* (mundane) daily lives resonated with the resurgent attention to the ethnic nation. Most fascinating about Kurata's analysis is his description of the eternal folk and the characteristics of their philosophy. In his 1947 essay "Jōmin no Tetsugaku" (Philosophy of the Eternal Folk), Kurata firmly planted the people within the Japanese village and discovered the foundation stone of the eternal folk in the village elders *(korō)*. In the philosophy of such elders, Kurata argued, one could see the shared ideas and opinions of the villagers in their views of humanity, society, nature, and the divine, accompanied by the "smell of the ethnic nation from the past" *(furukukara no minzokutekina nioi)*.[97]

Though some expected a strongly modernist portrayal of the people from this "American-influenced" group, Kurata presented a strikingly particularistic vision. He summarized the three central features in the philosophy of the eternal folk as collectiveness *(shūdansei)* or a social aspect *(shakaisei)*, historicity *(rekishisei)*, and concreteness *(gushōsei)* or matter-of-factness *(sokubutsusei)*.[98] That Kurata—a folklorist of Japan—was the first to frame the discussion of the people's philosophy was an early sign that the indigenous or native would be central in any discussion of the people and, later, mythologies of the *shimin*.

In the early stages (1946–50) members' attention focused on analysis of interviews and questionnaires. One of the earliest undertakings involved Tsurumi Shunsuke, Kazuko, Maruyama Masao, Taketani Mitsuo, and others interviewing a variety of prominent public individuals. This work resulted in a two-volume 1950 publication, *Watashi no Tetsugaku* (My Philosophy), which contained interviews with Ozaki Yukio, Tokuda Kyūichi, Shiga Naoya, Yanagida Kunio, and Sekine Hiroshi,[99] prompting Ronald Dore to observe that the publication spoke more about the "philosophy of the uncommon man in Japan" than it did to the consciousness of the populace.[100] Beginning in 1951, however, members turned their eyes toward less extraordinary individuals, researching the lives of geisha, nurses, firemen, doctors, fishermen, rural wives, farmers, and policemen.[101] During this early period, institute members also engaged in extensive content analysis of popular literature and other media, such as comic books, films, plays, *rakugo* comedy, and popular songs. Though never adequately theorized, such analysis provided an important insight for members into the popular mind.[102]

Far more important in the context of the people, however, must be the sketches of ordinary individuals written during the early 1950s under the rubric of biographies of the common folk *(shomin retsuden)*.

Most of these sketches appeared in the pages of *Me* (The Bud), a short-lived replacement for *Shisō no Kagaku* during 1953 and early 1954, and in a later 1955 edited volume, *Minshū no Za* (The Seat of the Populace). Among these, a few representative examples warrant mention. Under the pen name Sugimura Shichirō, in the March 1953 edition of *Me,* Tsurumi Shunsuke wrote of nineteen-year-old Oikawa Setsu, a "pale-skinned" girl whose "cheeks turned red as she spoke."[103] The piece adopted a documentary style, avoiding chronology in favor of description and concentrating on Oikawa's likes and dislikes, her frustrations with an overbearing father, her political views, and her dreams of marriage to the ideal man. Later in the same year, Tsurumi (again as Sugimura) penned a short biography in *Chūō Kōron* on Kadota Ine, the wife of a businessman.[104] More impressive than the biography's personal focus are its opening passages, however. "We believe in the wisdom of the common folk *(shomin no chie),*" Tsurumi declared triumphantly. "We shall prove that the daily life of the populace *(minshū no seikatsu)* contains both serious challenges and the wisdom to overcome these."[105] Within the first three paragraphs Tsurumi presented no fewer than four renderings of the people: the common folk *(shomin),* the populace *(minshū),* the Japanese *(Nihonjin),* and the Japanese populace *(Nihon no minshū)*.

In the April 1954 edition of *Me,* Watanabe Katsumi recounted the "life and thought" of Toda Ichizō, a "round-shouldered" coal miner whose "torso was out of proportion to his shoulders, arms, legs, and stout build."[106] Even more than Tsurumi's pieces, Watanabe's portrait of Toda balanced description with extensive direct quotation, drawing the reader into the coal miner's world and the logic he used to negotiate daily life. Rather than reading like scholarly analyses, such works read like textual canvasses. In them one can sense not only intellectuals' attempt to paint a verbal picture of the people but also their intense—almost desperate—desire to discard academic inquiry and simply empathize with subjects intuitively as fellow human beings.

Of course, empathizing with the people was by no means a seamless and unproblematic process. Intellectual historian Takeda Kiyoko, for example, recounted her troubling observations of life in a munitions factory staffed by young women in the later stages of the war.[107] "As the products of a history wherein society forced its rules" on the individual, workers had learned to disengage with social institutions, constructing their daily lives in a different world.[108] The result was a dual personality consisting of the "external self entrusted with portraying the human model demanded by the outside world" and another internal self, "concealed" yet nonetheless "rigorously defended"—the human shell *(kaigara ningen)* protecting the interior human *(nakami no ningen)*.[109] But where, then, was the true human? Was it the human shell built to survive society or the interior human, concealed inside?[110] And how did the workers perceive their own identity? What did they learn from this hypocritical dual existence?

For Takeda, being and living the duality of a human shell opened the ethical basis of these workers' psyche to criticism. "The shell has an intimate connection to the outside world. It has a basis in society. It is a humanity that changes in any way to suit the demands or shifts of society. . . . During the Pacific War it became the brave warrior and the industrial soldier, and when democracy suddenly became good, it quickly adopted the coloring and shape of democracy."[111] In short, it was an "instrumental way of living, produced out of convenience," and quite naturally, the interior human and the human shell had lost their "organic connection" and their "mutual understanding."[112] The interior human had no interest whatsoever in how the outer shell changed and, by consequence, no sense of responsibility. Indeed, there was no room for "subjective moral responsibility" in this duality, since the interior human was constructed around an ego "comfortably dozing" in a "primitive infancy" prior to "historicity" and "social responsibility."[113]

Takeda Kiyoko's ambivalent vision is a good place to step back and consider the overall yield of the project. Did the institute actually uncover a people's philosophy, and did its members' voluminous observations of the people condense into any kind of ideal sociological type? In broad terms, the answer is no—and we could hardly expect it to be otherwise, given participants' commitment to eclecticism. But, by the same token, after reading this literature one is left with an embryonic iconography in which the ethnic nation and the quotidian perspective resolve into an ethical—if all-too-human—vision of the people. Consider Tsurumi Shunsuke's acclaim for the prewar politician and activist Tanaka Shōzō (1841–1913). Son of a village headman and himself a wealthy land investor, Tanaka leapt to public prominence in 1891 when elected to the House of Representatives in the Japanese Diet. Tanaka's specific agenda in Tokyo was to question the government's policy regarding pollution of the Watarase River by the Ashio copper mine in his Tochigi electorate. Hereafter Tanaka became embroiled in a twenty-three-year battle to win compensation for the people of his beloved Yanaka village. In 1901, sensing the futility of parliamentary procedure, Tanaka appealed directly to the emperor—an action that stunned the nation and left many fearful for his life. Though Tanaka came through unscathed, the Ashio problem remained unsolved even at the time of his death in 1913.

According to Tsurumi, Tanaka was one of Japan's few truly original thinkers, not because he contributed to the "intellectual heritage of humanity," but because his thought was "remarkably in tune with the conditions of that age."[114] Though Tanaka's thought possessed no "original structure," for Tsurumi it contained a kind of intellectual "iron ore" from which thinkers could extract pure wisdom.[115] Indeed, Tanaka's life and thought presented a method for "understanding democracy from the perspective of the people's right to resist."[116] Tanaka's conviction that there was "no Japan other than Yanaka Village" *(Yanaka no hoka ni Nihon nashi)* presented an original and native conceptualization of democracy, according to Tsurumi.[117] By focusing on the rights of a minority, Tanaka mounted a criticism of the Meiji system as a whole, and this produced the vigor and originality in his thought. Even after seven long years of occupation, this was an aspect of democracy the Americans "could not teach" Japan, since it was the very weakness in Americans' own brand of democracy.[118] All the specificities of Tanaka's rootedness in his age, his consistency *(ikkansei)*, and his deep commitment to Yanaka as the authentic Japan supposedly gave his life and thought a "universalism" to be admired.[119]

Tsurumi's portrait of Tanaka Shōzō is about as close as any institute member ever came to an ideal typology of the people. Indeed, in Tanaka Shōzō we seem to have it all—or, at least, what institute members so desired: criticism *(hihan)* of the state, empathy *(dōjō)* with the dispossessed masses, and the guidance *(shishin)* of a self-made man. We have the perspective of an inhabitant of daily life *(seikatsusha)* and a representative of the common *(shomin)* and eternal *(jōmin)* folk. Moreover, in Tanaka's appeal to the emperor we see the possibility of protest through the empowering core of the ethnic nation *(minzoku)*. And perhaps we have a vision of the political citizen *(seijiteki shimin)* in Tanaka-as-politician. Of course, Tsurumi's essay on Tanaka must be read historically: in 1966 when he penned it, Japanese civic protest was on the rise with the spread of anti–Vietnam War groups throughout the country. Not surprising that Tsurumi should revive an indigenous Asian incarnation of radical democracy.

For a less romantic appraisal of the people and their potential at that historical moment, we might consider Tsurumi's 1955 essay, "On

Biography." Here he suggested that the philosophy of the people be understood as a kind of "mild cunning" *(odayakana zurusa)* embedded in the everyday. Indeed, it was wrong to expect the wisdom of the people to provide "progressive commentaries on the social structure or superior insights into the movements of world history." Such commentaries and insights, in fact, embodied the "wisdom of the child," while mild cunning represented that of the adult. "When the child becomes an adult, it forgets the knowledge of childhood," Tsurumi argued, "yet, during childhood the individual can never possess the knowledge of the adult." It would thus be necessary "to reconstitute the cunning, the conscience, and the creativity of the people in such a way that these connect[ed] to proper judgments about the movement of world history and to a resolve to move in a progressive direction." The challenge was to make the future by "turning around and facing oneself."[120] Bereft of naïve idealism, the people's mild cunning, Tsurumi argued, could become a new intellectual apparatus to elevate popular consciousness above and beyond everyday life—a kind of synthesis with no prior dialectic and politicality without contentious origins. Though they were ambiguously articulated here, Tsurumi was clearly heading toward an ethics and politics of daily life that would become central in later mythologies of the *shimin* and civic protest. Indeed, by shining a non-Marxist spotlight on the people, the project opened up a new strain of progressive thought in postwar Japan capable of rehabilitating the nation and infusing the private and the everyday with historical import. From the late 1950s it would be this same ethnic nation, this same daily life, and—above all else—this same people that Tsurumi and others would use to animate the *shimin* idea.

THE CULTURAL CIRCLE MOVEMENT: REVITALIZING GRASSROOTS ASSOCIATIONALISM

The project for a people's philosophy had more or less run its course by the mid-1950s, but initiatives to uncover and fashion an autonomous and democratic subjectivity at the grass roots of Japanese society continued. Among the impulses beating at the heart of the institute was its members' desire to have the people express their own ideas in their own words. Members' growing interest in the personal advice *(minoue sōdan)* columns of weekly magazines, so popular among 1950s youth, is instructive here.[121] More than academic interviews or surveys, such columns presented for Tsurumi Kazuko and others a purer and more unfiltered form of popular wisdom, since in them people could speak free of any intellectual intervention. Not coincidentally, members' interest in such popular forms of expression dovetailed with the rise of so-called independent cultural circle *(sākuru)* activism in the early 1950s. To an extent, of course, the Institute for the Science of Thought was itself a cultural circle (an elite one, to be sure) based on independent research, eclecticism, individual expression, and internally democratic methods.

Many other circles, in fact, would sprout from the intellectual seedbed of the institute in the 1950s, benefiting greatly from its early postwar attempt to liberate knowledge and cultural production from the academy. Institute members were greatly encouraged when ordinary people began to form cultural circles, with some members—such as Tsurumi Kazuko—working tirelessly to nurture these fledgling expressions of popular sentiment. For Kazuko and others, cultural circles were everything they had hoped for in the project for a people's philosophy: here were the silent masses acting and speaking for themselves. In the circles, they believed, the long-repressed consciousness of the people was beginning to move.

The term *circle (sākuru)* first entered the Japanese lexicon in the early 1930s when art critic and JCP member Kurahara Korehito brought it back to Japan from the fifth meeting of the Profintern. Writing in 1931, Kurahara defined circles as "support organs for spreading the political and organizational influence of the fundamental proletarian organizations (parties and unions) among workers and for mobilizing workers under the leadership of these organs."[122] In plain language this meant that cultural and other leisure activities among workers were to be used by the organs of the left to promote socialism and bring workers under party control. After a hiatus during the war years, in 1945 leftist organizations began to utilize cultural circles to manipulate workers' free time, resulting in a struggle between unions and managers for control over workplace recreation. Andrew Gordon explains how as early as 1947 workers in Kawasaki and Tsurumi were organized for "autonomous" activities such as music and theater. *Autonomous*, of course, had a very specific and almost inherently contradictory meaning: freedom from managerial control but not "independence from other affiliation."[123]

The reality was that the agents of the left were among the most active organizers of cultural circles, utilizing them as spaces to nurture workers' proletarian consciousness. Aspirations aside, however, leftist organizers' efforts were largely stillborn. Workplace cultural circles never lived up to their revolutionary potential, and participants often-times showed little interest in toeing the party line.[124] As Gordon notes, it was never clear how "recreation and self-cultivation," "the nurturing of a democratic citizenry," and the production of a "national political movement" were to be reconciled.[125] Faced with these contradictions and a rapidly changing workplace, the leftist-led cultural circle movement in workplaces had literally burned out by the 1960s, never even threatening to ignite the flame of revolution among workers. Significantly, cultural circle activism persisted, not in workplaces, but among independent groups, sometimes affiliated with socialist and communist organs but oftentimes not.

It was with the aim of studying these new experiments in associationalism that Tsurumi Shunsuke, Ōsawa Shinichirō, and other un-aligned progressives formed the Association for Groups (Shūdan no Kai) (hereafter, the association) in 1963. As Amano Masako notes, membership and participation in the association was extremely fluid.[126] A core of progressive intellectuals from the institute, such as Tsurumi and Ōsawa, were joined by a transient membership, including Amano herself and Kobayashi Tomi, who had played a crucial role in the citizen protests of 1960. The eight or so original members of the association met at a Chinese restaurant in Tokyo's Kinshichō area, which had a reputation as a gathering spot for "idle-chatting," "delinquent" youth.[127] This suited Tsurumi and others: for the price of one expensive cup of Chinese tea (fifty yen), the group could chat in the restaurant "cheaply" for hours on end. The group published its findings in a weighty volume covering circle activism from 1945 through to 1976.[128] What is interesting about this work is that its coverage stretches all the way from the early cultural circles of the 1950s to the later civic protest and activism of the 1960s—evidencing Tsurumi and others' perception that the one emerged from the other.

In the preface to the 1976 volume, under the title "Kono Hon no Hōhō" (This Book's Methodology), Sasaki Gen attempted to categorize the phenomenon, identifying six broad categories of circles:[129]

1. Friendship/affinity groups (travel groups, alumni groups, war veterans)
2. Common-interest clubs (stamp collectors, bonsai groups)
3. Study groups (literature reading groups)
4. Civic action groups (anti–nuclear weapons, antipollution, antiwar)

5. Cultural production groups (haiku, writing, life composition)
6. Research groups (workplace histories, mothers' histories, nature study)

Of course, Sasaki admitted such categorization could only be provisional, since many circles clearly fell under more than one category, and, moreover, activism had a tendency to morph from one category to another.[130] In their influential studies of postwar circle activism, both Tsurumi Shunsuke and Ōsawa Shinichirō traced the history of circles to the earliest days of the postwar period. Ōsawa described circle activism from 1945 to 1952 as an early attempt by Japanese people to create their own "conceptual spaces" and "life spheres" free of external control.[131] He identified an eclectic and dynamic array of movements during this period, such as the Exchange Market (Kōkanjo) in Tokyo's Nakano District. Here citizens dealt with postwar shortages through "mutual assistance" and "autonomous human relations" based on "self-support."[132] Ōsawa also highlighted mutual support groups formed by prostitutes and the homeless, such as the amusingly named Yamatani School for Pickpockets (Yamatani no Suri Gakkō).[133] In the same period, war survivor Shiratori Kunio established the Mountain Range Association (Yamanami no Kai) as a space to deal with war memories and the guilt of having survived.[134] This group would become a model for later independent civic activism.

The early postwar years also witnessed a flurry of independent association building among academics and other public intellectuals, as with the Institute for the Science of Thought and the Twentieth Century Research Institute. Representative of intellectuals' early attempts to stimulate popular political consciousness is the activism of philosopher-librarian Nakai Masakazu in Hiroshima. Beginning with a talk on Immanuel Kant to a small group in eastern Hiroshima in late 1945, Nakai's grassroots lecture tour extended throughout the prefecture to include men and women with diverse regional and class backgrounds. At the lecture tour's height in 1947, Nakai and his colleagues organized a "summer-term university," in which some forty lecturers spoke to local residents throughout eastern Hiroshima. As Leslie Pincus explains, Nakai's cultural movement represented more than intellectuals vainly attempting to enlighten the people. It was "a historically unprecedented social experiment" wherein people attempted "to understand their histories and restructure their souls along with their social existence."[135] Nakai's movement was years ahead of its time in many

ways, and Nakai himself was a rudimentary model for the citizen movement intellectuals of the coming decades. His belief that Japan was an
"aggressor nation" and that ordinary Japanese were complicit and,
hence, should "turn their critical faculties on themselves" prefigured
debates that anti–Vietnam War activists would resurrect again in the
mid-1960s.[136] Nakai's methodology and concept of the people resonated closely with members of the institute. Nakai believed that those
who visited his lectures were not there to "simply accumulate knowledge" but to "remake themselves" through a "revolution of consciousness." All they lacked was a "methodology"—something that he, as an
intellectual, had a duty to provide.[137] So the issue for him and others
was not how an intellectual vanguard should mobilize the masses but
how the people could be stimulated to organize themselves.[138]

The real takeoff for independent circle activism came in the 1950s
in response to a litany of controversies beginning with SCAP's (the
Supreme Commander of the Allied Powers) cancellation of the general
strike in 1947, the Red Purge of the early 1950s, the 1951 split of the
Japan Socialist Party into left and right factions, the JCP's turn to
extreme left adventurism, and the tragic events of Bloody May Day in
1952, when clashes with riot police over the peace settlement resulted
in the death of two protesters. Not only was the JCP severely demoral-
ized by the Red Purge, but also its support among more moderate
elements decreased sharply when, in the early 1950s, Secretary-General
Tokuda Kyūichi outlined a more radical program for revolution, effectively denouncing Nosaka Sanzō's early program of a united democratic
front and the creation of a "lovable" communist party.

This turn to so-called extreme-left adventurism *(kyokusa bōkenshugi)*,
though short-lived (it would be rejected at the party's sixth national
conference in 1955, the so-called Rokuzenkyō), had serious consequences for the party's wider political support, and by the time JCP
members realized this in 1955 it was too late for damage control. The
resolution of the JCP's 1955 conference noted, in a somewhat amusing
way, that Tokuda's 1951 thesis, though "entirely correct," contained
numerous "errors," not least of which was the turn to "extreme-left
adventurism." Correctly, the resolution noted how the party's "authority among the masses had been damaged, and the construction of a
national liberation democratic united front . . . made more difficult."
In short, extreme-left adventurism did nothing but weaken "ties with
the masses" as a result of its "high-handedness" and "unrealistic
demands," and in the end the masses were merely "alienated" and the

party left "isolated."[139] According to Tsurumi Shunsuke, the eventual taming of the ideological left by the state and moderate progressives forced activists to rethink their strategies and approach to activism, and it was through such reflection that the independent circle movement emerged as a possible alternative.[140]

But it was not only extremism on the left that shifted attention to independent cultural circles. Ironically, developments in Communist China alerted intellectuals to the possible use of circles to cultivate an antistatist ethnic-national consciousness. As Hidaka Rokurō recalled in 1959, the rising profile of grassroots circle activism coincided with the arrival—from Communist China—of the idea of the mass line *(taishū rosen)* method. Herein the intellectual was to enter into the world of the masses, learn their hopes and desires, and ultimately concentrate these into a revolutionary political program. In the process of this movement the political consciousness of the masses would supposedly be heightened too.[141] Enamored by the Chinese experiment, many within cultural circles showed an interest in the progressive potentialities of the ethnic nation: Ōsawa reported how numerous circles at the time faithfully read Mao's famous essays "On Contradiction" ("Mujunron," 1937) and "On Practice" ("Jissenron," 1937).[142] Similarly, the sinologist and Lu Xun specialist Takeuchi Yoshimi found an eager audience among many grassroots groups.[143] So independent circle activism was not simply filling a void left by the abortive workplace circle movement. As the attraction to Mao suggests, intellectuals saw in these groups indigenous pathways to democratization and liberation.

A case in point is the so-called life composition movement led by leftist teachers such as Muchaku Seikyō and Kokubun Ichitarō and progressive intellectuals such as Tsurumi Kazuko, Hidaka Rokurō, and playwright Kinoshita Junji.[144] Life composition—ordinary people gathering to discuss and write about their lives—had a long history in Japan. As early as 1913, progressive schoolteachers fostered the movement among school students in their attempt to correct the excesses of nationalistic, government-sponsored elementary education.[145] The movement began in the context of language education as a methodology to encourage the "unencumbered and 'pure' subjective written expression of the everyday thoughts and actions of ordinary people."[146] Ashida Enosuke, an elementary school teacher and founder of the prewar movement, began experimenting with classroom composition in the late 1890s primarily for language training.[147] But over the coming years Ashida's approach underwent dramatic change, particularly after he came into contact with the enigmatic figure Okada Torajirō in the 1910s.

Okada gained prominence among progressives during this period as a result of his innovative method of "quiet contemplation" *(seiza)*.[148] Originally an advocate of agricultural reform, Okada suddenly abandoned his wife and children in 1906, retreating into the mountains. After a period of self-imposed exile, Okada claimed to have healed his mental anguish through the formulation of an innovative method of seated contemplation. As Tsurumi Shunsuke and Kuno Osamu explain, Okada's movement thereafter spread as a kind of aesthetic of daily life, mutating eventually into a new religion *(shinkō shūkyō)*.[149] At its height, the movement attracted some twenty thousand proponents, and contemplation sessions attracted hundreds of devotees, including political activist Tanaka Shōzō. The movement remained popular until Okada's death at the age of forty-eight, in 1920.

What then of the connection to life composition? Together with the contemplative method, Okada also practiced a form of "nondirective counseling," which encouraged participants to define problems and formulate solutions independently with only facilitation from the counselor—what Tsurumi and Kuno amusingly characterized as a Zen-like method, similar to American psychoanalysis of the 1950s.[150] It was Okada's method that transformed Ashida's conceptualization of life composition. Originally drawn to Okada in 1912 in search of a cure for his own mental anguish through contemplation and nondirective counseling, Ashida found not only spiritual solace but also a new understanding of life composition as a method for generating a sense of subjectivity in young children. This discovery proved important in the subsequent development of the life composition movement. Freed into the hands of like-minded progressive teachers and in the comparatively liberal environment of Taishō period Japan (1912–26), the movement took on an overtly political agenda aimed at awakening the class consciousness of participants. The act of discovering individual subjectivity through composition, teachers discovered, quite easily transformed into a process of releasing submerged political consciousness. With the end of Taishō democracy, however, the movement came in for severe state suppression and went into an extended hibernation that would end only with defeat in war.

Progressive educators revived life composition among elementary school children in the 1950s. The most influential of publications were Kokubun Ichitarō's guidebook *Atarashii Tsuzurikata Kyōshitsu* (The

New Composition Classroom, 1952) and Muchaku Seikyō's *Yamabiko Gakkō* (Echo School, 1951), an unassuming collection of essays, poetry, and woodcuttings by elementary school students.[151] Muchaku's work, in particular, had a profound effect beyond education circles. The volume's appeal lay in its down-to-earth yet powerful decentering and reversing of knowledge production. By releasing the written word into the hands of his students, Muchaku directly challenged the modernist conceptualization of education as a unidirectional instrument for knowledge transmission. From a literary perspective too, *Echo School* challenged the notion that the written word belonged to or was the sole product of specialist writers—be they novelists, journalists, or academics. Children—what's more, unsophisticated country folk from the nether land of Yamagata Prefecture—could produce valuable meaning through the simple logic of the rural perspective. As Mari Yamamoto notes, *Echo School* also resonated with the general rediscovery of the ethnic nation in leftist circles: writing about everyday life helped children uncover "unique traits long embedded in Japanese society and its culture, language, and writing system."[152] In fact, in its most extreme forms, life composition was even mobilized as an ethnic nationalist attack on the American military presence in Japan, for example, as in *Kichi no Ko* (Children of the Military Bases), edited by Shimizu Ikutarō and others in 1953. The book was a compilation of essays by children living next to U.S. military bases, and Shimizu explained how the work expressed their trauma as inhabitants of a newly "colonized nation."[153]

From its beginnings among rural youth, the postwar life composition movement quickly spread, mostly among middle- and working-class housewives and young working women. At its height the movement even broke into the mass media. In late 1951 the *Asahi Shimbun* launched its innovative column, "Hitotoki," the first in Japan wholly devoted to reader contributions. Despite the limitations of the column in terms of sheer space, its creation, as Wesley Sasaki-Uemura notes, "represented a fundamentally different way of conceiving the media's function in society."[154] Where male editors had previously claimed a monopoly on expressing the voice of the people, "Hitotoki" let the people (i.e., women) speak for themselves. And, more significantly, in time such cultural spaces stimulated independent mobilization among groups of women throughout Japan in regard to a variety of political and social issues.[155]

Among institute members, Tsurumi Kazuko became most directly involved in writing circles after discovering *Echo School* in 1951 and meeting Muchaku and Kokubun at the National Conference for Composition Education in 1952.[156] Kazuko was attracted to life composition for a number of reasons: the way it supposedly broke down the barrier between student and teacher, the way it connected to everyday realities, its emphasis on self-renewal *(jiko kaizō)*, and its potential to become a literature of resistance.[157] By self-renewal Kazuko imagined a process in which ordinary people (especially women) solved their own problems through collective reflection and apparently without the intervention of intellectuals or the state (though she and other intellectuals were intimately involved, of course). Here she was influenced by Takeuchi Yoshimi—her self-proclaimed intellectual master—and especially the claim in his famous work on Chinese author Lu Xun that "revolution is when the people *(kokumin)* change themselves."[158] According to Kazuko, the process of life composition not only was one of catharsis but also involved sharing problems through discussion, criticism, rewriting, reconsideration, and repetition in daily life. By exposing their own internal contradictions and divisions, members forged unity and a recognition of the social significance of their experience.[159] As she stated in a 1961 essay, "The people who make history, write history, and through writing they remake themselves."[160] Or, at least, this was the ideal of life composition.

Kazuko's involvement in the movement developed in numerous spheres and evidences how some progressives were transforming themselves into movement intellectuals. Early on she became involved with a circle of female workers at the Toa Wool Spinning and Weaving Company in Mie Prefecture. Here labor activist Sawai Yoshirō mobilized women into the Association to Record Daily Life (Seikatsu o Kiroku suru Kai). Kazuko—together with Kinoshita Junji and later Hidaka Rokurō and others—edited the group's 1954 book *Haha no Rekishi* (Mothers' Histories) and the 1956 volume *Nakama no Naka no Renai* (Love among Friends).[161] In Tokyo, Kazuko also formed the Daily Life Composition Group (Seikatsu o Tsuzurukai) with working-class housewives, young female office and factory workers, and schoolteachers. In 1954 this group produced a book of compositions titled *Enpitsu o nigiru Shufu* (Housewives Holding a Pencil). The title was a jab at common wisdom: as Kazuko noted, women were supposed to be holding a rice ladle *(shamoji)*, not a pencil.[162]

Reflecting on the life composition movement in the 1960s, Kazuko explained, "They do not have the grand intention of producing 'works of literature.'"[163] Instead, the act of writing was simply an attempt to make their lives better. Members formed these groups as a way to "compare notes on daily life," not to come up with some alternative grand theory.[164] To date "the masses have shown their respect for (actually *avoidance* of) so-called intellectuals . . . but in their heart of hearts they are actually grumbling, 'what the hell are [intellectuals] talking about?' This is because those who speak on the radio and write in the newspapers have no idea about *reality*. Those who do know about *reality* simply clench their teeth and do their best to survive from day to day."[165] "In all these cases," Kazuko argued, the "motive" of "housewives" and "working women" to "write about their lives, is the correct understanding that, to the extent they leave this task to professional intellectuals, it will never be their own."[166] As one housewife remarked, "Up until now it was our turn to read, but I have the feeling it is now our turn to write. Most of the works I've read to date—mainly novels—are annoyingly written in a way that looks down upon their subjects. But I want to write in a way that represents the angle of those who are looked down upon."[167]

Kazuko (and Shunsuke) admitted that cultural circle activists often failed to see the link between the problems of daily life and the wider political, economic, and social structure. But, as I show in the following chapter, it was just such attachment to daily life that stimulated citizen protest beginning in the late 1950s. For instance, the *Asahi Shimbun* column "Hitotoki," discussed above, became a medium for the formation of so-called Grass Seeds Groups (Kusa no Mi Kai), many of which protested the U.S.-Japan Security Treaty renewal in 1960.[168] Similarly, the Children of the Cedars Association (Sugi no Ko Kai)—a reading group formed by a university professor and middle-class women in Tokyo's Suginami Ward—became an important impetus behind the anti-nuclear movement through its signature campaign in 1954.[169] Sawai Yoshirō of the Association to Record Daily Life in Mie Prefecture later became involved in the infamous antipollution movement among residents in Yokkaichi City during the 1960s. He was a member of two groups: the Association to Record Daily Life and Pollution (Seikatsu—Kōgai o Kiroku suru Kai) and the provocatively named Citizen Warriors Group to Fight Yokkaichi Pollution (Yokkaichi Kōgai to Tatakau Shiminhei no Kai).[170] Kazuko herself was later involved in the recording of life histories of Minamata poisoning victims in the 1970s as part of the progressive historian Irokawa Daikichi's famous 1984 work *Minamata no Keiji* (The Revelations of Minamata).[171] In short, cultural circle activism steeped in the indigenous daily life of the people could be political, and ultimately it did feed into citizen protest movements of the late 1950s and beyond.

Of course, we should be careful not to simply replicate progressive historical narratives that seamlessly slot cultural circles into a romantic tradition of independent grassroots protest. Liberation from the fetters of leftist dogma not only empowered organizers to foment a new politics of resistance but also exposed circles to the pull of new forces and the construction of civic activism around values often deeply at odds with the progressive vision. Nowhere is this clearer than the Green Association movement, one of the most high-profile cultural circles of the early postwar decades. With over one thousand local chapters at its height in the late 1950s, the association was the brainchild of the magazine editor Terashima Fumio, who imagined these spontaneously formed chapters as spaces for the unification of theory and praxis.[172] The movement developed by way of the magazine *Jinsei Techō* (Life Notebook), established in 1952 with Terashima as editor. The original idea for the magazine came from Daiwa Iwao, editor of *Jinsei Techō*'s predecessor, *Ashi* (The Reed), itself one of the early success stories of the 1950s human interest magazine *(jinsei zasshi)* boom.[173] Daiwa decided to establish *Life Notebook* after he became frustrated with an ideological dispute among editors of *The Reed* in the wake of JCP adventurism in the early 1950s. Looking for a new approach and a breath of fresh editorial air, Daiwa turned to his friend Terashima Fumio, editor and owner of a small publishing company. From the publication's low-key launch in 1952, Terashima went about fashioning a life composition magazine *(jinsei kiroku zasshi)* in which "nameless young men and women" could discuss their daily lives and contemplate life in general. By reading this magazine wholly composed of reader contributions, youth would supposedly realize that others like themselves led the same lifestyles and dealt with the same anxieties.[174] In the early 1950s *Life Notebook*'s readership comprised primarily working-class and agricultural youth in their late teens and early twenties, and some 77 percent of this readership resided in regional cities.[175]

Life Notebook hit the shelves at an opportune moment. The early 1950s witnessed a boom in life composition and popular participation in all forms of written media. After one year of publication the magazine had a circulation of ten thousand, and by 1956 this had grown sevenfold. Terashima, too, was very much a product of the ideological upheavals in 1950s Japan. As he explained,

I had an interest in farmers' movements and the JSP's farmer-worker activism from the beginning of the Shōwa period and, though only in a limited way, had participated in proletarian movements. . . . [In the postwar] I was primarily involved in publishing, and as a result of this experience . . . I came to the conclusion that nearly all of the cultural and political movements aimed at the democratization of Japan were self-indulgent organizations controlled by a small group of progressive elements who gave no consideration to the "conditions within Japan." I decided that they were fundamentally flawed.

Terashima imagined *Life Notebook* as a kind of antidote to this misguided "universalism" in progressive ideology. Social movements, he concluded, should not be controlled by "intellectuals who put theory first and do not accompany this with action." Better to produce autonomous individuals *(jiritsu shita ningen)*—nameless though they may be—who could stand up and say "this is my life, and this is what I think."[176]

Like Takeuchi Yoshimi, Terashima was deeply impressed by the Maoist Chinese model of nation building without "direct foreign importation" *(gaikoku choku yunyū)*.[177] This interest in the potential of the ethnic nation informed his interest in Ninomiya Sontoku (or Kinjirō, 1787–1856), an enigmatic intellectual and moral exemplar from Japan's Tokugawa period. Like many others of his age, under the wartime education system Terashima had been inculcated in Sontoku's teachings about sincerity, diligence, and frugality, and he remained particularly attached to Sontoku's insistence that learning sprouts from everyday life rather than from book learning. In the early postwar years he wrote a biography of Sontoku and became committed to revitalizing the image of this physiocracist *(nōhonshugisha)* "disavowed by postwar democracy."[178] As Amano Masako later explained, Terashima began a project for the "unity of theory and praxis"—a "noncontradictory unification" *(mumujunteki tōitsu)* of Sontoku's teachings with Maoism.[179] *Life Notebook,* the vehicle for this project, would become the mobilizing medium for Green Association chapters organized by youth interested in constructing their own lives on the basis of a pragmatic philosophy of the everyday. And, to emphasize the movement's ideological "nonalignment," it would be known as the Green Association. Unlike "red" *(aka)* groups based on "particular ideologies or ideas," the Green Association would be about the "imagination of a better daily life."[180]

Despite his rejection of ideology, however, around 1955 Terashima issued a "Green Pledge" (Midori no Chikai) with seven guiding principles for local Green Association chapters. Members collectively read out the pledge before every meeting.[181] The pledge encouraged them to "develop and implement positive ideas" and to "clearly state" what they thought. Like modern-day embodiments of Ninomiya Sontoku, members would constantly ask "why" and always try to find "better ways" of doing things. They would interact with others in a truly "genuine" *(sunao na kokoro de)* way, free of conceit and jealousy. They would recognize how trials and tribulations were a shared predicament among humans and would never "lose hope" or "give up." Problems would be opened up through discussion, collective consideration, and the "combination of energies." And, in keeping with the Sontokian overtones, members would be "proud" of their "work," regardless of its insignificance. Green Association chapters were to strive for a world in which work was "more and more rewarding." Terashima summed up the spirit of the Green Association with the words of his father. Years earlier Terashima had criticized Japanese society for his personal failure to enter higher education and find regular work. To this, his rustic father had retorted, "There's no trusting a man who can't swipe a fly away from his face!"[182] As Amano notes, this was an outright rejection of the "self-righteous" assumption that "without a change in the political system" an individual simply could not lay down a "life plan." Indeed, if society was really that "bad," all the more reason for the individual to "fervently persevere."[183] According to Green Association logic, old left progressives constantly focused on changing the "objective conditions," yet they failed to turn the objective spotlight on their own lives. They failed to ask, "What can I do to change?" or "How can I adapt?"

In the early to mid-1950s, Green Association chapters were the primary productive units for *Life Notebook*. Members used their meetings to discuss all aspects of life, ranging from family budgets to national politics. These discussions became the basis of written contributions to the magazine, making participants both readers and writers. Despite the focus on self-improvement, Sontokian ethics, and ideological "greenness," however, the stunning growth of local chapters from 1955 invited the suspicion of the state. With many laborers in their ranks, authorities (mistakenly) began to wonder if the Green Association was not merely a front for a communist comeback, and from the mid-1950s local chapters often faced official investigation. This negative state attention proved too much for many in the rank-and-file of the movement, and membership of local associations plummeted, not recovering until 1958.[184]

If the Green Association was "lime green" before this official attention, afterward leaders made sure they were "myrtle." Amano explains how contentious social issues disappeared entirely from the magazine in the late 1950s, replaced now with a strict focus on how to live.[185] Leaders fashioned *Life Notebook* and the Green Association into media for the formulation of life techniques: how to save for retirement, the benefits of marrying later, and the promotion of birth control. Rather than promoting human sentiment or ideas, magazine editors promoted techniques for self-expression, emphasizing the advice of specialists. By the 1970s, the Green Association and *Life Notebook* had completely transformed, focusing now on the "creation of a healthy body and spirit."[186] State intervention in the late 1950s certainly accelerated this process, but Terashima and other leaders' early rejection of socialist theory in favor of a Sontokian ethic of self-help deeply shaped the movement's evolution. In fact, the history of the Green Association speaks volumes about the development not only of circle activism but also of later civic activism. The movement certainly proved that, on the level of praxis, a quotidian ethic of self-help could be as powerful a motivating force as leftist revolutionary theory. But it also revealed the potential of movements either to degenerate into apolitical associations for self-preservation or, conversely, to reconstitute themselves into a nationalized project for a new community. Either path would raise serious questions about the fundamental politicality of grassroots groups mobilized after the near death of revolutionary leftist politics in the first postwar decade.

THEORIZING CIRCLES

Writing in the journal *Chūō Kōron* (The Central Review) in mid-1956, sociologist Sasaki Ayao suggested that cultural circles boldly confronted three historical challenges. First, the circle was a vehicle for popular consciousness *(minshū no ishiki)* to shed "ancient magical emotion" for "rational thought processes" *(gōritekina shikōhōhō)*.[187] The circle was a response and challenge to the "premodern elements of society" and hence a therapy for the feudal mind.[188] But for Sasaki, as much as they remedied premodernity, circles also defended against an intrusive hypermodernity. As he noted, "Though our society has its feet planted in the ground before modernity, its head protrudes into a hypermodern stratosphere."[189] Under the detrimental sway of America, Sasaki could not but lament the mass societization and mechanization of Japanese daily life. In the face of such forces, he believed, circles could be spaces for people to regain their "humanity" and "subjectivity." They could rejuvenate the alienated modern self through warm interaction. And finally, in their expression of humanism Sasaki saw circles as a bulwark against fascism, the manifestation of all "inhumane violence."[190] In the face of these forces, circles promised to become the basis of a new ethnic national culture *(minzokuteki na kokumin bunka)*.[191]

Sasaki was not alone: other proponents saw in circles a new model of association based not on imported dogma but on the indigenous democratic community. For Ōsawa Shinichirō, circles addressed desires and issues beyond the capacities of family, village, school, labor union, and political party. In these liberated, egalitarian, horizontally organized spaces, people could transcend established social norms and organizational rules, enjoying the sense of emancipation and energy possible only through direct human association.[192] The collective activities and objectives of circles grew out of this key interaction, and even when circles had a specific objective, the dynamic would always be such living interaction among members. This made circles fundamentally different from formal public organizations, which, according to another pundit, Tsurumi Shunsuke, were "bound to their self-committed long-term objectives." Conversely, said Tsurumi, circles were "amoeba-like movements without objectives; they assumed the exact same form as rudimentary life *(genshiteki-na seimei)*."[193] Indeed, Tsurumi felt strongly that circle activism could actually teach Marxists about direct democracy, individualism, liberalism, anarchism, and even existentialism. It could show Marxists that the rudimentary community *(genshiteki kyōdōtai)* was more than a repository of feudal backwardness.[194] Echoing his sister Kazuko's idea about circles being spaces for remaking the self *(jiko kaizō)*, Tsurumi saw in these associations an invigorating indeterminacy, fallibilism, and provisionalism which helped bridge the private world of individual desire with the public world of commitment. This made them fundamentally different political parties, labor unions and formalized organizations which demanded consistency from members.[195]

The circle activist and poet Tanigawa Gan brought a decidedly ethnic national flavor to his celebration of circles, situating them squarely within the communal traditions of the Asian village.[196] In a 1955 article he declared that the latent philosophy contained in the Eastern village was a kind of "isolated, anarchistic syndicalism in pursuit of peace and collaboration." It was the early form of the "innate progressive ideology of the ethnic nation."[197] And yet again in 1957 he claimed—as Tsurumi had—that "at the lower reaches of postwar democracy" was a "pure vitality" manifest as the "cunning of the Asian people."[198] Born in Minamata City, Kumamoto Prefecture, in 1923, Tanigawa graduated from the University of Tokyo, majoring in sociology. After a troubled eight-month stint in the army during the later stages of the war, Tanigawa signed on as a journalist with the *Nishinippon Shimbun* and began publishing poetry and social commentary at the same time. In 1947 he was fired from the paper for his involvement in a labor dispute and the following year joined with others to found a magazine for poets, *Boin* (The Vowel). Tanigawa became a member of the Japanese Communist Party in 1949, but his activism was constrained by a bout of tuberculosis in 1951. After an almost eight-year hiatus, Tanigawa and his companion, the writer Morisaki Kazue, moved to the Chikuhō region of Kyūshū to focus on circle activism among miners. The following year Tanigawa, Morisaki, and others established the short-lived but influential magazine *Sākuru Mura* (Circle Village) as a mouthpiece for themselves and circle participants.[199] *Circle Village* did not last long, however, disbanding quite inconsequentially in late 1961, and beginning in the mid-1960s Tanigawa drifted away from the world of activism. But Tanigawa's ideas had a great impact within the circle movement and on later citizen (and student) activism, especially his famous 1958 essay "Founding Declaration: A Deeper Exploration of Groups" and his concept of movement "facilitators" *(kōsakusha)*. Tsurumi Shunsuke viewed Tanigawa's activism and the magazine as a "new stage" in "Japanese intellectual history,"[200] while for Ōsawa Shinichirō, *Circle Village* represented the "perfect formulation" of a "method for transcending the transitional stage of modernity."[201]

In the "Founding Declaration" ("Sōkan Sengen"), Tanigawa located the genesis of circles in the traditions of the ethnic nation *(minzoku no dentō)*, especially the people's sense of solidarity *(rentaikan)* and its expression in communal organization.[202] Tanigawa saw circles as filters through which the "sentiment of the old commune" could be refracted as a "pure sense of solidarity" and the "most conventional expression of the logical world of Japanese civilization." By mediating the dark depths of the ethnic nation, circles also uncovered the "shameful parts" of this civilization, becoming physical expressions of the "sickness in Japanese civilization." The tendency of circles to be narrowly insular and self-defensive, he opined, displayed the older mindset of "peasant rootedness" and the self-defensiveness of the lowest commune.[203] Sounding much like a Russian Narodnik, Tanigawa declared that circles would thus become the "melting pots" and "bridges" by which the "fragments of the old community destroyed by capitalism" would "melt" into the "new cooperative organizations of the future." By forging a new logic of group creation *(shūdan sōzō)*, circles heralded a new historical stage in which the moment of community would subjugate *(kokufuku)* and sublate *(shiyō)* the moment of class.[204]

Of course, not all observers were convinced about the prospects for circles as progressive vehicles for a new associationalism in Japan. In early 1959, circle advocate Hidaka Rokurō worried about the troubling emergence of political nonalignment and ideological neutrality within many associations. Enamored with the communist experiment in China, Hidaka interpreted Japanese circle activism through the theoretical lens of the Chinese Communist Party's mass line approach *(taishū rosen hōshiki)*. What was significant for Hidaka was that in the Japanese case the mass line had taken root only *after* the Red Purge and the split within the JCP in the early 1950s. Lacking effective communist direction, the mass line approach manifested instead in a loose conglomeration of nonaligned *(mutō muha)* progressive groups, including the antinuclear movement, the Mothers' Congress (Hahaoya Taikai), and cultural circles.[205] Clearly at odds with Tsurumi Shunsuke, Ōsawa, and others who celebrated this eclecticism, Hidaka agonized about the extraordinary "ideological breadth" *(ideorogītekina haba)* that nonalignment made possible and the impact of this on political consciousness.[206] Released from the doctrine of the established left, the energy of many circles seemed to wane quickly and, even if they did not become overtly conservative *(hoshuteki)*, some groups seemed to wander away from their progressive roots. As Hidaka incisively put it, nonaligned reformist energy *(mutō muha kakushin seiryoku)* often degenerated into nonreformist nonalignment *(hi-kakushinteki mutō muhashugi)*, because circles lacked a strong logic of adhesion *(michaku no ronri)*, and members any sense of organizational commitment.[207] For Hidaka, this transformation of circles into modernist functional groups *(kindaiteki kinō shudan)* opened the way for nonreformist nonalignment. It signaled their co-optation into middlebrow culture and degeneration into groups "harmless to man and beast"—a perceptive insight given the trajectory of groups such as the Green Association.[208]

Attempting to address the problem Hidaka called for a third logic *(daisan no ronri)*.[209] He admitted that the current decline in circles had something to do with the link between the logic of adhesion and traditional Asian stagnation, but this did not mean activists should turn to "Greece," the "Reformation," or the "Renaissance." Necessary was some kind of marriage between rationalism and emotionalism—the Western and the Asian. Here Hidaka turned—once again—to Communist China: "When I hear the gentlemen of England and America speaking of how the People's Communes are a system of slavery, I can't help wanting to ask, 'Is what you have done in Asia actually a movement for the liberation of slavery?'"[210] Such "half-baked skepticism" of the Chinese experiment was Japan's reality too, and he could only criticize the shallowness of nationalistic fervor in Japan. The only solution lay in a third logic exemplified in the Long March or the People's Communes in China, where rationalism and emotionalism came together perfectly. Hidaka provided no further specifics on this third logic, but he was clearly pointing toward a Maoist concept of community capable of resisting the alienation of Western modernity while incorporating its rational thought processes—the Asian village as vehicle of modern revolution. That Hidaka would become a highly influential citizen movement intellectual in later decades makes his Maoist critique all the more intriguing.

Indeed, in Hidaka's ambivalent reflections we find ourselves at the high point of an early postwar moment that would have a deep and lasting impact on later *shimin* thought and civic activism—especially on ideas about the people, daily life, and the ethnic nation, and on the tension between nonaligned groups as models for a new associationalism in Japan and as repositories of the dark energies of the past.

CHAPTER 2

Mass Society, Anpo, and the Birth of the *Shimin*

Even a single match burning in the dark of night is still a
light. A light is a light.

—Sakaguchi Masaaki, citizen activist, 1960

My pregnant wife
Concerned for my safety, allows me to go in
   the demonstration
My aged father
Says he wants to live in a country without the fear of war
My aged mother
Says she does not want to lose a brother to war again
My friends
My younger brothers and sisters
And for all those yet to be born and for their future
For their sake
I walked.
Until the day that peace and democracy are safe
I will stand firmly on the earth, hand in hand with
   my colleagues,
For their sake I will walk again.
Yes indeed, let's walk for as long as it takes!

—Asagi Kazuyasu, "My Pledge," written while thinking of my
unborn child due in August (1960)

TWO STREAMS OF ACTIVISM: THE CONSCIENTIOUS AND THE PRAGMATIC

Reaching its apex in the summer of 1960, the struggle against renewal
of the U.S.-Japan Security Treaty (Anpo *tōsō*) witnessed some of the

largest mass protests in modern Japanese history. Hundreds of thousands of people flooded into the streets to express their anxieties about the treaty, the prime minister, and the apparent threat to peace and democracy in the country. As the pledge above evidences, some understood their protest as a moral crusade for democracy, a kind of definitive clash between the progressive forces of the future and those who would draw Japan back into its ill-fated past. Indeed, the Anpo struggle represents the first and last time that progressive forces would unite on such a large scale against the conservative establishment. It also marked the end of Japan's brief (1958–60) postwar flurry with national mobilizations and the "apogee of organized intellectual influence over mass political movements."[1]

Politically, of course, the protests accomplished very little other than forcing Prime Minister Kishi to resign in favor of a more moderate from his party. To this day the treaty remains the centerpiece of the U.S.-Japan security arrangement, and the conservative government responsible for its approval held almost uninterrupted power until 2009. From a politicohistorical perspective, the Anpo struggle was a grand defeat for the progressive camp and, as this chapter shows, one that had palpable effects on civic activism in the coming years.

Recognizing this defeat, however, should not blind us to the important breakthroughs of the Anpo struggle. Together with the organized mass movement, the struggle also witnessed the flowering of a new type of activism, brewing in cultural and other forms of grassroots activity since the early postwar years and invigorated by activists who now identified themselves as *shimin*. Unaffiliated with the formal opposition movement, these self-proclaimed *shimin* spilled into the streets during the protest, sometimes individually, but often in small, democratically organized protest groups. Progressive observers saw in these budding citizens' movements *(shimin undō)* the nativity of a performative citizenship in postwar Japan, and their articulations at the time suggest a good deal of optimism, despite the political trouncing. Pundits such as Ishida Takeshi, Shinohara Hajime, and Fukuda Kanichi, for instance, saw in the protests a new civic consciousness *(shimin ishiki)* and a vigorous civic spirit *(yakudō suru shimin seishin)*,[2] and *shimin* champion Takabatake Michitoshi spoke of a new form of civic resistance *(shiminteki teikō)*.[3] In the July 1960 edition of the progressive monthly *Shisō no Kagaku*—fittingly entitled *Shimin toshite no Teikō* (Resisting as Citizens)—philosopher Kuno Osamu triumphantly announced the formation of a civic ethos *(shiminshugi no seiritsu)*,[4] and his colleague

Tsurumi Shunsuke envisaged a new form of radical democracy *(raji-karu demokurashī)* powered by the ideas of the Japanese people.[5]

Even those outside the chattering classes gushed about the new movements: writing in a grassroots publication in late 1960, university student Maruyama Masahiro, of Yokohama, confessed that his unfulfilled dream was to join with citizens, to speak with citizens, and to rise up with citizens.[6] As late as the 1980s, even American observers looked back to the protests of 1960 as the moment when the idea of the citizens' movement was born in Japan.[7] Sure, there had been civic mobilizations before, but only in 1960, they opined, did Japanese activists develop a self-consciousness about belonging to a new political phenomenon.[8]

The Anpo struggle was indeed a breakthrough for civic activism in postwar Japan. That was the moment when movement intellectuals drew together the many strands of thought and activism from the early postwar years, molding these into a potent model for collective action—a mythology of the *shimin*.[9] Not that activity in the 1940s and 1950s had been apolitical, of course: the projects to define a people's philosophy and foster circle activism were wholly political—especially for those with an intellectual stake in guiding the amorphous masses. Yet to the utmost, circle activism and discussions about the people revolved around an introspective politics of cultural production and self-expression. Politics narrowly defined figured only in intellectuals' imagination of an amorphous and hegemonic Other. But the intellectual work and civic activism of 1960 went a step further. By focusing on concrete issues of parliamentary procedure, the law, and foreign policy, activists faced an all-too-real politics to be dealt with. The events of 1959–60 raised the stakes a notch for Tsurumi Shunsuke and others: autonomy, they realized, was not only about finding an ethical space for the masses. More crucially, it was about ordinary people dealing with the thorny questions of individual political engagement and motivation and the ways these related to daily life, the nation, the established left, the state, and, of course, democracy.

In this chapter I analyze civic thought and activism before, during, and soon after the Anpo struggle. I look first at the wider cycle of protest during the struggle to show how the national movement created a political opportunity for the new citizens' movements. I then trace the role of intellectuals—some in movements, some not—in rehabilitating and then reconceptualizing the *shimin* as a progressive activist identity in the years leading up to and during the events of 1960. Their conceptual work provided activists with an ideational tool to mobilize ordinary citizens. Thereafter I look closely at the ways movement intellectuals put the *shimin* idea into practice: the kinds of movements they mobilized in the name of the *shimin* and the ways they articulated their political objectives. The Anpo struggle, or, more pertinently, the *defeat* of this struggle, I argue, stimulated activists to forge two streams of civic activism: one a conscientious reaction to so-called conservative domination, and the other a more mannered, strategic, and pragmatic response. The former found form in later mobilizations, such as the anti–Vietnam War movement; the latter informed regional protests, progressive consumer cooperatives, local government reform, and eventually a movement for the reconfiguration of civic activism in the country.

Rather than narrating the *shimin* idea and civic movements during the Anpo struggle within the standard "*shimin* versus establishment" paradigm, I focus in this chapter on the impact of economic recovery and mass society on movement intellectuals' ideas and civic activism. High-speed economic growth was transforming the daily lives of Japanese at an extraordinary pace, and this could not but influence the aspirations and objectives that ordinary people brought to civic activism and the public sphere. If the *shimin* idea and civic movements represented the arrival of a truly autonomous and democratic subjectivity in Japan, then they just as powerfully spoke to potent, if unarticulated, desires for an affluent daily life.

The *shimin* idea itself actually entered political discourse in the mid-1950s in the context of a debate about this very issue: the impact of mass society on political consciousness. As J. Victor Koschmann explains, "Despite the revolutionary rhetoric of its Communist and left-wing Socialist elements, the movement was basically conservative in that it sought ultimately to preserve 'postwar democracy.'" Borrowing from Takabatake, Koschmann points out that the "movement was also undergirded by strong popular support not only for rapid economic growth but also for individualism and rationalism, consumerism, and the domestic happiness associated with *mai-hōmu* (my home)."[10] Similarly, in the Anpo protests sociologist Kurihara Akira sees a multifaceted defense of life *(seimei)*, daily life *(seikatsu)*, and identity *(aidentiti)*. The protest spoke simultaneously to a genuine belief in democracy and pacifism as ideals, to a rejection of Japan's militaristic past, to a commitment to new forms of mobilization centered on the individual, *and* to a desire to defend the actual and anticipated material gains of the postwar period.[11]

Indeed, we probably err by even assuming that these desires were somehow compartmentalized in the consciousness of citizen protesters. As Ueno Chizuko has noted, one of the primary reasons for the scale of the 1960 protests was the emergence of a form of daily life conservatism *(seikatsu hoshushugi):* people now had both the motivation and the financial elbow room to rise up in defense of these gains.[12] War memories, democratic aspirations, and desires for the good life blended in a way totally misapprehended by the organized national movement but not missed by citizen movement intellectuals and astute observers such as Maruyama Masao and Matsushita Keiichi. The defense of daily life had been of great import in civic thought and activism since the earliest days of the postwar period, but after the defeat of the Anpo opposition movement—and with the destruction of the established left—this defense came to the very center of activist consciousness. As Shimizu Ikutarō mordantly lamented, the Anpo struggle was a victory for mass society theory and one that would deeply influence the values and praxis of civic activism in the coming decades.[13]

THE SECURITY TREATY STRUGGLE: A NEW POLITICAL SPACE FOR CITIZENS' MOVEMENTS

Often ignored in histories of the Anpo crisis is the fact that, despite lively debate among intellectuals and other leftist groups on the issue beginning as early as 1957, the opposition movement did not reach a critical mass until April 1960, and, for the majority of people, the revision process remained highly technical and of little relevance to daily life. Only after the forced approval of the treaty on May 20 did large numbers of unaffiliated individuals join the protest. Kishi's highhanded attitude in the Diet and the implications of the treaty for Japan upset many people, but the real catalysts for action were the individuals, groups, and organizations that fervently called on the Japanese people to exercise their right of resistance. This is what helped ordinary citizens transform their antagonisms into political action. Before looking more closely at discourse on the *shimin* and the civic movements of Anpo, then, we need to reconsider briefly the wider protest movement of 1959–60, recognizing how this cycle of protest opened a window of opportunity for small-scale citizens' movements.

Interestingly, the national protest movement began around an issue only tangentially related to the security treaty: Prime Minister Kishi's move to amend the Police Duties Performance Law (abbreviated as

Keishokuhō in Japanese) in late 1958. The original Keishokuhō, enacted in 1948 under the U.S. Occupation, gave strong emphasis to the protection of individual freedoms and rights, arguably at the expense of police powers. Through the revisions, Kishi hoped to shift this bias, giving himself a tool to short-circuit any opposition to the long-term objective of treaty revision. The proposed amendments to the law gave much greater emphasis to the maintenance of public order than to the protection of individual rights and greatly expanded the preventative powers of the police with respect to interrogation, search, and arrest. Under the new law, police were permitted to act not only when a crime was in progress but also, more worryingly, if they *perceived* that a crime was about to happen.[14] Misuse of the law, opponents argued, could potentially result in extreme suppression of organized movements. The revision, critics pointed out, would allow police to enter and search almost any place, including hotels and meeting halls.[15] This immediately invoked the ire of hotel and inn owners, who feared that expanded rights of police entry would interrupt patrons' "freedom of love affairs" and hoteliers' "freedom of trade."[16]

In October 1958 some sixty-five groups led by the JSP and the labor organization Sōhyō formed the National Congress Opposing Harmful Revisions to the Police Duties Performance Law (Keishokuhō Kaiaku Hantai Kokumin Kaigi). The movement comprised many civic groups, including intellectuals, journalists, artists, innkeepers, and women's organizations, but not the JCP, which was excluded because of opposition from anticommunist labor groups. The National Congress organized a series of nationwide united actions *(tōitsu kōdō)* encompassing rallies, demonstrations, and strikes throughout October and November 1958. On October 28, for example, some eighty thousand mobilized in protest, and on November 5, over four million participated nationwide in the fourth united action of the congress. The Keishokuhō protest also broke ground ideationally, pitting the *shimin* against the state for the first time in political rhetoric. Most graphically, the National Congress's appeal for popular protest began with the inspiring "Fellow Citizens, Please Rise Up!" *(Shimin no Minasan, Tachiagatte kudasai).*[17] Congress leaders' use of the term here clearly anticipated many of the meanings later movement intellectuals would associate with the *shimin* idea, especially the right of people to defend their private lives and pursue their self-interest. As the Marxist historian Fujita Shōzō noted, affluent urbanites were drawn to the protest because they abhorred the idea of lowly policemen meddling in their daily affairs.[18]

Under growing pressure from the opposition movement, the media, and even opponents within the Liberal Democratic Party (LDP), in November 1958, Kishi announced that he would be scrapping the proposed revisions. More ironically for the prime minister, this move to stem future opposition to the treaty revision actually served to empower it. In March 1959, member organizations of the Keishokuhō movement reorganized into the National Congress to Block the Security Treaty Revision. This National Congress brought together some 134 civic and political organizations, including the JSP, the same labor group Sōhyō, the antinuclear group Gensuikyō,[19] the Women's Council for Safeguarding Human Rights, and the Alliance to Protect the Constitution. This time the JCP came onboard as an observer organization, something that partly explains why the National Congress to Block the Security Treaty Revision addressed most of its public rhetoric to the nation *(kokumin)* and not citizens *(shimin)*: after all, for communists, *shimin* equaled the petit bourgeoisie, and, moreover, communists saw the battle as an ethnic national struggle against U.S. imperialism— hence the appeal of terms such as *the nation.*[20] Like its predecessor during the Keishokuhō dispute, the National Congress began to organize so-called united actions at this time, holding over thirty such mobilizations until well after the crisis had ended in late 1960. For many it represented both the moral and effective leadership of the Anpo struggle.

The National Congress was not alone, however, as various non-aligned associations spontaneously mobilized in protest. In March 1959, for example, the Men of Culture Discussion Group on the Anpo Problem (Anpo Mondai Bunkajin Kondankai), formed by Shimizu Ikutarō, Minami Hiroshi, Hidaka Rokurō, and Ishimoda Shō, issued a public statement criticizing the Anpo revisions. Later renamed the Treaty Problems Research Association, the group submitted a highly publicized list of eight questions on the treaty to the foreign minister in December of the same year. Similarly, the International Problems Symposium (Kokusai Mondai Danwakai), formed in May 1959 by intellectuals Maruyama Masao, Shimizu Ikutarō, Tsuru Shigeto, Kuno Osamu, and Ishida Takeshi, released two influential discussions on the Anpo problem in the progressive monthly *Sekai* in 1959 and 1960: the first titled "Seifu no Anpo Kaitei Kōsō o Hihan suru" (Criticizing the Government's Conceptualization of the Anpo Revisions) (October 1959) and the second, "Futatabi Anpo Kaitei ni tsuite" (One More Time on the Anpo Revisions) (February 1960). As with its precursor, the Peace Problems Symposium, this group advocated the idea of active neutralism *(sekkyokuteki chūritsushugi)* and unarmed neutrality *(hibusō chūritsu)* in Japanese foreign policy and called for the immediate dissolution of the security treaty as a means to establish the independence of the nation *(waga kuni no jishusei no kakuritsu no tame).*[21]

In a similar vein, a month or so later the Group to Criticize the Security Treaty (Anpo Hihan no Kai) mobilized a mishmash of artists, performers, musicians, and intellectuals. As Hidaka Rokurō notes, this group had great appeal among ordinary citizens and especially housewives *(shufu)*, serving as an important model for later civic mobilizations because of its ability to transcend generational and ideological beliefs and the way in which its shared objectives enveloped (supposedly in a positive way) its internal diversity.[22]

One further group deeply shaped the cycle of Anpo protests: the student organization Zengakuren.[23] More specifically, I refer to the mainstream anti-JCP faction known as the Bund, or the Communist League, which took control of Zengakuren at the organization's rally in June 1956.[24] Ideologically, the Bund differed fundamentally from the JCP, which presented the treaty issue as an ethnic national struggle against U.S. imperialism. The Bund leadership argued conversely that Japan was already at the stage of "state monopoly capitalism" *(kokka dokusen shihonshugi)*, hence the target should not be the imperialist United States but the Kishi cabinet. On this point, the Bund not only took aim at the JCP but also mounted an attack on the legitimacy of "neutrality" put forward by liberal progressive groups, such as the International Problems Symposium. But it was not only—or primarily—the Bund's ideological stance that distinguished it during the crisis. More important were the high-profile tactics the Bund adopted as part of its strategy of direct action *(chokusetsu kōdō)*. Similar to many of the *shimin* theorists I discuss below, Bund members perceptively recognized the impact of socioeconomic change in late 1950s Japan. On the one hand, they believed that the Anpo issue represented a first step on the pathway to revolution, but on the other, they realized how the values of mass society were beginning to infiltrate and shape (perhaps politically anesthetize) the Japanese people. This interpretation informed Bund activists' strategy of direct and violent action throughout 1959 and 1960, as well as their critique of the united actions of the National Congress to Block the Security Treaty Revision, which they described as harmless incense-offering demonstrations *(oshōkō demo).*[25] Beginning with its invasion of the Diet precincts with young workers on

November 27, 1959, the Bund engaged in a series of protest activities that would bring it into direct confrontation with riot police and, by implication, keep the Anpo issue on the front page of the newspapers and in the television news.[26]

It would be wrong to conclude that there was popular support for either the ideological position or the violent, inflammatory tactics of the student radicals, but the Bund provided a theater that simply could not be matched by the more subdued approach of the National Congress and other groups. As one observer has noted, "Students' action against the treaty, by engaging that quintessentially 'postwar' demand that praxis be grounded in a socialized consciousness, was living out a moral injunction received from an earlier generation, and on that basis tapping a deep reservoir of popular sympathy. This is what pushed the anti-treaty movement forward."[27] Students reminded passive opponents of the treaty that political opposition became real only through performance—a message not lost on contemporary citizen movement intellectuals, who soon after fashioned their own vision of direct action around the *shimin* idea.

In terms of large-scale protests a number of moments stand out. On May 26, 1960, 540,000 came out in protest nationwide, 175,000 in Tokyo alone. On June 4, nationwide strikes led by the National Congress mobilized over 5.5 million workers. Some 20,000 small store owners in Tokyo, Osaka, Gunma, Hyōgo, Kyoto, and elsewhere held store-closure strikes while over 130,000 protested outside the Diet. Again on June 11, close to 2.5 million participated in the eighteenth united action of the National Congress, with 235,000 surrounding the Diet, in Tokyo. In a who's who of the civic protest movement, on June 14, the National Association of Academics and Researchers for the Protection of Democracy, the Grass Seeds Association (Kusa no Mi Kai), the Voices of the Voiceless Association (Koe naki Koe no Kai), the Young Japan Association, the Tokyo YWCA, the Buddhist Peace Conference (Bukkyōsha Heiwa Kyōgikai), the Japan Association for the Protection of Children (Nihon Kodomo o Mamoru Kai), and other groups staged a mass rally under the banner "the National Assembly for the Defense of Democracy" (Minshushugi o mamoru Kokumin no Tsudoi).[28] The following day—the infamous June 15, when student Kanba Michiko was found dead after clashes with riot police—brought out another 100,000 protesters around the Diet.

With the automatic renewal of the treaty in sight and growing public repugnance to escalating violence, however, the protests began to subside thereafter. On June 19, with the national movement waning, the treaty was automatically approved. Two days later the emperor gave his imperial attestation to the treaty, and it officially became law. On June 23, Kishi announced the resignation of his cabinet as quid pro quo for treaty ratification, and after some internal wrangling, his rival, Ikeda Hayato, emerged as president of the LDP and prime minister. With this, the furor over the security treaty ended. The largest street protests in Japanese history had certainly failed, but through their collective action the National Congress, the Bund, and other groups quite inadvertently opened up a new political space for movement intellectuals to both imagine and mobilize the first generation of *shimin* movements. From a historical perspective this was undoubtedly the most enduring legacy of the mass protests of Anpo.

RECONCEPTUALIZING AND MYTHOLOGIZING THE *SHIMIN* IDEA

With this wider cycle of protest in mind, we can turn now to the *shimin* idea and the emergence of citizens' movements during the struggle. I focus first on the *shimin* idea, not only because it preceded and was used to invigorate Anpo struggle citizens' movements, but also because its intellectual genealogy provides important insights into the kind of aspirations it spoke to. The *shimin* idea drew on any number of intellectual genealogies. As chapter 1 revealed, circle activism and early postwar imaginations of the people and indigenous democratic subjectivity were central, but of even more immediate impact were discussions about Japan as a mass society from the mid-1950s. Deeply influenced by socialist theory, theorists in this latter debate understood mass society as an insidious political and socioeconomic formation that threatened to anesthetize class consciousness. With the events of the Keishokuhō dispute and the Anpo struggle, however, some began to see rays of hope: rather than numbing political consciousness, popular attachment to the comforts of affluence conversely seemed to have stimulated active dissent. Enamored by the actions of this new middle stratum, some, such as Matsushita Keiichi, began to rethink the meaning of mass society and ultimately abandoned the socialist project for a new civic-national endeavor orchestrated and invigorated by Japan's rising legion of *shimin* and their citizen politics.

Literally translated, *shimin* means "the inhabitants of a city or town," though liberal intellectuals from the 1960s most often connected the term to ideas of universalism, spontaneity, equality, individualism, and democracy. Prior to its entry into political discourse in the mid-1950s, the *shimin* had been associated with a number of divergent meanings— some political, some not. In the Meiji period, for example, *shimin* was not generally used as a keyword for active political citizenship. In his best-selling *Seiyō Jijō* (Conditions in the West), the Meiji intellectual Fukuzawa Yukichi preferred to translate the French *citoyen* as *kokujin* (literally, "person of the nation"), whereas fellow intellectual Nakae Chōmin opted for *shi* (literally, "gentleman") throughout his translation of Rousseau's *The Social Contract*.[29] When Fukuzawa did use *shimin*— as in his 1875 *Bunmeiron no Gairyaku* (An Outline of a Theory of Civilization)—he presented it in a rather neutral sense to mean the inhabitants of a city *(toshi no shimin)*, against which he juxtaposed the natives of the countryside *(inaka no domin)*.[30] There is even evidence that the compound *shimin* was used to denote urban dwellers before the Meiji period.[31] Whatever its origins, however, *shimin* continued throughout most of modern Japanese history to connote the inhabitants of an urban area—a meaning further fortified with the creation of administrative municipalities, or *"shi,"* in the modern period.

But the term *shimin* was not completely disassociated from antiestablishment initiatives in the prewar period. Michael Lewis, for instance, has described the widespread occurrence of citizen rallies *(shimin taikai)* during the rice riots of 1918. Here speakers asked probing questions about wage declines in a growing economy and also about the paucity of popular political rights. As Lewis argues, such questions did not augur the rise of anarchism or social disintegration but, rather, signaled a demand for the "integration of popular interests within the Meiji constitutional order."[32] But it is unclear whether organizers of such rallies mobilized the term *shimin* in the sense of performative citizenship; more likely the term referred simply to their status as urban dwellers.

One further prewar usage of the *shimin* deserves comment: namely, in the context of Marxist discourse. In prewar (and postwar) Marxist discourse, *shimin* most often appeared in the compound *shōshimin* as a direct translation of *petit bourgeoisie*, and for this reason it had a negative connotation. The petit bourgeois mentality and the socioeconomic structure built around the capitalist class were things to be overcome, not aspired to. But the term was not always used negatively by Marxists. In the 1930s, under mounting state surveillance, some Marxists began to substitute *shimin* for the term *bourgeoisie* in an attempt to disguise explicit references to class. For example, in some discussions the terms *bourgeois revolution (burujowa kakumei)* and *bourgeois society (burujowa shakai)* were rendered into the safer *civic revolution (shimin kakumei)* and *civil society (shimin shakai)*.[33] Of course, the switch from *burujowa* (bourgeois) to *shimin* (civic or civil) was not entirely for self-defense. By substituting the one for the other, Marxist intellectuals at the time were also able to tap into ideas of universal human rights and freedom associated with the great civic revolutions in the West and the liberal thought of John Locke and others. For instance, in 1939 Kōza-ha Marxist Hani Gorō suggested in his book *Michelangelo* that *shimin* could denote the inhabitants of self-governing cities *(jichi toshi)*, as in the case of the citizens of Florence.[34] Earlier, Hani's Kōza-ha colleague Hirano Yoshitarō had freely interchanged the terms *bourgeois society* and *civil society* in his essay "Burujowa Minshushugi Undōshi" (A History of the Bourgeois Democratic Movement).[35] Such usage by Marxists proved crucial in opening up the possible meanings of *shimin*, because they effectively rendered the term into a Japanese translation for both *the bourgeoisie* and the French *citoyen* or the English *citizen*. In other words, *shimin* could represent both the narrow self-interest of a specific (urban) class and the universal values of freedom and equality—not to mention the neutral inhabitant of a city.[36]

After the war, the resurgent organs of the established left relegated *shimin*—once again—to its pejorative petit bourgeois status. With the proletariat now restored to its world-historical pedestal for orthodox Marxists, the *shimin* once again became a symbol for everything reactionary, and in the period from around 1945 to 1955, it appeared most often as the pejorative *shōshimin*. There were exceptions, of course. For example, as early as 1947 the literary critic Ara Masato used *shimin* in a positive way. Ara apparently mobilized the *shimin* idea to legitimize the role of the petit bourgeois intelligentsia—including himself—in the coming democratic revolution, at once challenging the notion of a unitary revolutionary subject and the JCP's privileging of politics over all else (particularly over artistic endeavors).[37] At the same time, as Oguma Eiji suggests, Ara's *shimin* stood in opposition to both the state and class. For example, Ara praised the notion of modern civil society in 1947 as a collection of horizontal connections *(yoko no tsunagari)* distinct from the vertical connections of the state and class.[38] For Ara, *shimin* implied a kind of universal humankind, and he saw the "humanism of modern civil society" reaching out to the "far horizon transcending the ethnic nation and class."[39] Ara's conceptualization of the *shimin* bears a striking resemblance to what would come later during the Anpo struggle, but in the late 1940s and, indeed, until the mid-1950s, such affirmative usage of the *shimin* idea by progressives—whether Marxists or modernists—was a rarity.

The question, then, is: Why and how did the *shimin* idea shed its pejorative baggage to become a new and vibrant vision of performative citizenship? The events surrounding the treaty renewal certainly provided an opportunity for movement intellectuals to refashion the *shimin* idea. Important too was the legacy of circle activism—especially that connected to the Institute for the Science of Thought. But in terms of language—that is, in terms of the word *shimin* and its progressive connotations—we must look to a new discussion unfolding from 1956, namely, the debate on mass society *(taishū shakai ronsō)*.[40] Here we can see how certain intellectuals' understanding of social, political, economic, and technological developments connected to a critique of established leftist strategy and concepts of class, and how this critique, in turn, paved the way for a rehabilitation of the *shimin* idea as the symbol for democratic subjectivity and revolution.

The key figure in this debate was Matsushita Keiichi, but the sociologist Katō Hidetoshi and the political theorist Maruyama Masao also made important interventions. The debate began with four articles on the subject in the November 1956 edition of *Shisō*, of which Matsushita's "Taishū Kokka no Seiritsu to Sono Mondaisei" (The Formation of the Mass State and Its Problems) proved to be the most influential and durable.[41] I would note, however, that the concept of mass society was not entirely new in Japanese intellectual circles. As early as 1951 Shimizu Ikutarō, in his book *Shakai Shinrigaku* (Social Psychology), portrayed *"masu sosaite"* as a "large-scale and critical disorder in contemporary society."[42] Shimizu's completely negative reading of mass society put him in the company of the majority of Marxists, for whom mass society theory—with its claims about class consciousness being superseded by mass apathy—hit an extremely raw nerve.[43] Shimizu seems to have stayed true to this position throughout the postwar period. Indeed, in his reflections on the failure of the Anpo struggle in late 1960, he could only lament the final victory of mass society theory, supposedly orchestrated and led by the citizen faction *(shimin-ha)* and their watered-down claims of protecting democracy and ousting Kishi.[44]

What Shimizu and other critics of mass society theory could not deny was that real socioeconomic changes were underway in Japan, especially in the cities. From a quantitative perspective, economic statistics show that the level of real per capita consumption in Japan exceeded its prewar level in 1954.[45] As Kenneth Pyle notes, from 1946 to 1954 real national income grew at an average of 10.8 percent, bringing the economy back to prewar levels of productivity, national income, and personal consumption. Remarkable economic growth continued for well over a decade thereafter.[46] Furthermore, the nature of consumption also underwent a revolution. After the early postwar years and until the mid- to late 1960s, the share of personal income spent on food showed a rapid decrease and was replaced by increasing consumption of furniture and household goods. Anecdotal evidence also supports these changes. John Dower locates the advent of postwar mass consumer culture in the mid-1950s with the commencement of the government's "citizen's car project" to replace the auto industry's earlier focus on trucks, buses, and taxis. Dower adds that 1955 also heralded the age of the electrified household *(katei denka no jidai),* when housewives dreamed of owning and using an electric washing machine, a refrigerator, and a television—the so-called three divine appliances *(sanshu no jingi).*[47]

The 1950s also witnessed countless other booms *(būmu)* or fads that similarly point to a reemergent mass culture in the country. In a fascinating essay on the topic, Matsuura Sōzō lists some of those major booms, including the electrical appliance boom in 1956, the department store boom, and, important for citizen politics, the *danchi* (apartment complex) boom in 1957.[48] By 1959, only two years after the *danchi* boom began, there were some five thousand complexes nationwide, housing around one million people. Matsuura notes that, at the time, the chance to live in one of these complexes was a dream among many urbanites. Even academics were captivated: a young sociologist writing in the popular magazine *Shūkan Asahi* about his research conducted at *danchi* exuberantly announced, "When I get married I'm going to live this way!"[49] It was large-scale and viscerally perceptible phenomena such as these, then, that formed the contextual backdrop to Matsushita Keiichi's, Katō Hidetoshi's, and others' descriptions of Japan as a mass society *(taishū shakai)* beginning in the mid-1950s.

Of course, for the young political theorist Matsushita Keiichi, things were not quite as rosy as the popular weeklies proclaimed, and the arrival of mass society was hardly a development to rejoice. Until the Anpo struggle at least, Matsushita, like most of his colleagues in the academy, remained committed to the socialist movement and hoped for the reform of socialist strategy to deal with the onslaught of mass societal conditions. In 1958, for example, he emphasized that the pursuit of civil liberties *(shiminteki jiyū)* did not mean imprisoning the socialist movement within a drive to protect liberty and democracy *(jiyū-minshushugi yōgo)*. In fact, in conditions of mass society, according to Matsushita, the latter movement actually "expanded the pathway to socialism."[50] But even in the late 1950s, when he still embraced a socialist resolution, Matsushita's intellectual activities reveal his rudimentary attempts to relocate Marxist theory within a broader historical and ethical framework of classical liberalism. Put schematically, beginning in the mid-1950s Matsushita's thought moved from the delineation of mass society to a critique of class-centered socialist strategy and, ultimately, to the lionization of the *shimin* idea and civil society. In the process of searching for a pathway to socialist revolution within mass society, Matsushita began to rethink the civil society idea of John Locke, Adam Smith, and other enlightenment thinkers, first in historical terms as a pit stop on the way to a Marxian utopia, but later through an enlightenment lens as an ethical ideal type for society. It was in this intellectual process that the *shimin* idea began to break free of its pejorative Marxist manacles.

In his influential 1956 article "Taishū Kokka no Seiritsu to Sono Mondaisei" (The Formation of the Mass State and Its Problems), Matsushita explained mass society as a social formation born from the stage of monopoly capitalism *(dokusen shihon dankai)*—most prominently in America and Europe but also Japan.[51] According to Matsushita, the shift from industrial to monopoly capitalism gave birth to mass production and mass communication. Technology, which up until that point had been contained within the production process, now spilled out into society, or as he put it, the intensification *(kōdoka)* in the structure of capital that facilitated mass production was made part of society or societized *(shakaika)*. The result was nothing short of a morphological change *(keitai henka)* in society itself.[52] Most significantly, the rise of mass society, according to Matsushita, witnessed the widespread proletarianization *(puroritariaka)* of the populace inclusive of a new middle class *(shin chūkan kaikyū)* populated by urban white-collar workers.[53] It was this massive working class with its white-collar element that mass society theory identified as the masses *(taishū)*.[54] According to the theory, the formation of this mammoth working class created new pressures. A natural outcome of proletarianization was the spread of unionization and the creation of workers' political parties.

Combined, such groups were able to force the state to implement
.certain progressive social policies that finally resulted in the formation
of the welfare state *(fukushi kokka)*.[55]

The significant point for Matsushita was that the working class had
nowhere been victorious under conditions of mass society: it could never
win political control, nor could it overcome the logic of monopoly capitalism. Indeed, in an ironic twist, the working class found itself transformed into the civic nation *(kokumin)* of a capitalist state, all on the
pretext of mass democracy and mass nationalism. The working class
apparently took possession of the motherland, and, as much as it was
liberated within the state, it was also acclimatized or, more graphically,
rendered passive *(judōka sareru)*, assuming a kind of pseudo- or false
subjectivity underneath the state *(kokka no giji shutai)*. The bottom line
for Matsushita was that the "formation of the mass state [in the West]
was not a sublation of capitalism itself,"[56] nor did mass transcend class,
since the former was but a special condition of the latter.[57] Moreover,
when combined with mass culture's *(taishū bunka)* leveling influence on
daily life, progressive state policies, such as social security and universal
education, only served to standardize the lives of the masses further.[58]
As Matsushita explained, mass democracy actually meant pseudodemo-
cracy *(giji demokurashii)*, because it left the people open to manipulation by elites—a kind of Caesar-style domination *(shīzāgata shihai)* or
mass-delegated dictatorship *(taishū inin teki dokusai)*.[59]

The question, then, was how to "overcome" *(kokufuku)* mass conditions. In 1956, Matsushita provided no answer, preferring instead to
warn that Japan, too, faced a similar challenge with the spread of
monopoly capitalism. Boldly setting himself apart from the modernizers
and Kōza-ha Marxists, Matsushita claimed that the problem for Japan
was not simply that of the feudal versus the modern. More pertinently,
modernity itself *(kindai jitai)* was now a problem in the form of monopoly capitalism and mass society.

Still seemingly committed to the socialist paradigm, Matsushita produced a flurry of essays in 1957 and 1958, reiterating his point that
Japan was a mass society and that socialism would do well to accept
this reality and deal with it.[60] But despite this commitment, in hindsight
we can clearly see in these essays how a liberal theory of civil society
was quickly replacing any Marxist future Matsushita claimed allegiance
to. For example, in 1957 Matsushita directly addressed the issue of
how a theory of mass society (and the accompanying collapse of civil
society) could be formulated from the perspective of historical material-

ism.[61] In other words, how were socialists going to deal with the implications of mass society: the co-optation of the working class and the political manipulation of the masses?

The solution, he suggested, lay in a rediscovery of civil society within Marxism. To be sure, in the Marxist lexicon, class *(kaikyū)* stood in opposition to bourgeois civil society, but, Matsushita claimed, even the proletarian class of communism had a civil-society-like structure *(shimin shakaiteki kōzō)* if this was interpreted as the harmonization of individual freedom and social union. Moreover, Matsushita noted, Marx himself admitted so much in the *German Ideology,* saying, "In the real community the individuals obtain their freedom in and through their association."[62]

Matsushita took this interpretation a step further in a fittingly titled 1958 essay, "Wasurerareta Teikōken" (The Forgotten Right of Resistance), published in *Chūō Kōron.* Here again, he admitted that the rise of mass society had hollowed out liberty *(jiyū no kūdōka)* by legitimizing passive private enjoyment among the Japanese masses. But the experience of the Reverse Course and other reactionary policies also forced the Japanese masses to understand and assert their liberty and attachment to democracy.[63] The problem was that such consciousness did not connect to any consciousness of a right of resistance *(teikōken).* For this, Matsushita blamed the established left and the tendency of many revolutionary ideologies in Japan to operate from the perspective of historical necessity. Of course, historical laws in themselves were not valueless, but the problem lay in the way the subject *(shutai)* tended to be buried within the substance of objective understanding.[64] Or, to put it in less abstract terms: historical materialism supposedly inhibited individual agency by subjecting it to the preordained rules of revolution.[65] For Matsushita, such abstract contraposition of capitalism versus socialism was by no means an effective ideological premise for concrete struggles, because it often amounted to no more than vanguard control over the masses.[66]

Instead of such imported sciences of revolution, then, Matsushita wanted the progressive camp to establish a subject-centered ideology from within the masses and, *only then,* attempt to connect this to objective understanding. Rather than foment a utopian passion for socialism, ideologies for change simply had to be constructed on the basis of resistance to any maladministration that would limit or inhibit liberty. As he argued, in postwar Japan liberty was a legal reality; moreover, it had taken root in the daily lives of the masses, who had begun to resist maladministration and transform themselves into the protectors of liberty.[67] Needless to say, though he still saw himself as a kind of reform socialist, Matsushita's logic here was clearly leading him away from orthodox Marxist theory and in the direction of a more classical liberal solution.

Though socialism was certainly an ideology of resistance, Matsushita argued that it was not a resistance based on individual freedom: it was all about revolution of the overall system. But present conditions demanded that the ideology of resistance be redirected from socialist revolution to the protection of liberty and democracy. Rather than conforming to historicist necessities, the Japanese masses needed to fashion a consciousness of the right of individual resistance, something they had never truly possessed.[68] Only then, he suggested, could Japanese democracy avoid yet another autointoxication—the nation poisoning itself. If Nazism and McCarthyism taught anything, it was certainly that democracy in the name of the majority could easily spiral out of control, morphing into fascism. Knowledge of the right of individual resistance, however, kept such tendencies at bay. It meant that the individual would not be swallowed up in the general will. It preserved individual judgment and appraisal vis-à-vis the government—the designated keeper of the general will.[69] To be sure, in conditions of mass society there was always a risk of liberty and democracy being hollowed out or of civil liberties degenerating into a vulgar liberty to consume.[70] But in the right of resistance, Matsushita claimed, lay an ideological switching device through which individual private interest could be turned into public politics.[71]

With the Keishokuhō dispute unfolding around him in late 1958, Matsushita had more or less set the theoretical stage for the comeback of the *shimin* idea and completed his own personal apostasy from Marxism. By late 1960 he was confidently speaking of an explosion of civic resistance born from new lifestyles, new forms of communication, and a general consciousness of the postwar constitution. In a time of political crisis (i.e., the furor of the security treaty renewal), the political conservatism of the new middle stratum had operated—conversely—as a spontaneous form of resistance.[72] As he would later claim, a new civic form of the individual *(shimin-teki ningengata)* had been born from the very womb of mass society in postwar Japan.[73] The freedoms of daily life and the pluralization of values and information had provided the masses with expanded political choice, and, supported by the institutional guarantee of the new constitution, this choice became a basis for the rise of civic spontaneity *(shiminteki jihatsusei)*. Matsushita pointed to civic groups such as the Grass Seeds Association (Kusa no Mi Kai) and the Voices of the Voiceless Association as examples of how civic political participation *(shiminteki seiji sanka)* expanded during the Keishokuhō and Anpo crises.

Moreover, he connected such activism to a civic prehistory: the anti-nuclear-bomb movement, the circle movement, and the earlier life composition movement.[74] The upheavals of 1958–60, however, were epoch making in that they emerged from truly civic political demands: the protection of daily life and parliamentary politics. It was in the protests of this period, Matsushita claimed, that civic resistance matured on a mass scale.[75] And, even more significant for him, the *shimin* idea was also detached then from its roots in Western history, signifying now a universal ethos based on ideas of self-governance *(jichi)*, equality *(byōdō)*, and a republican principle *(kyōwa genri)*.[76]

Of course, even after the summer of 1960, Matsushita recognized the persistence of a dual (class) structure in Japanese society, hence his turn to local activities and local politics. Moreover, he was painfully aware of the pathologies of mass society. But when the Keishokuhō and Anpo crises proved the limits of established leftist ideology and the potential of civic resistance, the temptation to mythologize the *shimin* proved almost too enticing. Though he would never directly say so, after 1960 Matsushita clearly believed that the future of Japanese democracy lay not in a socialist or Marxian utopia but rather in a utopia of the *shimin* and civil society. In fact, even by the late 1950s, Matsushita had already turned Marxist stage theory on its head, relocating socialism and communism *within* a grand classical liberal theory of civil society. In his 1959 book, *Shimin Seiji Riron no Keisei* (The Formation of Civic Political Theory), Matsushita argued that Locke's formulation of state versus individual (civil society) was alive and well in socialist theory. Marx's presentation of communism was nothing more than a vision of civil society *(shimin shakai)* based on the free association of liberated individuals who had come together as the proletarian class that would ultimately supersede the bourgeois state. Socialism, he said, was truly a legitimate successor of "society-ism"—in other words, civil society.[77]

For Matsushita, then, a Sorelian-type myth of the general strike was to be replaced by a myth of civic resistance. The great breakthrough of 1959 and 1960 for him was that the masses had shed their passive shell to become proactive *shimin;* in other words, there was a qualitative difference in their mentality. We can, no doubt, trace this romanticism, as well as Matsushita's idealized picture of Western civil society after feudalism, to his intellectual roots in classical liberalism—not to mention to the impact of the Anpo crisis. The point to keep in mind is that Matsushita came to see mass society less as a failure and more as a condition to be dealt with by *shimin,* the enlightened progeny of the masses.

Not all mass society theorists saw things this way, of course. Matsushita's contemporary, the sociologist and mass society theorist Katō Hidetoshi, for example, viewed civic consciousness not as a reaction to but as a natural outcome of the self-interested values of mass society. As Yonehara suggests, instead of a break in consciousness between the passive masses and the active citizenry, Katō posited a continuity *(ren-zokusei)* based on a kind of conservative defense of daily life.[78] Admittedly, there was only a shade of difference between Matsushita and Katō, since both saw a link between daily life *(seikatsu)* and civic activism. But in terms of civic imagery, the result in Katō's case was a rather more prosaic, if not wholly unromantic, vision of the *shimin* born of mass society. While Matsushita's *shimin* emerged like a lotus of civic consciousness from the mire of mass indifference, Katō's *shimin* reveled in the grime of private indulgence. Indeed, it was self-interest, not a republican spirit, that brought Katō's *shimin* out into the streets in protest.

Katō became interested in mass society theory in 1954–55, during his midtwenties, when he held a two-year research fellowship in the United States under the sponsorship of the Rockefeller Foundation. It was this experience that led him to rethink the development of culture *(bunka)* in postwar Japan, resulting in a series of essays published in the monthly *Chūō Kōron* during 1957 and later in the same year in a collected volume titled *Chūkan Bunka* (Middlebrow Culture). In a nutshell, Katō argued that culture had passed through three phases during the postwar years. From 1945 to 1955 highbrow culture *(kōkyū bunka)* dominated, most graphically in the intellectual-led *rondan* (debate) culture of magazines such as *Sekai, Chūō Kōron,* and *Kaizō.* In 1950, this highbrow culture began to be overtaken by lowbrow culture *(teikyū bunka):* radio quiz programs, dance halls, movies, and mass circulation publications such as *Heibon.*[79] Then in 1955 something interesting began to happen. With the spread of universal education and the impact of a national mass media, these two cultural poles began to merge into a middlebrow culture *(chūkan bunka)* marked by the rise of weekly magazines *(shūkanshi)* and the ubiquitous *shinsho,* or pocket-sized, books that presented specialized or academic knowledge in readable, everyday language.[80]

Katō's cultural dialectic was oversimplified, but of greater interest is his reading of the *impact* of this new middlebrow culture. According to Katō, for those socialized during the prewar and war years, social class, profession, and status had more or less determined a person's cultural preferences and ideological position. But with the leveling impact of mass society through education and the mass media, such disjunctures no longer mattered for the postwar generation.[81] The gap between white-collar worker and laborer or intellectual and nonintellectual was no longer so great, particularly in terms of cultural pursuits.[82] Katō suggested that the postwar generation *(sengoha)* shared the uniform values of daily life *(tōitsuteki seikatsu kachi),* and for this reason the masses *(taishū)* could be understood as a new civic stratum *(atarashii shiminsō).*[83] Certainly, significant wage differentials still existed, but, Katō quipped, if there were a machine to measure the level of fatigue among workers, then the gap between laborers and white-collar employees would definitely register a decrease compared with the past. Even Katō claimed that he felt less an intellectual and more an ordinary citizen *(futsu no shimin)* in the postwar era.[84]

But the postwar years witnessed more than a narrowing of culture and lifestyles; Katō also pointed to a middling of mass ideology.[85] The values of daily life had the potential to turn political, just as they had in Hiroshima in August 1955, at the first meeting of the World Conference against Atomic and Hydrogen Bombs (Gensuibaku Kinshi Sekai Taikai). This movement succeeded, Katō suggested, not because of ordinary people's affinity to progressivism but because people simply did not want to suffer another war. They did not want to die or to lose their house or other possessions. It was this simple attachment to life *(seimei)* and daily life *(seikatsu)* that brought citizens out in opposition—a fundamentally conservative impulse.[86] Needless to say, Katō anticipated here the very same sentiment that would drive the citizen protests of the Keishokuhō, Anpo, and beyond. Indeed, in an eerie portent of Kishi Nobusuke's famous 1960 comment, he remarked that the task for Japanese revolutionaries *(kakumeika)* would be to somehow excavate and politicize this petit bourgeois spirit buried within the voiceless civic throng *(koe naki shimingun).*[87]

Unlike Matsushita, then, Katō imagined the *shimin* (for the most part, at least) as a conservative and reluctant political participant, a sentiment he shared with others such as Maruyama Masao. Consider

Katō's essay "Nichijō Seikatsu to Kokumin Undō" (The National Movement and Everyday Life), in the special July 1960 edition of *Shisō no Kagaku,* in which he imagined civic motivation as a conservative impulse and drew a link between everyday life *(nichijō seikatsu)* and the national movement *(kokumin undō).*[88] For Katō, normal citizens had not risen up because of some moral awakening informing them that to focus on private life was wrong. Rather, "the energy source for countless numbers of people lay in the realization that in order to protect their 'lives,' political action was necessary."[89] After May 19, the social and political system that guaranteed citizens the right of unhindered enjoyment of daily life came crashing down. The social condition allowing fools *(ahō)* to be fools was stolen away, and, as Katō put it, fools-in-themselves *(sokujiteki ahō)* became fools-for-themselves *(kōjiteki ahō)*—in other words, *shimin.*[90] "Stated in extremis," he explained, citizens "participated in the opposition movement because they wanted to keep watching baseball. . . . It wasn't that baseball fans gave up baseball and took up political activism. . . . It was because baseball fans wanted to continue being baseball fans."[91] Hence his rather uninspiring definition of the *shimin* as "an individual who undertakes political action in order to guarantee an ordinary, peaceful daily life."[92] As Katō quite rightly pointed out, his *shimin* was essentially conservative: "The fool wanting to remain a fool is fundamentally different from the [ideology] of progressivism."[93] Here Katō clearly parted ways with many *shimin* advocates of 1960 who preferred a more romantic imagery for this new activist identity.

Katō's uninspiring portrayal of the *shimin* idea aside, his rehabilitation of the idea from the petit bourgeois scrap heap in Marxism also owed much to the discussion of mass society theory in the mid-1950s. The same can be said of Maruyama Masao, a University of Tokyo professor and high-profile critic of the government during the Anpo struggle. Though Maruyama tended to avoid the term *shimin* because he thought it ambiguous, there is no doubt that his attitude toward the idea and what he believed it could represent underwent a change during the late 1950s.[94] In the early postwar years, Maruyama apparently avoided using *shimin* for both pragmatic and ideological reasons. In 1947, for instance, he had divided the middle, or petit bourgeois, stratum into two types: a group comprising tradesmen, small business owners, factory managers, and the like, and another comprising urban white-collar workers such as journalists, academics, and professionals.[95] Though the latter group looks very much like Katō's new civic stratum, Maruyama chose to describe them at the time not as *shimin* but as intellectuals and the intelligentsia.[96] Conversely, it made no sense to classify the group of tradesmen and factory managers as *shimin*. Indeed, Maruyama suggested that this group, which he described as pseudointellectuals, was the very social foundation of fascism.[97]

Thus, in the late 1940s, Maruyama saw no strata of *shimin*, only the reactionary, pseudointellectual, majority middle strata and the less significant intelligentsia, which during the war had "largely lacked the courage to make a resolute defense of its inner individuality against fascism."[98] At the time Maruyama argued that the bearer of liberty *(jiyū no ninaite)* was not *shimin* but rather the "widespread working masses centered on laborers and farmers."[99] In his 1951 article "Nihon ni okeru Nashonarizumu" (Japanese Nationalism), Maruyama translated the French *citoyen* not as *shimin* but as *kōmin* (literally, "public person"). According to Oguma Eiji, employing the latter term—a combination of the Chinese characters meaning "public" and "people"—was a conscious attempt by Maruyama to avoid the negative petit bourgeois connotation of *shimin* prevalent at the time.[100]

So what was it, then, that caused Maruyama to reconsider the symbolism of the *shimin* idea and the potential of the middle strata? Three factors appear to be of significance here. First, as Tsuzuki Tsutomu and others have noted, in the late 1950s Maruyama developed an interest in Tocqueville via his reading of Fukuzawa Yukichi. In a 1956 essay for the magazine *Sekai,* Maruyama even discussed his "recent penchant for Tocqueville" *(chikagoro moppara Tokuviru ippentō).*[101] Specifically, Maruyama seems to have become more confident about the potential of intermediary associations *(chūkan dantai)* as vehicles for individual citizens to collectively resist the totalitarian tendencies of the modern state. Maruyama's Tocquevillian rereading marked a qualification of his earlier position that intermediary organizations (such as religions and guilds) were feudal and hence to be eradicated in the modernization process.[102] Second, and most obvious, the Keishokuhō and Anpo crises were pivotal events for Maruyama (and other citizen faction intellectuals), because they presented a sort of empirical evidence that a progressive civic consciousness could exist within the potentially fascist middle stratum.

But more than the Anpo struggle and Tocqueville were behind Maruyama's apparent reconsideration of the middle stratum in the late 1950s. The third and important factor was his evolving position on the impact of massification in Japan. As Hiraishi Takeshi has shown,

Maruyama was sensitive to the mass society problem as early as the late 1940s and continued to comment on the phenomenon intermittently until the events of 1960. As he opined in an important 1960 essay, after the war the Japanese people had reverted en masse from their status as subjects of the emperor *(shinmin)* to their natural state as the people *(tami)*. Thereafter, a bifurcation happened. A great majority moved toward the private *(watakushi)* realm and the values of mass consumerism—a complete reversal of the self-sacrificial and public-oriented ideology of the wartime period. A smaller group mobilized into an active renovationist movement *(akutibu kakushin undō)*, redirecting the wartime ethos of self-sacrifice into progressive initiatives.[103] Maruyama suggested that the conservative postwar establishment had shrewdly exploited this value divergence, playing on the political indifference of the masses as a means to contain the renovationist movement. To this extent, then, Maruyama felt that massification had had a deleterious impact on political consciousness and participation for at least one sector of postwar society—something Matsushita Keiichi had earlier pointed out.

But as with Matsushita, the protests beginning in the late 1950s forced Maruyama to rethink mass society, especially the link between self-interest and political involvement. In a 1961 discussion with Satō Noboru, Maruyama explicitly acknowledged the links among private self-interest, public engagement, and the new *shimin* ethos. Maruyama now even felt confident enough to call for a reconsideration of the more positive elements *(sekkyokuteki yōso)* of the masses.[104] This would entail a rethinking of the established socialist doctrine that positioned the proletariat as the most complete or perfected citizenry *(kanzen shimin)*— in other words, that the proletariat-as-vanguard was the contemporary incarnation of the Jacobin-as-complete-*citoyen*. For Maruyama, the marriage of self-interest *(shiri)* and public interest *(kōeki)* in this mythology produced an artificial image of the vanguard human *(zen'eiteki ningen)*.[105] For these perfected citizens, private desires became something disgusting *(kegarawashii)* and petit bourgeois, leaving no room to "nurture the practice of political *choice*" from the perspective of "one's own space" *(jibun no ba)*.[106] In reality, Maruyama felt there were very few—if any—such complete citizens, since the overwhelming majority of people possessed a private daily life *(shiseikatsu)* permeated by a multiplicity of everyday desires *(nichijōteki yōkyū)*. The point for Maruyama was that such individuals were also interested in the public realm and wanted to participate in public activities.

As the citizen protests of the Anpo struggle proved, a broad sector of the populace discovered their right of civil disobedience—what Matsushita called the right of resistance—and how this related to their rights as private citizens. Here Maruyama pointed to the symbolism of the Keishokuhō dispute with its slogan of "no more dates" *(mō dēto mo dekinai)*. That these protests inspired no revolutionary consciousness did not mean they were passive *(shōkyokuteki)*. On the contrary, self-interested civil disobedience was necessary in all societies—even socialist ones—because without it activism tended to become supportive of the system *(yokusan taisei teki)*.[107] The Anpo struggle proved for Maruyama that the self-interested masses could blossom into political *shimin* when their daily lives were threatened and they exercised their right of civil disobedience. The masses and their mode of behavior *(kōdō yōshiki)* were not to be separated into good and bad in an a priori way but, rather, had to be understood as potentialities *(kanōsei)* that could move in multiple directions.[108]

As Maruyama argued in a 1958 speech, politics needed to be imagined more broadly than the Diet or the political sphere; otherwise, there was a risk of confining it to interactions among a narrow group of political professionals. In reality, the majority of people shouldering the responsibility of democracy *(minshushugi o ninau)* engaged in professions outside politics. Indeed, Maruyama reminded his audience, democracy itself developed originally as a movement to liberate citizens from the monopolization of politics by a specific status group. The point for Maruyama, then, was that democracy first found support in the political concern *(seijiteki kanshin)* of apolitical citizens *(hiseijiteki shimin)* and in political expression and action from outside the political sphere—a form of reluctant political activity *(iya iya nagara no seiji katsudō)*.[109] As he explained in a May 1960 speech just before the forced renewal of the security treaty, Japan may not have had the deep tradition of direct democracy as in the Greek city-states, but it did have its own version of lay Buddhism *(zaike Bukkyō)* or, in political terms, the political activity of nonprofessional politicians. One need not take the tonsure to be involved in politics, he declared. Quite the reverse: democracy would be dead if political activity was limited to politicians, Dietmen, and political groups whose primary aim was politics in and of itself.[110] It was a reluctant sensibility to be sure—something citizens did because they *had no choice but to (yarazaru o enai mono)*. But it was precisely in this reluctant sensibility that the foundations of democratic consciousness lay.[111]

In the late 1950s and even more so after the Anpo struggle, Maruyama's imagination of the *shimin* idea incorporated both a public participatory aspect—the *kōmin*, or public person—and a self-interested motivation linked to daily life *(seikatsu)*—what he described as private interest *(shiri)*. The two aspects were mutually supportive: by recognizing the legitimacy of daily life, *kōmin* could resist the pull of pathological collectivities. Moreover, by actively participating in public matters *(paburiku no koto)* people could surmount the self-indulgent apathy born of mass society.[112] In 1961, Maruyama proposed the following definition of the *shimin:* "When I speak of the *shimin* as the bearer of democracy, I refer to both the *citoyen* aspect of proactive participation in various democratic decision-making processes and the aspect of protecting civil liberties *(shiviru ribatīzu)* and resisting state authority *(kōkenryoku)* and all other forms of social pressure from above and from the flank."[113]

Together, these ideas of Matsushita Keiichi, Katō Hidetoshi, and Maruyama Masao remind us about the close link between mass society (both as a concept and as a reality) and the imagination of the *shimin* idea. All three thinkers recognized that the new politics of the *shimin* depended as much (if not more) on prosaic concerns for a secure and affluent daily life as it did on any selfless commitment to Japan's nascent postwar democracy. Indeed, as Maruyama's definition of the *shimin* illustrates and as I have already explained, in the *shimin* idea idealism and realism blended seamlessly—the former in many ways fueled and invigorated by the latter.

Throughout 1960 Matsushita, Maruyama, and Katō were joined by a cadre of progressive intellectuals who discussed and advocated the *shimin* idea in highbrow monthlies, mainstream newspapers, grassroots publications, and in speeches and impromptu addresses to citizen groups. Not all of these individuals became directly involved in civic protest, so portraying them as movement intellectuals would be wrong, but their public articulations were important in that they helped identify and define an activist identity—the *shimin*—which movement intellectuals could use in their mobilizations. These discussions imparted the *shimin* idea with the intellectual breadth and conceptual modularity it would need in actual movements. While Matsushita, Maruyama, and Katō pointed out the *shimin* idea's prosaic roots in mass society, others focused on its links to a new civic consciousness, a professional ethos, a concept of the autonomous locale, and a rehabilitated ethnic nation.

Consider first some of the more classical liberal presentations of the *shimin* idea. In a 1960 discussion with Ishida Takeshi and Fukuda Kanichi, the political historian Shinohara Hajime identified in the Anpo struggle a large-scale civic ethos *(shimin shugi)* and the full expression of true citizen anger, making these protests qualitatively different from the earlier Keishokuhō protests, which were led by organized labor and motivated by material self-interest.[114] From now on, Shinohara suggested, progressive movements would be divided into established organizations *(kisei soshiki)* and nonaligned activists *(mutōha katsudōka)*—the latter group heralding a new age of progressive politics.[115] Fellow University of Tokyo professor Fukuda Kanichi agreed: the Anpo struggle had been driven by a more fundamental civic spirit *(shimin seishin)*, in which people organized themselves as though they were one person, one party *(hitori ittō)*.[116] As Fukuda noted in an essay for the journal *Sekai*, the outpouring of spontaneous public concern during the Anpo crisis represented a turning point in the cultural configuration of Japan. From now on individuals would have the independence to assume their public responsibility.[117] Political scientist Ishida Takeshi chimed in similarly, claiming that the historical import of the Anpo struggle lay in the extraordinary rise of civic consciousness *(shimin ishiki)*.[118] Before this event, democracy in the broadest sense had penetrated the white-collar class in terms of civic *(shiminteki)* modes of daily life *(seikatsu yōshiki)*. But it was only with the protests of 1960 that such values connected to a consciousness of political democracy. For Ishida, the struggle represented a real opportunity for civic revolution *(shimin kakumei)*—if only at the level of popular consciousness.[119] Even the Marxist historian Fujita Shōzō was drawn into the idealistic fervor of the moment, identifying a new civic sensibility *(shimin kankaku)* and calling on people to rise up "as *shimin*."[120]

Writing from a slightly different perspective was Kuno Osamu, a philosopher and the chairman of the Institute for the Science of Thought. Kuno, in fact, made the first attempt to delineate a theory of citizen activism in his highly influential 1960 essay "Shiminshugi no Seiritsu" (The Formation of a Civic Ethos).[121] Unlike Matsushita and Maruyama, who saw the *shimin* idea and civic consciousness as possible outgrowths of mass society, Kuno defined the masses as an inherently active group *(sekkyokuteki shūdan)*, going so far as to conflate *shimin* and *taishū* into a uniform construction: the *shimin-taishū*, or "citizen-masses." The point for him was that the masses were not a mob but a group with a shared emotional experience.[122] Also unlike earlier mass society theorists, Kuno rejected (or ignored) the link between self-interest and political action by this citizen-mass, preferring instead to paint a mythology of the *shimin* drawing on Western concepts of guilds, free cities, and the ethos of craftsmen. For Kuno the *shimin* was a human *(ningen)* who supported daily life *(seikatsu)* via a profession *(shokugyō)*. The key was that the line between work and daily life be clear: if profession invaded daily life, then the civic *(shiminteki)* human would not be born.[123] To be successful, citizen activists would have to sink two separate roots: one as professionals in the workplace and the other as inhabitants of daily life *(seikatsusha)*.[124] In both spheres, however, *shimin* had to be motivated by an ethos beyond self-interest. To be sure, Kuno did admit that local activism should partly focus on protecting and extending the benefits of daily life, but overall his *shimin* looked very much like that of Shinohara, Fukuda, and Ishida—that is, another rendition of the selfless public person.

While Shinohara, Kuno, and others defined the *shimin* within an enlightenment narrative of civic modernization, others preferred a mythology more closely linked to the nation and ethnic identity. Tsurumi Shunsuke is a case in point. Though he did utilize the *shimin* idea, Tsurumi preferred not to attach it to enlightenment narratives fashioned around the great revolutions of Europe and North America.[125] In a discussion with Shinohara and others in late 1960, he argued that the postwar revolution *(sengo kakumei)* was not a civic revolution *(shimin kakumei)* in the Marxist sense of that which occurred before socialist revolution but something more akin to civic protest during the 1956 Hungarian Revolution.[126] Tsurumi likened the appearance of *shimin* during the Anpo struggle to the ethnic national revolt by Hungarian citizens against the Soviet Union and its client state in their country. In a July 1960 essay, "Nemoto kara no Minshushugi" (Democracy from the Base), Tsurumi explicitly distinguished the civic revolution of the Anpo struggle from the English, American, and French revolutions,[127] calling instead for a Japanese form of radical democracy *(rajikaru demokurashī)*.[128] Tsurumi connected the popular protest to a broader quest for national self-determination, saying, "I want Japan to carve out a path for Japan *(Nihon jishin no michi)* in the world" by rebuilding "Japanese public policy" from the "private roots" *(shitekina ne)* contained in the "thought of the Japanese people" *(Nihonjin no shisō)*. Through engaging a nonaligned *(mutō muha)* mass movement, the Japanese people could address the interlinked problems of bureaucratic despotism, monopoly capitalism, and perhaps even U.S. policy

in Asia.[129] Tsurumi carefully avoided using the term *shimin* as a historical actor in the essay, preferring instead the terms *the Japanese masses
(Nihon no taishū), the Japanese people (Nihonjin),* and *the civic nation
(kokumin),* which he juxtaposed to *the Japanese state (Nihon kokka)*
and *America (Amerika).* Together with the *shimin* of mass society theorists or that of enlightenment idealists such as Shinohara, Tsurumi's
ethnic nationalism pointed to deeper motivations informing the civic
protests of 1960 and, by consequence, to a mythology of the *shimin* in
which the nation occupied a legitimate—indeed, an essential—space.

MOVEMENT INTELLECTUALS AND ANPO CIVIC ACTIVISM

Public intellectuals and academics did much to legitimize and broadly
define the *shimin* idea on a theoretical level before and during the Anpo
struggle, but it was movement intellectuals (some from the former
groups) who used the emergent mythology to inspire and directly mobilize people into action. In this section I move from ideas to the actual
civic mobilizations of the struggle, focusing specifically on the role of
movement intellectuals in inspiring, defining, and directing civic movements. An instructive point of departure is Hidaka Rokurō's work on
the events of Anpo published in late 1960, in which he identified three
types of civic organizations in the protests: professional groups *(shokunō
dantai),* political and cultural circles *(seiji sākuru, bunka sākuru),* and
residents' organizations *(kyojūsha soshiki).* I have already discussed
some of the major professional groups, such as the International Problems Symposium and the National Association of Academics and
Researchers for the Protection of Democracy. To these we might add
the Maebashi Democratic Chamber of Commerce (Minshū Shōkōkai),
which staged store closure strikes in protest,[130] and the National Union
of Meteorological Employees, which issued a statement lambasting the
government for claiming that U2 jets landing at U.S. bases in Japan
were for "weather forecasting purposes."[131]

Such groups certainly added to the civic flavor of the protests, but
in the context of citizens' movement history, the last two groups in
Hidaka's typology—political and cultural circles and residents' organizations—were far more important. Among political and cultural circles,
a number of groups deserve mention: the Voices of the Voiceless Association (Koe naki Koe no Kai), the Mountain Range Association
(Yamanami no Kai), and the Grass Seeds Association (Kusa no Mi Kai),

all of which traced their roots to circle activism during the 1950s.[132] Though far less visible, the Anpo protests also witnessed a surge in residents' organizations, especially in the Tokyo area. Such groups tended to mobilize in the large housing complexes *(danchi)* or in local neighborhoods, such as Tokyo's Suginami Ward. Movement intellectuals in both forms of activism tapped into the imagery of the *shimin,* but, interestingly, their conceptualization and use of such imagery was remarkably different.

For greater clarity, I will separate the grassroots civic groups of the Anpo struggle into two streams of activism. Political and cultural circle groups can be positioned in a stream of *conscientious civic activism,* and residents' organizations in a stream of *pragmatic civic activism.*[133] Movements in the conscientious stream pursued fundamental yet somewhat intangible questions of rights, democracy, and pacifism and engaged primarily in street protest and other forms of symbolic dissent. Activists' war memories and remorse about the past deeply informed the ethos of these movements and found expression in both their often-rigid antiestablishment stance and their passionate commitment to political democratization. In terms of issues, conscientious movements focused on defending the constitution, opposing the U.S. military presence in Japan, and (to a lesser extent) advocating the rights of peripheralized groups such as ethnic minorities, the infirm, and people in the geographical hinterlands. Such activism was not new, of course: its roots can be traced to the cultural circle activism of the 1950s and earlier large-scale mobilizations such as the Mothers' Congress or the anti-nuclear-bomb movement. There were also more small-scale precedents such as the Children of the Cedars Group (Sugi no Ko Kai), originally a housewives' study group but later a leading light in the anti-nuclear-bomb movement.[134] Activism in this stream fed, most prominently, into the anti–Vietnam War movement beginning in 1965.

The pragmatic stream of activism born during the Anpo struggle unfolded at the local level, focusing on prosaic bread-and-butter issues relating to daily life, such as sewage, education, and garbage disposal. The failure of mass protest during the struggle undoubtedly promoted such activism, but so too did movement intellectuals' vision of civic activism. Even during the mass street protests of 1959–60, leaders distinguished their small-scale, nonhierarchical movements from the National Congress to Block the Security Treaty Revision and the organs of the established left, which accommodated only organized, affiliated protesters in a nationally focused movement. The key movement intellectuals in this stream were Matsushita Keiichi and his colleagues in the Tokyo Municipal Research Association (Tosei Chōsakai).[135] Far from seeing 1960 as a defeat, movement intellectuals such as Matsushita saw pragmatic activism at the local level as the best conduit to promote popular democratic consciousness in the country as well as to mount an assault on conservative rule from below. In the long run, this pragmatic stream proved far more durable and became far more widespread than movements in the conscientious stream, charting a developmental pathway to the antipollution and antidevelopment residents' movements *(jūmin undō)* of the late 1960s and 1970s, the progressive lifestyle consumer cooperative movement, the diverse citizens' activities *(shimin katsudō)* from the 1970s, and ultimately the nonprofit organizations (NPOs) of the 1990s and beyond.[136] The defeat of the Anpo protests undoubtedly played a role here. But as I show below, important too were the ideas of movement intellectuals that helped define and direct the contours of civic activism in the years thereafter.

CONSCIENTIOUS MOVEMENTS: THE VOICES OF THE VOICELESS

The Voices of the Voiceless Association (hereafter "the Voices") is invariably described as the pioneer of citizen activism in postwar Japan—the nursery of the *shimin* we might say—so any investigation of civic mythology should begin here. The first point to note about the Voices is that, despite the mythology of spontaneity surrounding the group, there was nothing really spontaneous about it at all. Kobayashi Tomi, a key movement intellectual in the group, was already active in grassroots movements by the time of the protests. In the 1950s she had participated in numerous circle groups organized by the Institute for the Science of Thought. From 1958, for example, she participated in the institute's Modern Art Circle as well as a group to discuss the political strife in Hungary. "I felt at home in their circles," Kobayashi recalled, "so I joined up with various chapters here and there."[137] Important as well, Kobayashi also belonged to the institute's Subjectivity Circle (Shukan no Kai), which traveled around Tokyo and its environs making audio recordings of ordinary people, such as actors and juvenile delinquents. It was in the midst of such activism in late May 1960 that Kobayashi and her colleagues first considered some form of active protest against the revision of the treaty.

Despite her participation in such groups, Kobayashi later claimed that she "was the kind of person who didn't belong to any organization" and, until the Anpo struggle, "hadn't participated in any political demonstrations," merely "sitting at home becoming more and more annoyed" as she "listened to the daily news and read the newspaper."[138] All this apparently changed during her conversation on the train on May 30. "We decided to participate in the June 4th demonstrations, the day of the planned general strike. We decided that we would appeal to those unorganized individuals, the ones brooding at home with no way of expressing their feelings."[139] On June 2, two days before their first demonstration, Kobayashi and her group gathered in the basement of the Newspaper Institute at the University of Tokyo, where they made up placards for their march. In hope of attracting a wide array of participants, they made up signs reading "Just walk with us for ten minutes," "Walk with us for fifty meters or even ten!" "Call an Election," "U2 Jets Get Out!" and the group's primary placard reading "The Voices of the Voiceless Association, Anyone Can Join."

The association's name was not original, borrowing from a statement by Prime Minister Kishi in late May 1960. Kishi had argued that because the majority of Japanese were not out in the streets protesting, by implication they supported his move to renew the security treaty by way of parliamentary majority. "In fact it's the voices of the voiceless *(koe naki koe)* that I have to lend an ear to. Right now all we have are the voices of the audible *(koe aru koe)*. What I'm talking about is so-called public opinion."[140] He announced, "If we give in to the movement outside the Diet, we will not be able to protect Japanese democracy. I have faith in the support of the voiceless voices of the nation."[141]

Turning this notion on its head, Kobayashi and her colleagues decided to become self-appointed voices for those among the silent majority who were apparently opposed to the treaty and Kishi. Of course, the Voices never developed into anything close to a mass movement, so its claims about representing the silent majority must be read critically. At its height the movement seems to have attracted the participation of only around three thousand or four thousand, and rallies after the crisis month of June attracted tens—and not thousands or even hundreds—of participants. Indeed, the Voices' significance lay in its ideational legacy rather than its impact (or lack thereof) on national politics. Kobayashi and her colleagues showed how the mythology of the *shimin* could motivate ordinary citizens frustrated by political developments but lacking a space in which to express opposition comfortably. The group's marching refrain, written by the movement intellectuals Takabatake Michitoshi and Yasuda Takeshi and handed out at rallies, expressed this sentiment most clearly:

> Come on Citizens, let's walk together
> Even for five minutes, or a hundred meters, let's walk together.
> We don't have a particularly outstanding opinion,
> Nor do we have a loud voice to declare our position,
> But the Voices of the Voiceless have the prudence to distinguish what
>   is right.
> Let's walk together and quietly show that we really have the will to
>   protest against the government.
> We know that you are busy at work every day and, moreover,
>   embarrassed to participate in a demonstration,
> But if we give up here and now and fall silent
> Japan will never improve for the better.
> At the very least we want to act now so that someday, when
>   our children ask, "What were you doing then?" we will not
>   be ashamed.
> So that we do not passively approve the tactics of May 19,
> Let's have the Diet dissolve immediately and start again with a
>   clean slate.
> Prime Minister Kishi did his duty to America and suppressed the
>   people. Let's have him resign.
> Moreover, let's have them call off Ike's visit—which Kishi will make
>   the most of—until the day that we can willingly welcome him.
> Come on citizens, be brave!
> Let's walk together and express how we feel.
> ("The Anybody Can Be Involved Voices of the Voiceless March," by
>   Takabatake Michitoshi and Yasuda Takeshi)[142]

Voices participants also left a graphic record about what attracted them to this movement. Consider the comments of a woman who joined Kobayashi's march on June 4, 1960: "I just couldn't stay at home today," she explained, "so I brought my son from his exam prep-school and came to the Diet. Then I saw your placard, so I joined in. This is just wonderful. To turn around and go home at this stage would have been a real letdown. I participated in May Day this year, but it was kind of uncomfortable to mix in with the labor unions and their red flags."[143] The *Asahi Jyānaru* recounted the story of a business owner involved in a collective bargaining dispute with company workers. Unable to resist his teenage daughter's lamentations about the treaty renewal, he had come out to demonstrate. But as he explained in the interview, since he was in management, there was no way he would join in a union march and, hence, had ended up in the Voices march.[144] The same was true for a middle-aged housewife, persuaded to join the Voices group as she stood watching on the sidewalk: "In the morning I told my children the following, knowing full well that it probably wasn't true. 'Today I'm going to participate in the "Election for Idealists Association" at the House of Councilors Assembly Hall. It's close to the Diet, so I'll probably go watch the demonstrations, and there is a chance I may even participate in a demonstration.' My kids laughed, saying that if I tried to join a demonstration I would be thrown out." And later, as she stood on the sidewalk watching the demonstration: "A young-faced person called out to me, 'Won't you walk together with us?' I was surprised at the informality of this person's request, so I turned around and saw [her] sunburned face. I hesitated for a moment wondering if it could be true, if insignificant 'I' could in fact join the march. I looked at the person's face once again. Then I took the hand of my friend who stood beside and said, 'Let's go together,' 'let's join.' And with that we took a deep breath and joined the march."[145]

Empathizing with Kobayashi's endeavor, Takanashi Saburō, a high school teacher from Setagaya, organized his own Voices of the Voiceless group on June 11. "We didn't belong to any organization," he explained. "In the beginning I participated in the students' demonstrations, but when I got to the Diet I ran into some other unaffiliated people like myself. I realized then that I wanted to make a marching association for solitary citizens who could not participate in the opposition [movement]. We shared the common feelings of isolation in being nonaffiliated and also a [sense of] opposition to Anpo and [a desire] to protect democracy. I consulted with some friends and then made up banners reading 'The Voices of the Voiceless Association' and 'Anyone can join!' Twelve of us assembled outside the Education Ministry on June 11. We did one lap of the Diet, and as we passed the Patents Office on our way to the U.S. Embassy our ranks had swelled to nearly three hundred people. Nearly all were first-time demonstrators. The next time we [demonstrated] on June 18, there were far more people than we had expected. There may have been as many as two thousand."[146]

After the Anpo protests, the Voices movement transformed into a liaison group for budding citizen activists and progressive grassroots associations. Most notably, in September 1960 the Voices hosted a meeting of grassroots groups in Kichijōji, in the eastern part of Tokyo.[147] The meeting attracted some 150 activists from groups in *danchi* complexes, Tokyo neighborhoods such as Setagaya, Itabashi, Nerima, Shinjuku, and Suginami, as well as outlying areas such as Fujisawa City. No serious resolutions were adopted, but all agreed on an antiwar stance, more demonstrations, the creation of more regional branches, and the establishment of a lifestyle consumer cooperative (though this never eventuated).[148] Perhaps the most durable activity of the Voices was its publication of the movement newsletter, or *minikomi, Koe naki Koe no Tayori* (Correspondence from the Voices of the Voiceless).[149] Takabatake Michitoshi came onboard as the newsletter's first editor, and it became a mouthpiece for both movement intellectuals such as Kuno, Tsurumi, and Takabatake, who outlined programs and suggestions for civic groups, and ordinary citizens, who submitted their own contributions. The pamphlet was published monthly (occasionally bimonthly) from 1960 to 1995.

In terms of concrete political activism by the Voices group, two mobilizations warrant mention. First, in preparation for the general elections of November 1960, the Voices produced a chart of Diet members indicating how they had voted on the Anpo renewal.[150] The group followed this up with a questionnaire to political parties, pushing them for clarification on key policy issues.[151] *Tayori* also ran a number of interesting "how to" articles such as "Conducting a One-Man Election Movement" in its November 1960 issue.[152] The article encouraged members to "approach people at rallies or those on the street," to "send letters to friends and acquaintances," and to "make use of the telephone." It warned against "carrying placards or distributing pamphlets supporting a specific candidate or party—since this violated electioneering rules." Moreover, the article advised that if the police appeared, "you should accompany them only if they say 'You're under arrest' "— everything else was just scare tactics. It reminded members of their "right to remain silent and to have a lawyer" once at the police station. The article encouraged them to stay "committed to their beliefs" in such a situation but also to be sure not to "insult the police officers personally or professionally."

Similarly, beginning in mid-1961 the Voices attempted to mobilize a movement opposing the government's newly introduced Law to Prevent Acts of Political Violence (Seijiteki Bōryoku Kōi Soshi Hō, known by the abbreviation Seibōhō). The LDP claimed that the new law was necessary because of recent acts of political terror, such as the murder of the JSP secretary general Asanuma Inajirō. In reality, the law was another attempt—similar to that of the Keishokuhō—to strengthen policing powers over radical antigovernment demonstrations. The proposed law took specific aim at groups such as the mainstream faction of Zengakuren, prohibiting "collective violence" and action "in or around the Diet or prime minister's residence." It empowered authorities to prohibit groups from holding rallies, demonstrations, or printing pamphlets for up to four months and authorized the state to order groups to disband.[153] The bill was ultimately scrapped by the LDP for political reasons, not because of pressure from protests outside the Diet. In fact, the mobilizations against the bill by the National Congress Opposing Harmful Revisions to the Police Duties Performance Law and groups such as the Voices failed to gain any real public interest or support. Just as in the earlier election movement, many within the Voices group were left downhearted by the general lack of interest in the Seibōhō issue and the sense that their movement had really played no part in the eventual outcome. The Seibōhō letdown only compounded the failures of the earlier Anpo struggle and the election of late 1960, and from 1961 to around the middle of 1963 the movement waned almost to the point of extinction.

Organizational failures aside, the period from the Anpo crisis to 1963 proved to be a formative moment in the articulation of a new political praxis by movement intellectuals in the Voices movement. In the first issue of *Tayori* in July 1960, Tsurumi Shunsuke called for the formation of citizens' assemblies *(shimin shūkai)* with four basic characteristics: political nonalignment *(mutō muha)*, diversity of opinion *(sengen meidai)*, avoidance of political opportunism (i.e., finding allies in the conservative camp), and direct democracy by political amateurs.[154] At the year-end meeting of Voices groups in 1960, Takabatake Michitoshi proposed his own four pillars *(yotsu no hashira)* for the fledgling movements: first, staunch opposition to the now-renewed security treaty; second, the creation of residential organizations *(kyojūchi soshiki)* to link politics to daily life; third, participation on the basis of free will and an ethos of individual self-renewal *(ningen o mizukara kaete iku)*; and finally, avoidance of organizational resolutions *(ketsugi)* in the name of respect for individual autonomy. Better to keep the movement one for delinquent citizens *(furō shimin)*, Takabatake argued.[155] Addressing the issue of social mission, philosopher Kuno Osamu proposed in the fifth edition of *Tayori* that Voices groups take on a third role *(mitsume no yakuwari)*, that of a faith group *(shinkō shūdan)* in civil society, which he rendered into Japanese as *bunmei shakai*, or civilized society.[156] Kuno saw civic groups such as the Voices as a kind of clearinghouse for specific issues faced by residential groups *(kyojūchi soshiki)* and professional groups *(shokunō soshiki)* in their respective spheres.

Of course, after a series of abortive protests it was difficult for many to see their movement as the beginning of a new wave. Kobayashi Tomi spoke of how she was overwhelmed by disappointment and a sense of powerlessness.[157] By 1965 she was ever more confused by her *shimin* status: "Actually, it's very hard to know what is really going on in the world just by reading the newspaper. For example, when I saw the Japanese flag raised during the [1964] Olympics I froze up—on the one hand I thought it's not so bad after all, but on the other, I felt that it just wasn't right. I was really confused."[158] For Kobayashi and many other citizen activists, the shift from street protest to the humdrum of everyday life was a difficult process. It was tricky to resist the pull of the mainstream—to remain conscientious. Kobayashi felt that social movements seemed to be becoming more irresponsible. She complained, "It seems as though those who [resist] the hardest are always left behind; it's crazy!" For Kobayashi this irresponsibility among citizens stemmed in part from the disjuncture between activism and daily life. To be sure, conscientious citizen activists still gathered in small groups to debate problems and plan activism, but when they went home they returned to a realm of conventionality. "It's disappointing when you realize that it is just the same kind of people clustered together here and there who are doing all the talking. Moreover, the discussion is more and more about aspects of daily life."

Most telling of the downbeat mood among conscientious activists after the Anpo protests is the following analysis contained in a 1962 retrospective on the Voices movement titled *Mata Demo de Aō* (Let's Meet Again at a Demonstration). The extract outlines six reasons for declining rates of participation:

1. The movement has not extended its power in mainstream politics.
2. The association has no rules. The association holds meetings but doesn't make any resolutions. It's not clear who is responsible for doing things. It's not clear what we should be doing.
3. Some prefer [formal] organizations, so they are dropping out. An association of nonorganized individuals will never change politics. It's frustrating to not know how much power we have [or don't have].
4. I don't have the energy to spare.

5. I'm not a *shimin*; that's why I'm quitting. The Voices of the Voiceless Association say they are an assembly of *shimin*. But what actually is a *shimin*? Rather than making a noise about *shimin*, we should value the *shomin* (the common folk).

6. We aren't in a period of crisis now, so I'm dropping out. Should we enter a period of crisis, then I'll be active again.[159]

That activists at the time saw such factors in negative terms is understandable: their movement *was* in decline. But from a historical perspective, these very same factors evidence the extent to which Kobayashi and other movement intellectuals were defining and forging a new style of civic activism. Practices of nonalignment, amateurism, informalism, pluralism, spontaneity, and multivocality—though undoubtedly frustrating at times—were what made these movements new and appealing to many Japanese previously politically active only in a formalistic way. This was the real breakthrough of Kobayashi and her fellow movement intellectuals in the Voices of the Voiceless movement of the Anpo struggle.

PRAGMATIC MOVEMENTS: THE LOCAL SOLUTION

The other important story of citizen activism during the Anpo struggle is the emergence and spread of localized, pragmatic citizen groups.[160] Different from the conscientious stream, which tended to stagnate after the anti–Vietnam War movement, the pragmatic stream fed into a nuts-and-bolts set of theories about the attainment of local democracy *(chiiki minshushugi)*, the reform of local politics *(jichitai kaikaku)*, citizen participation *(shimin sanka)* in local government, and nonprotest forms of activism beginning in the 1970s. In other words, although it is often slighted in the Anpo struggle master narrative of "*shimin* versus establishment," the pragmatic groups' impact was actually more far-reaching than that of the conscientious *shimin* groups, which tended to disband quietly after the crisis.

Matsushita Keiichi, Narumi Masayasu, and their Tokyo Municipal Research Association, the Tosei Chōsakai, became the intellectual nucleus of this stream, and their work at the time provides a useful window into the emergence and internal dynamics of residential organizations mobilized in mid-1960. Envisaged as a JSP think tank, the Tosei Chōsakai was established in 1955 as a unit of the Tokyo Conference of Allied Labor Unions (Tōkyōto Rōdō Kumiai Rengō Kyōgikai or Torōren).[161] Though the Voices of the Voiceless took the lead in bringing citizen groups together immediately after the struggle, the Tosei Chōsakai very soon became the primary hub for local groups in and around the capital.[162] In May 1961, the Tosei Chōsakai hosted the inaugural Liaison and Discussion Group for Local Organizations (Chiiki Soshiki Renraku Kondankai), effectively replacing the meeting convened by the Voices in September 1960. The Tosei Chōsakai hosted a unique confluence of individuals: activists from local movements, supporters of local government reform, and, important to note, individuals such as Matsushita and Narumi, who would conceptualize a reformist local vision for civic groups. To the extent that it produced theory regarding the new movements, the Tosei Chōsakai also transcended its role as a Tokyo-centered organization, reaching out to other urban (and in some cases rural) movements throughout the country. Moreover, after the nationwide local elections of 1963, many academics within the Tosei Chōsakai took on positions as public policy advisers for the newly elected progressive administrations.[163] Here they pursued policies to foster local activism and reform local politics.

It was Tosei Chōsakai members who first coined the phrase "local democracy" *(chiiki minshushugi)* after their survey work with groups such as the Suginami Association soon after the Anpo struggle. In a May 1961 article, "Chiiki Minshushugi no Kadai to Tenbō" (The Challenges and Outlook for Local Democracy), in the scholarly magazine *Shisō*, Matsushita Keiichi put forward local democracy, local association building, and the reform of local politics as key challenges facing post-Anpo citizen groups. He argued here that the national movements mobilized during the Keishokuhō and Anpo crises revealed how the sensibility of the new constitution had struck roots among the new middle stratum *(shinchūkansō)*, developing into a consciousness of the right of resistance *(teikōken)*.[164]

The problem, however, was that the civic energy of the Anpo struggle had failed to take root in the localities where old middle-stratum *(kyūchūkansō)* conservatives still doggedly retained control through neighborhood and small business associations.[165] Matsushita described this situation as a kind of dual structure in postwar Japan: the cities belonged to new middle-stratum individuals who had escaped the village and, through higher education, moved into the bureaucracy and large corporations and now enjoyed the bounty of an affluent mass society. The countryside and the localities, however, remained conservative strongholds both politically and economically. Cognizant of mass society, conservatives had transformed their strategies of control such that those in the new middle stratum were effectively isolated on returning to their bedroom towns.[166] Matsushita felt that the commitment of the progressive political parties and the labor movement to workplace struggles *(shokuba tōsō)* did nothing to alleviate this situation.[167]

Rather than proposing a movement of conscientious citizens, Matsushita and his colleagues in the Tosei Chōsakai proposed a pragmatic set of strategies for post-Anpo citizens' movements. Activists would need new applied theorizations on local organization, they would need more local specialists, they would have to forge links with progressive local bureaucrats, and they would have to focus all of this on the reform of local government.[168] As Matsushita explained to readers of *Tayori* in March 1961, transforming street protests into residential organizations, creating links with local progressive groups, and nurturing local leaders would be of real significance for future activism.[169]

We get a clearer picture of the movements that Matsushita had in mind in the survey work of fellow Tosei Chōsakai member Narumi Masayasu, conducted soon after the Anpo struggle. Consider, for example, Narumi's report on the Central Nerima Citizens' Association in Tokyo, established by four groups during the height of the protests in June 1960.[170] One year after the Anpo demonstrations, Narumi reported that the association was broken up into six squads, and most of the 136 members were either housewives or individuals working in other regions.[171] Academics and local intellectuals took a leading role in the organization, for example, as in February 1961, when they commenced the Nerima Citizen Lectures (Nerima Shimin Kōza). As part of its activism, the organization also gathered information and conducted surveys on such matters as the national pension scheme, the need for more high schools, the rising cost of train fares, and the murder of the Japan Socialist Party chairman Asanuma Inejirō—a colorful mixture of issues both close to home and also focused on national politics. Echoing this eclecticism, the group's founding statement stressed, "We want to use this 'Citizens' Association' . . . to problematize the most important facets of our daily lives *(seikatsu)*. For example, from large questions such as capitalism or socialism, which party to vote for in the upcoming general election, whether or not the national pension scheme is good or bad, all the way to problems closer to home such as sewage and trash buildup."[172]

Narumi also reported on the Koganei Citizens' Association for Peace and Democracy (Heiwa to Minshushugi o Mamoru Koganeishi Shimin no Kai), established in April 1960.[173] Though the group's regulations stipulated nonalignment with specific political parties, as their activities developed members began to perceive the limits of doggedly independent activism and, in turn, to explore new ways to engage with established progressive parties and labor unions. Group members began discussions on school education with the local branch of the radical communist-aligned Japan Teachers Union, and they called on leftist parties and labor groups to join them in a drive for expansion in government social security expenditure.[174] Over time this willingness to engage among pragmatic civic groups fostered not only deeper ties with progressive organizations but also, more interestingly, a greater willingness to discuss public policy issues with local bureaucrats and even conservative LDP politicians.

In Narumi's report on the Suginami Association (Suginami no Kai) in Tokyo, we get a glimpse of the kinds of motivations fueling these new residential organizations. In 1961 Narumi, together with local activists and members of the Tosei Chōsakai, produced a highly influential report on the movement and ward politics, titled *Daitoshi ni okeru Chiiki Seiji no Kōzō* (The Structure of Local Politics in Large Cities).[175] Narumi noted how the group began as a "residential organization of activists" intent on "establishing local democracy," *not* as a "citizens' organization" *(shimin soshiki)*—the latter obviously referring to conscientious groups like the Voices.[176] On the contrary, the Suginami Association developed a concrete set of initiatives for ridding their locality of old-style conservative control. As one activist lamented, "Suginami has been lumped with the nickname 'the city of culture where mosquitoes buzz.' "[177] The phrase harshly revealed for him the reality that even Tokyo qualified in ways as a village *(mura)*. It proved that progressives had "given up midstream" in the face of an "all-powerful conservative pipeline" recently reorganized into neighborhood associations that "skillfully drew on the everyday demands *(nichijō yōkyū)*" of local residents.[178]

Not to be discouraged, however, the association took its activism to a second stage. It appointed block leaders within the region to mobilize support for the group. Each block was assigned specific issues ranging from price raises, infant paralysis, and even the proposed site for construction of new municipal offices. Association members also became involved in the Seibōhō protest movement.[179] The aim in all of this was to hit at the roots of conservatism: the neighborhood association and traditional community leaders.

The emergence of citizen associations in *danchi,* the large residential complexes in Tokyo, Osaka, and other metropolitan centers, also caught the attention of the Tosei Chōsakai. In northern Tokyo, for example, a women's study group developed into the Higashi Fushimi Danchi Nineteenth Association (Higashi Fushimi Danchi Jūkunichi Kai). As with most other citizen organizations, the group demanded that Kishi immediately resign and the Diet be dissolved.[180] After the crisis, the Higashi Fushimi group continued to meet monthly, holding a social studies class for adults *(otona no shakaika),* which provided an opportunity to hear lectures and hold discussions among members.[181] Similarly, residents at the Tamahei Danchi in Hino City dealt with issues of democratization in everyday life. Its early activism focused on the prosaic issue of rising sewage rates. Narumi noted that progressive parties and organizations had not developed in the Hino area during the postwar era; hence, the new Tamahei Danchi Association became the center of a drive for democratization in local politics. The association tackled the problem of corruption among local government officials. Together with unionists, the group formed the Discussion Group on Democratization of City Politics (Chōsei Minshuka Kondankai), which subsequently developed into a recall campaign against the local mayor.[182] Tamahei Danchi Association members also adopted a self-study path. During July and August 1960 they invited professors living in the *danchi* to speak on topics such as the "relationship between the security treaty and the constitution," "the security treaty and the Japanese economy," and "the student movement."[183]

Reflecting on his survey work out in the localities during this period, Narumi argued that the crucial significance of the Anpo struggle was that it was the first time a new stratum of individuals had spontaneously mobilized in a political movement to protect democracy.[184] After the struggle these individuals fanned out into the localities to create local democracy. "The historic Anpo struggle was a valuable experience for us," he suggested, and it was "also a moment of learning."[185] Citizens, through the painful defeat of 1960, realized that politics could be transformed only from the bottom up, hence, the need for democracy from the grass roots *(nemoto kara no minshushugi)* and local democracy *(chiiki minshushugi).*[186]

Although it did not come onto the Tosei Chōsakai's radar screen, one more innovative Anpo movement deserves mention in any discussion of the development of pragmatic activism: the Seikatsu Club (Seikatsu Kurabu), a lifestyle cooperative union. I will return to this movement in greater detail in later chapters, but for the time being note its importance as a forerunner of pragmatic activism. Iwane Kunio, the ideological force behind the early movement, was drawn into activism as a result of his work photographing the protests of 1960. Soon after the crisis ended he signed up in a youth organization of the JSP and made an unsuccessful bid for a council seat in Tokyo's Setagaya Ward. Growing more and more frustrated with the hardline ideological stance of the established progressive parties, Iwane—together with his wife and other supporters—decided to pursue their own pragmatic, self-supporting, grassroots movement for democratization. Their movement began with an antinuclear signature campaign and sales of cheap milk and eventually developed into one of Japan's foremost independent lifestyle consumer cooperatives.

What is interesting is how Iwane and his colleagues arrived at the consumer co-op model (which was by no means new to Japan). Angered by the tactics of Kishi and the LDP, Iwane was originally drawn to the Japan Socialist Party but soon became disenchanted with what he saw as its rigid devotion to ideology. This led Iwane and fellow activists to concrete activism at the local level focused on daily life and, in particular, issues of concern to urban housewives. As with many other movements in this pragmatic stream, the Seikatsu Club's realistic and concrete approach to activism, though initially envisaged as a form of resistance to the established order, ultimately fed into a broader logic among civic groups in the mid-1970s supportive of constructive activism based on engagement with the state and market. Moreover, movement leaders' presentation of *shimin* subjectivity as *seikatsusha* (inhabitant of daily life) informed a kind of grassroots ethnic nationalism so prominent in Japanese civic groups throughout the postwar period. As we shall see in the coming chapters, Iwane shared a great deal in common with other movement intellectuals who blamed free market capitalism, the "West," and most of all the United States for just about everything they felt to be wrong with their country.

Although it was civic and not ethnic nationalism driving their project, we can see a similar progression away from the established left to a so-called new politics of the *shimin* in the Tosei Chōsakai's theorizations. Matsushita Keiichi's ideational evolution is instructive: his early rethinking of mass society; his generally positive appraisal of civic activism during the Anpo struggle; and his dissatisfaction with the workplace strategy of the established left. After the summer of 1960, localized grassroots activism became for Matsushita the most rational and practical way to overcome the deep roots of conservative power and the polarized demographics of contemporary urban society in Japan. In articulating his model of pragmatic citizen activism and actively abandoning earlier leftist strategies of local struggle *(chiiki tōsō)* and struggle for local government *(jichitai tōsō)* in favor of reformist programs such as local activities *(chiiki katsudō)* and local government reform *(jichitai kaikaku)*, Matsushita began to articulate an emergent mindset that would sink deep roots among intellectuals, bureaucrats, and politicians of all political hues over the coming decades. Like Iwane and the Seikatsu Club, Matsushita and local democracy advocates would further distance themselves from the established left—so much so, in fact, that their objectives came to be wholly divorced from socialist theory and redirected toward the formation of a civic nation by sovereign, yet patriotic, socially responsible, self-disciplined, and largely apolitical *shimin* subjects. Unlike conscientious movement intellectuals committed to steadfast resistance, Matsushita and those in the pragmatic stream of activism began to fashion a mythology of the *shimin* and a theory of civil society directed *toward* rather than *away from* the institutions of conservative hegemony. The defeat of the Anpo struggle certainly played a role in provoking this pragmatic response, but it was movement intellectuals and civic group advocates who articulated how the response should unfold and what its ultimate aims should be.

THE LEGACIES OF ANPO CIVIC ACTIVISM

The Anpo struggle was one of those historical moments when multiple streams of thought and action were unwittingly drawn together in a vortex of society-wide unrest. One outcome was a potent new mythology of the *shimin,* first hinted at in debates about mass society, then put into practice by movement intellectuals intent on mobilizing and shaping a burgeoning sphere of civic activism. The Anpo struggle left a number of legacies for later civic thought and activism. First, it revealed that the people's visceral—if uninspired—attachment to an affluent daily life informed their democratic consciousness at the very deepest level. Second, it set in motion two streams of civic activism, one focused on conscientious dissent and the other on pragmatic grassroots initiatives. Third, it proved that, even in the face of defeat, movement intellectuals could use the *shimin* idea to mobilize and fashion civic movements.

CHAPTER 3

Beheiren and the Asian *Shimin*

The Fate of Conscientious Civic Activism

There is one thing we want to say: "Peace to Vietnam."
This is not only our voice; it is the voice of most
  people throughout the world. Indeed, it is the voice
  of humankind.
From this corner of Asia, Tokyo, we raise our voices. Our
  voices may be small. But one echo invites another and
  rapidly but surely it will spread throughout the world. For
  example, to America, to China, and, of course, to
  Vietnam. And those voices will move our governments.
—Invitation to protest, April 15, 1965

We are ordinary citizens.
Ordinary citizens means company employees, elementary
  school teachers, carpenters, their wives, newspaper
  journalists, florists, men who write novels, and boys
  learning English.
In other words, that means you, the person reading
  this pamphlet.
And there is one thing we want to say,
"Peace to Vietnam!"
—From a protest flyer, April 24, 1965

"PACIFISM," ETHNIC NATIONALISM, AND THE *SHIMIN*

For many, Beheiren—the Citizens' Alliance for Peace in Vietnam—is the quintessential Japanese new social movement.[1] Beginning in early 1965 after the commencement of U.S. bombing in North Vietnam, the movement diversified into over three hundred local chapters in its nine years, making it one of the most broad-based and high-profile civic mobilizations in the postwar era. Building on the model of the conscientious civic activism of the Anpo struggle, Beheiren promoted nonalignment, organizational pluralism, individual autonomy, small-scale mobilization, and single-issue politics. Participants intentionally avoided hierarchical organization in the mode of the old left, forming instead a loose alliance among any who agreed with three objectives: peace to Vietnam, Vietnam for the Vietnamese, and an end to Japanese governmental cooperation in the war.[2] People—movement intellectuals—also linked Beheiren to the earlier Voices of the Voiceless Association and the Institute for the Science of Thought. It was Tsurumi Shunsuke and Takabatake Michitoshi, for example, who first hatched the idea of an antiwar movement in early 1965; it was Takabatake who coined the acronym "Beheiren";[3] and it was the same two who handpicked the movement's intellectual leader, the novelist and social critic Oda Makoto.[4]

In his history of the postwar period, Masamura Kimihiro describes Beheiren as an extension and deepening of the civic aspects *(shiminteki yōso)* born during the Anpo struggle, and it was.[5] Under the guidance of Oda, the novelist Kaikō Takeshi, Tsurumi Yoshiyuki, and a new crop of citizen movement intellectuals, Beheiren complemented the Anpo-struggle model of civic protest with a novel range of strategies such as the provision of safe houses for U.S. deserters, provocative street marches, antiwar newspaper advertisements, international peace conferences, speaking tours by U.S. activists, and creative mobilizations against munitions manufacturers, such as Mitsubishi Heavy Industries.[6] Movement intellectuals consciously broke away from the serious demonstrations of the old left, promoting instead (though not always) a festive style of activism, replete with balloons and bouquets.[7]

In terms of political outcomes, however, Beheiren did not accomplish very much. It did not have a palpable impact on Japanese governmental policy vis-à-vis the Vietnam War, nor did it significantly contribute to the ending of hostilities. It did not precipitate a mass movement opposed to the U.S.-Japan security alliance, nor did it foment widespread dissatisfaction with the military-corporate nexus in Japan. Nevertheless, Beheiren became a model—in fact, an ideal—of how to *do* and *be* a conscientious citizens' movement in a postwar way. Kuno Osamu—a participant in both the Voices and Beheiren—saw Beheiren as a breakthrough movement in this sense, describing its flower bouquet marches as somehow artistic.[8] Activist Iida Momo even proclaimed that Beheiren was Japan's first truly self-starting movement—a spontaneous alternative to the slow-starting established left and peace movements.[9] Takabatake Michitoshi compared the spirit of Beheiren to the Renaissance, which "symbolized the flowering of long-suppressed individualism and the liberation of emotional sensitivities." He also likened Beheiren to the Reformation because of the movement's "emphasis on forming organizations of fellow believers."[10] Takabatake suggested that Oda Makoto's focus on the ordinary person was a direct challenge to old left ideologies, which placed the worker at the center of social change. In distinctively quixotic prose, he depicted Beheiren's ethos as an "aspiration for universalism through the wholeness *(zentaisei)* found in actual human beings."[11] Individual autonomy, he opined, transformed the movement into something bright and playful.[12]

To be sure, Beheiren did inherit the tradition of conscientious activism begun by the Voices, priding itself on its fundamental differences—ideological, organizational, and strategic—from the established left. Beheiren was, indeed, a loosely organized movement, and its members intentionally avoided the language of Marxism and class. Anyone was free to start up a Beheiren movement (provided they opposed U.S. military engagement in Vietnam, that is), and members could engage in any type of activism they pleased. Beheiren's leaders succeeded in both transferring the *shimin* idea to a new issue and in using it to mobilize thousands of people in support. They proved that the Anpo struggle model of autonomous citizen activism (the new collective action frame) had vitality years after its formulation in that earlier protest. As the new social movement proponent Amano Masako explains, Beheiren and other similar mobilizations articulated a powerful critique of advanced industrial society and its supposedly corrosive ideology of economic growth above all else. For Beheiren activists, *shimin* were "people who kept a distance from the state" and were "cautious" and "critical" of all "state and political power."[13] Their motivation to protest came from the perspective of "daily life," from being a "weak individual" *(yowai kojin)*.[14] These elements, according to Amano, attracted a new stratum of participants to the movement and made it fundamentally different from earlier models for political and social change.

In light of all this, Beheiren clearly fits the mold of a new social movement and, from a global-historical perspective, probably deserves recognition as one of the landmark movements in this genre. But, as I noted in the introduction, while NSM approaches elegantly situate movements within a post-1960s zeitgeist, they tend to obscure as much as they capture, and this does not make for balanced history. If we are to faithfully traverse the "unprocessed historical record" of movements like Beheiren, we need to look in all corners of the historical field, not only at levels of theoretical fit.[15] Beheiren may well have been an NSM, but for a deeper understanding of the movement and the values that motivated its participants we need to look further.

In this chapter I focus on the role of Beheiren's spokespersons and the ideas they used to grow and shape the movement. I am interested in the movement intellectuals' engagement with questions of race, ethnicity, and nation, because, despite such aspects having been largely ignored to date, in them we uncover the core intellectual foundations of Beheiren.[16] In the ideas of Oda and others, we see war memories blending together with anti-Americanism, Pan-Asianism, third worldism, and Black Power. We see a movement deeply opposed to the Japanese state, supposedly rendered into an impotent client of the United States. And we also witness a gradual investigation of individual aggression and complicity in the deeds of the state. While the Anpo struggle ended with *shimin* as the defenders of an affluent and autonomous daily life, Beheiren's leaders championed an Asian *shimin* who questioned the very foundation of Japan's autonomy and affluence and longed for a spiritual return to the East.

By stepping away from the NSM paradigm and adopting the lenses of race, ethnos, and nation, a different—and more deeply fascinating— Beheiren is revealed. Consider, for example, the generally accepted image of Beheiren as a pacifist movement.[17] This portrayal is misleading. Oda certainly claimed that his basic principles were absolute pacifism *(zettai heiwashugi)* and nonviolence *(hibōryoku)* and that these were the reasons he fought so hard to defend Article 9 of the Japanese constitution.[18] But, regardless of such claims and despite the movement's official name—the Citizens' Alliance for *Peace* in Vietnam—and its mostly nonviolent activism, Beheiren was not about absolute pacifism and nonviolence if we understand these to be the ideology of opposition to all forms of violence.[19] Though movement intellectuals endlessly called for an American cease-fire and withdrawal from Vietnam, one is hard-pressed to find any of its leaders asking the North Vietnamese to lay down their weapons and practice nonviolent opposition. On the contrary: Oda Makoto openly said that it was antiwar activists' duty to support the armed struggle of the Vietnamese. On numerous occasions he declared his affinity for the National Front for the Liberation of Vietnam, the Vietcong, and their armed struggle for ethnic liberation. Oda even admitted to this double standard running through his pacifist antiwar movement: "To be honest, I contradict myself," he confessed.[20] For some, such as novelist Kaikō Takeshi, unconditional support for the North Vietnamese proved too much. Kaikō became more and more disillusioned with both sides of the conflict after his sojourns as a reporter in Vietnam for the magazine *Shūkan Asahi*. Kuno Osamu recalls Kaikō lamenting over the terrible methods of both the Americans *and* the Vietcong and how he had become nihilistic after seeing this and wanted to quit Beheiren, which he eventually did.[21] To be fair, in its own activism Beheiren never resorted to violent tactics; it was the epitome of nonviolent civil disobedience. But we need to consider such tactics in the context of the movement's overall support for the ethnic liberation of Vietnam by force. Understanding this subtle yet important point will help us comprehend Oda and others' attraction to the tactics of black and third world revolutionaries.

Race, ethnos, and nation pervaded movement intellectuals' public articulations. In May 1965, for example, Hidaka Rokurō and other Beheiren leaders issued a statement with a fascinating mix of Pan-Asian and progressive civic nationalist rhetoric. "As members of Asia," they declared, "we strongly express our desire for peace, justice, and humanitarianism, and we keenly feel the obligation to work for these." Hidaka and his colleagues claimed that large-scale opposition to the war in Japan was a "manifestation of the conscience of the *Japanese nation (nihon kokumin)*." And, in one of the earliest statements of what I call Beheiren's peace constitution nationalism, the same statement demanded that "in the spirit of the antiwar peace constitution," the Japanese government "must not lend assistance" to the Vietnam War or any other "combat activities" in Asia.[22] Oda Makoto argued that each and every Japanese person was bound to the Vietnam problem, because they were Asians tied to America through the security treaty.[23] More provocative were the following claims made by Beheiren at a 1966 conference with U.S. activists. Lambasting America's "extremely vicious and inhumane" methods, such as "indiscriminate bombing, napalm, and destruction of food and housing," the statement concluded, "The promotion and use of such weapons for the genocide *(tairyō gyakusatsu)* of the Vietnamese people *(betonamu minzoku)* shows that the American government sees very little worth in the colored peoples of Asia *(ajia no yūshoku shominzoku)*."[24]

Indeed, Beheiren's leaders asserted, the Vietnam War was an "attempt to annihilate an ethnic group" and, "in essence," a "continuation of the French-Indochina War."[25] Such statements and ideas were not isolated rhetoric. Even a cursory glance at the discourse of Beheiren's intellectual leadership reveals that intermingling with universalism, humanism, and pacifism were other more complex ideas about race, ethnicity, and nationalism.[26] In the thought of Oda Makoto, Tsurumi Yoshiyuki and others, we see the appeal of an Asian imaginary and the mobilization of ethnic nationalism *(minzokushugi)* and ethnic self-determination *(minzoku jiketsu)* as vehicles to resist the imperialism *(teikokushugi)* and aggression *(shinryaku)* of a white *(hakujin)* controlled and deeply racist U.S. government. We see the important influence on Beheiren of black and third world nationalism through their reading of, or meetings with, black American activists such as Malcolm X and Stokely Carmichael. And, most interesting of all, we see an intellectual struggle within the mindset of Beheiren activists to find a place for Japan in a world seemingly polarized into the white, racist, capitalist, American camp versus all the oppressed colored peoples *(yūshoku jinshu)* of the world (including those within the United States). Beheiren's leaders labored endlessly over Japan's ambiguous status both as an honorary white nation through its security treaty with the United States and as a colored race by way of its geographical and cultural Asianness. This is the sentiment we must plumb if we are to grasp the complex mobilization that Beheiren was and the ways that movement intellectuals deployed the mythology of the *shimin* therein.

SHIMIN AS VICTIMS IN JAPAN AND VIETNAM: TWO INFLECTIONS OF VICTIMHOOD

We might profitably begin by tracing the intellectual linkages in Beheiren among war memories, the general sense of victimization, and the Vietnam conflict. In March 1965, Takabatake Michitoshi approached Tsurumi Shunsuke with the suggestion of starting a movement to oppose the U.S. bombing of North Vietnam. Tsurumi agreed, and the two decided to spread the word through the various civic organizations already in existence, such as the Voices of the Voiceless Association. In early April, activists met in Tokyo to plan their strategy. All agreed that the movement needed young leaders and should not merely be a repeat of the Anpo demonstrations of 1960. As Tsurumi later recalled, "The reason was that we were all worn out, and rather than ourselves, we wanted to be led by young people."[27] At this point the name of Oda Makoto came up as a potential spokesperson. A graduate of Tokyo University and later an exchange student at the Harvard Graduate School, Oda was one of the few young Japanese to have extensively traveled abroad in the late 1950s, recording his experiences in the bestseller *Nandemo mite yarō!* (I'm Gonna See It All!). Tsurumi and Takabatake approached Oda, and after a meeting in Tokyo, he agreed to be spokesperson for the new movement.

Ordinary citizens, for their part, joined Beheiren for a variety of reasons: dislike of war, dislike of American intervention, a commitment to humanitarianism, and simple fear of Japanese involvement in the conflict.[28] One young Beheiren participant's mixture of humanitarianism and fear of war neatly captures this sentiment: "As a nursing student and also as an individual human being, I am extremely concerned about the Vietnam War," she said. "If Japan gets tangled up in this war, nurses will be the first to be sent to the battlefields."[29] Though motivations for opposition were diverse, movement intellectuals took the lead in shaping the movement's basic ethical standpoint. Oda Makoto and Kaikō Takeshi, in particular, superimposed their own wartime experience as victims of the Japanese state and the United States onto that of the Vietnamese. Here they tapped into the powerful symbolism of victimhood in the postwar peace, antinuclear, and antiwar movements in Japan.[30]

In an important 1966 speech, for example, Oda asked, "Why am I opposing the Vietnam War?" Moreover, he probed, why were Beheiren activists opposing America's policy in Vietnam, and why were they criticizing their own government's approach? In answer, he explained to his audience, "The most important factor for me" is the "war experience of twenty-one years ago," the "experience of a victim."[31] When he saw newspaper photographs of injured or dead Vietnamese, his own war experience welled up inside, reigniting his terrible memories of wandering among the bombed ruins of Osaka in 1945. He recounted this experience most graphically in an essay, "Nanshi no Shisō" (The Ideology of Meaningless Death), published in the magazine *Tenbō* in January 1965: "When I think of the deaths of August 15, it is not the deaths of those right-wing youth that comes to mind. What I recall—or rather, what is permanently etched into my memory—is the deaths of those people murdered in the great Osaka air raid of the previous day."[32]

Their deaths, Oda lamented, were not glorious deaths for great public causes, like those of the suicide squads. No, they were meaningless deaths *(nanshi)*, "the deaths of so much scum."[33] Oda believed there had really been two Pacific wars: the war of official rhetoric and glorious death on the one hand, and the meaningless deaths of ordinary people on the other. As he explained, "I was born in the midst of war, and grew up with war. Since I didn't know peace, war seemed to be the most natural of all things. Different from that of intellectuals, my connection with the war was rather like that of the masses. They didn't have the intermediaries of principle and romanticism with which to connect to the war. Quite unconsciously the war soaked its way into their bodies. And by the time they realized this, they had been drawn into the whirlpool of the war." For ordinary people—like Oda—there was no theory of total war *(sōryokusen riron)*, no philosophy of world history *(sekaishi no tetsugaku)*, and no overcoming modernity *(kindai no chōkoku)*.[34] "I had no meditations on dying, such as the *Manyōshū* paperback edition or *Hagakure*," he recalled. "In my world, at that moment, I didn't have a single one of these." As he put it, "I connected directly with the war," or rather, "like it or not, the war connected itself to me." To be sure, ordinary people knew catchphrases such as the "ideal of a Greater East Asian Co-Prosperity Sphere" and "for His Majesty the Emperor," but unlike intellectuals they had no private realm of principles and romanticism. For the masses, left with nothing to connect "public matters" to "private matters," the private was reduced to the suppression of speech, conscription, starvation, and ultimately death. The masses had no conceptual "cushions" to soften the collision between these two realms of private and public. Death, too, took on a public and private manifestation for Oda: it was pitiful, devastating, and ultimately meaningless for the mass of Japanese engulfed by public matters. And nothing could be more emblematic of the absolute meaningless of their deaths than the carnage of the American air raids in Osaka on August 14, 1945.[35]

Not that the Pacific War in itself had been completely bad. Oda recognized that economic recovery in Japan had stimulated people to rethink the meaning of the war, and this was only natural. The "restoration of Japanese [self-]confidence" had "aroused nationalism" and directed people toward "history." And it was also only natural, Oda explained, that the grand undertaking *(igyō)* of the Pacific War be prominently reflected in their vision. And, Oda added, the war was indeed a "grand undertaking" and "in effect . . . resulted in the liberation and independence of Asia and Africa."[36] The issue, however, was that this grand undertaking and the way it was remembered afforded little credit to ordinary folk. Oda pointed to the Yasukuni Shrine, where only state-sanctioned deaths were remembered.[37] Most ordinary Japanese had died unrecognized in the service of nothing, just as innocent Vietnamese were dying under U.S. bombs.[38]

Oda was by no means the only Beheiren leader who appealed to a narrative connecting Japan's wartime experience of victimization to the plight of the Vietnamese. Irena Powell has described a similar tendency in the thought of Kaikō Takeshi. As she notes, "The hardship and the tragedy of the Pacific War that Kaikō's generation experienced form a constant referent in his descriptions of the conflict in Vietnam. They form a funnel through which the bombing, the death, the extreme deprivation that he witnessed in Vietnam are viewed. The reader is encouraged to draw a parallel between the Japanese, who were deceived by their State and left unprotected to suffer death from American air strikes and hunger in the Second World War, and the Vietnamese, who are seen as the helpless victims of ideological and physical warfare, caught in a conflict over which they have no control. Both peoples are identified as the casualties of war and both wars are viewed from the victims' perspective. From this it is the Americans who appear as the perpetrators and there is no room in this scenario for, nor is any consideration given to, Japanese aggression in Indochina or anywhere else."[39]

We might contrast Oda and Kaikō with Tsurumi Shunsuke. As we saw earlier, Tsurumi's war experience began in the United States, extended into Southeast Asia, and ended in Japan. In other words, Tsurumi experienced the war not only as the Pacific War between Japan and America but more significantly as Japan's Fifteen-Year War in Asia, hence his interminable expressions of regret and remorse. Though Oda, Kaikō, and others in Beheiren were certainly sensitive to and deeply concerned about the legacy of Japanese wartime aggression in Asia, this does not appear to have been the primary locus of their emotional connection to the Vietnamese. On the contrary, the Pacific War and the Vietnam War emerged quite naturally for movement intellectuals in Beheiren as interconnected cases of U.S. aggression, incursion, and, indeed, imperialism in Asia. At times, the Vietnam and Pacific wars were even connected to the longer history of Western imperialism in Asia—all of which tended to shift attention away from Japan's past and toward the United States as a historical villain.

Put simply, a deep-seated ethnoracial consciousness underpinned the idea of victimization within Beheiren. For example, in his influential novel *Kagayakeru Yami (Into a Black Sun)*, Kaikō spoke of "Asian death" at the hands of America.[40] At a 1968 conference in Kyoto with antiwar activists from abroad, even Tsurumi Shunsuke broached the issue of white American racism toward Japan (and, by extension, all of Asia). He read a letter by one Ernest MacDonald sent to Beheiren in reaction to an antiwar advertisement that Beheiren had published in an American newspaper.[41] In the most repulsive language, MacDonald had asked, "How can you slant-eyed, yellow-skinned Japanese with your unreadable language complain to us? . . . We are trying to bring civilization to you Asians by fighting in Vietnam. Anyone who keeps complaining about a bomb dropped on Hiroshima years ago is wrong."[42] Tsurumi could laugh off the sheer small-mindedness of MacDonald's language but not the implication of his statement. As though answering MacDonald, Tsurumi suggested to his conference audience, "The American government knew that . . . even if they did nothing [Japan] would self-destruct." Moreover, the idea that the bomb "limited American army casualties" was a lie. "I can't accept this explanation," he said, because the bomb was really dropped as a "political display of force to the Soviets."

But even worse than Hiroshima, Tsurumi added, was Nagasaki, for which there were only two reasons. First, the American government simply wanted to try out a different kind of bomb, and, second, it was dropped because of racist attitudes toward Asians. These were truths the U.S. government would never admit to. Of course, states everywhere told lies, he admitted. Before and during the war, Tsurumi recalled, Japanese textbooks had proclaimed the actual existence in the palace of the so-called three sacred treasures of the emperor. Postwar historians later disproved this claim. But, Tsurumi said, compared with America's lies about why it dropped the A-bombs, the myth of the three sacred treasures was actually quite a "charming lie."[43]

Oda, too, often recounted his sense of disjuncture with white Americans when it came to remembering the Pacific War. While traveling with a white American woman in Paris in the late 1950s, Oda recounted how the pair had come across a group of French war veterans at the Arc de Triomphe singing "The Marseillaise" in homage to their fallen brethren. Deeply moved by the ceremony, Oda began to cry. Afterward the American woman inquired about Oda's tears. "Because I remembered the war dead in my country," he had replied. "I see," said the young American. "I understand how you feel—because we fought against each other." Oda, however, could not believe her empathy: "Actually, she didn't really understand how I felt," he confessed. "I was crying because at that moment I remembered all of my fellow countrymen who had died without recompense. You might argue that there were war dead in France and America too. But to that I would say one thing. They had the objective of defeating Nazism and fascism. But what did my countrymen have? Their deaths were absolutely meaningless. And until very recently one of the ringleaders who sent them to their deaths was prime minister of our 'democratic government.' "[44]

Oda described a similar disconnect with the anthropologist Marshall Sahlins as they sat in the library at the University of Michigan in the late 1960s. Oda expressed his surprise to Sahlins at the number of pages in the *New York Times* in 1945. He told Sahlins that in Japan at the time, the newspaper was merely a one-page tabloid print. "Sahlins nodded his head with an 'is that so' kind of expression," Oda recalled, "but I'm sure he didn't really understand what I wanted to say." Oda confessed, "Occasionally I felt a painful gap between him and me. We were about the same age and should have shared the same memories of the Pacific War. But though the memory of 'Pearl Harbor' was fresh for him, he had no memory of 'August 15,' for example." Oda noted how many Americans mistakenly believed that August 15 was the day of Hiroshima, yet, by the same token, most clearly remembered the day of German surrender—as though the war against Japan was really just an afterthought. "In other words, what for we Japanese was a desperate fight to the death, for Americans was merely a trivial war." Oda told Sahlins of his terrifying experience in Osaka. How he had picked up a pamphlet dropped by American attack planes, reading, "The war is over." But if the war was over, then why were all those people murdered in the air raids? As he explained to Sahlins in the quiet library with "adrenalin running through" his body, their deaths "amounted to nothing. Not a thing. And then, a short twenty-four hours later the 180-degree turn in values began." Oda told Sahlins, "That was my war. How about you?" But to Oda's disappointment, Sahlins could reply only that "the honest truth" was that he "didn't really remember." In fact, Oda was more than disappointed in Sahlins, adding, "I always felt as though he had dodged my question."[45]

As we will see, Beheiren activists experienced quite different emotions in their meetings with black Americans, but before I address this issue,

let me try and characterize once again the links among victim consciousness, war memories, and Vietnam in the oeuvre of Beheiren's intellectual
leadership. I am suggesting that the empathy Beheiren expressed toward
the Vietnamese people was not only an expression of humanism. As
Kaikō wrote in September 1965, "I felt that *'Heiwa'* (Peace) is a rather
soiled Japanese word. I also decided not to think of my action and sentiment in terms of . . . 'humanism' *(hyūmanizumu)*. *'Heiwa'* was too large
and superficial; it made me stray off course; it enveloped me."[46] Oda,
Kaikō, and on occasion even Tsurumi Shunsuke saw the connection as
Japanese and as Asians who had previously been victimized by the United
States and the Japanese government. With the injection of racialized
discourse into such perceptions, it became quite easy for Oda and others
to see themselves and, in fact, the Japanese nation as part of an Asian
ethnic struggle against white American aggression. And, needless to say,
in this narrative, the conscientious *shimin* was imagined as much as a
Japanese and an Asian individual as he or she was an ordinary human
being—contrary to public proclamations of Beheiren at the time and
many later depictions of the movement.

VICTIMS AS AGGRESSORS AND AGGRESSION AS SELF-VICTIMIZATION

Of course, one of Oda's (and by association, Beheiren's) great intellectual breakthroughs was supposedly to transcend the victim consciousness so entrenched in postwar pacifist thought and activism in
Japan. Beheiren's leadership was at pains to distinguish the movement
from this tradition. Tsurumi Yoshiyuki (Shunsuke's American-born
cousin), for example, argued that the postwar peace movement in
developed nations concentrated on nuclear weapons at the expense of
questions about ethnic self-determination. The result, he said, was a
bifurcation in the global peace movement. After the Bandung Conference of 1955, Asia, Africa, and Latin America actively took on the
problem of ethnic self-determination in their struggles for colonial
liberation, but the peace movement of the developed countries stuck
rigidly to its anti-nuclear-bomb campaign.[47] The Korean War certainly
raised the issue of peace and ethnic liberation and independence
(minzoku no kaihō to dokuritsu), Yoshiyuki conceded, but the Vietnam
War was undoubtedly the moment when the idea of a war of ethnic
liberation *(minzoku kaihō sensō)* took center stage.[48] The problem with
the antinuclear-focused peace movement, then, was apparently that it

worried only about "what might happen to us," never about "what we might be doing to others."

It was Oda's suggestion that Japanese people were not only victims but also aggressors in the Vietnam War that supposedly propelled Beheiren beyond the peace movement of victimization and narrow nuclear disarmament to an honest interrogation of individual complicity. But even the discovery of self as aggressor in Beheiren was deeply colored by Oda and others' comprehension of *what* made the Japanese people into aggressors in Vietnam, and again this connected deeply to the Pacific War experience. Moreover, rather than leading away from the nation or toward a critique of it, admission of one's aggression almost demanded a reengagement with that nation—the ethnic nation—as a possible vehicle of liberation for Asia. In other words, the trajectory from victim to aggressor was not simply one of Japanese recognizing their complicity as humans or, for that matter, of internationalism replacing the nationalism of victimhood. Just as they had done with victimization, Beheiren's leaders tended to connect the concept of individual aggression to the nefarious marriage between the Japanese and U.S. governments more than they did to any meaningful exploration of the past. The state as client of the United States made Japanese people aggressors in Vietnam, an aggression made only more terrible for its betrayal of an Asia and a third world to which Japan owed its allegiance. As Tsurumi Shunsuke said in a 1968 speech, only when the dropping of the A-bombs was connected to the conflict in Southeast Asia would the Japanese be able to understand the Vietnam War.[49] Indeed, only then would they truly understand how history had rendered the Japanese people—once again—into aggressors over another ethnic nation of Asia.

Nowhere did Oda and others advertise this message more strongly than at the so-called Japan-U.S. Citizens' Conference for Peace in Vietnam (Betonamu ni Heiwa o! Nichi-Bei Shimin Kaigi), held in August 1966. The conference came at the tail end of a series of exchanges between Beheiren activists and their counterparts in the antiwar movement in America. In June of the same year, for example, Beheiren had hosted the American historian Howard Zinn and the Student Non-Violent Coordinating Committee activist Ralph Featherstone on a speaking tour of Japan.[50] Much later Zinn fondly remembered his encounter with what appeared to him as the Japanese counterpart of the American New Left.

I was enormously impressed with the people in Beheiren. Oda Makoto, who conveyed us from one city to another (I especially remember a plane ride to Hokkaido) kept up a running lesson on Japanese history and politics. He was famous in Japan for his books and for his political courage. Muto, thin, always with a cigarette, seemed the epitome of the Left intellectual, with an incisive analysis of Japanese and world affairs. Tsurumi Yoshiyuki had one foot in the Establishment (his father had been a consul in Los Angeles, as I recall) and one foot in Beheiren and had the connections to get things printed in mainstream publications. (A few years after our trip he phoned me from Japan to arrange a meeting between an American anti-war person and the deserting sailors of the U.S.S. *Intrepid*.) Tsurumi Shunsuke was our host in Kyoto, with marvelous stories about his time at Harvard, and his imprisonment after Pearl Harbor because he refused to profess loyalty to the United States or to Japan, and was therefore termed an anarchist. He certainly was an impressive thinker.[51]

Oda was similarly impressed by the message his visitors brought, especially Ralph Featherstone's likening of the plight of the Okinawans to that of black Americans: both were linked by America's colonial policy and the resultant distortion and destruction of democracy.[52] In the late 1960s Oda would extend this idea, arguing that the U.S.-Japan Security Treaty made not only the Okinawans but all the Japanese into a third world people.[53] The June tour also proved to be an important learning experience tactically for Japanese activists, as Zinn and Featherstone explained the mechanics of nonviolent civil disobedience.[54] Following on the heels of the tour, the August 1966 conference was the next logical step, bringing together activists from around the nation to exchange ideas and debate tactics and, moreover, to mobilize support for Beheiren in an overtly public way.

Held at Tokyo's Sankei Hall, the conference brought together participants from America and Japan and numerous other foreign observers from as far afield as France, Canada, Mongolia, Pakistan, Argentina, India, and the Soviet Union. In another who's who gathering of *shimin* advocates, Oda, Tsurumi Shunsuke, Kuno Osamu, Kaikō Takeshi, Katō Shūichi, Maruyama Masao, Hidaka Rokurō, Ishida Takeshi, and others represented Japan, prompting one observer to ask, "Is this really a conference of *shimin*? It seems more like a conference of intellectuals."[55]

Proceedings began with a greeting by Kuno Osamu, followed by keynote speeches from Oda and the American pacifist David Dellinger. Iida Momo gave an important talk on the state of the Japanese peace movement—Beheiren in particular—and there was a presentation on the U.S. peace movement. The second and third days of the conference were its meat and bones, so to speak, given over totally to discussion and preparation of three central documents: The Japan-U.S. Citizens' Antiwar Peace Convention, An Appeal to the Citizens of Japan and America, and Actions for Peace in Vietnam. American participants were left bewildered as the Japanese side battled over the semantics of using *shimin* or *jinmin* for *people* in the Antiwar Peace Convention. Finally, on August 14, participants engaged in an international teach-in attended by over seventeen hundred, followed by a reading of the three official documents and the signing of the Antiwar Peace Convention. For a movement that prided itself on informalism, the conference, with its official documents and signing ceremony, emerges as a strangely orchestrated and rigid affair.

Moreover, irritation with lofty statements about peace and humanism continued to bubble beneath the surface. Commenting on the document Actions for Peace in Vietnam, activist Hariō Ichirō argued that, yes, "we should struggle against all inhumanity and cruelty in ourselves. But in this case I think we should struggle against the policy of the United States of America as manifest in the Vietnam War, and also as Japanese people struggling against the policy of the Japanese government."[56] Others wanted even more specificity: Kitakōji Satoshi suggested that the document Actions for Peace in Vietnam be renamed Actions to Stop the War of Aggression in Vietnam.[57] Kaikō Takeshi chimed in with another denunciation of peace: "*Heiwa* is a Japanese word I really hate," he declared. "Why do I dislike it? It's because the word has no aroma *(nioi)*. It has no punch *(chikara)*. There are things it obscures. Why? Because there is Washington Peace, Beijing Peace, Moscow Peace, Paris Peace, Tokyo Peace, and Hanoi Peace. Moreover, during the last twenty years we have used this word '*heiwa*' way too much. And I believe the word is simply worn out. So I think it might be better in future if our movement for peace in Vietnam use the Vietnamese word '*hoà bình.*' At the very least it should make people stop and pay attention."[58]

Kaikō's call for *hoà bình* as opposed to *heiwa* was a shrewd intervention, because it signified two interconnected issues: first, that the war was one of ethnic liberation vis-à-vis the West and not some kind of deracinated universal peace, and, second, that the U.S.-Japan Security Treaty was providing the United States with a staging ground on Japanese soil for a war of aggression against other Asians. As Kaikō and others rightly sensed, in the U.S.-Vietnam equation, Japan was not only a victim; its government and economy were also intimately bound to the conflict as *Asian* aggressors. One only had to consider the U.S. military facilities dotting the Japanese landscape in Okinawa, Sasebo, Yokosuka, Yokota, Iwakuni, Misawa, Sagamihara, and elsewhere, not to mention the indirect ways that Japanese government agencies and corporations were helping to feed the U.S. war effort (via so-called special procurements).

Actually, Oda Makoto had already begun to address the ambiguous and compromised position of Japan vis-à-vis Vietnam before the conference in his suggestion of a victim-aggressor mechanism at work in the Japanese psyche. This was arguably one of the most important intellectual steps forward in a postwar peace and antiwar movement dominated by victim consciousness. It apparently marked a shift from a comfortable mythology of national victimhood to a new morality founded on individual responsibility for both the past and the present. Of course, for Oda and others in the movement, the rejection of national victimhood does not seem to have amounted to a rejection of the nation, nor did they see a kind of internationalized individual as a solution. On the contrary, for many in Beheiren recognition of the victim-aggressor mechanism seems to have represented an opportunity to relocate the moral individual in a rehabilitated nation that could in turn challenge the true (and "foreign") source of aggression itself.

Oda discussed the victim-aggressor mechanism on many occasions beginning in the mid-1960s, but his original and most powerful statements on the issue are to be found in two influential essays published in August and September 1966 and in his speech at the 1966 conference.[59] Consider his warning on the first day of the conference:

> We must not forget that, today, some twenty-one years after the war, we have joined hands with America, our former enemy, and are fighting in Vietnam. At the same time, on an individual level we must demand that America—which is entrapped in this situation—stop bombing North Vietnam, that U.S. forces withdraw immediately, and that the Japanese government end its involvement. It is the strong recognition of self as aggressor—the hand committing atrocities against the Vietnamese people may be our very own—and action to sever ourselves from this that can become the fundaments of civil disobedience. We should not obey merely because the state orders us to. As with the principle of the Nuremberg Trials, the obligation for citizens, and their right, is to "follow the universal principles of humanity over and above the state."[60]

Oda understood his Pacific War experience and that of most Japanese in terms of *nanshi*—the meaningless death of victims. As he noted in 1966, "There is no doubt that at the base of our August 15 experience—the departure point for the postwar—is our strong self-awareness as victims" of state "deception." Herein lay the "excellence," "stupidity," "strength," and "weakness" of postwar thought. The most important legacy of this victim consciousness for Oda was that it set Japanese "face to face" with a state that had always been "absolutely powerful," "absolutely just," and always "good." Victim consciousness also gave legitimacy to private concerns where only public concerns had existed before, undermining the state's very reason for existence. The victim experience also undergirded the Japanese people's commitment to absolute pacifism *(zettai heiwa shugi)*. Indeed, their consciousness as victims made it all the easier, Oda argued, for Japanese to take on "peace, democracy, freedom, and equality—despite their being conferred from without."[61]

But, Oda admitted, this victim consciousness contained a fatal flaw. By focusing the weight of blame on the state and not the nation, the Japanese people had comfortably avoided their own complicity in the war. "It was the state that was completely wrong, and we were easily able to cut off the individual from this state by means of our experience as victims. And, as a result, the agent responsible for 'deception' could only become a strange abstraction in the form of a state lacking the people of which it was composed." Conspicuously lacking was a consciousness of the fact that at a given moment the individual victim may also have been an aggressor. According to Oda, the only "grotesque conclusion" was that everyone was a victim, indiscriminately and without limit. This made it impossible to ask just who was an aggressor and how or just who had done the deceiving and why.[62]

Indeed so. But Oda did not provide any clear answers. He did not specify what the complicity and aggression of the Japanese people may have been. Was it that they had let the state mismanage the war? Was it the Japanese Army's war crimes in Asia? Was it the surprise, yet foolhardy, attack on Pearl Harbor? Or was it that the Japanese people had given in to a state in the thrall of Western imperialism? How, in short, had the Japanese people been aggressors in a war that Oda himself described as a grand undertaking? Oda did not dwell too much on the past, not as he did when discussing his experience of victimhood. In fact, in 1968 he suggested that the war and war crimes *(sensō hanzai)* should be seen not only as a problem for the Japanese *(Nihonjin no mondai)* but also more broadly as a problem for human beings *(ningen no mondai)*. Approaching such issues as a Japanese person first was certainly acceptable, but if the problem was not also understood as a problem for all humankind *(zenjinrui)*, it could have no universal applicability: what the Japanese had done would remain a problem for the Japanese alone. According to Oda, that logic immediately disconnected people from different nations. For example, Japanese people would consider the brutal crimes of whites against blacks in the American South as someone else's problem. But universalizing Japan's past transgressions—its war crimes and war of aggression in Asia—made it possible to rise up against the American war of aggression in Vietnam.[63]

In Oda's discussions about victimization and the *nanshi* experience, cause and effect were always very clear: the Japanese wartime state and the U.S. bombings victimized innocent Japanese people—aggressor and victim were existentially distinct. But the causal chain is more complex in his explanation of aggression by ordinary Japanese during the war, because aggressor and victim conjoin. In other words, aggression is always a function of victimization. Oda and other Beheiren leaders certainly believed that ordinary Japanese had been aggressors, because they cooperated with or failed to resist a state that had violated Asia. Oda said so much. But as he carefully explained, what made the Japanese aggressors also made them victims. Crucially, his mechanism implied that the Japanese people, by lining up with the state, became aggressors against themselves as well. By relinquishing power to the state, the nation produced a grotesque mechanism in which the aggressors victimized themselves. As Oda himself said, the victim-aggressor experience was something national. Aggression, as Oda understood it, emerged from the individual's relationship to the state and its principles. And, even more generally, it emerged from one's location within the conditions of a specific society and ethnic national history.[64] As much as it was a call for Japanese to settle accounts with Asia, then, Oda's victim-aggressor mechanism also apparently exposed the vicious cycle that had ensnared the Japanese people, a kind of self-inflicted wound that could be healed only when the people recognized their true home in Asia and, more generally, among the colored peoples of the world.

Conventionally, Oda's victim-aggressor mechanism might be understood as a discussion about Japanese aggression toward Asia—Japanese violating Asians.[65] There is no denying that this is partly what Oda wanted to say and that people partly understood his message in this way. But this was not the totality of his message, nor was it the totality of its reception. By giving up to the logic of the state—a state deeply shaped by Western imperialism since the early Meiji period—Oda was also suggesting that the Japanese people had turned against themselves as Asians. Hence, for him and others, the solution for the Japanese nation became one of breaking away from the state—the conduit of aggression—and lining up with all of the other victims of white imperialist belligerence throughout the world. This is a position fundamentally more complex than a straightforward engagement with Japan's crimes against Asia during the war. It might be better to understand the notion of aggression in Beheiren as a problem of the Japanese nation dealing with its betrayal of self and its Asian ethnic brothers. In other words, just as with victimization, Oda and Beheiren's denunciations of aggression owed as much to ethnic and racial proclivities as they did to any universalistic or humanistic motivation. Admission of aggression was a rejection of the white imperialist within and, at the same time, an apology to Asia for ethnic apostasy. And what could have been more appropriate for a movement deeply committed to the ethnic self-determination of Vietnam and staunchly opposed to so-called U.S. imperialist aggression in Asia?

This rethinking of Oda's victim-aggressor mechanism is not merely an attempt to mark out some new interpretative territory. Rather, it is based on a largely (and perhaps purposely) ignored, yet powerfully influential, set of ideas that Oda and movement intellectuals such as Tsurumi Yoshiyuki discovered, wrote about, and advocated beginning in the late 1950s. I refer here to Beheiren's engagement with black America, Asia, and the third world. As a world traveler, Oda's impact on Beheiren here—once again—was crucial, but the American-born Tsurumi Yoshiyuki also played a role. It was through these experiences that Beheiren's ideas about victimization and aggression became closely linked to concepts of race and ethnicity.

THE SMELL OF AMERICA, THE SMELL OF THE BLACK MAN, AND THE INESCAPABILITY OF ASIA

Tsurumi Shunsuke said that during the war he had been in a struggle with Japan, but in the postwar his fight was with America.[66] The level of animosity—hatred in some cases—of Beheiren's intellectual leadership toward the U.S. government and society cannot be overstated. It is at least as palpable as, if not more so than, Beheiren's sympathy for the Vietnamese. Again, activists' wartime experiences were formative, but so too were their encounters with America after 1945. In fact, Beheiren cannot be understood intellectually until we come to terms with its leaders' absolute estrangement from an America that, ironically, had nurtured their own intellectual development and critical capabilities.

Actually, Oda Makoto began his diatribe against America well before the Beheiren movement in his 1961 best seller *I'm Gonna See It All!* written during the height of the Anpo protests in the summer of 1960. The book recounts Oda's experiences while traveling in America, Mexico, Europe, the Middle East, and Asia during the late 1950s after completing a Fulbright Scholarship at Harvard University—an American scholarship, I would note, that he utilized without hesitation, gratitude, or regret. Written in a lively journalistic style, the book captured the hearts of young Japanese at a time when overseas travel was extremely limited. But, far more than this, the book had popular appeal because it explored "the relationship between the US and Japan as well as the deracinated relationship between Asia and Japan." It suggested that "all Asians regardless of social status were equal when it came down to the postwar generation's struggle for daily survival."[67] In fact, *I'm Gonna See It All!* was more social commentary than travel diary, more introspection than description. It was the staging ground for Oda's full-scale attack on everything American—its values, its government, and most of its people. And, though Oda may have set out to see it all, what he found was a conformist, racist, patronizing, and self-indulgent United States; a sliver of hope in the resistance of black Americans; a wholly ignored, exploited, and poverty-stricken Asia; and a Japan trapped hopelessly between the white imperialist and the colored victim. Though Oda would call on his countrymen to uncover the aggressor within, works such as *I'm Gonna See It All!* lay bare Oda's belief that it was America—and, more generally, the West—that had facilitated the sudden and pathological mutation for aggression in the Japanese psyche. America, as Oda would later note, was the hopeless point of arrival of a decadent twentieth century—a truly degenerate end of history.

Oda had an overtly patriotic agenda in *I'm Gonna See It All!* He recalled how at the time both the left and right were saying how bad Japan was. The book, he hoped, would show that Japan had its own Japanese value.[68] It could be a message to other Asians that under the new constitution many Japanese were striving to avoid a repeat of the past. Moreover, it would be a rebuke to patronizing Japan specialists in the West, one of whom had claimed in *Time* magazine that the Japanese were "still children" who "occasionally behaved violently" such that "there was no telling what they might do."[69] Oda's repugnance toward the Japanese studies establishment in Europe and America should not be underestimated. He recalled his frustration with a French professor from the Sorbonne who, assuming that Tokyo was certainly smaller than Paris, had asked if the city's population was around two million.[70] At almost every opportunity Oda took aim at the Harvard history professor and U.S. ambassador to Japan Edwin Reischauer and his "patronizing" attitude toward Japan and Asia in general. Oda felt that Reischauer and others of his generation believed—admittedly with goodwill and affection—that it was their duty to instruct and guide the so-called backward regions of the third world (including Japan).[71] In his meetings with the professor, Oda had felt as though there were a "plastic membrane" separating them.[72] *I'm Gonna See It All!* then was an attempt to answer such critics and patronizers of Japan. But more than this, the book also became Oda's earliest statement of what he would later call open-minded nationalism *(hirakareta nashonarizumu).*

Consider Oda's sentiments on returning to Japan at the end of the book: "I was happy to be a citizen *(kokumin)* of a 'small nation.' I was even proud," he wrote.[73] After all, as Japan's terrible forays into China, Korea, and Asia proved, his country had no business replicating the imperialism of England, the United States, and other great nations.[74] Looking over his bow-shaped archipelago, Oda could not believe it was simply a stationary point on the map. On the contrary, he felt that Japan was alive—that it was in movement *(ugoite ita).*[75] For Oda, it was as though the whole of Japan was moving in a single direction. And put quite simply, he explained, this direction was a good direction *(yoi hōkō).* The nation was becoming more affluent, and the standard of living of the people was rising.[76] "Foreigners visiting Japan," Oda explained, "are surprised at Japanese busyness, their diligence, and the extreme energy that is the sum total of all this."[77] Uncharacteristically, here he borrowed from the Japanese studies insider Edwin Reischauer, who in a moment of overstatement had described Japan as the "most alive country."[78] On this point, at least, Oda could only agree with the great professor—the nation was something to be proud of now, even if the energy of its individual citizens still lacked a strong sense of collective direction. As Oda's Beheiren colleagues would later recall, such sentiments made the book read like a treatise from the new rightwing.[79] There is certainly no doubt that it marked the beginning of Oda's project to rehabilitate Japan as part of Asia and, simultaneously, to excrete any vestiges of the white imperialist mentality.

Excrement, in fact, is an appropriately repulsive metaphor for Oda's reaction to 1950s America, which he felt was the extreme form of a twentieth-century civilization at a dead end and in search of an exit.[80] "Americans all eat the same (terrible) food, wear the same clothes, live in the same houses, think in the same way, speak in the same way, and act in the same way," Oda scorned.[81] For Middle America, of course, the 1950s were fondly remembered as the good old America—the days of the Eisenhower presidency and beautiful clean cities. "Clean," Oda reminded readers, because all of America's problems—including the issue of black Americans—were "shoved into the trash can."[82] What remained was standardization and alienation.

Interestingly, it was not toward the white picket fences of suburbia or even the patronizing attitude of Reischauer and the Asian studies community that Oda directed his most scathing invective. This he reserved for the Beatniks and gays, whom he found the most repugnant of all. They, he explained, were escapees from the standardization of America with their modern jazz, their love for the bongo, their habitual drug taking, their weird sweaters and slacks, and their squeaky readings of the most obscene poems.[83] But although they rejected conformism, they did not have the energy to smash that ideology or to change their society fundamentally. Hence, they represented for Oda a kind of infantile regression: like a spoiled child they were bawling and having a tantrum before society. "They are self-appointed young brats," he wrote, whose "response and reaction to conformism" was more conformist than any other group in society. "Perhaps this is the essence of the 'smell of America' *(America no nioi)* I refer to. And, unfortunately, the way out has not been found."[84] Yes, he concluded, "American society" had "fallen ill." "One hundred and fifty million people" were checked in to an "exceedingly extravagant and expensive hospital," and every day they were fed "the same awful tasting food." Yet strangely, he observed, the "majority of people seem to be satisfied with this."[85] But America, he explained, had a much deeper sickness. The Beatniks liked to think of themselves as invalids *(byōsha)* while all others were squares. But in Oda's opinion even the squares were invalids, since they too were members of the massive "hospital" that was America and, more generally, the "mechanized civilization" in which all people were entrapped. Mirroring Alexandre Kojève's depiction of American affluence as a pathetically animalized end of history, Oda saw in America the darkest of futures, in which everyone would be *"Sick, Sick, Sick."*[86]

Not that no one was looking for an exit. Beheiren's intellectual leadership was quick to see the potential of black American activism for the ethnic struggle in Vietnam and, more generally, for twentieth-century civilization. In the late 1960s, Tsurumi Yoshiyuki recognized not only how black Americans were an indigent class excluded from American affluence but also how they bore the brunt of racial discrimination, received only second-class civil rights, and lived as foreigners *(ihōjin)* within the state. They were an excluded class, shut out of the welfare state and forced to bear the most terrible of human suffering.[87] Yet, from this position of absolute weakness—from the "trash can" of America, to use Oda's metaphor—black Americans had created the Student Non-Violent Coordinating Committee (SNCC) and the idea of Black Power. Blacks had realized that winning the vote did not solve poverty or substantially improve their legal standing. Moreover, they began to suspect that leaving contemporary society the way it was and enjoying the benefits of the welfare state might, in fact, constitute a betrayal of the liberation struggles of colored peoples of the third world currently under the thumb of American pressure *(appaku)*. Accordingly, explained Yoshiyuki, black activists concluded that the liberation of black Americans would simply have to proceed together with the liberation of the Vietnamese people. This would be the only way for them to grasp a truly equal power. "Black Power is an outstanding concept of international solidarity," Yoshiyuki declared. "If [it] is developed to its fullest it will certainly mean the liberation of the world from American wealth and productive power." He said that Black Power, as a result, was not only a criticism of American society from within but also a criticism of America's position in the wider world, and, hence, this made it an ideology open to all oppressed peoples of the world.[88]

In 1968, soon after the assassination of Martin Luther King Jr., Yoshiyuki wrote in the progressive weekly the *Asahi Jyānaru* of his meeting with SNCC leader Stokely Carmichael. Carmichael told Yoshiyuki how vanguard new left black activists did not feel as though they belonged in the country, and this, Yoshiyuki observed, produced their movement for self-rule through the creation of alternative institutions—what Yoshiyuki saw as a kind of parallelism. Stokely Carmichael, for example, became honorary prime minister of the Black Panthers in 1968. Yoshiyuki noted that the political anti-Americanism of the SNCC and the Black Panthers was an attitude of active resistance to perceived human manipulation by imperialistic state power. Yet, Yoshiyuki could not agree with Carmichael's claim that all white antiwar activists were motivated by simpleminded humanitarianism *(jindōshugi)*, since Yoshi-yuki personally felt that many whites had moved beyond a critique of Vietnam to a critique of America itself.[89]

But there is no denying that Yoshiyuki was deeply moved by Car-michael's resolute position on the issue of race, expressed in one par-ticularly powerful moment during their 1968 interview. "In colonized Vietnam there are some Vietnamese who are cooperating with the colonial powers," Yoshiyuki suggested, and "similarly, there may be some black people in America who are cooperating with the colonial powers. What would you do about this?" Without a note of hesitation Carmichael answered, "Kill 'em." These were certainly "cold-hearted" words, but as Yoshiyuki admitted, in Carmichael's southern drawl, "kill 'em" made him feel a sense of "simplicity," "sweetness," and "goodwill." "And as if we were both aware of the simple naïveté [of those words], together we shared a quiet laugh." Yoshiyuki told his readers, "I have nothing but fear and uncertainty toward the idea of killing another, so I cannot adopt his position. But since he is in a situ-ation where he may be killed, I have no right to question him morally."[90] Yoshiyuki recognized that behind Carmichael's bold declaration was the peculiar predicament of black Americans who found themselves living in conditions similar to the most backward of nations in the most developed of the developed nations.[91] For this reason, Yoshiyuki rec-ognized, black activists had been forced to come up with a completely new method for revolution. "Good luck, brother," Carmichael said as the two parted. And, as Yoshiyuki noted, he could not help but feel that the word *brother* almost instantaneously narrowed the distance between them. And, he concluded, "he is, without doubt, a brother of us Japanese." "Given his difficult circumstances," Yoshiyuki added, "it is I who should be praying for the good fortune" of this "openhearted, spirited, yet melancholy brother."[92]

Tsurumi Shunsuke was equally moved by the activism of black Americans, more so for the tactics and free-style organization of the SNCC than for its ideological challenge to white racism. In 1969 he even went so far as to say that if he were to rewrite his early work *Amerika Tetsugaku* (American Philosophy), he would do so from the perspective of blacks or Cubans—in other words, focusing on how such minority groups had influenced and produced an American philosophy.[93] Tsurumi had certainly come a long way from his focus on James, Dewey, Holmes, and Mead, but the switch is less dramatic if we recall his early fascination with Otto and the philosophy of the ordinary citizen.

But, it was Oda Makoto—not Tsurumi Yoshiyuki or Shunsuke—whose experiences in America and Asia most powerfully shaped ideas about race and ethnicity in Beheiren, especially through written accounts of his encounters in the Deep South of Jim Crow, in the black bars of Harlem and Chicago, in postrevolutionary Cuba, and in the slums of India.

Disappointed with the Beatniks and gays, Oda traveled to the American South in the late 1950s to experience white racism firsthand. Here he encountered not only the "smell of America" but also the unavoidable "smell of the black man" *(kokujin no nioi)*—a smell that forced him to confront his own racial ambivalence head on.[94] What shocked Oda most of all in the South was the blatant segregation of African Americans and other people of color: benches, buses, toilets. It was here, he claimed, that he truly understood what racial discrimination was about. For the first time since birth he had entered a world in which the same human beings were differentiated by the color of their skin.[95] As he recalled, this was a shocking moment—something "thrust up from below" that "jolted" his entire existence from the very root. In fact, he admitted that until this time racial problems had been something far from home for him, but not anymore.

Oda learned that whether one liked it or not, in the South you simply had to choose between black and white; you had to take sides. And, to his great dismay, he chose to be white, sitting rather uneasily on whites-only benches, looking through glass windows at them—the ones living in that filthy other world *(kitanai bessekai)*. Indeed, it was in this state of absolute internal contradiction, Oda explained, that he felt true indignation and made a vow to struggle for the rest of his life for them *(karera)*.[96] Oda traveled the South in an "oppressive state of mind." Even though the people were warm and friendly, the separation of whites and coloreds made it very difficult for him. Even though he felt constant indignation toward racial discrimination, his decision to remain safely anchored in the world of whites relentlessly "weighed down" on him, exposing his aggression in a sense. "In the South, I visited black areas, I drank with them, and I watched movies in their designated cinemas. But, frankly speaking, the 'white' perspective within me followed wherever I went."[97]

On his return to the North, Oda found himself sitting between an old black woman and a white youth at a bus station. "Between black and white, once again," he thought to himself. But after seeing the South, he lamented, he could no longer find sanctuary in this ambivalent no-man's-land.[98] While in New York, for example, Oda spent some time mixing with the denizens of Harlem in local bars. On more than one occasion, he recounted, he had glanced at a wall mirror while chatting and drinking with his black friends, only to be surprised that one "white person" *(hakujin)* was within the group. But on closer inspection he discovered he was looking at his own reflection.[99] At a black jazz bar and radio station in Chicago, he and his companion were introduced by the DJ as a "beautiful white lady" and her "gentleman boyfriend." The black DJ had continued, "He's not white. So what is he? A nigger? No, he's Japanese. *He stands between black and white.*"[100] So he was not black. In fact, Oda also recalled how when he held hands with the most white *(hakujinteki)* and northern European ("pure white skin" and "blond hair") of American women, he clearly saw a *"slight coloring"* in his skin *(sukoshi iro ga tsuite iru).*[101] Moreover, this slight coloring was useful sometimes: it gave him access to the black bars of Harlem. It meant he could attend black political rallies. Only once was he stopped by a doorman for being white, but even then an onlooker had stepped in, telling the guard to "look at his skin" and that Oda was an "ally."[102]

But Oda's experience with race and racism in America forced him to choose sides for the first time. He noted that among his Japanese roommates in the United States, *hakujin* (white person) was a word invoked only as the opposite of *kokujin* (black person), never in reference to other colored races *(yūshoku jinshu)* such as themselves. But the relationship among whites, blacks, and Japanese, he opined, could be imagined variously. In one scenario whites and blacks could unite as Americans against Japanese in a kind of nationalistic consensus. In another, Japanese and whites could distinguish themselves from blacks simply because the latter were "niggers" *(kuronbō).* And then there was Oda's most preferred scenario after his experiences in the South: Japanese and blacks uniting against whites on the basis that they were both colored races and hence should struggle against racial discrimination. But, Oda was forced to admit, such consciousness was more or less absent among Japanese—even those living in America, who, on the contrary, had somehow (and unfortunately) become whites *(nantonaku 'hakujin' ni natte shimattiru).*[103]

Oda, however, only became more committed to the third world and Black Nationalist perspective throughout the 1960s. Consider his rethinking of history and race after an encounter with a former Cuban revolutionary in the late 1960s. As Oda's Cuban interpreter explained, it was only with the revolution that this Cuban man knew of the word *historia (rekishi)*. "Before, [history] did not exist in his world. Or rather, before, he had no history. When he learned the word '*historia*' his history began." Listening to the words of the black Cuban interpreter, Oda was reminded of Malcolm X and his indictment of history: "I read the 'father of history' Herodotus. No, better to say I read about him. And I read the histories of various nations, which opened my eyes gradually, then wider and wider, to how the whole world's white men had indeed acted like devils, pillaging and raping and bleeding and draining the whole world's nonwhite people."[104]

Oda could only agree with Malcolm X's spiritual teacher Elijah Muhammad that history had been made white *(hakujinka sarete kita)*. The Pacific War, for example, could be interpreted through a nonwhite lens, as Malcolm X's friend John Oliver Killens had done in his novel *Then We Heard the Thunder*. Oda recounted the powerful finale to this novel about white racism during the Pacific War, when white soldiers massacre their black counterparts. The novel raised serious questions about the endless U.S. government appeals to defeat fascism and to defend liberty and democracy. For blacks, Oda learned from the novel, there had even been a degree of anticipation—if not hope—after the Japanese attack on Pearl Harbor. On hearing news of the attack, some black people in Harlem set off celebratory firecrackers. A black soldier onboard a ship bound for the battlefield dreamed of how the colored race of Tojo would conquer the world.[105] When they met, Killens gave Oda a copy of his 1965 essay collection *Black Man's Burden*. He directed Oda to a passage about Hiroshima and Nagasaki, which suggested that many black people believed these bombs were dropped because the Japanese were a colored race *(yūshoku jinshu)*. Killens suggested that the same could be said of America's involvement in Vietnam. As he said to Oda, "I—no, we—think that the Vietnam War is a race war *(jinshu sensō)*. If the Vietnamese were white, America would not be dropping napalm or burning down villages so indiscriminately."[106]

Oda sensed that the idea of Vietnam as a race war seemed to have many proponents within the civil rights movement: he heard similar views from youths in the Harlem Writers Guild, from *Freedomways* editor John Clarke, and from Chicago's Southern Christian Leadership Conference leader James Bevel. Moreover, such individuals saw a substantive connection among Hiroshima, Nagasaki, and the Vietnam War; the same racism was at work at the base of all these events.[107] He recalled an experience at a black bookstore in Harlem. When Oda had entered the store, its elderly owner—affectionately known as "the professor"—immediately turned to another customer and began to discuss Hiroshima and Nagasaki. Oda remained silent throughout, and when the professor finished speaking, he turned to Oda and said, "Japanese are always silent. So I spoke for you." Oda recalled how the professor kept photos of his favorite colored leaders at the rear of the store: Gamal Abdul Nasser, the Egyptian president, for instance. The professor also spoke about the Vietnam War, which he too saw as a race war.[108]

That there could be an affirmative nonwhite interpretation of history made absolute sense to Oda—it confirmed things he had been feeling since at least the late 1950s, especially with respect to Asia and Japan. "How I wish I could have translated Fukuzawa [Yukichi]'s words for Malcolm X," Oda lamented. "I wonder how he would have responded?" The Meiji intellectual Fukuzawa, after all, had carefully documented white American racism toward Native Americans. Fukuzawa realized that America originally belonged to the Indians *(Injiyan)* but that they had been driven aside to make room for the white people. As a result, Fukuzawa had concluded that American civilization had been made white and hence could not be called American civilization.[109]

But Oda felt that very few Asians—including himself—had taken hold of their own history in this way. He recalled his own shameful reaction to the shocking poverty of India while visiting in the 1950s: "In the face of poverty, rather than opening my eyes and probing the essence of the problem, I tried to deceive myself with [memories of] Copenhagen and pure white-skinned women. . . . If that isn't cowardice, then what is?"[110] And here was the painful truth for Oda—the realization that he, too, had been colonized and deceived by the West and the allure of "pure white skin." He had even felt "pleasure" when treated "just like a white" in the American South.[111]

> But if I were to run away [from Asia], where would I go; where could I go? If I were a "Westerner" I could return to Copenhagen into the arms of a blond-haired, pure white-skinned woman—in other words, to things "Western." But I—this Asian me—has no choice but to return to Asia. I must descend to the base of Asia, which includes the Japan of which I am a part. All I can do is to descend there. We alone must confront head on that which awaits us there, even if it is naked and unconscionable poverty.[112]

On his return to Japan in the late 1950s, Oda recounted his "unprecedented action" of going for a haircut to "remove the germs that most certainly attached themselves" to him "in the various regions of Asia."[113] But though he may have removed the Asian germs from his body, exorcising them from his mind proved impossible. Oda's Indian and American experiences only made him think more deeply about Japan and its tenuous relationship to the third world. He said he did not feel history in India as one might expect, say, by looking at the Taj Mahal or the Ganges River. Nor did he perceive it in the historically rooted castes of India. For Oda, India was a place that had not taken hold of its history, nor were the people even trying. "In other words, a negative fact conversely made me aware of history—my own history *(jibun jishin no rekishi)*." He began to feel the Meiji Restoration keenly after seeing India. He saw a Japan fighting to maintain independence in the face of an extraordinarily powerful West, and in the poverty-stricken street people of Calcutta and Benares he saw the populace of the Bakumatsu and Restoration period—as though these two worlds had been super-imposed, one on the other. This was not the Restoration of television dramas *(terebi dorama)*; it was that of the ordinary person—the ordinary *Asian* person.[114]

But this was not all Oda had felt in India. Again, he stressed his feeling that Indians were without history. Contemporary Indian society had forgotten the spontaneous civilization constructed from within.[115] In the condescending attitude of an Indian university professor toward the street people, Oda saw remnants of the former English colonialists. And to make matters worse, these very same intellectuals spoke of the evils of British imperialism in "beautiful English." "When I met such university professors," Oda recalled, "I came to the conclusion that they had not taken possession of their history." Yet, this was a self-reflexive discovery: "Do I actually possess my own 'history'?" he wondered.[116] If India was still in the thrall of a Western history, then what of Japan? Oda could only admit that Japan's Restoration had not been about Japanese people taking hold of Japanese history but, instead, a rush to become Western—something a colored race could never do.[117]

Hence, Oda's admiration for Malcolm X, who had realized that history would become their own—it would exist for the colored races of the world—only when they recognized and exorcised the white domination from their past. Malcolm X had rejected great thinkers like Schopenhauer, Kant, and Nietzsche. "But his heart opened up to Spinoza," Oda stressed, "because Spinoza was a Jew with the blood of a black man. In short, it was because he was 'black.'"[118] Oda agreed that black activists from Martin Luther King onward had made good progress by moving beyond the "Uncle Tomism" of the National Association for the Advancement of Colored People. He noted that the black liberation movement of King and others was originally based on the principles of Western civilization, which should rightly have been universally applicable to all humankind but in reality were the property of a select few (i.e., whites). Oda agreed that this approach met with a degree of success. But the world was still one in which supposedly universal principles were not applicable to all. At this point there was an awakening. Black activists began to question the very nature of these universal principles. Or, at the very least, they began to feel that they would have to remake these principles as their own. This led them, according to Oda, to two further realizations: discovery of the third world and discovery of socialism as an ideology with the potential to change the particularized civilization in which they lived.[119]

India and Japan may have failed in this project, but Oda saw hope in Japan's Asian neighbor, Communist China. For him, the Chinese Cultural Revolution was a powerful example of third world socialism. Whether one agreed with it or not, Oda asserted, the undeniable fact of the Cultural Revolution was that it was a reconfiguration based on the Chinese people's idea about what socialism should be. He argued, "Through the process of the Cultural Revolution, China seems to be beginning to engage with the principles of socialism. There is no telling what the future may bring, but there is no denying that China has the intention of producing something it can unequivocally present as its own socialism *(jibun no shakaishugi)*." He admitted that the Cultural Revolution might have had a certain overlap with Stalinism and the absurd cult of personality or idolatry. But it was still an example of a principled engagement with Chinese socialism. In fact, Oda could proclaim that the new China had for the first time begun to take hold of its own distinctive history. China, he suggested, was "attempting to insert a rupture in its own history." And from this perspective, Oda could feel empathy for the Red Guards' destruction of history and their "foolish attempt" to remove Western books from bookstores. All of this folly he understood as a crucial expression of the third world creating and taking hold of its own history.[120]

Imagining how Mao must have thought, Oda asserted that anything short of a Cultural Revolution–style solution would have left the new socialist society of China as merely another extension of Western civilization and, moreover, trapped within the model of Chinese history of old.[121] In short, the Cultural Revolution, as Oda saw it, was an attempt by the Chinese to forge a distinctive history and, to this extent—and regardless of the outcome—he could express nothing but approval for its original intent.[122] The Cultural Revolution emerged as a concrete manifestation of third world liberation in Asia, and, for Oda, it transported Malcolm X across the Pacific.[123]

Oda claimed that, together, all of these movements heralded a rendering of the whole world into a third world *(daisansekaika)*.[124] The movement in Japan, for example, involved a serious questioning of democracy, once a self-evident principle but now the focus of popular dissatisfaction. The direct democracy of citizens versus the parliamentary democracy of political professionals expressed this new sentiment perfectly, connecting Japanese citizens to the wider global movement for third world liberation.[125]

Echoing Oda's sentiment, in 1971, the Beheiren secretary general Yoshikawa Yūichi argued that the elimination of ethnic and racial discrimination within Japan would be the starting point for citizens to join the struggle against white imperialism. Yoshikawa said that to the extent the Japanese people viewed American aggression and Vietnamese resistance from the perspective of outsiders *(daisansha)*, the problem of Japan's minorities would remain concealed. After six years of activism against American aggression in Vietnam and Indochina, Beheiren members had finally begun to realize that this was not something happening in a place totally disconnected from themselves. In fact, Yoshikawa explained, "It has forced us to take a look at the daily lives of us citizens. . . . By thinking about the people of Indochina, the abused peoples of Asia, and other oppressed peoples, and by considering our solidarity with those people, we have come to think about the society we find ourselves bound up in, and the [nature] of our position therein." Yoshikawa argued that citizens' movements simply had no choice but to recognize discrimination within Japan against resident Koreans, other Asian ethnic minorities, and former outcaste groups. Citizens' movements that failed to recognize such minorities, Yoshikawa warned, would actually assist in "intensifying" discrimination. In other words, the "civil rights" *(shiminteki kenri)* so prized by citizen activists would become a tool of imperialist oppression.[126]

We might pause for a moment to think about the possible implications of Yoshikawa's ideas. In effect, he was saying that to the extent the Japanese people (especially Beheiren activists) discriminated against Asian minorities within Japan, they could not truly participate in the international movement to stop American aggression in Asia, nor would they walk the beautiful path of third world liberation. So more than an appeal for ethnic equality on the basis of universal human rights, then, Yoshikawa's problematic emerged as one of ethnoracial consciousness—or lack thereof. After all, he called for Japanese to recognize discrimination (aggression) toward resident Asian minorities because Japanese themselves were Asian, and this was an assertion that connected directly to Oda's victim-aggressor mechanism. It was the pathology of a Japan that betrayed its ethnic core via the great deception of the universal. And, as Oda asserted, in an age of third world socialism, the only solution would be to take "illusory" universal principles and "thrust" them into "particular circumstances." This "phony universalism" could then be "removed," and in its place "universal principles" made into "something new."[127] The lead actors in this project would be ordinary citizens, not people of some standardized global culture, but those rooted in their historical nations and united in a chain of solidarity among the colored nations of the third world as well as any whites who might pledge allegiance to the cause.

NATIONALISM OF THE VANQUISHED AND ITS HISTORICAL MISSION

Actually, not long after Oda's articulation of the victim-aggressor mechanism, Beheiren found itself presented with a golden opportunity to strike at the heart of "phony universalism." In late 1967 four American servicemen jumped ship in Yokosuka City in an apparent show of conscientious objection to the Vietnam War. Fittingly, perhaps, the group became known as the "Intrepid Four" after the carrier from which they had fled: the U.S.S. *Intrepid*. Beheiren responded immediately, providing safe houses in the short term and eventually passage to Sweden for the four by way of the USSR. In true Beheiren style, an independent organization, JATEC (the Japan Technical Committee for Assistance to Antiwar U.S. Deserters), mobilized to provide support and, over the coming months and years, helped some twenty conscientious objectors to flee U.S. military facilities in Japan. As Thomas Havens has noted, the *Intrepid* incident caused an immediate media sensation, which was only intensified when Oda, Tsurumi Shunsuke, and Yoshikawa screened a film of the deserters for journalists at a press conference in early November.[128] For Beheiren, the incident marked a new stage of activism propelling the movement beyond flower bouquets and white balloons to the borderlines of legality. Moreover, the media attention raised Beheiren's profile and attracted many new participants into the movement. Around the same time, Beheiren also provided assistance for Korean deserters and, interestingly, for a Japanese national who had been drafted while staying in the United States.[129]

There are many fascinating cloak-and-dagger stories of Beheiren's covert assistance for deserters—anecdotes about infiltration by phony runaways, stories of pursuit by dark-suited agents in black limousines, and courageous flights to the northern reaches of Japan. I will leave such tales for others, however, and focus here on the intellectual impact of the deserters on Beheiren, especially as a manifestation of how *shimin* could smash the victim-aggressor mechanism. Beheiren's intellectual leadership saw these mobilizations as more than an opportunity for individual citizens to break away from the Japanese state and its U.S. patron. More interestingly, they also saw such support as a manifestation of a new postwar nationalism based on the peace constitution, the authenticity of daily life, and the distinctive ethnic identity of the ordinary Japanese person. Here, in fact, was an opportunity for Japanese to prove their mettle as Asians, as peace constitution nationalists, and as standard bearers for the third world.

Oda was particularly impressed with the patriotic sentiment of the four deserters. In their official statement released at the November press conference, the four referred to themselves as patriotic deserters *(aikokuteki dassōhei)* and portrayed their opposition to the war as that of true Americans with no affiliation to any political party.[130] Deserter John Michael Barilla described himself as "just one American" acting for what he believed was right. His colleague Michael Lindner demanded that he be "characterized as nothing other than an American who refused to support military genocide." Nineteen-year-old Richard Bailey resolutely announced, "I am an American," and "the spirit of our constitution will prevail."[131] As Oda later explained, since their principles were what they considered to be truly American principles *(Amerika no genri)*, no matter where they went, they would be Americans.[132] In other words, the nation and its principles apparently resided within the individual alone—they were not the property of the state or even the collective mind of a national community.

But Oda went much further. He suggested that if the deserters' principles conflicted with the current principles of their motherland, they should pack up and go elsewhere. If they could find another society or state with principles matching their own, then it would be quite acceptable to adopt this place as their new motherland. And, quite predictably, Oda imagined his Japan as a place where they could find spiritual solace and a national imaginary constructed on the principle of absolute pacifism. Oda pointed to the example of Korean deserter Kim Jin Suh, detained by Japanese immigration authorities for illegal entry in 1965. After Kim served time in a Fukuoka jail, authorities transferred him to the Ōmura Detention Center for illegal immigrants, in Nagasaki.[133] It was around this time that Beheiren activists mobilized a full-scale movement to prevent his deportation to South Korea, which had a death sentence for desertion. Though Beheiren was unable to stop Kim's deportation, it did succeed in having him "returned" to North Korea.[134] Oda claimed that, by seeking out the protection of Japan's peace constitution, the Intrepid Four and other deserters such as Kim were expressing their oneness with a motherland that was Japan. Their actions sent a powerful message to the world about the significance of Japan's "admirable" peace constitution.[135] Tsurumi Shunsuke agreed, suggesting that Kim came to Japan because of its peace constitution. Through support for such individuals, Tsurumi believed, Japan would be a country that anyone who hated war could believe in.[136] In the most optimistic of imaginations, Japan would become a motherland to any who believed in and loved the principles of peace.

Beheiren's engagement with deserters and asylum seekers certainly unfolded as an active engagement with aggression, but, as the articulations of Oda and Tsurumi reveal, it also provided movement intellectuals with an opportunity to attempt a rehabilitation and an endorsement of the Japanese nation and its peace constitution. Oda, for example, imagined the dry cleaners and bean curd salesmen—in other words, the *shomin* (the ordinary folk)—and the deserters they helped as part of a community of destiny *(unmei kyōdōtai)*. If there was a Japan for him, Oda said, then it was to be found in the connection among all of these people, including the deserters with their strange-colored hair.[137] After all, many deserters desired to live peacefully under the Japanese constitution, and this, he argued, made them far more qualified as Japanese than even Prime Minister Satō Eisaku and his conservative henchmen. This connection, Oda wrote, could be expressed only as a kind of nationalism conjoined with internationalism or an open-minded nationalism *(hirakareta nashonarizumu)*,[138] whereby the realization of the principle of democracy within an individual nation was directed toward the attainment of international democracy.[139] And, Japan, with its peace constitution, was in an excellent position to take the lead here as a kind of visionary community that had transcended the nation-state structure.

We can see this peace constitution nationalism at work in the thought of Tsurumi Yoshiyuki, who, in the course of the Beheiren movement rejected his place of birth (the United States), discovered the third world and Asia, and reimagined the meaning of Japan. Consider his important 1967 essay, "Nihon Kokumin toshite no Dannen: 'Kokka' no Koku-fuku o Ika ni Heiwa Undō e Kesshū suru ka" (Abandoning Japanese Nationality: How to Mobilize a Peace Movement That Overcomes the "State").[140] The title suggests a straightforward attack on the state from the perspective of universalistic pacifism, but the piece is written from the perspective of a patriot and a nationalist deeply committed to the Japanese ethnic nation and to the production of a progressive national-ism from below.

In the essay Yoshiyuki confesses that he was beginning to doubt his commitment as a Japanese national *(Nihon kokumin)* domiciled with the Japanese state. Indeed, this feeling had become so intense that he was even considering abandoning *(dannen)* his nationality. He admitted that such feelings stemmed partly from a commitment to the philosophy of natural rights, which "rejected the state's complete absorption of individual rights and ideas." But his discomfort with Japanese national-ity was by no means the product of some cosmopolitan sentiment. As he explained, he was not pleased *(yorokobumai)* at the way state insti-tutions extended the authority of the Japanese state, and, hence, aban-doning Japanese nationality was the sole contribution he felt he could make to the world as a Japanese *(Nihonjin dearu watakushi)*.[141] Such an assertion may sound somewhat contradictory, but we need to keep in mind the way Yoshiyuki, Oda Makoto, Tsurumi Shunsuke, and others in Beheiren distinguished between membership in the ethnic nation and citizenship in the state. There was no universal citizen here: Yoshiyuki was resolutely speaking from the perspective of the *shimin* as a constituent of the ethnic nation *(minzoku)* deeply opposed to the state *(kokka)*. "To be sure, we should be proud of the ethnic nation," Yoshiyuki argued, "but we need to formulate nationalism from an entirely new perspective so that this pride will not degenerate into self-imposed subservience within the power relations of the great nations."[142] Rejecting Japanese nationality, then, was to become an expression of a new Japanese nationalism—an "incredulous" and rather "half-hearted" assertion perhaps, but also, Yoshiyuki argued, a "proactive key for the creation of a new world."[143]

And the vehicle for this new antistate nationalism would be none other than the Japanese constitution, which, Yoshiyuki asserted, was the "first international declaration" of the "death of the state."[144] He pointed to Article 9 of the constitution, which in his reading implied a stance of absolute demilitarization. And, in Yoshiyuki's opinion, since the final guarantee of state sovereignty was military power, then any state that renounced this right automatically declared its own bankruptcy. For the Japanese state, the constitution was actually a statement of "self-destruction." And, taken to its logical conclusion, it implied that Japan would no longer exist as a state but would become an absolutely new kind of collectivity beyond the state yet cognizant of the ethnic nation as a binding force—a historical formation yet to be named.[145] Yoshiyuki argued that the postwar Japanese constitution presented just such a vision to the world. The antiwar promise of Article 9 was something that spoke out to the various states and various ethnic nations of the world.[146] Through such peace constitution nationalism, the Japanese people could apparently bypass the state and make a contribution as a concrete ethnic group. The "constantly debated and somewhat banal formula" of "nationalism leading to internationalism" would be realizable, Yoshiyuki asserted, only when the Japanese "completely discarded their weapons" in the spirit of Article 9 and abandoned the state and their place as nationals *(kokumin)*. Until such a time, any national sentiment or love of native place *(kyōdoai)* would simply be swallowed up by the state and its single-minded mission as a militarized organization.[147]

Despite claims of open-mindedness, however, Oda and Yoshiyuki's imagination of a progressive nonstatist nationalism must be read against the backdrop of their Pacific War experience, their discovery of black nationalism and the third world, and their revulsion toward first world (American) nationalism. These experiences taught that some nationalisms were simply better than others. Consider again Oda's important 1965 tract on the *nanshi* experience. Here he suggested three kinds of contemporary nationalism: victor's nationalism *(senshōkoku nashonarizumu)*, vanquished nationalism *(haisenkoku nashonarizumu)*, and emerging-nation nationalism *(shinkōkoku nashonarizumu)*. Needless to say, Oda assaulted victor's nationalism with a kind of indignant rage. In this nationalism, he scoffed, there were no contradictions *(mujun no nai nashonarizumu)*. "Think about the American or Soviet soldiers during the war," he said. They were fighting to smash fascism or to protect their homeland from it. And not for one moment did they have cause to doubt the legitimacy of this objective, even some twenty years after the war. Certainly a few picked up the "terrible stench" of imperialism in such nationalism, but their voices were inaudible. Victor's nationalism made all deaths meaningful—even those citizens who died in air raids. Every death was in the name of an absolutely legitimate higher cause. And to make matters worse, this nationalism empowered such countries to set out on new missions—against Cuba and Vietnam, for example—all in the name of defending liberty *(jiyū no yōgo)*. Here again, Oda's view of history melted into a seamless narrative about Western imperialist expansionism wrapped up in the "phony universalism" of victor's nationalism.[148]

On the other side of the coin—and, for Oda, there was always another, truly legitimate side—lay vanquished nationalism. Those from the victorious nations, he announced, could simply not comprehend the complexity of vanquished nationalism. In the case of Japan, for example, ordinary people were faced with the undeniable fact that any commitment to defend the motherland automatically made them accomplices in a war of aggression *(shinryaku sensō)*. "Whenever I explained this to Americans, they were at a loss for words," he noted. "And, as if questioning myself, I always asked them, 'What would you do?' "[149] One is reminded of Oda's dissatisfaction with Marshall Sahlins, who he felt had dodged questions about the war. The difference here, of course, was that it was Oda himself doing the sidestepping—responding to a question with a question.

But vanquished nationalism was more than a mechanism to explain the wartime complicity of ordinary Japanese. Oda saw a way to the future through vanquished nationalism, because, for him, it emerged from the perspective of pacifism and private concerns, not from the romanticism of just causes. For this reason it had the potential to become a non-state-indigenous nationalism *(dochakuteki nashonari-zumu)*, born, for example, from the desire to defend one's family and friends and one's daily life. Japan's experience as the only nation to have suffered nuclear bombing *(yuitsu ni hisaikoku)* made its vanquished nationalism something altogether unique. Traveling the world, Oda explained, revealed to him that the Japanese possessed a distinctive nonmilitary thought: the way they considered things, their psychology, their actions all lacked any consideration for things militaristic.[150] And, in a modern-day world where public concerns had begun to run rampant, vanquished nationalism undergirded by pacifist thought *(heiwa shisō)* and private concerns was needed more than ever.[151] In other words, the unique indigenous nationalism of the victimized Japanese people represented one antidote for the white poison infecting colored nations of the world. It found a place beside Black Nationalism and other third world movements for ethnic liberation. Indeed, from Oda's perspective, here antiwar *shimin* activists found meaning, if not their historical mission.

THE COMPLICITY OF DAILY LIFE

Oda and Tsurumi Yoshiyuki's rehabilitation of Japanese nationalism brings me almost to the end of my rethinking of the *shimin* idea in Beheiren. But as I mentioned in the introduction, one theoretical loose end in the antiwar movement would play out in paradoxical ways in future citizen activism. I refer here to the problem of daily life *(seikatsu)* and its supposed complicity in the sins of the state and corporate Japan.

As early as 1966, activists within Beheiren recognized the implications of Japan's growing military-industrial complex and its links to daily life. Writing in the May 1966 edition of *Beheiren Nyūsu,* Tsurumi Yoshiyuki noted that very few recognized how deeply Japanese society was contributing to the Vietnam War and how the overall structure of society was implicated. "The thing that worries me," Yoshiyuki commented at the time, "is that the various forces capable of moving Japanese society—politicians, bureaucrats, capital, the mass media, labor unions, and citizens—have no factually based overall perspective on Japan's contribution to the Vietnam War. We are connected to the Vietnam War through so many atomized routes that we can no longer see the total structure of these countless routes." Yoshiyuki rightly pointed out that the term *special procurements (tokuju)* not only referred to munitions supplied by Japan to the United States but also included the whole range of Japanese support for U.S. forces stationed in Japan under the arrangements of the security treaty. Indeed, under this agreement, special procurements were a permanent, institutionalized system. And even more worrying for Yoshiyuki was this system's promotion of Japanese remilitarization and the growth of a Japanese military-industrial complex *(gunsan fukugōtai)* through corporate giants such as Mitsubishi Heavy Industries and Ishikawajima Harima.[152]

Wada Haruki, professor of Russian history at Tokyo University and prominent citizen activist, was a key figure in publicly exposing the complicity of Japan's war industries. In a series of *Asahi Jyānaru* articles in 1971 and 1972, Wada produced exposés of Japanese businesses involved in Indochina, opening the way for a new wave of Beheiren activism.[153] The list of companies, Wada's so-called Hyena

Corporations, was an amazing who's who of corporate Japan: Mitsui Bussan, Mitsubishi Shōji, Marubeni, Itōchū, Nisshō Iwai, Mitsubishi Jūkō, Toyota, and Sony. Together with members of his Ōizumi Citizen's Association, Wada actively pursued Sony and Toyota, both of whom had their sights set on market development in postwar South Vietnam. Sony came in for the greatest criticism when in 1972 a U.S. Air Force colonel blurted out that so-called smart bombs were equipped with Sony TV guidance systems on their warheads. Terrified by the potential market backlash, Sony's senior managing director immediately released a press statement claiming, "We haven't got all the details yet, but I can say that it's impossible to transfer TV, which is for home use, into something for military use. Our product receives clear images only within a radius of 100 meters."[154] The following day U.S. military officials made yet another public blunder, attempting to clarify the U.S. colonel's earlier statement: the camera in the warhead of the smart bomb was actually manufactured by Texas Instruments, "it was the TV screen used in *guiding* the bombs that was Sony's contribution."[155] Needless to say, this clarification caused a storm of protest against Sony—if only because of the sheer irony of it all: the very same Sony televisions depicting the pain in Vietnam were being used to inflict that pain. On June 30 after a deluge of protest from irate citizens, Sony's president, Akio Morita, issued a written petition to the U.S. Embassy in Tokyo: "If Sony TV is being used in weapons, it is not in accordance with our wishes. We design and produce TV equipment for home use. We hope that our products will be used only for peaceful, nonmilitary needs, which is their proper purpose."[156]

Through such exposés, Oda and others in Beheiren slowly began to recognize how the victim-aggressor mechanism played out not only between the state and the individual citizen but also between the market and the consumer. Writing in the journal *Tenbō* in late 1967, Muto Ichiyo articulated the new conceptual mindset beginning to take root among Beheiren's intellectual leadership, mounting a frontal attack on postwar-style peace and democracy and lambasting its contradictory and bourgeois self-righteousness. As he explained, the problem lay in a one-dimensional transition from ideals to activism. The battle against the past, he said, implied unquestioning acceptance of current conditions. "As a single consistent ideology, 'peace and democracy' sought to understand the whole of society—it claimed that it could. But actually it did not illuminate the whole of society, merely the gap between civil society and the political superstructure. In the name of 'peace and democracy,' movements and activism focused entirely on the sphere of the political superstructure. Thus, the whole of class-based civil society disappeared as a target for activism in the name of 'democracy.'"[157] This more or less murdered the potential for revolution or, in Muto's words, made the "abortion of postwar revolution" a foregone conclusion.[158] In a sense, peace constitution nationalism sheared activists' field of view.

Muto thus traced the hollowing out *(kūdōka)* of peace and democracy to more than just the advent of high-speed economic growth. Peace and democracy came into this period already "hollowed out" and subsequently "developed obediently within a civil society under the hegemony of the ruling class." But it was during this period that peace and democracy reached the height of paradox. Muto cited public opinion surveys taken before and after the Anpo crisis in 1960. Respondents were asked, "What would you be willing to make any sacrifice for?" Prior to the events of 1960, most had responded, "family well-being." But thereafter this had shifted to "peace." The point for Muto was that these two—family well-being and peace—were perfectly interchangeable in mainstream consciousness. Indeed, "'peace' had already been absorbed by 'family well-being' before the crisis. So long as 'family well-being' was unthreatened, then 'peace' could not be regarded as threatened." Peace was privatized, commodified, and depoliticized.[159] The Anpo struggle confirmed once and for all that peace and democracy meant nothing more than the status quo, nothing more than vulgar "my homism." Thus, peace and democracy, fatally flawed from the outset, were only further emasculated with the onset of high-speed economic growth.

Here Muto saw the intersection of U.S. militarism, Japanese corporate domination, and the daily life of ordinary citizens:

> The thing that emasculated this antiestablishment principle of peace and democracy was, primarily, rationalism. It produced the weakness in postwar democracy, restained the postwar individual as a "my home"–style individual, knit a theory of rational nationalism (realism), and, at length, formed a single long, long belt running all the way to the Pentagon. In Japan, this rationalism developed as an integrating force . . . born of the corporate rationalism central to civil society and preceding any political integrating force. While we were fighting against the "war criminal Kishi," "high-speed economic growth" continued to tie this infinite belt.[160]

Oda could only agree that all roads unfortunately led to the Pentagon. "As a human being, I eat," he noted, and "whether we like it or not, the fact of the matter is that the political has forced its way into the act of eating." For example, the price of rice, the price of meat, the price of vegetables—all these things, he agreed, "cannot escape the political." On a more individual level, Oda admitted his own indirect complicity in the Vietnam War. "I pay tax," he noted, and of that tax a percentage was used by the government to assist America in the war.[161] Moreover, to the extent that people bought and consumed things, they would at some point become implicated in the war too. After all, sooner or later one would buy a product from a company profiting from the Vietnam War.

So what could *shimin*—trapped as they were in the logic of peace and democracy—do to resist the enemy that was postwar rationalism? How could the belt to the Pentagon be cut? Muto could prescribe only in broad strokes: "If Beheiren has an ideology, then it is an ideology of action," he noted. "If establishment rationalism has an Achilles' heel, then it is right there."[162] Borrowing from Oda Makoto, he argued— quite ambiguously—that citizens needed first to break away *(kiri-hanashi)* from the network of establishment rationalism and thereafter to take sides *(katan suru).*[163] But this was easier said than done. Citizens could easily protest against corporate merchants of death *(shi no shōnin),* which they did in the 1970s in a high-profile single-share movement aimed at Mitsubishi Heavy Industries. But dealing with the complicity of daily life required a completely new strategy—something *beyond* protest: a constructive, as opposed to a *destructive,* approach.

As anti-Mitsubishi Heavy Industries activist Moriyama Yūichi pointed out, opposing munitions production was not simply action in a disconnected political realm. "Politics simply cannot be separated from 'culture,' which is the synthesis of our sensibilities and values," Moriyama argued. Political revolution had to occur in conjunction with cultural revolution. Citizens also had to step back from their own daily life and genuinely interrogate this space, this spiritual home that formed the basis of their identity. Only then would they see that their "lives were completely bound to a culture born of a system forged by the authorities." And only then would the task become clearer. Cultural revolution implied more than opposing the system; it meant fundamentally deserting the system *(datsu-taisei).* "Since our 'culture' is denied by the system," Moriyama continued, the "enemy, first and foremost, is all the Japanese people—including ourselves—who substantially shape this system." The task for citizens was to create and display a new and advanced culture that could be a model for society.[164]

But what would be the content of this new emancipated culture? Neither Moriyama nor anyone else in Beheiren provided an answer. But Beheiren's engagement with the complicity of daily life did broach an issue that would be of crucial importance in the future for citizen activists. How were citizens going to deal with a complicit daily life that formed the emotional, ethnic, ethical, and intellectual foundation for their activism and one root of their "open-minded nationalism"? Where were they to go after abandoning the state and discovering that their yet-to-be-named historical formation was deeply implicated in the sins of late-capitalist society? These questions percolated at the base of grassroots activism in the mid-1970s and, in time, would give rise to a new generation of activists who, picking up on the ideas of scholars such as Matsushita Keiichi and the loose ends of Beheiren, would propose the creation of alternatives to the mainstream capitalist establishment. In fact, here were the roots of a fascinating transformation in *shimin* thinking from the ethics of protest to the realism of alternatives, participation, proposal, marketization, and symbiosis.

From the perspective of Beheiren, the great irony was that its rejection of the state, rehabilitation of the nation, and interrogation of the individual in daily life actually became one foundation for a movement that began in the 1970s, empowering *shimin* movements through reengagement with receptive arms of the state and through mining untapped opportunities in the market. What linked these two seemingly divergent approaches was the activists' fundamental belief that *shimin* could bring about change through individual action, whether as members of an ethnic nation vociferously opposing U.S. imperialism or as inhabitants of daily life constructing alternative institutions. The difference was really only one of strategy and tactics.

Ideologically, of course, the *shimin* idea could accommodate both approaches quite seamlessly—so much so, in fact, that very few, if any, recognized the fundamental changes under way in citizen activism and *shimin* citizenship in the years after Japan's period of high protest. But before I pick up this narrative, we need to step back once again to the mid-1960s. While Beheiren activists searched for an authentic identity as Asian *shimin*, the stream of pragmatic activism born during the Anpo struggle was charting its own path toward a vision of the *shimin* firmly located within an authentic (and often worryingly parochial) daily life.

CHAPTER 4

Residents into Citizens

The Fate of Pragmatic Civic Activism

ENVIRONMENTAL PROTEST, SELF-HELP, AND CITIZEN PARTICIPATION

The history of Beheiren reveals how a conscientious model of civic activism born during the Anpo struggle could be married to more parochial and deep-seated commitments to the ethnic nation and the Pan-Asian struggle against so-called U.S. imperialism. Detaching (and purifying) the nation from the state freed movement intellectuals to remake the *shimin* as a patriot, a good-willed internationalist, and an envoy for other "colonized" Asians. This was certainly a vision with broad appeal in 1960s Japan, but it was by no means the only vision: while Oda and others plumbed their primordial impulses to fashion a movement of Asian *shimin,* still others with a more nuts-and-bolts agenda conceptualized civic movements as pragmatic and rational instruments for institutional change. They argued that citizen activists should focus on solving specific problems in daily life through strategic local activism and active political participation.

These were not new ideas, of course. During and soon after the 1960 Anpo protests, Matsushita Keiichi and the Tosei Chōsakai began to promote and actively pursue local democracy and government reform. Some of the citizens' movements mobilized against Kishi also refocused their attention on more mundane problems of daily life after the crisis subsided. But it was not until around 1963–64 that the pragmatic model of civic activism started to come of age theoretically and in practice. Around this time too, citizen movement intellectuals began to conceive of civic movements not only as instruments for antiestablishment protest but also as fully institutionalized political actors—a conceptualization that would greatly shape civic activism in Japan in the coming years.

The period from around 1963 to 1975 is generally understood as the high point of citizen protest in postwar Japan. Pressure from thousands of antipollution and antidevelopment movements forced elites in business and government to address the dark side of economic growth through legislation, administrative reform, and technological innovation. From a national perspective, such protest was largely successful: by the mid-1970s Japan had turned the corner on industrial pollution, producing what some have called a "pollution miracle" in the country.[1] This is an important history, because it speaks to the success of protest movements in stimulating (if not actively directing) environmental policy in Japan.

Rather than turning to the history of environmental policy in this chapter, however, I turn to movement intellectuals and their role in developing this model of pragmatic civic activism. I trace two interconnected processes: first, the development of ideas about self-help and self-reliance in local activism and, second, theorizations and experimentations on citizen participation (shimin sanka) in local government. I argue that the cognitive framework that movement intellectuals erected to support these strategies had a palpable—if paradoxical—impact on later civic activism. As I show in chapter 5, movement intellectuals propelled the mythology of the shimin in bold new directions beginning in the mid-1970s, intentionally disassociating civic activism from protest and accusation and linking it to a communitarian vision of constructive activism based on symbiotic relations with the state and the market. This apparent shift certainly connected to activists' dissatisfaction with earlier civic movements, but as I show in this chapter it also built on the ideas of movement intellectuals in the period of high protest. The logic of self-help was applicable as much to the quietist construction of daily life alternatives as it was to local protest, and the process of citizen participation drew civic energies as much into service of an elite-defined public interest as it directed them into a pluralistic politics. This is not to say that local protesters and citizen participation advocates of the 1960s and early 1970s intentionally set out to undermine contentious activism. On the contrary, their aim was to defend daily life from corporate and state interference and to challenge conservative hegemony from the bottom up. What they could not control, however, was the direction their ideas would take in practice and when released into the hands of savvy local bureaucrats and other political entrepreneurs.

The first process, which I will call the "discourse on self-help," grew out of the various residents' movements *(jūmin undō)* mobilized in opposition to local development and pollution in the early 1960s. Activists, advocates, and scholars almost immediately began to theorize on the meaning and prognosticate on the future of the new movements, some even claiming that they heralded a revolution in grassroots democratic practice and consciousness in Japan. In schematic terms we can identify three relatively distinct interpretations of the new movements: a class approach (the class faction, or *kaikyū-ha*), a localist approach (the resident faction, or *jūmin-ha*), and a civic approach (the citizen faction, or *shimin-ha*). I want to show how these interpretations resonated, conflicted, or otherwise interacted and what legacies they bequeathed to later imaginations of the *shimin* and civil society. Each of these groups clung to its own distinctive aspiration for the new movements: Miyamoto Kenichi and the Marxists wanted local activism to escalate into a national movement against monopoly capitalism; local activists such as Miyazaki Shōgo saw residents' movements as the harbingers of a new locally determined "public interest"; and Matsushita Keiichi and *shimin* advocates imagined the movements on an evolutionary scale that would culminate in the civic type of human.[2]

There was almost total agreement, however, that the strength of the new movements lay in their thoroughgoing strategy of self-reliance and self-help. Winning movements, most observers recognized, used a range of innovative strategies, from direct confrontation all the way to negotiation and unabashed collaboration. They usually avoided formal political affiliation and highly ideological language, preferring instead to build a nonpartisan *(mutō muha)* alliance of protesters. Many were happy to seek the assistance of both conservative and progressive politicians. Most cared very little about big political or ideological issues, preferring instead to focus on protecting their own backyard—even if this meant polluting somebody else's. More than anything else, winning movements confirmed that victory was a function of a movement's ability to mobilize and exploit institutional, financial, and ideological resources strategically. A sure-fire recipe for defeat was to rely on the benevolence of elites. In short, the message was that self-help worked *sometimes* and that this was far better than the *never* in earlier strategies of dependence and appeal.

The second process, which I will call the "discourse on participation," drew most directly on the ideas of Matsushita Keiichi and the Tosei Chōsakai and found concrete manifestation in the numerous progressive local administrations elected to office in the early 1960s. Building on widespread resentment toward excessive development and pollution, these administrations promised to bring a civic perspective to local governance through direct participation, local government reform *(jichitai kaikaku)*, and the implementation of civil minimums *(shibiru minimamu)*. Though progressive administrations in Tokyo, Yokohama, and elsewhere genuinely attempted to implement such policies, the outcomes, in terms of the democratization of public administration, were at best mixed, often deteriorating into tokenism and political opportunism.

Matsushita and his political supporters, however, saw the rise of progressive local governments as a golden opportunity to make locally egoistic *jūmin* (local residents) into fully fledged *shimin* who would spontaneously and selflessly work for the construction of a new civic nation. They conceptualized citizen participation in terms of civic republican ideas about responsible participation and spoke of good citizens *(yoki shimin)* with appropriate civic discipline *(shimiteki shitsuke)*. The objective of all this, of course, was to bring an end to so-called conservative domination, but Matsushita and others' ideas—by lionizing civic nationalism and communitarianism on the one hand and demonizing contentious activism on the other—tended to undermine their project for political reform. As local politicians and bureaucrats quickly realized, the concept of citizen participation could be made into a useful ideological device for fostering soft volunteerism in areas of official concern, such as social welfare provision and community building. Just as with the logic and praxis of self-help in local movements, then, conceptualizations and processes of citizen participation threatened to shape and contain civic energies as much as they promised a greater voice for citizen activists in mainstream politics and administration.

PREVENTION MOVEMENTS, LOCALISM, AND THE DISCOURSE ON SELF-HELP

Nineteen sixty-four was an important moment in postwar civic thought and activism, especially as these related to pragmatic local protest. The landmark events happened in the cities of Mishima, Numazu, and Shimizu, located in Shizuoka Prefecture to the south of Tokyo, where local residents successfully mobilized to prevent construction of a large-scale petrochemical complex, or Konbinato (from the Russian *kombinat*), planned for their region.[3] The movements attracted national attention for a number of reasons: because of their organizational, tactical, and political innovations; because of their threat to the government's prodevelopment policies, and, most of all, because they succeeded: the complex was not built. For citizen movement advocates, the broad alliance of fishermen, housewives, intellectuals, schoolteachers, businessmen, organized workers, and political parties heralded a new style of local organization that transcended traditional party lines.

Tactically, the movements in Shizuoka evidenced a new level of sophistication at the grass roots. In February 1964, for example, the anti-Konbinato movement in Mishima presented the local mayor with a list of specific questions concerning the possible environmental impact of the project. Dissatisfied with the response, Mishima activists began their own investigation into the issue. Investigatory groups—including local conservative politicians—visited petrochemical complexes in Chiba, Mizushima, Kawasaki, and the infamous Yokkaichi City, where they saw the impact of development firsthand. To help explain the intricacies of industrial pollution, local schoolteachers conducted over a thousand teach-in sessions for local residents, utilizing a range of visual and physical specimens to communicate their message. Outside the classroom, teachers, local doctors, and scientists from the nearby National Institute of Genetics conducted environmental impact research. Using simple but persuasive experimental science, the teachers arranged for hundreds of carp streamers to be lined up downwind of the planned complex, graphically demonstrating the likelihood of air pollution in residential areas. All of this data they collated into a powerful report, whose findings contrasted greatly with those of the official Kurokawa Commission, sponsored by the government. Mishima farmers lent assistance, too, by engaging in a land-sale boycott and encouraging their neighbors in Numazu and Shimizu cities to do the same. Under pressure from this activism and scared by massive rallies involving thousands of residents, mayors in all three cities were left with no choice but to oppose the planned complex, and around two years after the movements began activists in Shizuoka could claim absolute victory.[4] It was the first time local residents had succeeded in stopping a major industrial development supported by corporate interests, the conservative national government, and all levels of the bureaucracy.

As Iijima Nobuko explains, the Shizuoka movements had a number of concrete outcomes. They put the brakes on a frenzied lobbying war among local governments to attract industry and undoubtedly encouraged construction-prevention movements elsewhere, such as in nearby Fuji City and, later, as far away as Shibushi Bay, in Kagoshima Prefecture. And to a lesser extent, their success provided inspiration for pollution victims to take their plight into the courts beginning in the late 1960s.[5] When they reconsidered the movements in 1975, pollution researchers Miyamoto Kenichi and Shōji Hikaru suggested three reasons for the Shizuoka victory. First, the movements were mobilized on a local level in the name of local interests, opening the way for a broad-based coalition of residents with varying interests. Second, residents helped themselves through scientific research and grassroots educational activities, making the movements cultural and educational. And, third, because of their horizontal organization, the movements encompassed both unity and diversity. Together, these three aspects produced a victory that Miyamoto and Shōji believed could be replicated elsewhere.[6] Miyamoto articulated the sentiments of many activists when he claimed that the Mishima-Numazu-Shimizu movement represented an epoch-making shift from grassroots conservatism to grassroots democracy.[7]

In hindsight, of course, we know that Miyamoto's optimistic prognostications went largely unrealized, but his words captured the spirit of the moment. Conservatives, for instance, found the Shizuoka movements profoundly disturbing, not only because they could happen anywhere, but also because they represented a highly organized, mostly legal, and thoroughly rational challenge to progrowth economic policies. Miyamoto's optimism and conservatives' worry were not unfounded: by the mid-1970s over three thousand antipollution and antidevelopment movements existed throughout the nation, involving hundreds and thousands of people.[8] *Kōgai* (pollution) soon became a major issue in the mainstream press, supported at the grass roots by a vibrant sphere of movement newsletters *(minikomi)*.[9] Residents also began to forge rudimentary networks, such as the Independent Lectures on Pollution (Kōgai Jishu Kōza), started by scientist Ui Jun in 1970, and the Residents' Library (Jūmin Toshokan), established in Tokyo in 1976. Shōji Hikaru and Miyamoto Kenichi succinctly captured the mood of the moment in their highly influential and well-timed 1964 publication, *Osorubeki Kōgai* (Fearful Pollution).[10] Along with presenting a pollution map of Japan, the book devoted over twenty pages to a pollution diary, which documented a chilling litany of pollution cases stretching from one end of the archipelago to the other. Putting a sardonic twist on the department store boom of the time, some even announced that Japan was in the midst of a pollution boom with its very own pollution department stores *(kōgai no depāto)*.[11]

Though nobody welcomed pollution and overdevelopment, many implicitly admitted that in the realm of popular political activism these two excesses seemed to have had some ironic benefits. In April 1971, for example, the progressive *Asahi Jyānaru* ran an upbeat article titled "Kono Wakitatsu Teikō no Nami" (This Fermenting Wave of Resistance), in which Yokoyama Keiji, of Chūō University, prophesied new positive developments in regional politics as a result of residents' movements.[12] The historian Irokawa Daikichi similarly suggested that "these local citizens' movements and new communities must be watched closely; they may hold the key to Japan's future."[13] Other readings were far less subdued. The political scientist Tsurutani Taketsugu argued that the new era of Japanese politics was of historic import because it combined "the ideal of democratic citizenship and the necessity for the autochthonic growth of political systems and processes." Tsurutani pronounced that "the 1970s may well produce, for the first time in history, 'Democracy—Made in Japan.'"[14] Echoing these sentiments, Matsushita Keiichi predicted that these movements would change the nature of politics in Japan, opening the way for citizen participation and citizen self-governance *(shimin jichi)*.[15] Indeed, Matsushita saw nothing short of a civic revolution *(shimin kakumei)* under way in Japan.[16]

Such bold predictions aside, however, as with the earlier Anpo upheavals it is important to keep in mind that the new movements emerged very much on top of various socioeconomic and institutional transformations under way in the early 1960s. Large-scale urbanization was a major contributing factor, as it had been at the time of the Anpo dispute. To give a sense of the transformation: in 1950 around 37 percent of the population lived in urban areas, which accounted for 5.4 percent of the total land area of Japan, but by 1960 the urbanized population had risen to 63 percent, and urban land area accounted for 22 percent of the total land area.[17] On the positive side, Matsushita Keiichi, his Tosei Chōsakai colleague Narumi Masayasu, and other *shimin* advocates pointed out how urbanization had promoted new values. Narumi explained how the maturity of mass society had stimulated a new constitutional sensibility *(shinkenpō kankaku)* among the younger generation.[18] The affluent new middle stratum *(shinchūkansō)* possessed both the willingness and the financial ability to engage in politics beyond established organizations and, if rationally organized, could pose a threat to the entrenched conservative old middle stratum *(kyūchūkansō)*.

Of course, urbanization and high-speed growth had their downsides. Rapid urbanization resulted in chronic rural depopulation and, on the other side of the coin, in urban overpopulation with all its associated problems. Moreover, progrowth economic policies clearly gave short shrift to the environment and diverted national resources from social infrastructure.[19] As Miyamoto explained, Japanese capital had concentrated in and around large cities, providing the greatest densities of private capital, public infrastructure, and labor power. This stimulated an urban migration explosion, which was further exacerbated when bureaucrats diverted public spending from housing, the environment, education, and public transport to proindustry infrastructure, such as roads.[20] As Endō Akira asserted in 1971, pollution was not—as some claimed—a "transitional distortion" caused by high-speed growth, nor was it the result of a lack of care or mistakes on the part of elites.[21] Pollution had to do with the voracious accumulation—intensive accumulation *(kyōchikuseki)*—inherent in the high-growth model.[22] One did not have to be a Marxist to agree with Shōji and Miyamoto that the "history of pollution was also the history of capitalism."[23] As the scientist Ui Jun mordantly concluded, understanding pollution as a distortion or a consequence was a mistake. On the contrary, just like low wages and protectionism, pollution made high-speed growth possible; it was the third pillar *(daisan no hashira)* of the miracle.[24]

The Japanese state certainly had much to answer for when it came to pollution. The National Comprehensive Development Plan (Zenkoku Sōgō Kaihatsu Keikaku, or Zensō) released by the Economic Planning Agency in 1962, for example, planned for an extensive industrialized Pacific belt running from the northern reaches of the archipelago to Kyūshū Island, in the south.[25] The grand plan envisaged an integrated transportation and communications infrastructure connecting these areas like the "beads of a Buddhist rosary."[26] In the process everyone would supposedly benefit, including traditional industries such as fishing and agriculture. The plan was concretized in a number of specific laws: one to promote new industrial cities (NICs) and the other to foster special industrial regions (SIRs). Ultimately, fifteen areas were selected as NICs and six as SIRs.[27] Economic planners hoped these strategic sites would stimulate development in surrounding areas in a kind of industrial wave effect, enticing people back from the cities and stimulating local demand.[28] But as early as 1965 a prime ministerial advisory committee already recognized that Zensō had done very little to solve the movement toward intensive urbanization around Tokyo, Osaka, Nagoya, and northern Kyūshū.[29] In addition, selected localities discovered the cold realities of rose-colored development when they were forced to foot massive infrastructure bills for incoming industry. The hoped-for employment opportunities did not eventuate either, and, to make matters worse, local communities found that their new next-door neighbors brought a whole range of unwanted "gifts," such as air, water, and various other forms of pollution.[30]

Government foot dragging on environmental legislation also exacerbated the pollution problem. Although a number of laws regulating water quality, industrial dumping, and smoke emissions were passed beginning in the late 1950s, not until 1967 (after numerous high-profile pollution cases) did the government make any significant legislative moves. Basic Law for Environmental Pollution Control (Kōgai Taisaku Kihonhō) of that year was a first step, setting out the responsibilities of corporations and government vis-à-vis pollution prevention, concretizing the polluter pays principle, and identifying the need for regional environmental standards.[31] But the basic law of 1967 was a toothless instrument, since its early health-first provisions were replaced by a harmony clause requiring that measures for protection from pollution complement (i.e., yield to) the "sound development of the economy."[32] The defanged basic law did not last long, however. In response to growing public, media, and legal pressure over the pollution issue and fearful of an electoral backlash, the Satō administration revised the law in 1970, removing the harmony clause and strengthening measures for pollution prevention at the local level.[33] In the same session of the so-called Pollution Diet (Kōgai Kokkai), the Diet passed fourteen pieces of legislation, including the amendment to the basic law, giving Japan some of the toughest environmental standards in the world. In the long run this legislation contributed to the mitigation of the worst aspects of industrial pollution; however, it did nothing to contain the fermenting wave of resistance at the grass roots and, if anything, probably encouraged it.

In terms of a rough typology, we can identify two categories of antipollution and antidevelopment citizen mobilizations during this period: compensatory movements and prevention movements. The former, sometimes referred to as victims' or first-generation movements, sought relief and compensation for injuries sustained or loses incurred as a result of development and pollution. Such movements have a long history in Japan that can be traced back to at least the Meiji period, when Tanaka Shōzō led the struggle to save Yanaka Village and the Watarase River. After the war, fishermen in Tokyo Bay protested against industrial effluent as early as 1958, resulting in some early water-quality legislation. But the most high-profile victims' movements mobilized in the 1960s, culminating with the so-called Big Four Pollution cases. From 1967 through 1969, plaintiffs in Kumamoto, Niigata, Mie, and Toyama prefectures filed lawsuits against polluting industries regarding the incidence of Minamata disease, Yokkaichi asthma, and *itai-itai* disease, and, with varying degrees of success, all were victorious by 1973.[34] The public impact of these movements and their victories cannot be overstated. Not only did they push the government to take substantive legislative measures to deal with pollution, but also, as McKean notes, they taught grassroots activists that the postwar legal system was more than a slave of the conservatives and that litigation could be successful.[35] And, even more significant, pollution victims' use of the courts hinted at the possible utility of state institutions and resources.

But while victims' movements made some important breakthroughs, in terms of movement praxis—the nuts-and-bolts of mobilization—it was prevention movements like those in Shizuoka that most interested *shimin* advocates and activists. To agree with Hasegawa Koichi, the organizing processes, strategies, and tactics of these second-generation environmental protest movements would deeply affect later mobilizations.[36] After the Mishima-Numazu-Shimizu movements, for instance, residents in nearby Fuji City mobilized successfully for both compensation and prevention of pollution from paper pulp processing. The so-called *hedoro*, or industrial sludge, there not only produced dangerous gases and foul-smelling fumes but also poisoned fisheries and farming land. Similar to participants in the earlier movements, teachers in the region organized study meetings, activists ran for public office, and in 1970 the movement filed suit against the prefectural governor and the implicated pulp companies.[37] In 1966 in one of the most high-profile prevention movements of the postwar, farmers and locals from Sanrizuka and Shibayama, in Chiba Prefecture, mobilized against government plans to construct the New Tokyo International Airport in their locality. By late 1967 they had been joined by radical student-activists from

Zengakuren, and in subsequent years numerous violent clashes would occur between this farmer-student alliance and state authorities.[38] Though definitely aimed at prevention, the violent tactics and unconventional membership of the Sanrizuka movement clearly disconcerted many *shimin* advocates who preferred to mention rather than truly analyze this militant version of localism.

Troubling in a different way for *shimin* advocates was the anti-freight-line movement in Yokohama, led by pragmatic localist Miyazaki Shōgo beginning in 1966. I deal with this movement later, but for the moment note its significance in concretizing the logic of localism and challenging a bureaucratic-defined public interest. Finally, taking prevention to a new level, residents of Oita (Buzen City) and Hokkaido (Date City) prefectures instigated environmental rights *(kankyōken)* suits in the 1970s on the basis of their rights under Article 25 of the constitution.[39] These movements met with little success, but they do confirm the lasting impact of the prevention-based mobilizations in Shizuoka.

What then of prevention movements' long-term significance? First, these movements clearly influenced local government policymaking, not only with respect to industry, but also in city planning matters, such as amalgamation and zoning. Second, short-lived though they may have been, prevention movements also challenged a public interest that was defined by bureaucrats and was unconditionally supportive of national economic growth. And third, because prevention activists had to convince local residents that the pollutive downside of industry outweighed its promises of affluence, they were forced to develop sophisticated strategies and inclusive organizational practices. Even more than struggles for ex post facto compensation, aiming for prevention almost demanded engagement—sometimes antagonistic, sometimes not—with political, economic, and legal institutions, and this is where we see the intersection of local activism and the participatory paradigm later advocated by Matsushita Keiichi and others.

It is worth reiterating, however, that very few prevention movements succeeded after the high-profile mobilizations of Mishima-Numazu-Shimizu and Fuji City. Farmers' attempts to stop construction of the airport in Chiba produced only stalemate and failure, as did the Yokohama anti-freight-line mobilization. The environmental rights suits instigated by activists in Date and Buzen proved far too progressive for the Japanese legal system, though other, more moderate suits, such as those involving sunlight rights *(nisshōken)*, did result in amendments to local zoning regulations in some cities. Yet despite this general lack of success, observers and theorists remained decidedly upbeat. Marxists, localists, and *shimin* advocates all agreed that the new movements were here to stay and that, with just a little luck, they might challenge the logic of unrestrained growth and awaken the populace from its delusion of affluence. What impressed observers and activists more than anything else was the promise of self-help as a strategy for movements to win.

THE CLASS FACTION: THE DISJUNCTURE
OF OBSERVATION AND THEORY

How the antipollution and antidevelopment movements are to be understood—their significance—is a deeply political question, and switching the ideological lens can redefine any given movement in an instant: a parochial local dispute can be fed into an enlightenment narrative of civic resistance or even into the struggle of proletarian masses against monopoly capitalism. As I noted above, we can identify three broad positions or interpretations of the new movements: a Marxist perspective (the class faction, or *kaikyū-ha*), a localist perspective (the resident faction, or *jūmin-ha*), and a civic perspective (the citizen faction, or *shimin-ha*).[40] Admittedly, this characterization is somewhat overly schematic, because these were not mutually exclusive positions, but rather had a degree of theoretical overlap—something akin to the circles of a Venn diagram. Though Marxists and localists tended to avoid the term *shimin* in favor of *jūmin* or some other term, this was not always the case. Moreover, those committed to either localism or Marxism quite happily published in magazines such as *Shimin*, explicitly associating with the new politics of this term. For clarity, however, I want to trace each of these positions separately, and then come back to ask how they may have resonated or conflicted and what the implications of this may have been for later imaginations of the *shimin* and civic activism. To clarify my ultimate destination up front: I argue that beyond their ideological differences, the three approaches tended to gravitate around an affirmative vision of local activism based on self-help, inclusivity, and ideological neutrality. This vision not only drew on earlier developments in civic activism; it also brought the notion of constructive self-help to the very center of *shimin* mythology—a position it retains to this day.

Consider, first, the ideas of the class faction. As evident in the thought of Miyamoto Kenichi and Endō Akira, the class faction's position on the new movements grew out of its reading of postwar capitalism as a relentless process of intensive accumulation and colonization of everyday life. Had the members of this faction closely abided by the orthodox line, such conditions would have necessarily connected to class struggle, and the energy of local movements would have been interpreted in the context of a world-historical task. To an extent Miyamoto and others in the class faction did stay faithful to this position, but, as committed empiricists, they could not deny or ignore the ways in which local activism broke with established socialist ideology and strategy. The class faction never reconciled this gulf between theory and discovery, and, if anything, their findings tended to support the narrowly parochial vision of the resident faction.

Miyamoto's description and reading of prevention movements reveal just how difficult it was for committed Marxists to position the new movements. Ideologically, he noted, residents' movements had no strategy for revolution, and their sense of purpose (mokuteki ishiki) was weak. Organizationally, they possessed no rigorous regulations and had no centralized power structure, coming together instead as a collectivity of free individuals and groups.[41] Endō Akira echoed this position, saying that residents' movements must rely on spontaneity, and leaders were to take control only at important moments, the rest of the time merely proposing a strategic agenda.[42] In terms of victory, what seemed to matter most, both recognized, was that movements unfolded around single issues in the context of local governance. As Miyamoto observed, movements tended to win when they focused on a concrete issue justified on the basis of love of native place (kyōdoai), the equivalent of modern-day regional self-governance (chihō jichi).[43] Ironically, on this point, Miyamoto was actually voicing not the class faction's position but that of the localists and their parochial brand of local egoism.

Miyamoto and Endō's identification of a form of localistic synergy in residents' movements only further undermined a class-based reading. Local fishermen, for example, could provide the explosive energy of a revolt, while workers, with their capacity for tolerance, could contribute durable and organized activism.[44] Local political parties, too, played a role, and, as Endō carefully explained, successful movements tended to mobilize party energies from *all* sides of politics. This not only opened up resources on both the left and right but also protected movements from so-called red attacks (aka kōgeki—i.e., from accusations of communism). Endō even recognized how winning movements tapped into the energy of conservative local organizations, most notably neighborhood, village, and self-rule associations *(chōnaikai, burakukai, jichi-kai)* and business groups. Victory resulted when such organizations were brought into the movement, even if they had to be "dragged along."[45] Invoking the powerful mythology of Tanaka Shōzō, Miyamoto recalled how this popular martyr had appealed to a variety of groups across the political-ideological spectrum, such as socialists, Christians, and even emperor-system humanitarians (not to mention the emperor himself).[46] Of course, Tanaka Shōzō's movement was a dismal failure, but for Miyamoto, Endō, and others in the class faction the lesson from both the past and the present for movement strategy was that localized, specific, nonideological activism often linked to victory—no doubt, a somewhat disconcerting conclusion for a Marxist.

Empirically, of course, this all made good sense, but on the downside it deposited the Marxist position on residents' movements in a kind of ideological no-man's-land. Nevertheless (and essentially ignoring their own empirical insights into local activism), Miyamoto and fellow Marxists remained doggedly committed to a unity of residents' movements on both the national and the international levels.[47] Endō Akira agreed, arguing similarly that the more autonomous the personality, the more necessary it became for an individual to participate in and strengthen organizations.[48] There was no contradiction, he asserted, between being an autonomous individual and being a member of an organization.[49] For Endō it was a small group of *shimin* ideologues with their stance against communism that was preventing the formation of a united front with citizens' movements. Branding the name *shimin* onto the working class and working residents, he announced, was nothing short of disarming oneself in front of the enemy.[50] If the citizen faction's influence could be eradicated, such a united front would not be impossible, he asserted.[51] So, as with Miyamoto, Endō seems to have either misconstrued or intentionally ignored his own description of the new movements in order to stay faithful to a Marxist vision of the future.

The class faction's logically tenuous conclusions revealed just how difficult it would be to slot the new movements into a Marxist framework. Their praise for the strategic realism of the new movements and their concentration on local resources clearly resonated more with the political instrumentalism of localists and the participatory logic of the citizen faction than it did with theoretical purists in the party. Moreover, from a historical perspective, the tension between theory and observation in the writings of the class faction suggests that the idea of a new *shimin* paradigm was not all hot air: there was indeed a new style of activism that could not be neatly slotted into established leftist categories.

But before we relegate the class faction to the scrap heap of citizen movement history, one point is worth noting: by at least *attempting* to link pollution and overdevelopment to systemic proclivities and institutional actors, and by suggesting the necessity of a broad alliance among those at the receiving end, the class faction stayed faithful to a politics of contention. Admittedly, this position contained a dogmatic and often intractable commitment to theory, but what it lacked in expediency it made up for in critical posture. The same cannot be said of many localists and *shimin* advocates, who often enthusiastically compromised principles in the name of pragmatism and results.

THE RESIDENT FACTION: SELF-HELP AND A PLURALIST CONCEPT OF THE "PUBLIC INTEREST"

Not surprisingly, the resident faction, or localist perspective, on the new movements found its most ardent supporters among individuals actually involved in local mobilizations. These individuals had neither the time, nor the energy, nor the resources to entertain mythologies of class or *shimin;* their activist logic had to be rough and ready and, above all else, effective. Ironically, however, one of the most high-profile proponents for the *jūmin* perspective was Ui Jun, who was not a local protester but an academic employed at the apex of elitism, the University of Tokyo. As a graduate student on the Faculty of Engineering in the early 1960s, Ui, along with a colleague, was among the first to confirm scientifically that methyl mercury poisoning caused Minamata disease, but lacking the confidence to go public he and his colleague held back this information—something Ui would greatly regret in later years. This discovery, however, was life altering for Ui, and from the mid-1960s, as an instructor in urban engineering at the University of Tokyo, he became more and more involved in pollution research and activism. These activities reached a high point in 1970, when Ui convened the first in a series of forums known as the Independent Lectures on Pollution (Kōgai Jishu Kōza). To Ui's surprise, the first *jishu kōza* attracted some three hundred observers, and in the series' first year over eight hundred participants came from all over the nation.[52] The lectures provided a space for activists, politicians, advocates, and intellectuals to compare notes, formulate movement strategies, and—significantly—to debate the localist perspective of the resident faction.

After Ui's initial presentations on pollution and the local protest against it, the lectures were opened up to a variety of presenters: the JSP dietwoman Doi Takako, the progressive Yokohama mayor Asukata Ichio, the Yokohama activist and proud local egoist Miyazaki Shōgo, and Matsushita Ryūichi, a tofu maker and novelist protesting power plant construction in Oita Prefecture. The independent lectures movement was also active on an international level. Much to the chagrin and embarrassment of government officials, in 1972 the group produced an English-language report titled *Polluted Japan*, neatly timed to coincide with the Stockholm Conference on the Human Environment,[53] and two years later it organized a bus tour for foreign students and journalists to visit pollution sites such as Ashio and Fuji City.[54] Ui was supported throughout by an executive committee consisting of university students, white- and blue-collar workers, and housewives.[55] Soon after the lectures began, the group rented an apartment near the university, and over time this became a contact point for individuals committed to the struggle against pollution—very much like Beheiren's antiwar office at Kagurazaka. As Ui recalled, participation happened in stages: first people came to hear the lectures; then they joined the organizing committee; and after this they very often became deeply involved in a local struggle, such as in Minamata or at Shibushi Bay.[56] Firmly committed to the autonomy of local movements, Ui saw the independent lectures as no more than a telephone exchange to relay information (and people) among the myriad local mobilizations.[57] He carefully pointed out that the various specialist committees dispatched to assist local struggles were there to serve *(sābisu)*, not to guide *(shidō)*.[58] Ui's self-confessed phobia about organizations *(soshiki kyōfushō)* meant that the Kōgai Jishu Kōza would never develop into a centralized organ for the control of local movements.[59]

Ui's characterization of the independent lectures was essentially on the mark: the forum was, indeed, a loose gathering of individuals opposed to pollution. But it also served as a mouthpiece for influential intellectuals to define and disseminate the localist approach to activism and, most notably, Ui's idiosyncratic vision of local self-help. Ui accepted that the problems of pollution prevention and conservation were deeply rooted in Japan's polity and economy, but he disagreed that such problems would be solved only by sweeping transformation of the overall system.[60] For example, he strongly believed that pollution eradication, if it focused solely on dismantling the U.S.-Japan security alliance, would actually short-circuit activism. In a thinly veiled attack on the established left, he complained that people had "incessantly repeated this argument for almost thirty years," but "in reality" it had "not helped solve any actual problems." On the contrary, it had served as a convenient excuse for doing absolutely nothing about pressing pollution issues.[61] Successful residents' movements, on the other hand, tended to avoid debates about the overall state of affairs *(daijōkyō)*, focusing instead on the urgent problems at hand.[62] Of course, this did not mean movements could be oblivious to the political situation; rather, they needed to have a keen sensitivity toward the macro- *and* micro-aspects of politics.[63]

Ui never explained how this macro- and microconsciousness should manifest in actual mobilizations, preferring instead to elucidate the tactical and organizational pragmatism running though antipollution and antidevelopment movements.[64] He identified a vertical and horizontal principle *(tate to yoko no gensoku)* for residents' movements.[65] If Minamata, Toyama, and other victims' movements taught one thing, it was certainly that mobilizations based on lobbying *(chinjō)* governmental authorities for relief inevitably resulted in failure.[66] Bureaucrats could simply shuffle victims and their petitions to other agencies or levels of government. The only approach with a chance of success was one premised on the assumption that the differing levels of government possessed a degree of self-autonomy—that they were not simply appendages of a gigantic conservative Leviathan. So rather than struggling for comprehensive relief from the outset, activists would fare much better by molding strategies to fit the compartmentalized structure of the bureaucracy. In other words, Ui argued that activists should make specific—if modest—demands on local officials within their discretionary limits, even if this did not amount to a complete solution.[67] Far better, Ui argued, to have an occasional piecemeal victory through such strategies than the predetermined defeat of old-style lobbying.[68]

Beating at the heart of Ui's reasoning here was a profound commitment to citizen activism as a form of self-help and a conviction that the real problem for the Japanese people was their proclivity to depend absolutely on elites for relief and redress—whether conservative or progressive. "The strength of a movement," he suggested, "is proportionate to the distance it has walked."[69] By walking, of course, Ui was referring to activists taking matters into their own hands. In Shizuoka, for example, activists discovered the way to win when they "walked" outside and began to study wind direction.[70] In Kōchi Prefecture a housewife uncovered hydrogen sulfide pollution after noticing a discolored coin in a local river. In Toyohashi City, residents mapped out diseased pine trees to trace the pollution source,[71] and in Oita Prefecture, locals represented themselves in a suit for environmental rights. All of these examples revealed for Ui how local citizen activists had produced a self-styled praxis by clarifying matters for themselves.[72]

When residents walked, Ui explained, they began to question the current state of Japan and the truth of the various assumptions they had unquestioningly accepted. They were pushed to emancipate their thinking and no longer rely on others. The one piece of psychological devastation *(seishintekina kōhai)* brought about by high-speed growth, Ui lamented, was an unquestioning belief in the continuity of daily life, that even if the foundations of existence began to collapse, people would survive by relying on the authorities. This was nothing more than an illusion. The most formidable "brick wall" for residents' movements, he suggested, was an "overconfidence in bureaucracy," that the authorities would "look after things."[73] More than anything else, Ui argued, the Japanese people needed a political discussion that stressed the absolute necessity of economic and spiritual autonomy for residents in their localities.[74] In the absence of such autonomy, institutional change would amount to nothing. Indeed, only after local residents discarded the established notion of trusting institutions could the real movement begin.[75]

Here, of course, was yet another inflection of the autonomy so central in antipollution and antidevelopment activists' concept of civic activism. Inasmuch as it implied independence from the established left and resistance to a hegemonic state or an all-encompassing market, this autonomy shared commonalities with the citizens' movements of the Anpo struggle and Beheiren. But we should also recognize how this model of autonomy differed from and, indeed, added another dimension to notions of autonomy extant in the sphere of *shimin* discourse. Given that physical and material things were at stake, the pursuit of autonomy for resident faction movement intellectuals tended to manifest itself more in terms of realpolitik and ideological neutralism, since this stance broadened the resource pool and made the chances of success greater. Not that this meant local movements were somehow softer or co-opted; quite the opposite: they were among the most doggedly relentless and confrontational of all grassroots movements in the postwar period. But, as the Shizuoka movements reveal, local autonomy as a movement objective often tended to encourage strategic utility at the expense of wider political principles. More to the point, since it was a parochially imagined autonomy, it often came at the expense of any concern for overall fairness, a wider common good, or fundamental political reform—something akin to a stance of "anywhere *other than* my backyard." Conceptualized in this way, the autonomy and self-help advocated by the resident faction and practiced by many actual movements of the time take on a far more complex ambience.

Nowhere is this hard-edged pragmatism of localism clearer than in the thought and public activism of Miyazaki Shōgo, a defiant and controversial protester from Yokohama. Here, Ui Jun's inspiring treatise on self-help as a path to autonomy found a home in unabashed local egoism. Miyazaki's movement began in mid-1966 after residents in suburban Yokohama learned of the intent of Japan National Railways (JNR, later Japan Railway Group) to construct a freight line through their neighborhood. According to JNR, this new line running from Tsurumi to Totsuka would allow conversion of the main Tōkaidō freight line into a commuter track and alleviate rush-hour pressure. Since there was no room to run another line through the built-up center of Yokohama, this diversion through the rear suburbs of the city was unavoidable according to JNR. Both JNR and local officials claimed legitimacy for the project on the basis of the public interest *(kōkyōsei)*: after all, why ride agonizingly overcrowded trains day after day when a simple solution was at hand? Local residents along the proposed route saw things quite differently, of course, complaining that the new line— decided upon without any local consultation—would result in the destruction of their quiet residential communities. Deeply opposed to the project, residents promptly organized in protest. In Miyazaki Shōgo's locale, disgruntled residents were quick to mobilize, selecting seven representatives to act as a central organizing committee. By early 1967 opposition movements along the proposed route had joined together in the Conference of Alliances Opposed to the Yokohama New Freight Line (Yokohama Shinkamotsusen Hantai Dōmei Rengō Kyōgikai).

In response, the progressive Yokohama administration of Asukata Ichio attempted to assuage local animosities by addressing the pollution issue head on. In 1970 Asukata formed the Pollution Countermeasures Conference (Kōgai Taisaku Kyōgikai), comprising specialists, bureaucrats, and hand-picked citizens not directly involved in any of the opposition movements. Such moves ended in utter failure, however, and by the mid-1970s Mayor Asukata had all but given up on engagement and now openly denounced the egoism of a few residents *(ichibu jūmin no ego).*[76] In 1974 the minister of construction effectively rubber-stamped the project when he gave official permission to invoke the Compulsory Purchase of Land Act (Tochi Shūyōhō). Soon after, JNR began surveying activities, which resulted in numerous confrontations with local residents. By this point, relations between protesters and the Asukata administration had more or less ceased. In a last-ditch attempt to win, Miyazaki and his colleagues pursued a number of innovative but ultimately fruitless strategies. The movement ran its own candidate, Okuda Michifumi, in mayoral elections, gathering only twenty thousand votes. It also instigated two legal actions: a civil suit to stop the freight line construction and an administrative lawsuit (gyōsei soshō) against the Ministry of Construction's (MOC) approval of the project. When all else had failed, local residents announced their intent to secede formally from Yokohama and become an independent administrative unit. This endeavor ended in failure too, and in October 1979, residents made room for the vibrations and noise of a shiny new embodiment of the public interest.[77]

Miyazaki's anti-freight-line mobilization was significant for a number of reasons. First, the movement represented a test case for the wave of progressive local administrations elected to office beginning in 1963. It was a moment of truth for leftist politicians' lofty claims about citizen participation in local government and the establishment of civil minimums to protect daily life. I discuss both of these policies in detail below, but note that, in the Yokohama movement, both citizen participation and civil minimums were largely ignored by elites. Second, the movement represented the most sophisticated statement of localism, based as it was on a radical redefinition of the public interest as the sum total of private local interests rather than any agreed societal standards. And third, the movement took the ideas of autonomy and self-help to new extremes, in the process opening up diverse possibilities in citizen activism.

Miyazaki articulated four concrete reasons for opposing the freight line. First and most obvious, residents opposed the plan because it threatened to disrupt their daily lives and living environment—what some would later conceptualize as an infringement of the right to daily life (seikatsuken). This had nothing to do with monopoly capital or the security treaty system, Miyazaki stressed; it was simply a question of protecting one's backyard. Second, Miyazaki and other residents questioned the veracity of the objective of easing commuter congestion. The construction of the freight line, they believed, was really part of a larger national government policy for radical modernization of the transport infrastructure, and given the National Comprehensive Development Plans floated during the 1960s, such claims were not without substantiation.[78] And, if what the residents believed was truly the case, then officials' claims about the public interest would tumble like a house of cards. Third, activists pointed out the absolute lack of democratic consultation in the freight line project. Though local residents would be most affected, at no point were they included in the planning or decision making for the freight line. Quite the opposite: as Miyazaki explained, JNR and the MOC kept a lid on the project until it was approved. Residents were then asked to accept a done deal without any discussion of its merits and demerits.[79] On this point, Miyazaki and fellow protesters could hardly be blamed for wondering just what "citizen participation" actually meant.

Finally, activists rejected outright the so-called Yokohama Method (Yokohama Hōshiki) of the Asukata administration. In simple terms, this was a method for preventing pollution at the local level by requiring industry to enter pollution prevention agreements *(kōgai bōshi kyōtei)* with local governments before they could set up operations. Yokohama City was among the first local administrations to enter such an agreement, and in the coming years hundreds of similar agreements were signed between industry and local governments throughout the nation. Yokohama City became a model of pollution control. For freight line protesters, however, this policy line was nothing more than a pollution smoke screen *(kōgai surikaeron)* that drew attention away from the rights and wrongs of the project itself.[80] It focused all the attention on the issue of pollution and relevant countermeasures, bypassing local residents' concerns about siting.[81] Residents argued that the Yokohama Method actually worked to the advantage of the aggressor industry, because it implicitly sanctioned certain levels of pollution. After all, if this was not the case then why demand pollution control measures in the first place?

As Miyazaki noted, the Yokohama administration could demand only that industry do what it was capable of doing, because setting the bar too high would encourage industry to go elsewhere. In a counterintuitive way, according to Miyazaki, pollution agreements provided an official stamp of approval for certain levels of pollution.[82] And to make matters worse, the terms of such agreements were determined by local officials and industry in the total absence of local residents. In sum, then, Miyazaki and affected residents were upset by the project itself, the decision-making process, and the supposed progressive policy line of Asukata Ichio and his administration. It was this curious recipe of factors that shaped Miyazaki and other movement intellectuals' localist strategy and ideology.

Ironically, though the movement was completely trounced, Miyazaki geared his tactics and strategies to winning and nothing else. As he put it, winning was the objective *(katsukoto koso mokuteki)*, because losing left people with nothing, regardless of how their understanding may have deepened or their consciousness been enhanced.[83] And because winning was all that mattered, activists needed to pursue the most instrumental of strategies. Both the enemy and the issue, Miyazaki advised, were to be defined as specifically as possible.[84] In this case the issue was the construction of a railway line—not monopoly capitalism, not U.S. military bases, not the Vietnam War, not the security treaty, and not even pollution. Why was it, Miyazaki wondered, that systemic problems were given precedence over local problems when the two had no vertical connection?[85] Such an approach only muddied the issue and drew people's attention away from the pressing question at hand: Would the freight line really reduce congestion?

The same could be said of the enemy. The big mistake of movements, to date, Miyazaki argued, was the tendency to adopt the logic of anti-capitalist struggles and—by default—identify the Liberal Democratic Party and the bureaucracy as the enemy. But the reality was that freight lines affected anyone who lived beside them, even LDP dietmen and business executives.[86] Making an enemy out of the conservative camp only alienated potential supporters on both the left and the right. Much better, Miyazaki advised, to define the enemy as only those individuals in JNR and the government who supported the project; that way, everyone else was a potential ally.

Miyazaki's approach manifested itself in local organization as well. To the greatest extent possible, the movement was to unfold on the basis of an ethos of local struggle *(genchi tōsō shugi)*, and never was it to be monopolized or become the demesne of the progressive camp.[87] Keeping things local and neutral, he explained, had a number of concrete advantages. It meant that activists could mobilize the support of local conservative organizations such as neighborhood associations. Miyazaki noted that, though activists were wary of such associations, most agreed that their nonparticipation would be a minus.[88] Rather than alienate local conservatives, why not create a movement so strong that they were left with no choice but to join? And, if conservatives came onboard, the movement would inoculate itself against any red attacks that might arise. There was absolutely no advantage in movements allying themselves with the left, Miyazaki asserted. Leftist claims of an alliance between workers and residents were nothing more than a process of proletarianizing residents *(jūmin no rōdōsha ka)* and making them subcontractors for the nationwide struggle.[89] If the anti-airport movement in Chiba Prefecture proved one thing for Miyazaki, it was that residents' movements made a tactical error when they joined hands with the left: by adopting a red weapon to ward off the red attack, the movement at Sanrizuka had lost its focus, he claimed.[90]

What was so wrong with an ideology of local egoism *(chiiki egoizumu)*, Miyazaki wondered, and what was a public interest that sacrificed the daily lives of residents?[91] Miyazaki believed it ludicrous that the public welfare *(kōkyō no fukushi)* should conflict with or contradict residents' efforts to improve or protect their localities.[92] On the contrary, the absolute premise for the public interest was actually a regional egoism that served to protect the daily lives of the people. Miyazaki imagined the public welfare instead as an accumulation of regional egoisms or as an extension of them.[93] On this point Miyazaki found moral support in the thought of anticolonial champion Frantz Fanon, who, in his classic, *The Wretched of the Earth,* argued:

> If the building of a bridge does not enrich the awareness of those who work on it, then that bridge ought not be built and the citizens can go on swimming across the river or going by boat. The bridge should not be "parachuted down" from above; it should not be imposed by a *deus ex machina* upon the social scene; on the contrary it should come from the muscles and the brains of the citizens. Certainly, there may well be need of engineers and architects, sometimes completely foreign engineers and architects; but the local party leaders should be always present, so that the new techniques can make their way into the cerebral desert of the citizen, so that the bridge in whole and in part can be taken up and conceived, and the responsibility for it assumed by the citizen. In this way, and in this way only, everything is possible.[94]

So, for Miyazaki (and Ui Jun), localism was about residents' taking responsibility and making decisions about their own living environment—and not relying on officials.

But localism was to be far more than this. Indeed, by reappropriating the public interest from the state, Miyazaki was suggesting the possibility of a national and international imaginary produced through a synthesis of particularistic localisms. Here again, he was deeply influenced by Fanon's claim that "national consciousness, which is not nationalism, is the only thing that will give us an international dimension."[95] As

Fanon had explained in *The Wretched of the Earth,* "It is at the heart of national consciousness that international consciousness lives and grows," and "the building of a nation is by necessity accompanied by the discovery and encouragement of universalizing values."[96] Reworking Fanon's romantic vision into a powerful endorsement of localism, Miyazaki located the foundation of all universalism in a nonlocally egoistic localism *(chiikisei).*[97] On this point Miyazaki's worldview came very close to that of Meiji activist Tanaka Shōzō, who had similarly imagined the nation as a somewhat paradoxical extension of localisms, expressed most famously in his quixotic claim that there was no Japan other than Yanaka Village.[98] And though Miyazaki's movement was worlds apart from that of Beheiren, Miyazaki's logic clearly resonated with the Beheiren movement intellectuals Oda Makoto, Tsurumi Yoshiyuki, and, of course, Tsurumi Shunsuke, who were searching for universalism and open-minded nationalism through a marriage of *shimin* and *minzoku.* The difference, of course, lay in the structural composition of this particularism: for Miyazaki Shōgo it was the locale, whereas for Beheiren activists it was the ethnic nation.

Miyazaki's exaltation of localism found voice elsewhere too. In Date City, Hokkaido, the anti-power-plant activist Masaki Hiroshi asked a judge if there was no public interest in growing vegetables.[99] Tomura Issaku, chairman of the anti-airport protest in Chiba, brought a decidedly messianic flavor to localism, proclaiming that Sanrizuka was his crucifix *(waga jūjika)* and a space where locals rose up in the fields *(no ni tatsu)* and lived in struggle *(tatakai ni ikiru).*[100] In Fuji City, Shizuoka, the *hedoro* pollution protester Kōda Toshihiko sang praises of the natives *(domin)* and their native language *(dogo).* "We think about things in native language," he explained, since this was the only way for local residents to express their thoughts and their anger. Residents' movements, he argued, had to "crawl through the folds *(hida)* of the village," because "native language lived in the customs of the village" as the "one common language produced by those customs." He confessed, "Native language is our mother tongue," and if "dialogue" was to "pierce the heart," then it simply had to proceed through the language of localism.[101]

Matsushita Ryūichi, protesting power plant construction in Buzen City, Oita, agreed with Miyazaki's portrayal of localism as the basis of universalism, but he brought a softer, more bucolic flavor to the assertion. "'Affluence' is a question of attitude," he suggested. "It's a question of what you actually need to feel affluent. Having a house full of things does not amount to affluence. Even with half the income of those in the big cities, we still enjoy living under our big blue sky and collecting shellfish from the shallow coastal waters."[102] In a short essay penned for the *Asahi Shimbun* in the early 1970s Matsushita proposed a philosophy of the dark *(kurayami no shisō)* to combat the powerful rhetoric of economic growth. "This isn't a metaphor," he explained; "it is literally about darkness *(kurayami)*." Nor was it a simpleminded polemic about returning to the age of topknots (i.e., before modernity) but rather a suggestion that people step back and reconsider the naturalized discourses of economic growth and affluence. "To the extent I am living in the present, I will not completely deny electric power," he admitted, but "what I am saying is that we should think about the culture and lifestyle we have constructed at current levels of electricity." Ordinary Japanese needed a quiet moment to deal with the pollution at hand. The philosophy of the dark would supposedly help people see realities beyond the modern myth that development was unquestioningly necessary. "Why don't we have a 'power-off day' *(teiden no hi)* once a month?" Matsushita proposed to readers. "One night a month, let's part from our televisions and submerge into the 'philosophy of the dark.'" Here people could discover the scam of Japan's illuminated culture. They could begin to question and think beyond a society wherein both work and leisure were overheated. Only in this darkness could citizens discover true emancipation: turning off the lights made the individual free, if only for a few short moments.[103] Matsushita brought this philosophy into his movement's unsuccessful environmental rights *(kankyōken)* suit against the Kyūshū Electric Company, and his thought gained nationwide exposure via Ui Jun's independent lectures and Matsushita's movement newsletter, *Kusanone Tsūshin* (Grassroots Report).[104]

Matsushita's ideas can, indeed, be located in the parochial rhetoric of localism, but they also represent the formative moment of what would become a self-reflexive trend in *shimin* thought and citizen activism in the mid-1970s. In chapter 5, I discuss how advocates and activists called on ordinary people to scrutinize their own patterns of consumption. Instead of blaming or accusing the state or corporate Japan, the task for *shimin*, such individuals claimed, was to improve themselves and their living environments through proposing alternatives and hands-on activities. Here, indeed, was one logical outcome of self-help at the local level: turning the critical eye on the self, then remaking daily life.

While some localist discourses imagined the locale as a conduit to universal values, in most cases this did *not* imply a final Hegelian-like sublation of the locality into some higher communal imaginary or stage of civic consciousness. The localist perspective culminated in a community autonomous of both the nation and the state (though not necessarily hostile to them). As Yasuda Tsuneo argues, local egoism was nothing other than a pejorative rendering of the wholly legitimate right to daily life *(seikatsuken)*, and for this reason actually embodied an alternative (if not more legitimate) expression of the public interest *(mōhitotsu no kōkyōsei)*.[105] Moreover, not only was local egoism an alternative, but also localists' appropriation of the rhetoric of the public interest pointed toward a novel reconceptualization of the public sphere, in which local movements could *overcome* localism through mutual discussion—an imagination of associationalism we have already seen in the circle movement of the early postwar decades.[106]

THE CITIZEN FACTION: THE SPIRAL OF UNIVERSALITY FROM *JŪMIN* TO *SHIMIN*

Committed, as they were, to a civic republican model of citizenship, the citizen faction (most prominently Matsushita Keiichi and Shinohara Hajime) could not be satisfied with the static and parochial vision of local activism espoused by local protesters. Just as the class faction dreamed of local movements' subsumption into the wider proletarian struggle, the citizen faction clung doggedly to an enlightenment mythology of the new movements: the parochial *jūmin* ripening into the universal-minded *shimin*. And though by no means did the citizen faction have an ideological monopoly, their ideas (brewing since the mid-1950s) came to dominate discussions of state-society relations and the proper configuration of civil society in the coming years. Specifically, in the early 1960s, citizen faction ideas deeply influenced the attitudes of progressive local governments toward citizen involvement in policy-making and the legitimacy of independent civic activism. Moreover, these ideas helped local and national officials recalibrate practices of self-help in civic movements into government-supported programs for social welfare volunteerism and community building.

Consider first the ideas of Shinohara Hajime, a political scientist at the University of Tokyo and an activist in Tokyo's Nerima Ward. Shinohara has been a key figure in the development of civic thought and politics in the postwar era, popularizing the *shimin* idea during the

Anpo struggle; becoming deeply involved in local politics and activism and helping formulate the concept of citizen participation in local politics in the early 1970s; and, in the 1990s, vocally advocating civil society and citizen politics *(shimin seiji)*. What interests me here, however, is his interpretation of residential activism opposing pollution and overdevelopment.

Writing in the activist publication *Shimin* in May 1971, Shinohara argued that the egoism of citizens' movements had the potential to stimulate people to defend their right to live *(ikiru kenri)* as individual citizens *(ichishimin toshite)*.[107] This was certainly praiseworthy, but to the extent that movements stagnated in local egoism, they would not become an influential *(yūryoku)* political and social force.[108] As he asserted in the progressive *Asahi Jyānaru* in 1968, *shimin* first became complete when they developed a social aspect *(shakaisei)* and a sense of solidarity as citizens *(shimin toshite no rentaikan)* with other Japanese and citizens of other countries.[109] Contrary to Miyazaki Shōgo's parochial interpretation, Shinohara's belief was that local problems garnered the support of residents precisely because these problems connected to more fundamental questions. Residents mobilized in the anti-freight-line movement in Yokohama, for example, because the movement was also opposed to urban environmental destruction.[110]

Similarly, Shinohara saw his own drive for publicly elected mayors in Tokyo's Nerima Ward in terms of the more fundamental principle of public elections. In short he perceived a qualitative difference between citizens' movements and residents' movements in that the former tended to sublimate *(shōka)* local particularity *(chiikitekina tokushu)* into a greater universality *(yori ōkina fuhen)*.[111] His assertion, of course, was that universalism was not only qualitatively (ethically?) better than localism but that it represented a more functionally useful value in concrete struggles for democratic rights. Many local protesters disagreed, no doubt, but Shinohara's position was emblematic of the citizen faction's evolutionary approach to the new movements. There could be no development, he and others believed, until residents transformed themselves into citizens *(jūmin kara shimin e)*.[112]

Drawing on some of Shinohara's central assertions, the University of Tokyo sociologist Nitagai Kamon made a valiant—if abortive—effort to explain how this transformation in values might happen. What began as a simple desire to protect the living environment often developed into a rights consciousness *(kenri ishiki)*.[113] When people realized that living *(sumu koto)* in the localities was the most natural and reasonable of things, they understood for the first time that daily life was a natural right *(shizen no kenri)*.[114] With this realization, movements transformed from passive opposition *(shōkyokutekina hantai)* to the proposal of constructive issues *(sekkyokuteki na kadai teiji)*.[115] Mobilizing some Marxist categories, Nitagai saw the subjectivity of residents' movements emerging as they clarified the use value *(shiyō kachi)* of the tools or means of daily life.[116] He saw a fundamental difference in such consciousness when compared with earlier social movements in Japan, which had denied everyday life on the basis of principles and doctrines—what he called ideological self-restraint. It was through just such an operation that earlier movements established their subjectivity.[117] But residents' movements were different, because their sense of community was based, first, on the relationship between people and things (including space or place), and, second, on the sense of the collective social relations *(kyōdō no shakai kankei)* that emerged from this.[118] In other words, Nitagai was suggesting that the fundamental motivation for residents' movements lay in a local meeting of the minds vis-à-vis the importance of the local living environment.

But though localism empowered people to imagine a collective we, to develop a rights consciousness, and to organize in collective protest, it did not, according to Nitagai (and Shinohara), produce any social aspect *(shakaisei)* in the consciousness of locals, and this was its major flaw.[119] For this, activists would need to develop a transregional perspective that rose above the parochial interests of groups in different regions. Here Nitagai hinted at a broader conceptualization of activism in which social movements voiced the collective interests of society against the state and the market. In other words, he imagined the new movements as the backbone of a civil society. In support, Nitagai invoked civil society theorist Hirata Kiyoaki's notion of the shared civic relationship *(dōshimin kankei)* among citizens as they protected their collective interests from public authority *(kōkenryoku,* i.e., the state) and capitalism *(shihon,* i.e., the market).[120] His point was that the moment of localism contained within it the potential for civic awakening, which, in turn, would become the dynamic energy for a civil society in Japan.

The mechanism for overcoming local egoism, Nitagai argued, lay in a front-on engagement between residents and state authorities *(kōkenryoku, ōyake)*[121] and, specifically, through interaction with local government *(jichitai),* a contradictory node *(mujun no kessetsuten)* susceptible to control from above yet receptive to appropriation from below.[122] Pitting bureaucratic or politicized definitions of the public interest against residents' communal perspective would produce a contentious or critical version of the public interest *(hihanteki kōkyōsei)*, akin to that in the ideas of Miyazaki Shōgo.[123] The moment of intellectual transformation would supposedly come about when residents connected this critical perspective to their rights *(kenri)* and duties *(gimu)* as conscientious citizens *(jinkaku o motsu shimin)*. At this point their regional egoism would apparently fade away and be replaced by the brilliant radiance of civility *(shiminsei)*.[124] Moreover, Nitagai confidently concluded, through resident participation *(jūmin sanka)*— that is, bringing the energies of these conscientious citizens into the structure of governance—the local bureaucracy would itself be made civic *(shiminteki)*.[125]

Nitagai's model had much in common with the Tosei Chōsakai and clearly drew on ideas that were percolating among that influential group beginning around the mid-1960s. Both Matsushita Keiichi and Narumi Masayasu had described the new movements as a civic revolution *(shimin kakumei)* and claimed that they evidenced the birth of a modern civil society *(kindai shimin shakai)* in Japan.[126] It was in citizens' movements, Narumi added, that autonomous citizens *(jiritsuteki shimin)* matured in great numbers, providing, in turn, the impetus for progressive local governance in the 1960s and 1970s.[127] But like Shinohara and Nitagai, Narumi could not be content with localized struggle, envisioning instead a process of spiraling ascent from resident *(jūmin)* to citizen *(shimin)*, then to Japanese national *(kokumin)*, and ultimately to world citizen *(sekai shimin)*.[128] Jūmin were, for Narumi, the "inhabitants of daily life" *(seikatsusha)* and—invoking Hegel—the embodiment of desires *(yokubō no gugensha)*. Theirs was an isolated existence with no aspiration for things universal *(fuhentekina mono)*, hence the tendency for expressions of local or individual egoism. Of course, this was only to be expected: Japanese modern history was a tale of sacrifice and obliteration of the individual for the sake of the state *(kokka)*. Egoism—the ideology of absolute self-interest *(isshin dokuji)*—Narumi admitted, was probably the only way for the Japanese people to discover their right to live *(ikiru kenri)*.[129] But to the extent that consciousness stagnated in the egoism of residents' movements, the Japanese people could not become the legitimate heirs of postwar democracy.[130] The resident *(jūmin)*, he explained, was little more than a point of departure *(shuppatsuten)* on the way to becoming a fully fledged citizen *(shimin)*.[131]

Narumi imagined the stage of the citizen as qualitatively different from that of the resident, because becoming a citizen was all about the subjective conquest of the ego.[132] It was a process of examining the standards for action within the self—a search for commonality among the values and aspirations of people in their respective life spaces, similar to Hirata Kiyoaki's notion of the shared civic relationship. Narumi posited a transformation from an ideology of egoism, rights, and resistance at the resident stage to the attainment of self-education *(jiko kyōiku)* and self-discipline *(jiko kiritsu)* at the stage of modern citizenship *(kindaiteki shimin)*.[133] But recognizing the sheer vulnerability of such logic, he carefully stressed that it would be wrong to explain the shift as simply one from *"jūmin* = rights" to *"shimin* = rights + duties."* Such rhetoric, he noted, had long been a claim of the establishment, which hoped to subdue and control civic energies. The point was not about juxtaposing rights and duties but about understanding both rights and duties as rights in themselves. Thus, the aim of citizens and their movements was the imagination of a new mode of daily life based on civic self-governance *(shimin jichi o fumaeta atarashii seikatsu yōshiki no sōzō)*.[134] At the citizen stage, people asked how they would construct a new civic morality *(shiminteki moraru)* and produce a civic ethos *(shiminteki ētosu)*.[135] For Narumi, this stage, if taken to its logical conclusion, would quite naturally produce at full maturity a new vision of the Japanese citizen *(kokumin)* transcendent of simple nationalism *(tan naru nashonarizumu)* and connected to cosmopolitanism *(kosumoporitizumu)* or a vision of the world citizen *(sekaiteki shiminzō)*.[136] As he put it, more than anything else the whole process hinged on the transformation of the *jūmin* into the *shimin*.[137] The *shimin* would be the primary agent *(shutai)* in the formation of a new ethos, and local government would be the strategic fortress for the construction of this ethos *(shimin keisei no senryakuteki horui)*.[138]

Matsushita Keiichi's definition of the *shimin* in his influential 1966 essay, " 'Shimin' teki Ningengata no Gendaiteki Kanōsei" (The Contemporary Potential of the "Civic" Type of Human), neatly summed up the spirit of the citizen faction position. "The *shimin* can be understood as a spontaneous type of human *(jihatsuteki ningengata)* capable of both private and public self-governing activities," he explained. "Today the *shimin* is to be understood as the individual political disposition upon which democracy is premised; in other words, [it is] the ethos of 'civility' *(shiminsei)*." Matsushita admitted that the citizen emerged first as a distinct status ethos *(mibun ētosu)* in the context of

Western history, but in the present day it had come to signify a civic type of human possessed of the universalism produced by mass democracy *(taishū minshushugi)*. The task for this new *shimin* was to construct civic spontaneity through political participation as a citizen of a nation *(kokumin)* and within class movements *(kaikyū undō)*.[139]

Similar to advocates of the class and resident factions, Matsushita, Shinohara, and other citizen faction advocates recognized how strategies of self-help fueled antipollution and antidevelopment movements. But they could not accept local struggle as an end in itself. For them, residents' movements were never anything but egoistic and, hence, had to be subsumed into the democratic project of expanding popular political participation. Such conclusions were wholly compatible with the project for local democracy and government reform that Matsushita and others had been pursuing since the defeat of the Anpo struggle. The difference now, in the midst of a rising wave of resistance and progressive local governance, was that a civic conquest of conservative hegemony actually seemed possible. The key, Matsushita and his political allies concluded, would be institutional reform that empowered *jūmin* to shed their egoism and blossom into civic-minded *shimin*—in other words, a program for full-scale citizen participation. Given the progressive fervor of the 1960s, this project was one that made good sense—so much so that very few stopped to wonder about the merits of a political program that not only attempted to institutionalize civic energies into a new national imaginary but also branded dissenting activists as egoists and bad citizens.

THE DISCOURSE ON CITIZEN PARTICIPATION: THEORIZING *SHIMIN SANKA*

If 1964 was a revolutionary year for local activism in Japan, then 1963 was arguably an epoch-making one for local government. In the nationwide local elections of 1963, progressive administrations came to power in Yokohama, Kyoto, Osaka, and Kita-Kyushu, as well as many other small- and medium-sized administrative areas, such as Asahikawa, Kushiro, Tochigi (City), Ueda, and Niihama.[140] The icing on the cake came in 1967, when the "smiling" statistician Minobe Ryōkichi was elected governor of Tokyo. The progressive onslaught continued into the 1970s: after the local elections of 1971, progressives controlled one-third of the nation's local governments,[141] and by 1975, 10 of the 47 governorships and 20 percent of the 642 mayoral positions nationwide were in the hands of progressives.[142] At least two factors were behind this political realignment at the local level. First, it was clearly a reflection of widespread discontent with the less-palatable aspects of high-speed growth, such as pollution and urban overcrowding. Second, progressives also helped themselves with shrewdly crafted promises of citizen politics based on institutional reform, direct citizen participation, and the setting of civil minimums.

Matsushita Keiichi, Narumi Masayasu, and others in the Tosei Chōsakai were quick to mobilize after the progressive electoral landslide of 1963. Apart from Matsushita, who preferred to contribute from the safety of the academy, members of the Tosei Chōsakai fanned out as advisers and officials in the new administrations. In Yokohama, Narumi Masayasu took on the position of policymaking bureau chief for Mayor Asukata, writing the mayor's speeches, formulating his civic policies, and, more generally, transforming Asukata's image from far-left JSP dietman to progressive champion of the ordinary citizen.[143] Narumi skillfully refashioned Asukata's public image, injecting a *shimin* flavor into almost everything the mayor said or did. As Michiba Chikanobu explains, at the outset Asukata and Narumi were ideological oil and water. Steeped in socialist revolutionary dogma, the progressive mayor was initially opposed to the idea of incremental structural reform, and, as Narumi put it, he was an "old Bolshevik" whose penchant for ideology was in serious need of control. Conversely, Asukata viewed his citizen faction adviser as a matter-of-fact "Weberian" and a rational supporter of systemic reform. As Asukata quipped, the resulting policy was one of "Marx dressed up as Weber," although the mayor undeniably conceded more ideologically than his adviser.[144] Narumi was joined in the Yokohama administration by fellow Tosei Chōsakai member Tamura Akira, who acted as chief engineer in the Planning and Coordination Bureau. In Sendai City, the Tosei Chōsakai's Sugiwara Yoshihisa joined the progressive Shimano administration as a special secretary *(tokubetsu hisho)*, in the same capacity that Yasue Ryōsuke joined Minobe Ryōkichi's Tokyo governorship in 1967.

From such strongholds, the Tosei Chōsakai group set about making local democracy and local government reform a reality. But the excitement of a progressive future would not last long, because, as we have seen, almost immediately the shiny new administrations came face to face with the reality of local protest and the institutionalized conservatism and corruption of local politics. Not only did residential protest movements hinder local reform, but also, and more worryingly, they threatened to expose promises of citizen participation and civil minimums as a deceptive citizen faction ruse to sort out the good (i.e., cooperative) citizens from the bad. Rallying in defense of the *shimin* model, Matsushita, Narumi, Shinohara, and others set about concretizing their ideas in both theory and pragmatic policy programs for local governance.

As I explained in chapter 2, from around the late 1950s Matsushita had begun to argue that Japan was transforming into a mass society as it shifted from industrial capitalism (the stage of modernity, or *kindai*) to monopoly capitalism (the stage of contemporaneity, or *gendai*). The gradual proletarianization of the population, the emergence of a professionalized new middle stratum in the cities, the spread of new technologies, and the leveling of traditional social classes, he argued, called for a fundamental rethinking of established Marxist theory, especially with respect to the dynamics of revolution. In an age when mass democracy pacified the people and mass nationalism obscured their vision, historical change lay not in direct socialist revolution but in a united front of forces for liberty and democracy.

Despite his somewhat pessimistic reading of mass democracy, Matsushita parted ways with orthodox mass society theorists, who viewed the new social formation as the end of popular political involvement. For Matsushita, mass society was as much an institutional problem (if not more so) as it was a psychological one, and, hence, he saw a way out through the exercise of individual political agency by civic individuals—his civic type of human *(shiminteki ningengata)*. More concretely, Matsushita argued in the early 1960s that the key lay in the masses recognizing and utilizing their forgotten right of resistance against new forms of manipulation and domination. The Anpo struggle and failure revealed a number of things for him. The inability of the established forces of the left—especially enterprise-based unions—to crack the central locus of power proved for him that the orthodox socialist line could simply not deal with the new social formation of mass society. But, on the positive side, spontaneous citizen protest heralded a new form of civic resistance. Recognizing the persistence of conservative control in the countryside and the urban bedtowns, Matsushita and his colleagues in the Tosei Chōsakai began to promote a program of local government reform *(jichitai kaikaku)* for the realization of local democracy *(chiiki minshushugi)*. Here was one source of his mid-1960s advocacy of citizen participation.

To this we need to add one more theoretical development from the late 1950s: namely, the theory of structural reform, or *kōzō kaikaku*. For specialists of contemporary politics in Japan, *kōzō kaikaku* no doubt invokes images of bureaucratic downsizing, government cost cutting, deregulation, and privatization of public utilities—in other words, a wholly neoliberal agenda. The interesting historical twist is that *kōzō kaikaku* first entered Japan in leftist political discourse and, subsequently, in progressive theories of citizen participation. Discussion of structural reform theory began in a number of late-1950s Marxist publications, such as in the three-volume *Gendai Marukusushugi* (Contemporary Marxism, 1958), edited by Kozai Yoshishige, and in the 1959 magazine *Gendai no Riron* (Contemporary Theory).[145] The idea originated in the Italian Communist Party's so-called new political line, or Salerno Turn, of the 1950s. Building on the thought of Antonio Gramsci and directed by Communist Party leader Palmiro Togliatti, this Marxist revisionism (or reformism) rejected all forms of violence in favor of democratic and socialist reconstruction.[146] The aim was to extend the boundaries of democracy to the greatest extent possible in pursuit of a new democracy. More significantly, the agents of change were to be from the petty and middling bourgeoisie and the working class, operating in alliance.

The central assertion of structural reform theory was that, since the contradictions of capitalism were rapidly intensifying, it would be possible to construct a socialist society in a peaceful and democratic way without any need for violent revolution. As Narumi explained, in simple terms structural reform meant change through complete implementation of the constitution (peace, independence, democracy), popular participation in politics, and a citizen-worker alliance against monopoly capitalism.[147] In the late 1950s, the theory found supporters in the JSP, the JCP, and among academics, activists, and even government bureaucrats who apparently saw it as a breath of fresh air after the official revolutionary theory of the old left. The JSP chief secretary Eda Saburō was among the theory's chief proponents, even attempting to incorporate it into official Socialist Party policy in 1961. The JSP rejected the theory in 1962, but it found a new constituency in Matsushita Keiichi and other proponents of local government reform. In a paper published just months after the Anpo crisis, Matsushita praised the tenets of structural reform, noting how in late capitalist nations it increased policy elasticity (especially from a leftist perspective).[148]

Important to note, Matsushita linked the theory of structural reform to his evolving ideas about local government reform and the possibility of democratic revolution through active yet peaceful civic involvement.[149] Structural reform offered solid leftist—albeit revisionist—theoretical support for incremental, system-affirmative political action, not by revolutionaries, but by civic-minded citizens and in this sense provided a theoretical stamp of approval for the Tosei Chōsakai's notion of citizen participation.

Fittingly, Yokohama mayor Asukata Ichio served as editor (at least in name) for the first important theoretical work on citizen participation: the 1965 *Jichitai Kaikaku no Rironteki Tenbō* (A Theoretical Survey on Local Government Reform). Along with theoretical essays by Matsushita, Narumi, and others, contributors also presented case studies of progressive local government reform. Asukata, for example, outlined his idealistic proposal for a meeting of ten thousand citizens *(ichiman-nin shimin shūkai)*, and others discussed local governance in Germany, England, Italy, the Soviet Union, and China. In his contribution to the volume, Matsushita noted that although many progressive local administrations had come to office, governance still tended toward kind bureaucracy *(shinsetsu gyōsei)*—that is, sincere attempts by good-willed officials to make local government more responsive to residents but not geared toward any fundamental change in the practice of bureaucratic rule. But as Matsushita explained, the aim now was not kindly change from above by enlightened despots but transformation from below through residential activism and joint struggle in local government.[150] Progressive administrations simply had to foster the people's ability to govern, in the process transforming individuals from political beneficiaries into political subjects. Matsushita saw political training in local government as the essential foundation of popular sovereignty and regional self-governance as the school of democracy.[151] The new administrations needed to arouse political spontaneity among residents by fostering local movements that both criticized and created in the sphere of local government.[152] At the same time, he added, local governments needed to guarantee a certain level of citizen services, or what he called civil minimums *(shibiru minimamu)*.[153]

In 1971 Yokohama City mayor Asukata attempted to make a case for kind bureaucracy, arguing that, though it was merely a rudimentary form of direct democratic participation, it was unavoidable early on as an educational measure to enlighten the citizenry.[154] But, concurring with Matsushita, he also recognized the need to surmount *(kokufu)* this stage.[155] In Yokohama, for example, public participation in the form of citizen-determined construction objectives for the city supposedly evidenced this trend away from bureaucratic control toward citizens making decisions about their own living environment. Narumi, mirroring his presentation of spiraling civic consciousness from resident to citizen and beyond, imagined a similar evolutionary progress for local government. At stage one, enlightened bureaucrats established a kind bureaucracy, lending a sympathetic ear to the requests of the people. Stage two involved the transcendence of kind bureaucracy through dialogue *(taiwa)* and citizen participation *(shimin sanka)*. Finally, at stage three the authority of local government faded away almost completely, replaced now by progressive self-governance *(kakushin jichi)* through citizen management and decentralization of authority.[156] But as Michiba Chikanobu incisively notes, Narumi gave very little concrete description of how these levels would work or how the transitions would come about.[157]

Matsushita provided no more clarification either, other than suggesting that the key lay in institutionalizing civic energy. In 1971, he argued that citizen participation had to be seen as a dynamic system involving both accusation *(kokuhatsu)* and participation in planning *(sankaku)* on the part of citizens.[158] Because citizens' movements participated in politics as external entities, their criticism of the internal logic of politics was inevitable. Echoing the earlier ideas of Maruyama Masao, such amateur political participation *(shirōtoteki seiji sanka)*, he opined, had a refreshing vitality compared with professional politics.[159] But although recognizing this extrainstitutional vitality, Matsushita remained firmly committed to a systematic incorporation of civic energies into local governance. Matsushita, Narumi, Shinohara Hajime, and other proponents of citizen participation ultimately saw no long-term value in extrainstitutional protest, not even as a token expression of minority dissent. Citizen participation, after all, made such good sense on paper. Not only was it the most elegant and intuitive of enlightenment-inspired social scientific models; it also promised to propel academic theory to the very heart of democratic practice and nation building.

So how did this beautiful theory play out in practice? Citizen participation did indeed find a home in the policy platforms of many progressive local administrations. In Tokyo's Chōfu City, Mayor Honda Kaichirō set up the permanent Citizen Consultation Office (Shimin Sōdanshitsu) to listen to the "candid voices of citizens" with his "own ears."[160] Honda held annual meetings with citizens to discuss local governance, such as with the Housewives Group to Discuss City Administration (Shufu to Shisei o Kataru Kai) and the amusingly named Citizen Consultations by the Train Station in the Evening Cool (Nōryō Ekimae Shimin Sōdan).[161] All of this was apparently a reflection of his policy for city government moving in unison with the citizenry (shimin to tomo ni ayumu shisei).[162] In Ueda City, Nagano Prefecture, Mayor Koyama Ichirō, sounding remarkably like someone issuing wartime calls for total mobilization (sōdōin), pursued a policy of total citizen participation in city government (shimin sōsanka no shisei). In an effort to bring the voice of the citizenry into city administration, he implemented a number of novel initiatives, such as the send-a-letter-to-the-mayor campaign (shichō e no tegami), the Group to View City Facilities (Shisetsu o Miru Kai), and the innocuously titled talkback radio program Moshi Moshi Shichō-san (Hello, Mr. Mayor).[163]

Elsewhere citizen participation took on a more systematic and institutional flavor. Musashino City, for example, attempted to structure its long-term policy planning process (chōki keikaku sakutei) around so-called citizens' committees (shimin iinkai). A 1971 city publication titled Shimin Sanka ni yoru Chōki Keikaku Sakutei to Sono Tenkai (Long-Term Policy Planning through Citizen Participation and Its Development) explained how the new committees were fundamentally different from earlier advisory organs, which simply offered feedback on plans already drafted by bureaucrats. In contrast, citizens' committees would take the initiative in researching, formulating, and implementing policies. The report described an impressive range of committees dealing with health, city greening, community building, trash disposal, cultural activities, and the creation of civic facilities. Perceptibly absent, however, were any committees for bureaucratic and political oversight or for representation of citizen rights vis-à-vis city administration (i.e., independent ombudsmen). The report gushed optimistically on the prospects for citizen participation, expressing officials' high hopes for the independent judgment (jishuteki na handan) of ordinary citizens and the lively development (iki iki to tenkai suru) of a flexible institutional structure (danryokuteki kōzō). Of course, for all their liveliness, the proposals of such committees were not legally binding, nor do they appear to have dealt with any of the more politicized issues of local government, such as infrastructure expenditure.[164]

The same was true of the citizens' committees set up in Higashi Osaka City, although here they took on a decidedly autonomous character with seemingly little bureaucratic interaction at all. As the Higashi

Osaka administration described in its 1974 report *Fureai no Machizu-kuri* (Building an Interactive Community), citizens' committees were to be spaces for citizens to create new rules for coordinating their individual interests through mutual contradiction *(mujun)*, opposition *(tair-itsu)*, and debate *(tōgi)*.[165] Unlike the town meeting style in which officials and citizens met to discuss area-specific issues, citizens' committees in Higashi Osaka City would be dialogue meetings *(taiwa shūkai)* in which citizens autonomously participated in discussions about city planning and management. The report advised that, in the interests of gathering the opinions of various citizens, committee membership should cover a range of civic strata, including intellectuals, workers, businessmen, locals, and housewives.[166] The city administration would assist in logistical ways, but to the utmost, committees would be citizen-led *(shimin-shudō-gata)*, and according to the report, these spaces for independent citizen debate would be fundamentally different from those of existing bureaucrat-led *(gyōsei-shudō-gata)* citizen participation.[167] But as with Musashino City, proposals emanating from such debates had no formal or legal character, and, as the report noted at least three times, it was ultimately up to bureaucrats to strive *(doryoku)* for the reflection of civic ideas in city governance.[168] Moreover, the central assertion of the report—that citizens should try to solve problems mutually *before* utilizing the bureaucracy—was a clear indication of how state officials conceptualized civic energy. It was a conceptualization that Matsushita Keiichi would later term *shimin gyōsei*, or civic bureaucracy—citizens helping themselves.

The two most high-profile and arguably influential examples of citizen participation, of course, were the Yokohama administration of Asukata Ichio, beginning in 1963, and the Tokyo Minobe governorship, beginning in 1967. Like progressive mayors in Musashino, Ueda, and elsewhere, Asukata implemented a number of glossy populist initiatives, including send a letter to the mayor *(shichō e no tegami)*, citizen consultations *(shimin sōdan)*, meetings of ten thousand citizens *(ichi-man-nin shimin shūkai)*, and various meetings of neighborhood residents and ward inhabitants *(jūmin shūkai, kumin shūkai)*. Obviously no longer a "Bolshevik," Asukata explained how he responded personally to letters from residents, often visiting people directly. The mayor also participated in various local residents' meetings, apparently aimed at solving specific regional issues. Asukata's meetings of ten thousand citizens almost failed to get off the ground after being rejected by the conservative-controlled Yokohama assembly on three occasions. Unperturbed, the mayor went ahead, unofficially, with the support of independent groups in 1967 and 1970, but no concrete policy shifts or innovations resulted.[169] Asukata envisioned the meetings as pure manifestations of citizen participation, with citizens and administrators deciding big policy issues through healthy civic debate.[170] But, as Michiba notes, in hindsight he was rather disappointed with the meetings, which often degenerated into mundane discussions about trash collection and the like.[171]

Nor was everyone enamored of the new mayor and his citizen participation. Still a student at the time, the academic and activist Nakamura Kiichi recalled his feeling that such events reeked of political propaganda.[172] Not surprisingly, Miyazaki Shōgo agreed, denouncing the meetings of ten thousand citizens as nothing more than public relations for the mayor and an opportunistic chance for him to blow his own trumpet *(jiga jisan no hanashi)*.[173] After all, Miyazaki complained, the meetings were held only twice, and this hardly amounted to institutionalized citizen involvement; they were more like an empty advertising balloon floating overhead.[174] So too with Asukata's residents' meetings, which Miyazaki portrayed as a clever mechanism to manage residents *(jūmin taisaku)* by having them engage in a lot of abstract debate among themselves.[175] Admittedly, Miyazaki hardly presented an objective opinion on citizen participation in the Asukata administration, given his perspective as a disgruntled opponent of development in the region. But his intense animosity reminds us that the unfolding of citizen politics was not a seamless process, especially for those contentious individuals who were considered too egoistic to qualify as *shimin*.

Even more high profile than Yokohama City was the Tokyo governorship of Minobe Ryōkichi. Soon after coming to office in 1967, Minobe made his famous Dialogue Declaration (Taiwa Sengen), which articulated the new administration's commitment to candid dialogue with city residents *(tomin to no taiwa no shisō)*. Minobe imagined this more expansively than bureaucrats simply listening to the claims of citizens. Instead it was to be a process whereby bureaucrats stood in the shoes of citizens, citizens recognized the various obstacles faced by bureaucrats, and together both groups laid out the direction for city governance.[176] After its Meeting to Unite City Residents and City Officials (Tomin to Tosei o Musubu Tsudoi) in July 1967, the Minobe governorship became known as the Tokyo dialogue administration *(taiwa tosei)*, and thereafter citizen participation found concrete form in so-called dialogue meetings *(taiwa shūkai)*.[177]

As in Yokohama, however, such initiatives proved less than successful. Even Matsushita Keiichi leveled a brutal criticism, labeling the
meetings Minobe Kōmon's Tokyo Travels (Minobe Kōmon Tōkyōto
Manyūki), which, of course, likened Minobe to the famed Tokugawa-
period samurai Mito Kōmon, immortalized in a popular television
series documenting his apocryphal quests to help the common folk.[178]
Stung by such criticism, Minobe shifted gears from dialogue to full-
scale participation (sanka) in 1971. The Minobe administration adver-
tised its policy shift in a booklet published that year, Hiroba to Aozora
no Tōkyō Kōsō (Plan for a Tokyo of City Squares and Blue Skies),
wherein the term city squares referred to the official policy of citizen
participation in municipal governance and blue skies denoted the establishment of civil minimums, not only for the environment, but also with
respect to social welfare and public infrastructure.[179] But as Yonehara
points out, the shift from dialogue to participation, while certainly a
knee-jerk reaction to citizen faction criticism, was also just as much
about having citizens' movements shed simple opposition (tannaru
hantai) in favor of constructive participation in local government.[180]

The creation of civil minimums was undoubtedly the most sophisticated attempt to institutionalize shimin values comprehensively in local
governance. The idea of civil minimums drew on William Henry Beveridge's notion of the national minimum set out in his classic 1942
work, The Beveridge Report: The Way from Freedom and Want. This
report brought together various strains of thought on social welfare,
providing a grand framework for the postwar welfare state in Britain.
In Japan, however, Beveridge's national minimum found a home not
in policies for poverty eradication but rather in the context of urban
problems caused by excessive economic development.[181] Komori
Takeshi first aired the idea of civil minimums in his 1965 work, Toshi-
zukuri: Toshi Mondai no Genjitsu to Mirai (Building Cities: The Reality
and Future of Urban Problems), in which he proposed the establishment
of a citizen minimum (shichizen minimamu).[182] Matsushita later modified Komori's terminology to civil minimums, which, according to
Narumi, articulated Matsushita's understanding of them as a citizen-
side antithesis (shimingawa kara no anchitēze) to high-growth policies—a theory of civil society imagined against the dominant theory of
industrial society.[183]

In a flurry of early-1970s publications on the topic, Matsushita
defined civil minimums as normative standards for the fulfillment of
social security (shakai hoshō), social capital (shakai shihon, meaning

public infrastructure here), and social health *(shakai hoken)* in a modern urban society.[184] They guaranteed bottom-line standards with respect to both the rights of daily life *(seikatsuken)* and political appeal *(seikyūken)*.[185] Moreover, they set policymaking standards *(seisaku kōjun)* that supposedly institutionalized civic spontaneity *(shiminteki jihatsusei)* in local government and made possible the redistribution and systematic reorganization of both public and private social surplus in the national economy.[186] Stated more systematically, civil minimums, in Matsushita's view, fulfilled at least five objectives: guaranteeing environmental and living standards; securing popular participation in government; setting procedural standards for local government administration; providing concrete guidelines for the redistribution of wealth; and becoming an institutional means for transforming local egoism into universalistic civic action.

Civil minimums found form in numerous local government plans, most notably in the Tokyo Midterm Plan (Tōkyōto Chūki Keikaku), of 1968—a three-year rolling plan subject to yearly revision.[187] Parroting Matsushita, Minobe explained that civil minimums referred to the minimum required standards for the daily life of Tokyo residents—the basic institutions and facilities expected of a modern urban metropolis.[188] Apart from Tokyo, progressive administrations in Asahikawa, Yamagata, Aomori, Kanazawa, and Musashino cities brought civil minimums into their mid- and long-term plans, and in its 1970 report "Kakushin Toshi-zukuri Yōryō: Shibiru Minimamu o Sakutei suru tame ni" (Principles for the Creation of Progressive Cities: Planning Civil Minimums), the Nationwide Association of Progressive Mayors positioned civil minimums as a cornerstone in local government policymaking.[189]

As an administrative response to urban and environmental problems, the implementation of civil minimums was generally a success. In fact, it was so successful, Narumi notes, that by the late 1970s even conservative administrations had to include civil minimums in their policy platforms.[190] Of course, broad acceptance was also a double-edged sword, because the moment conservatives adopted civil minimums into their policies, the idea was, by default, no longer progressive. Moreover, as much as civil minimums remedied urban and environmental problems, little evidence suggests that they fundamentally shifted power relations between state and citizens. If anything, they gave further theoretical credence to the idea that civic energies were better domesticated and institutionalized than not.

Matsushita, for instance, believed that the formulation of civil minimums through mutual discussion and transcendence of individual egoism would imbue citizens with an active public-mindedness. He foresaw civic group representatives forming into regional civic councils *(chiiki shimin kyōgikai)* for lateral communication among citizens and the transformation of specific claims into responsible policy decisions *(sekinin aru seisaku kettei)* for the whole area of local administration.[191] In the midst of such dialogue and negotiations among civic leaders, individual egoisms would give way to a new system of self-rule and civic values—a new public interest.[192] Matsushita conceptualized these civic councils as Japanese incarnations of the American town hall meeting, the French commune, the Russian soviet, and the Chinese communist-liberated zones *(kaihōku).*[193]

As he explained in 1973, once people discarded the normative laws of heaven or those of a monarch or bureaucracy, they had to create standards for governance by establishing objective rules to mediate the infinite needs of people.[194] In this sense, civil minimums were autonomous standards by which civic needs *(shimin no hitsuyō)* were transformed into civic reason *(shimin no risei)*. Citizens had to realize that the first step toward their own self-conquest *(jiko kokufuku)* lay in the effort to establish such rules. As Matsushita put it, citizens were to be "planks" spanning a "ravine"—the "ravine," of course, being their very own needs and self-interested desires.[195] Thus, not only were civil minimums a set of guarantees for urban standards of living, but also they hit at the very heart of modern civic consciousness.

Although members of the citizen faction praised the independence of citizens' movements, they could not be satisfied with anything less than the absolute institutionalization of civic energies into the very fabric of the state. Historically speaking, this was a very interesting position, because it meant that a *shimin* defined, legitimized, and indeed mythologized against the state could be complete for them only when he or she was fully integrated back into that state. As Matsushita Keiichi admitted in 1984, the victory of progressive local government theories (local democracy, civil minimums, citizen participation, local government reform) was a double-edged sword. On the one hand, now even conservative mayors could not bypass ordinary citizens in the policymaking process, so, at least in a formalistic way, citizen participation had become national common sense. But on the other hand, the incorporation of these ideas by conservatives more or less left the progressives without an agenda; there was no longer any point of theoretical confrontation. And more worryingly, there was a risk that a new generation of conservative mayors might pull the rug out from beneath the progressive mayors by hijacking their innovations, if only rhetorically.[196]

In time, Matsushita lamented the ritualization of participation *(sanka no gishikika)* in the Blue Sky Meetings of local mayors and even at the national level, as in Prime Minister Fukuda Takeo's budget making through popular participation *(kokumin sanka no yosan-zukuri)*.[197] Not that this was anything new, of course: many of the citizen participation initiatives during the 1960s and 1970s, such as Asukata's meetings of ten thousand citizens, had amounted to little more than tokenism. As Matsushita pointed out as early as 1971, citizens' movements had to vigilantly guard against the tendency to degenerate into auxiliary organizations *(gaikaku dantai)* for local administrations all in the name of *sanka*.[198]

Here Matsushita shared an unusual consonance with local activist Miyazaki Shōgo. Institutionalizing procedures for citizen participation within the overall structure of local administration, Miyazaki argued, acted as a kind of mass mobilization of the populace to reinforce *(hokyō)* the authority of the bureaucracy.[199] After all, by including hand-picked *shimin* representatives in various decision-making processes, bureaucrats could always forestall later complaints with the argument that citizens had been involved from the very outset and had no right to grumble once plans were set in motion. Citizen participation, Miyazaki concluded, was the current-day version of the wartime general mobilization structure *(sōdōin taisei)*.[200]

Though hardly as acerbic, Shinohara Hajime also recognized how citizen participation constantly faced the "enveloping maneuvers" of those in power. As he explained, the shrewd administrator would welcome the participation of citizens as a form of administrative economy *(tōsei no keizai)*. After all, even though participatory politics took longer, it was a far more energy efficient *(enerugī setsuyaku)* process than coercion.[201] Rather than contending with movements spontaneously mobilized from below, citizen participation empowered elites to mobilize citizens' movements strategically, pitting the one against the other and eventually eliminating opposition and winning popular support for themselves.[202] Even *shimin* champion Narumi Masayasu admitted that the idea and practice of citizen participation always had the potential for civic mobilization *(shimin no dōin)* through division.[203] In other words, it could become an ingenious device for separating out the good citizens *(yoki shimin)* from the bad citizens *(warui shimin)*—that is, the local egoists.[204] Because citizen participation put emphasis on the nurturing of civic reason *(shimin risei no ikusei)*, it was difficult, he admitted, to stop participation from morphing into cooperation or full-blown support *(kyōsan)*.[205]

Yet for all these concerns about citizen participation, Matsushita, Narumi, and others continued to believe in it as the most rational and practical way to forge authentic popular democracy in Japan. Indeed, by the late 1980s the idea of opposition and extrainstitutional protest had all but vanished from Matsushita's thought. In his 1987 *Toshigata Shakai no Jichi* (Self-Governance in Urban Society), he imagined a civic bureaucracy *(shimin gyōsei)* staffed by self-disciplined citizens providing voluntary and community activities and working side by side with the official bureaucracy and corporate Japan.[206] Matsushita confessed his hope that such volunteerism would replace the neighborhood and village associations of old.[207] Civic bureaucracy founded on volunteerism and community activities, he declared, would be a truly meaningful expression of civic self-governance *(shimin jichi)*.[208] On this point Matsushita remained unflinchingly confident: citizen participation and civil minimums were the most authentic and rational theories for a modern Japanese citizenry. Only there did *shimin* find their ethical and historical place.

WHITHER SELF-HELP AND PARTICIPATION?

How, then, are we to understand the wave of new movements and the drive for citizen participation of the 1960s and early 1970s? There is no doubt that antipollution and antidevelopment activism stimulated authorities to act legislatively and administratively to alleviate the downside of high-growth economics. Furthermore, the persistence of local protest up to the present shows how the new movements became an ideational resource for later activists, providing a kind of master frame for protest. As Jeffrey Broadbent has noted, "This continuance [of protest] indicates that once the progress frame had gotten tarnished, and the pollution frame had become widely recognized, environmentalism became a permanent part of the popular subculture."[209] In this respect, Ui Jun, Miyamoto Kenichi, Miyazaki Shōgo, Shinohara Hajime, and others certainly carved out a place for themselves in movement history, regardless of their sometimes conflicting perspectives.

But where there were positive legacies, there were also other, more complicated outcomes. As both Frank Upham and Miranda Schreurs point out, governmental support for pollution legislation was primarily about damage control—a means to cool down the wave of grassroots protest and, more to the point, to keep citizens out of the courts, where judicial decisions always threatened to narrow the boundaries of bureaucratic discretion. The government quickly enacted meaningful legislation and implemented a bureaucratic-led system to direct and control pollution disputes at the local level, effectively taking the "wind out of the sails" of the antipollution movement.[210] For some, such as Nakamura Kiichi, this damage control marked the beginning of what activists would call the ice age (*fuyu no jidai*, literally, "winter period") of citizens' movements, beginning (for him) roughly in 1978 with the forced opening of the new international airport in Chiba Prefecture. According to Nakamura, with the onslaught of modernity, the *jūmin* and ideas about localism and native language were driven almost to extinction. The bubble economy and the neoliberalism of the 1980s and beyond only served to weaken community ties further as private self-interest took center stage, he claimed. Moreover, the 1980s drive for internationalization *(kokusaika)*, he opined, also negatively affected localism, as the native language of local residents was forcefully rejected in favor of English—the language required to be truly human. The invasion of computers and mobile telephones drove a wedge between fellow residents who had previously gathered on the streets. What remained, in Nakamura's dark vision, was a hegemony of the *shimin* as a lone wolf in a neoliberal world. With the governmental turn to small government in the 1980s, Nakamura explained, also came an expectation that strong citizens *(tsuyoi shimin)* would emerge in regional society. The dense localism *(nōkōna chiikisei)* of residents was diluted by citizens, and the locality became a universal space governed by the market *(shijō ga shihai suru fuhenteki na kūkan)*. For Nakamura, in a civil society ruled by a Hegelian system of desires, the rise of the *shimin* gave birth to a world of survival of the fittest and the appearance of winners and losers.[211]

Nakamura's dark vision of a neoliberal future for civil society rings true in some respects, but we need to modify his somewhat-oversimplified juxtaposition of *jūmin* and *shimin*. As I argued throughout the chapter, though Marxists, localists, and the citizen faction disagreed on the objectives of the new movements, many points of commonality also fed into later imaginations of the *shimin* and civil society. In particular, theorists' collective endorsement of self-help and political instrumentalism proved useful for a new generation of activists who imagined the triangular relationship among the state, the market, and civil society in terms of cooperation, proposal of alternatives, and self-responsibility. On this level, theorists in all political camps were implicated, not only the citizen faction. While the pollution and antidevelopment movements of the 1960s and early 1970s did indeed fashion a model for later protest, they also articulated and concretized ideas—such as local self-help—which could and would be used to legitimize and nurture social activism tailored to the needs of a neoliberal age.

What then of citizen participation? Let me continue for a moment with the thought of Nakamura Kiichi, because it provides a wonderful arc from this chapter to the next. In the beginning of the 1970s, he explained, activism was all about protecting the local environment and challenging bureaucratic definitions of the public interest. At the base of this was a strong localism (chiikisei) and sense of self-governance (jichi). But in the late 1970s, Nakamura suggested, local government politics (jichitai seiji) gave way to local government management (jichitai keiei), and with this residents' movements acquiesced to a new, more palatable form of activism called citizens' activities (shimin katsudō). Nakamura lamented how these new citizens' groups forfeited the tense relationship established between local bureaucrats and residents' movements, essentially discarding any vestige of autonomy from the bureaucracy. Many citizens' groups, he argued, were enveloped and utilized by local officials, because their stance of cooperation sanctioned such incestuous ties. Although Nakamura did not reject state-civil society relationships outright, he was deeply troubled by the hegemony of a discourse in which citizens' activities were seamlessly attached to the bureaucracy. It was as though no one even suspected that civic energies could be subcontracted by the state all in the name of maximizing the vitality of the "private sector." In time, Nakamura argued, the symbolic and institutionalized vessel of citizens' activities, the NPO (nonprofit organization), came to be seen as the leading actor in civil society. Not only did the government call for cooperation between NPOs and the bureaucracy; it also facilitated greater incorporation through institutional and legal reform.

To put my own spin on Nakamura's interpretation, we might say that the state began to recalibrate its mode of governance over civic groups by endorsing some of the key aspects of the citizen movement paradigm, such as self-help, autonomy, participation, and institutionalization—a story I trace in the following chapter.[212]

So as much as citizen participation proposed a method for popular political participation, in the hands of shrewd officials it also had the potential to become a legitimizing ideology and method for the incorpo-ration and domestication of civic energies. It is worth noting that in the coming decades citizen participation manifested itself not only or even primarily as a device for open political debate between administrators and citizens but also as a tool for coordinating civic energies into social welfare and community-building *(machizukuri)* activities.[213] In other words, citizen participation ultimately had much more to do with the infusion of civic energies into social service than it did with the institu-tionalization of civic advocacy. Though Matsushita and others had another future in mind, their grand theorizations and policy interven-tions of the 1960s and 1970s undoubtedly fed into such developments.

By the 1980s, the *shimin* idea had come a long way theoretically and in practice, thanks to the interventions of citizen faction intellectuals, local activists, and supportive Marxist onlookers. But the story of the *shimin* does not end here. What we need to keep in mind is that from the perspective of activists and progressive intellectuals in the mid-1970s, the *shimin* paradigm remained very much an emblem for the project to fumigate conservative domination and bring about true democracy. The paradoxical potentialities I have identified in *shimin* thought and citizen activism remained latent, and they are visible to us only with the perspective of hindsight. To explain how the latent became overt, we need to reconstruct a fascinating process in which changing institutional priorities intersected with a new approach to civic activism at the grass roots. As I show in chapter 5, the period from around 1975 to 1995 witnessed an interesting meeting of the minds among bureaucrats, corporate elites, politicians, private think tanks, and leading civic movement intellectuals. Picking up the theoreti-cal, symbolic, and tactical tools of their forebears and dismissing the more unpalatable and contentious aspects of the past, these groups began to converge around a vision of the new citizen, or *shin-shimin,* transcendent of protest and located within a communitarian civil society of symbiosis, self-help, and full-scale marketization.

CHAPTER 5

Shimin, New Civic Movements, and the Politics of Proposal

Compared with back then (ten years ago), the meaning of
the term *shimin* has changed. There is no need to get caught
up in past complications.

—Deliberative Council on National Lifestyle, 2006

A NEW PARADIGM FOR CIVIC ACTIVISM

In the mid-1970s, citizen activism in Japan was at a crossroads—or, at
the very least, many at the time seemed to have thought so.[1] Pointing
to the waning of local protest, some observers predicted a period of
decline *(taichōki)* and even the onset of an ice age *(fuyu no jidai)* for
citizens' movements.[2] In 1976, the *Asahi Yearbook* noted how people
had begun to speak of the bells of winter *(fuyu no fūrin)* for residents'
movements, as though a glorious age of protest was slowly drawing to
a close.[3] There is no doubt that civic activism began to change substan-
tively and ideationally in the mid-1970s: movements of protest did
decline, and in their wake emerged a generation of new civic movements championing constructive activism and engagement with former
foes. A number of factors fueled this shift. First, bureaucrats at all levels
of government had a palpable impact, on the one hand, by preempting,
obstructing, or otherwise preventing widespread protest and, on the
other, by reaching out to groups whose vision of civic activism matched
their own policy objectives. The waning of environmental protest in
the mid-1970s, for example, is largely attributable to state intervention:
first, via stringent legislation that remedied many of the problems, and
second, through the establishment of a system for bureaucratic
mediation that diffused conflicts before they escalated into protest
or litigation.[4]

Governmental response to the student movement also had a great influence on activists in the new civic movements in the 1970s. Many civic activists of the 1970s cut their activist teeth in the student movement, and—as the metaphor implies—this had not been a wholly painless experience. Some became disenchanted with extremism—a disenchantment greatly intensified by the negative public backlash and the rapid and often-violent response of the state. Emerging from this experience and in many cases from jail time, these former student radicals began to recalibrate their approach to the state and market. As some of them would later explain, radicalism had simply failed and needed to be replaced by strategies that took civic groups inside the state-business nexus, from where they could launch a guerrilla-style program (albeit a peaceful one) for fundamental social change.

The attitudes of bureaucrats and corporate elites toward certain forms of activism underwent change at the same time, influenced in no small way by the spread of policies for citizen participation in local administrations throughout the nation. Moreover, faced with lower economic growth after the first oil shock and a rapidly aging population, bureaucrats (especially in welfare) began to actively support independent forms of volunteering and civic activism in the 1970s. Their evolving vision of a new community of civic-minded and self-motivated citizens from this time resonated with and, indeed, helped to legitimize influential activists' embryonic message about civic activism based on proposing and constructing alternatives.

Corporate actors also began to forge a new relationship with the civic sector in the early 1970s, reaching out to receptive movement intellectuals and sponsoring grassroots initiatives. The memory of vociferous environmental protest no doubt fed into the changing corporate mindset, but important too was the experience of Japanese companies in the United States, where philanthropy was both expected and tax beneficial. The new civic movements benefited greatly from corporate logistical and financial support, which raised their public profile and enabled them to forge influential movement networks. State and corporate actors helped to shape civic activism, then, through a combined strategy of prevention on the one hand and carefully guided empowerment on the other.

But, as I argue in this chapter, the changes in civic activism and the rise of new civic movements beginning in the mid-1970s in Japan are not wholly explained by contingent historical factors, state and corporate intervention, or even public disillusionment with contentious activism. Historical actors—movement intellectuals—intervened at this moment, articulating a bold new vision of the *shimin* idea centered on notions of creative, engaged, and financially sustainable activism. These new citizens *(shin-shimin)*, as later pundits would call them, propagated a pervasive logic of proposal-style *(teian-gata)* civic activism. They contrasted their new movements, which pursued alternatives to mainstream practices and institutions (e.g., organic farming, recycling, welfare volunteerism), rather crudely with protest groups of the 1960s and the early 1970s, which had supposedly adopted losing strategies of opposition and bureaucratic dependence. They argued that true movement autonomy would come about only through nuts-and-bolts activism and pragmatic engagement with the state, the market, and society in general. Beginning in the 1970s and increasingly in the 1980s, activists injected their model into movements for the disabled, women, the elderly, foreigners, social welfare, health, education, community businesses, food and agriculture, ecology, international cooperation, peace, and human rights.

A 1992 Toyota Foundation pamphlet, aptly titled *Jiritsu to Kyōsei o Mezashite* (In Pursuit of Autonomy and Symbiosis), neatly summed up the new mindset: absolute opposition and struggle against political oppression may have been necessary in the past, but citizens' movements that merely opposed for the sake of opposition *(hantai no tame no hantai)* were inevitably drawn into a quagmire without solving anything. The role of citizens' movements now, the report concluded, was to present problems to society and come up with solutions.[5] Structural conditions certainly facilitated this 1970s shift in civic activism, but change happened, I argue, only when movement intellectuals identified new social needs, articulated a novel vision, and actively mobilized people into a new generation of civic movements.

These movement intellectuals by no means spoke for every civic group, and not all movements bought in to the new mindset, preferring to remain resolutely undomesticated. But absolute consensus was not necessary for the new logic to become dominant. Moreover, as we saw in Beheiren, the Tosei Chōsakai, and some antidevelopment movements and as I explore further in this chapter, the new mindset in civic activism also had much to do with activists' own self-reflexive interrogation of daily life. The notion of constructive activism was not merely a knee-jerk reaction to institutional barriers; it was also born out of a long postwar tradition in which movement intellectuals called on activists to think about their own complicity, responsibility, and duty with respect to social, economic, and political problems. Recall the refrain of the father of Terashima Fumio, the Green Association founder, that there was no trusting a man unable to swipe a fly away from his face. This mindset's harmony with bureaucratic and corporate designs for civic activism and its endorsement—albeit unintentional—of the domestication and institutionalization of civic activism in postwar Japan should not blind us to the important role of movement intellectuals in shaping this trajectory of activism from the 1970s onward.

In this chapter I trace the emergence of new civic groups from the 1970s onward. I am interested in the philosophy articulated and put into practice by influential movement intellectuals and the ways in which their model shaped the civic movement sector in Japan. Like earlier civic groups, the new civic movements beginning in the 1970s can be understood as a Japanese form of the new social movements so prevalent in industrialized nations since the 1960s. The focus of movement intellectuals on issues of daily life, their attention to nonclass identities, and their preference for practical initiatives are all quintessential elements of the NSMs. Leading activists' emphasis on self-reflexivity—approaching social, political, and economic issues first through personal self-examination—also lends credence to an NSM reading of these movements.

Nevertheless, in this chapter, as I have done throughout the study, I set aside the NSM paradigm for two reasons. First, much of what movement intellectuals claimed to be new about their movements actually drew liberally on elements of earlier *shimin* thought and activism, especially notions of self-help, participation, nation, and community. To be fair, their use of these ideas drove civic activism in new directions and into new spheres of activity, but that use was hardly a sudden rupture from earlier movement practice. Second, the new civic movements and their leaders effected changes that NSM theory—with its progressive assumptions about civic activism—simply cannot explain. Movement intellectuals' lionization of constructive activism and their demonization of contentious politics, while understandable, clearly had a number of deleterious outcomes. Not only did this logic tend to marginalize those groups whose agendas were either incompatible with or hostile toward the state and the market; it also reinforced bureaucratic and corporate imaginations of civil society as a harmonious space for socially contributive initiatives by largely apolitical civic groups. Movement intellectuals in the new civic movements certainly set out to remedy the excesses of Japan's Iron Triangle, but their ideas and activities facilitated an ironic convergence with the very institutions they had set out to transcend. What they gained in social legitimacy they arguably lost in the sphere of ethical political dissent.

Below, I trace this convergence from three perspectives: the state, the new civic movements, and corporate Japan. Though developments came in fits and starts and not everyone agreed, starting in the 1970s we can see a gradual meeting of the minds about the significance and meaning of civic activism and, more broadly, civil society. By the late 1980s there was a broad consensus among bureaucrats, interested political and corporate actors, and influential movement intellectuals about the utility of the new civic groups and the necessity for regulatory reform. This consensus fed into and fueled the political movement for nonprofit legislation allowing certain civic groups to incorporate— something eventually realized in 1998 and heralded as an epoch-making moment in state-society relations in Japan.

STATE PROMOTION OF CIVIC ACTIVISM

Historians and other social scientists have noted the long-term and extensive nature of state involvement with civic groups throughout modern Japanese history.[6] Even if we limit our purview to the new constitutional regime of the postwar period, intensive state involvement has continued through regulation, official appointments, subsidies, subcontracting, brute force on occasion, and a variety of informal means. To give just a few examples: until legal reform in the late 1990s, Japanese civil society organizations faced a strict regulatory regime under the Civil Code—a legal straitjacket, as Pekkanen puts it.[7] The Civil Code gave the state great leverage over the kinds of groups that were afforded legal legitimacy and significant powers with respect to oversight of their operations. In the early years of the postwar period, state ministries, in addition to wielding their regulatory powers, began to reconstitute and establish various forms of so-called state-appointed volunteers (gyōsei ishoku borantia). The list is too extensive to reproduce here, but examples—some of which trace their roots back hundreds of years—include district welfare commissioners (minsei-iin), voluntary probation officers (hogoshi), youth guidance officers (shōnen shidōin), and the ubiquitous voluntary firefighting groups (shōbōdan). The state has also mobilized various local groups—notably neighborhood associations—for initiatives such as recycling, cleaning, and community policing. State officials have been particularly active in promoting forms of welfare volunteerism, working through the National Volunteer Promotion Center (NVPC) and the thousands of affiliated local volunteer centers.

Given the great diversification of civic activism since the 1970s, the diversity of state responses that we see is not surprising. Many officials' initial encounter with the new civic groups was in the context of protest, beginning with the Anpo struggle in 1960, then stretching into the Beheiren movement and later into the thousands of antipollution and antidevelopment protests.[8] As we have seen, by the late 1960s, corporations and government officials were faced not only with a plethora of troublesome local mobilizations but also with worrisome citizen-initiated court cases that threatened the crown jewel of bureaucratic discretion and the sovereignty of progrowth policies. Officials dealt with antipollution and antidevelopment protest in a number of ways: regulatory reform (notably the Pollution Diet of 1970), the establishment of nonjudicial, bureaucratic-led mechanisms for dispute resolution, and policies promoting citizen participation. Though only partly successful and often tokenistic, these early experiments served as models for later interactions between the new civic groups and state officials, especially at the local level. Furthermore, as Sheldon Garon explains, after the first oil shock of 1973, many civic groups and bureaucrats "discovered common ground" in "conservation and restraints on mass consumption." Significantly, local governments "appropriated the language and organization" of the new civic groups, promoting initiatives such as "tidying up parks, furnishing school-crossing guards, or helping the elderly."[9] So, though many of these groups began quite spontaneously, officials moved quickly to forge linkages with the ones engaged in potentially useful activities.

Governmental interest in the new civic groups of the 1970s also needs to be understood in the context of a cluster of linked debates among elites: the so-called reconsideration of welfare *(fukushi minaoshiron)*, the aging society *(kōreika shakai)* problem, and the official movement for administrative reform.[10] One of the key concepts to emerge from these debates was that of a Japanese-style welfare society *(Nihongata fukushi shakai)*. Rather than blindly following the welfare states of the West, Japan would apparently draw on the creative vitality inherent in liberal economies while pursuing a path unique (and apparently most suited) to the country. In this story, welfare provision—*Japanese* style—was to proceed through individual self-help efforts and the solidarity of regional society, neighbors, and family (i.e., housewives), thereby avoiding the pitfalls of Western welfare states or, more color-fully, afflictions such as the "English Disease."[11] Of course, as John Campbell and others note, state provision of certain welfare goods continued to expand, and Japan in many ways came to resemble the welfare states of the West.[12]

But the idea of Japanese-style welfare was not all rhetoric or a "warmed-over version of Thatcherism or Reaganism."[13] In the reformist context of the Second Temporary Commission on Administrative Reform, or Rinchō, the idea evolved into the conceptualization of a dynamic welfare society *(katsuryoku aru fukushi shakai)* and later into a citizen-participation-style welfare society *(shimin sanka-gata fukushi shakai)*, both of which spoke to notions of self-help *(jijo)*, autonomy *(jiritsu)*, and self-responsibility *(jiko sekinin)*—ideas that state officials and activists themselves had long championed. As Kōroki Hiroshi later explained, the state became more and more interested in the use of volunteers in the 1970s, when welfare services for the elderly and other groups in need shifted from an emphasis on government-run institutions to local and community care. Throughout this period the nurturing of volunteerism slowly moved its way up the policy agenda at both regional and national levels. At the time, Kōroki explains, bureaucrats were not ready to characterize volunteerism as a citizens' movement, nor did they accept the logic of volunteerism as a tool for the creation of autonomous citizens *(jiritsu shita shimin)*. Their preferred language was *mutual support (tasukeai)* and *goodwill activities (zen'i no katsudō)*.[14] Over time, however, bureaucrats came to embrace the symbolism of the *shimin* and civil society, especially the communitarianism implicit in earlier ideas of citizen participation.

One concrete outcome of the Japanese-style welfare discourse was an intensive effort on the part of welfare bureaucrats to foster and promote widespread civic engagement in volunteerism. The state continued its support for institutionalized volunteerism via a plethora of state appointees: counselors for the disabled *(shintai shōgaisha sōdanin)*; counselors for the mentally ill *(chiteki shōgaisha sōdanin)*; women's counselors *(fujin sōdanin)*; family counselors *(katei sōdanin)*; district welfare commissioners *(minsei-iin)*; childcare commissioners *(jidō-iin)*; single-mothers' counselors *(boshi sōdanin)*, and so forth. But in the 1970s officials also began to take notice of and support the growing number of spontaneously formed volunteer groups. A 1976 survey by the NVPC found that, *excluding* state appointees, some 3.4 million volunteers existed nationwide, 1.2 million of whom belonged to independent volunteer groups.[15] Such statistics were crucial in convincing welfare and other bureaucrats of the benefits of promoting certain kinds of new civic groups. Nowhere is the state response to new civic groups more evident than in the national government's promotion of independent volunteerism in the 1970s and the various state surveys and reports on the new civic groups in the 1980s.

Consider first the myriad of state policies for the promotion of independent welfare volunteerism and volunteer groups. In the early 1970s, what was then the Ministry of Health and Welfare (MHW) began proactively supporting the establishment of volunteer centers throughout the nation. These centers had their roots in the early 1960s, when social welfare council *(shakai fukushi kyōgikai,* or *shakyō)* offices in Oita and Tokushima prefectures established so-called Goodwill Banks (Zen'i Ginkō) to provide logistical and financial support for welfare-focused volunteer groups. In 1963 there were 530 of these banks nationwide, and by 1971 the number had increased to around 1,200.[16] State support for the volunteer centers came in stages: financing for 84 centers in prefectures and specified municipalities in 1973; funding for the establishment of centers in 289 municipalities in 1975; and funding for the upgrading of the Central Volunteer Center (est. 1975), which became the NVPC in 1977.[17] In 1985 the MHW instituted the Volunteer Community Building Project (Fukushi Borantia no Machizukuri), or Voluntopia (combining *volunteer* and *utopia;* Borantopia in Japanese), in which selected volunteer centers received state subsidies. With the stated aim of excavating and nurturing a new generation of volunteers, these funds were used to establish Volunteer Activities Promotion Councils (Borantia Katsudō Suishin Kyōgikai) in municipal *shakyō* offices; to expand volunteer educational programs (called volunteer schools); to increase volunteer registration; and to promote various volunteer-organization-building projects.[18] Such state funding for independent citizen volunteers and groups continues to the present.

OFFICIAL CONCEPTUALIZATIONS OF THE NEW CIVIC GROUPS

Together with increased funding for volunteerism, state surveying and reporting on the new civic groups—especially in the 1980s—also reflected the growing official interest in tapping into the energies of the new civic movements. Particularly fascinating is the perceptible shift from an overtly managerial tone in the reports of the early 1970s, when the official stance was one of *dealing* with citizen groups, to a language of individual empowerment and self-responsibility in a participation-style welfare society by the late 1980s and early 1990s. In 1968, a landmark report of the Japan National Council of Social Welfare (Zenkoku Shakai Fukushi Kyōgikai, or Zenshakyō) lamented how urbanization and the growth of nuclear families had undermined traditional institutions of mutual support, such as extended families and neighborhood units. At the same time, citizens now demanded higher-quality social welfare services, but given chronic welfare labor shortages, the current system could simply not provide such support.[19] The bottom line was that such demands could be adequately met only through new forms of volunteerism. Although the report spoke of the need for a strong consciousness of civic solidarity *(tsuyoi shiminteki rentai ishiki)* in groups, its overall tone was still rather managerial. For instance, *shakyō* officials and volunteer leaders were instructed to strive intentionally and purposefully to connect the naïve goodwill and voluntary cooperation of citizens to the problems and spaces in most need of them. This naïve goodwill of volunteers, it warned, was not always appropriate or immediately useful for social welfare, and, hence, the correct development *(tadashii hatten)* of volunteerism would depend greatly on officials' ability to coordinate and unify voluntary activities, which, ironically, it defined as independent activity based on "spontaneity."[20]

In 1984 the MHW *Kōsei Hakusho (White Paper on Welfare)* discussed volunteerism in the context of dealing with escalating welfare demands. In the sphere of welfare, the *White Paper* pointed out, voluntary activities were shouldering an ever more important role; however, according to a survey conducted by the prime minister's office at the time, although some 60 percent of respondents were interested in volunteer activities, only 23 percent had actually participated. The key then, according to the report, was to facilitate the participation of the remaining 77 percent through government funding for volunteer centers, the provision of volunteer insurance, and the promotion of volunteerism among youth, housewives, and the elderly.[21]

The MHW devoted another large section of its 1991 *White Paper* to volunteerism, but the most forceful push came in 1993, when the MHW, its Central Deliberative Council on Social Welfare (Chūō Shakai Fukushi Shingikai), and Zenshakyō released a series of interlinked reports on the importance and promotion of independent welfare volunteerism. As the report by the Deliberative Council indicated, the official aim was now threefold: to make volunteerism "easy" and "enjoyable" "whenever," "wherever," and by "whomever"; to have one-quarter of the people participating in volunteerism by the end of the century; and, in the long term, to have the majority of the population volunteering.[22] To this end, the government and *shakyō* offices would promote a whole range of initiatives, including welfare education starting in childhood, conferences to promote voluntary activity, programs for the elderly and disabled, more volunteer centers, the appointment of three hundred thousand volunteer advisers and thirty thousand volunteer coordinators, the promotion of paid employee volunteer leave, and more funding for volunteerism throughout the country. Rather than a Japanese-style welfare society, centered on the extended family and traditional community organizations, the objective now was a participation-style welfare society *(sanka-gata fukushi shakai)*, based on partnership *(pātonāshipu)* and collaboration *(kyōdō)* between the state and new forms of volunteerism and civic activism.[23]

According to MHW official Kobayashi Masahiko, the emergence of this discourse of volunteer participation reflected the trend away from volunteerism as simple service *(hōshi)* to volunteerism as participation in policymaking and implementation by autonomous citizens.[24] Perhaps this is true, but we should also keep in mind the concrete government policies fueling the participation-style welfare society. Citizens may well have been spontaneously forming new civic groups to address challenges in local communities, but welfare bureaucrats were also crafting policies to promote and shape such activities, all the while singing the praises of civic autonomy *(shiminteki jiritsu)*.

The MHW and Zenshakyō officials were not the only state institutions interested in the new civic groups and independent volunteerism. Indeed, the Economic Planning Agency crafted the broadest and most comprehensive vision of this emergent sphere in government circles from the 1970s onward. EPA officials' interest in civic activism began as early as 1969, when the influential Deliberative Council on National Lifestyle (CNL) released a report titled *Komyuniti: Seikatsu no Ba ni okeru Ningensei no Kaifuku* (Community: The Restoration of Humanity in the Space of Daily Life).[25] But not until 1981 did the agency initiate a systematic investigation of civic activism with its comprehensive survey on volunteerism. The survey revealed that the number of independent civic groups engaged in social welfare was on the rise, especially in urban areas—an important message given official concerns about aging and welfare provision. In a 1983 report, the CNL announced that in the future improvements in national welfare would have to be conceptualized through a combination of activities in both the formal and informal sectors.[26] The report defined independent social participation activities (the EPA's term for the new civic groups) quite broadly as "independent participation by people with a common objective in a group in the informal sector" and suggested that the role of the bureaucracy was to support such activities through the provision of facilities, personnel, information, and subsidies. Important too, the report added, would be the creation of a relationship of trust between such groups and a bureaucracy respectful of their independence.[27] Thereafter the EPA and its CNL continued to publish and release statements on a range of connected issues, including volunteer trading systems (1990); special employee volunteer leave (1991); a volunteer credit system (1992); volunteerism for schoolchildren (1992); methods for promoting civic activism, such as tax exemptions on donations (1992); and retraining for civic activism after retirement (1993).

The culmination of these ideas was articulated in a 1994 report of the CNL aptly titled *Jikaku to Sekinin no aru Shakai e* (Toward a Society of Self-Awareness and Responsibility). Replete with terms such as *autonomy (jiritsu)* and *self-responsibility (jiko sekinin)*, the report explained how constructive involvement in social participation activities depended greatly on people's civic consciousness *(shimin ishiki)*. Since the government could not manage everything, it was now up to each and every Japanese national *(kokumin)* and citizen *(shimin)* (the report used both terms side by side without distinguishing them) to make constructive efforts for the creation of society.[28] Citizens had to realize that they received benefits from society and, hence, must give something in return. Japanese society, the report explained, had to move away from the negative cycles of dependence and irresponsibility and reliance and criticism (the CNL's characterization of earlier contentious citizen activism) toward the positive cycle of self-responsibility and mutual trust (the CNL's depiction of the new civic groups).[29] Particularly important in the context of an aging society, the report suggested, would be the role of welfare volunteers and private nonprofit activities.[30] Through such activities people would apparently stimulate their consciousness as citizens *(shimin toshite no ishiki)* and help create a civil society *(shimin shakai)* based on self-awareness and responsibility.[31] The relationship among state, market, and nonprofit sector, as a result, would purportedly move to a new level of engagement based on relations of cooperation *(kyōchō kankei)* and partnership *(pātonāshipu)*—all the while preserving a healthy yet critical distance among the three *(kinchō kankei).*[32]

Apart from reflecting bureaucratic hopes for the new activism, the 1994 report evidences how much bureaucrats had incorporated the language and aspirations of new civic groups by the 1990s. Whereas official discussions about volunteerism in the 1970s and 1980s often spoke about state support and guidance for civic activism—the legacy of an age when officials felt they needed to *deal* with civic groups—articulations were far more sophisticated by the early 1990s. The 1994 report, for instance, stressed that the state would need to ease regulations in order to nurture self-responsibility and civic consciousness. Specifically, the report envisaged the creation of a legal framework to support incorporated nonprofit organizations and facilitate them with preferential tax treatment.[33] The important point, however, is that the state was actively involved in supporting and legitimizing certain forms of new civic activism from the 1970s onward. Moreover, ideationally, it adopted and adapted the language of new civic groups (itself the legacy of some three decades of *shimin* thought and activism), directing it into a rhetoric of community self-help in an age of self-responsibility.

MOVEMENT INTELLECTUALS DEFINING A NEW AGENDA

State agencies certainly reached out to volunteers, citizen activists, and civil society advocates from the 1970s onward, but their efforts would have amounted to very little had it not been for an influential group of citizen movement intellectuals who advocated a new approach to civic activism and a reworked vision of the *shimin* idea. As I indicated, around the mid-1970s observers began pointing to a rhetorical and substantive change in citizen activism in Japan. Although evidence of the mood swing is anecdotal, we get a good sense of it in the pages of the *Asahi Jyānaru,* Japan's highest circulating progressive weekly at the time. At the height of the environmental protest movement in 1971, the magazine published a list of citizen movements boldly titled "The Fermenting Wave of Resistance," but in 1986 it announced the arrival of a "new wave of daily life proposal-style citizens' movements" in an article of that title.[34] This latter article optimistically explained how in every sphere such movements were proposing and putting into practice an alternative *(orutānatibu)* lifestyle and an alternative society. As these new citizen groups critically inspected the crises unfolding deep within Japan's affluent society, they were "attempting to create—in a bright and enjoyable way—a new kind of daily life, work, and society."[35] In the same article, the young recycling guru Takami Yūichi noted how, until recently, citizens' movements had been all about criticism *(hihan)*, struggle *(tōsō)*, and accusation *(kokuhatsu)*. He pointed to the frustration of the student movement and the supposed dogmatism, shadiness, and crudeness of the consumer movement as the negative outcomes of these "flawed" strategies. Though earlier antipollution movements certainly had needed to criticize, for Takami student and consumer activism proved that such strategies would not bring an end to environmental destruction and pollution. Takami believed that a fundamental change in values and lifestyles was the one and only key.[36]

Elsewhere, the organic food distributor Fujita Kazuyoshi promoted the new civic movements as a kind of remedy to earlier student insurgency, which he portrayed as wholly self-destructive—quite understandably, because Fujita had spent time behind bars for his own student radicalism.[37] From a more humanitarian perspective, an advocate of the disabled, Harima Yasuo, portrayed the new movements as an attempt to revive symbiotic—as opposed to contentious—human relationships, which had been destroyed by the rationalism of the market and the state.[38] And finally, for Iwane Kunio and Yokota Katsumi, of the progressive consumer cooperative Seikatsu Club, citizen activism was to be a vehicle for the creation of an alternative Gramscian-style hegemony that would eventually transcend the evil of modern (i.e., Western) capitalism. Though each had his own ideological idiosyncrasies, all of these activists were united by a flagrant, and often somewhat contradictory, realism when it came to activism: to effect change against the might of the bureaucracy and big business, they argued, movements simply had to abandon criticism and struggle for strategies of engagement, participation, and proposal.[39]

Of course, as I indicated above, not all activists agreed, and contentious movements continued to mobilize sporadically thereafter. It would be wrong to claim that these individuals spoke for the totality of the civic movement sector. Nevertheless, I argue that these movements and the model of social activism they promoted came to dominate not only public discussion of civic activism and civil society in the coming decades but also the internal dynamics of a great many civic groups in the country.

From the mid-1970s onward, we see nothing short of the rhetorical overshadowing—if not the thorough delegitimization—of contentious strategies by activists and advocates intent on promoting a refurbished vision of the *shimin* idea and civil society. Some proclamations have an almost Wellsian science-fiction-like ambience, such as the 1988 report titled *Dokokade Nanikaga Hajimatteiru!? Suimenkade Ugomeku Mōhitotsu no Shakai Keisei e no Kokoromi* (Something Is Starting Somewhere!? Squirming below the Surface: An Attempt to Establish an Alternative Society), by the Toyota Foundation program officer Watanabe Gen.[40] Here Watanabe traced the new civic groups to the resistance *(teikō)* and accusation *(kokuhatsu)* movements of the 1960s, born of rapid industrialization and urbanization and led by individuals attempting to defend their life spaces from the distortions *(hizumi)* of the social system. Over time these adversaries (government and business versus the civic movement sector) had come to recognize their mutual interests and, at times, were even able to cooperate *(kyōryoku suru)*. Civic activists realized there was a limit to opposition *(tairitsu)* and discord *(kattō)*, and state and corporate actors accepted that they could no longer ignore the situation of citizens. This signaled a mutual recognition on both sides in Watanabe's telling and in the late 1970s set the stage for participatory *(sanka-gata)* movements that united citizens and bureaucrats in constructive initiatives, such as community-building projects *(machizukuri)*.

Building on this base in the 1980s, a new kind of activism—a creative *(sōzōteki)* and autonomous type *(jiritsu-gata)*—emerged in which civic groups not only solved problems by themselves but also proposed and implemented an alternative set of principles for daily life *(mōhitotsu no seikatsu genri)*. Three things distinguished the new groups for Watanabe: the belief that activism should be enjoyable; the commitment to financially self-sustaining organizations; and the pragmatic approach to political and economic institutions.[41] Watanabe's characterizations were more or less on target, although I would add one more element: the oft-articulated stance that civic groups should create, propose, and collaborate rather than protest, complain, and oppose. In a sense, this was merely a sophisticated restatement of the "good citizen–bad citizen" dynamic first articulated in the 1960s and early 1970s by progressive politicians and *shimin-ha* intellectuals, such as Matsushita Keiichi. What differed now, of course, was that the voices of the so-called bad citizens— the Miyazaki Shōgos of the world—were almost inaudible, drowned out by a mellifluous chorus of good citizens advocating positive activism.

That said, civic activism did indeed expand and diversify from the mid-1970s onward. Data from the time, such as movement networking lists and *minikomi* publications, evidence a range of new groups engaged in community building *(machizukuri)*, environmental protection, international aid and cooperation, organic farming, consumer cooperatives, social welfare, and cultural activities.[42] The question of why these movements appeared when they did is complex. Changing values and expectations brought about by affluence no doubt played a role, as did new issues arising from the shift to advanced industrialization—issues such as aging, low fertility rates, and environmental degradation. Urban movements—especially progressive daily life consumer cooperatives— clearly benefited from affluence, drawing their membership from a stratum of relatively affluent housewives (what Matsushita Keiichi had earlier called the new middle stratum). The state, as I discussed above, contributed by bringing some of these issues to the forefront of public consciousness and actively engaging with cooperative grassroots groups. When bureaucrats realized the limitations of the extended family as the provider of Japanese-style welfare, for example, they slowly began to engage with civic groups providing in-home welfare services and the like, eventually making it possible for these groups to enter the welfare provision sector formally.

State support also contributed to the growth of international non-governmental organizations (NGOs) in Japan during the 1980s and 1990s.[43] As Kim Reimann has shown, beginning in the late 1980s state recognition of and financial support for international development NGOs increased noticeably as bureaucrats accepted international norms for the role of nongovernmental groups in global issues; in other words, pressure from without facilitated a change in state attitudes.[44] The corporate sector also played a role. Economic expansion abroad exposed Japanese companies to new ideas about corporate citizenship and philanthropy, prompting some—such as the automaker Toyota— to establish funding foundations similar to the Ford Foundation and other organizations in the United States. In 1990, Keidanren (the Federation of Economic Organizations) established its 1% Club after conducting a mission to investigate corporate philanthropy in the United States. Individual and corporate members of the club contribute 1 percent of disposable income or operating profits to socially worthwhile causes and third sector activities. A year later, in 1991, Keidanren established the Social Contribution Division (Shakai Kōkenbu) to deal full time with corporate social responsibility activities (CSR).[45] Reflecting this "civicization" of the corporate sector, in 1990 the Japan Management Association (Nihon Nōritsu Kyōkai) warned members that, in the future, companies without the support of *"shimin"* would simply "not be able to survive."[46] All of these factors—affluence, value change, new issues, the state, the corporate sector, and international pressures—either directly or indirectly provided stimulus for the new civic movements starting in the 1970s.

But, in keeping with my ideational focus, here I stress the important role of prominent movement intellectuals and their progenitor movements in providing a rationale and a model for the new wave of activism. By progenitor I refer not only to the novelty of the issues and tactics of such movements but also, and just as important, to the high-profile role these movements played in promoting a reconfigured—some might say neutralized—vision of civic activism.[47] In other words, these were the movements that intentionally blended the *shimin* idea with notions of collaboration, proposal, alternatives, and symbiosis, at the same time rebuffing strategies of contention, protest, and opposition. The high profile of their leaders and their role in key events and organizations brought these movements to the center of attempts to reconfigure the *shimin* idea and citizen activism in the 1970s.

Consider first the Association to Protect the Earth (Daichi o Mamoru Kai, or Daichi), established by the former student activist Fujita Kazuyoshi and his colleagues in 1974. Working in publishing after his release from prison in the early 1970s, the twenty-seven-year-old Fujita became concerned with agricultural pesticide use. After unsuccessfully approaching numerous urban consumer co-ops, Fujita and a friend—in concert with Tochigi Prefecture farmers—began to sell organic daikon radishes in Tokyo. The enterprise proved a success, and in mid-1975 Fujita, together with some three hundred producers and consumers, formed Daichi, or as it was then known, the Citizens' Association to Protect the Earth (Daichi o Mamoru Shimin no Kai). Joined by the former Zengakuren leader Fujimoto Toshio after his release from jail and financially supported by Fujimoto's celebrity wife, the folksinger Katō Tokiko, Fujita incorporated the movement in 1977 as a stock company *(kabushikigaisha)*, with Katō as the major shareholder. Eventually Daichi managed to buy back and redistribute shares to movement members and staffers, mostly on a single-share basis—an egalitarian practice it borrowed from Beheiren's earlier single-share protest against Mitsubishi Heavy Industries. Fujita envisioned his movement as different from consumer cooperatives, of which Daichi was extremely critical. Instead, Daichi's leaders presented it as a kind of neutral intermediary between easily egoistic consumers on the one hand and victimized farmers on the other. As Fujita explained, Daichi aimed at protecting both agriculture and the global environment. To this day it continues to eschew consumer imagery, promoting itself instead as a for-profit company defending daily life and the environment through grassroots networking.[48]

At the time of its inception in the mid-1970s, Daichi was emblematic of the new movements on numerous levels, not least of which was Fujita's characterization of earlier social activism as involving nothing but accusation *(kokuhatsu)* and self-gratification *(jiko manzoku)* and lacking any substantial connection to everyday life *(nichijō no kurashi-kata).*[49] "Our '60s- and '70s-style struggles were an attempt to overcome modernism *(kindaishugi),*" Fujita concluded, "but looking back, I don't think we ever transcended the framework of modernism we were trying to overcome."[50] Fujita told of how he "shrank back" from the enlightenmentism *(keimōshugi),* mass mobilization *(tairyō dōin),* and politicism of earlier social movements.[51] Indeed, if anything, his experience in the student movement (and, no doubt, in prison) pushed him toward a kind of parochial, neotraditional, cultural nationalist position—in many ways reminiscent of the physiocratic or agrarian nationalism *(nōhonshugi)* of the prewar period.[52] The student movement experience convinced Fujita that outright opposition, regardless of its ethical purity, did not produce anything and in the end amounted to no more than self-indulgence. As the extended struggle to prevent construction of the New Tokyo International Airport proved for Fujita—a dispute in which he was involved as a student radical—opposition often led to stalemate and, in some cases, violence at the hands of the state. The mistake of student radicals at Sanrizuka, he believed, was to focus on broad, abstract issues such as Japanese imperialism or the Amakudari State, when the airport problem was solvable only as a single issue in its own small universe. To be sure, Sanrizuka was linked at the very deepest level to the political and economic structure of conservative rule, but this did not automatically demand a movement of similar scale.

Fujita was similarly dissatisfied by the supposedly accusatory posture of environmental and consumer movements, which in his view ignored the cultural aspects *(bunkasei)* of agriculture and the concrete daily life world *(gutaiteki seikatsu sekai)* of farmers.[53] Best understood as a kind of cultural concentrate *(bunka no katamari)*—the product of regional

weather patterns and climate, the fertility of the soil, and the experience, toil, and sentiments of local farmers—agricultural produce had
become no more than a commodity for consumption. The consumer
movement with its rhetoric of the wise consumer *(kashikoi shōhisha)*,
Fujita argued, championed daily life but slighted farmers' situation,
reducing the fruits of their labor to a commodity. Such logic, he claimed,
encouraged consumers to switch easily to imports because they were
pesticide free. Moreover, when consumers saw tomatoes or cabbages,
for example, they no longer saw the reality of farmers' lives, since their
consciousness was arguably trapped within "consumption."[54] So Fujita
saw the challenge as bringing culture back into consumers' consciousness of food, thereby breaking the cycle of pesticide use. Here, he turned
to the old Chinese principles of eating:[55] know who grew the produce;
know where it was grown; and eat it as close as possible to where it
was prepared.

Given his vehement rejection of the supposed fundamentalism in
earlier social movements, Fujita's romanticized and essentialist presentation of agriculture reads somewhat ironically. Yet, at the same time,
his was an essentialism that connected not to programs of radical social
change through mass mobilization—after all, he believed these had
failed—but to the transformation of individual values and practices.
And, on this level, his vision reverberated with ideas about self-help
and self-responsibility long prized among *shimin* advocates. One need
only look at the proclamations of Daichi to its consumer-members to
see this. In a 1981 Daichi newsletter Fujita reminded members that the
objective of the movement was not obtaining safe produce but rather
formulating a way to reconsider individual lifestyles and the current
age: the objective was to produce "food for thought" *(kangaeru sozai)*.
Nobody wanted to eat pesticide-covered vegetables, he admitted, but
members had no right to accuse farmers. Articulating a core value of
the new civic movements, Fujita argued, "We need to escape from a
world in which others are criticized and denounced, where people abuse
each other, and fight for things. . . . You want organic vegetables, don't
you? I want them too. Our movement will stand at its starting point
for the first time, when we create a world in which people begin to
think about what they can do *together*."[56]

Daichi supported its almost-religious commitment to consumer self-
examination with an equally rigorous dedication to self-help. As Fujita
put it, "Rather than cry out a million times about the danger of pesti-
cides, why not grow, deliver, and consume pesticide-free vegetables—

even if it is just one daikon radish?"[57] In the long term, Fujita imagined the creation of an independent people's daily life world *(minshū no jiritsushita seikatsu sekai)*—what others would call an alternative daily life—opposing the commodified world of mass consumption.[58] This life world not only included Japan but also extended to a Pan-Asian community in which farmers would form an alternative bloc based on national food self-sufficiency and resistance to globalization.[59] In the 1990s, Daichi began to establish contacts with farming organizations in Thailand, Korea, Taiwan, and Indonesia in order to resist the international commodification of agricultural products represented, for instance, by the Uruguay Round of GATT.[60] Of course, such Asian imaginaries were always predicated upon the movement's fundamental objective of protecting local farmers.

Moreover, although Fujita and his movement rejected the rationalizing tendencies of modern global capitalism, Daichi was a model capitalist enterprise as a for-profit stock company. In fact, Fujita even admitted that this was what made the movement different from the accusation-style mobilizations of old. True independence, as Fujita saw it, was nothing other than the creation of material strength: so long as movements relied on donations and free lunches *(gochisō)*, their members would not become independent. Activists had to aim for an organization in which people could earn a living *(undō de kasegeru)* and feed themselves *(kutte ikeru soshiki)*.[61] As Fujita explained, he and his partners were not worried about the vehicle for their movement, nor were they concerned about borrowing an already established form of incorporation. Since the for-profit model connected to what Fujita called "social material strength," he and other members felt no need to cling to so-called progressive alternatives such as the consumer cooperative model.[62]

Daichi thus spoke to a number of interesting developments—and continuities—in the *shimin* idea and citizen activism: a commitment to local and, more broadly, Asian ethnic culture in the face of Western capitalist expansion; a strong ethic of self-examination and active individual self-help; and a belief that there could be a nonviolent, nonoppressive form of capitalism. It was an interesting, if somewhat contradictory, concoction, but in the mid-1970s Daichi's message clearly found many sympathetic activist ears wearied, one assumes, by a decade of "accusation."

Presenting a similar message was the Kobe resident Takami Yūichi, founder of the recycling movement in postwar Japan. While still a nineteen-year-old university student and self-proclaimed hippie, Takami and a group of friends started the pioneering Kansai Recycling Movement Citizens' Association in the Kobe region of Hyōgo Prefecture in 1977. After some initial setbacks, Takami expanded the movement to Tokyo in 1984, establishing the Japan Recycling Movement Citizens' Association. Building on the success of the movement's "free markets" (i.e., flea markets) and recycling exchange programs, Takami expanded his operations into organic produce distribution, also founding Radish Boy (Radishu Bōya), a stock company with many similarities to Daichi. In 1993 Takami was elected to the national House of Representatives in the Japan New Party (Nihonshintō), and during his single term in office he focused on the creation of an "NGO law," as he called it at the time.

Takami appealed to a *shimin*-style catharsis through self-examination and self-help. In newspaper interviews and books, he repeatedly recounted his own environmental epiphanies. As a high school truant hitchhiking in Kyūshū in the 1970s, he recalled encountering a strange smell in the air, only to discover—from a road sign—that he was on the outskirts of Minamata. Fearing the smell of "infection," he had fled, only to be ravaged by a deep sense of shame and guilt later, on learning the city's methyl mercury poisoning was to blame. His second encounter with environmental contamination came while camping on a pristine island in Okinawa. Waking up in the morning, he discovered the perfect white sand of the previous day blackened by oil waste.[63] These experiences, Takami explained, shaped his activist mission.

Like Fujita, Takami was hypercritical of earlier social protest, characterizing 1960s and 1970s citizens' movements as being all about accusation *(kokuhatsu)*, struggle *(tōsō)*, and criticism *(hihan)* toward government, bureaucracy, and corporations.[64] He felt many had opposed for the sake of opposition, had no comprehension of social realities, and had adopted a stance in which their position was always right and that of others wrong. Those who agreed were considered allies, and those who opposed in even the slightest way were considered enemies. Takami concluded that such self-righteous strategies of dissent were the primary reason citizens' movements found it difficult to gain any social recognition or legitimacy.[65]

When I looked at the collapse of the student movement and the accusation style of the consumer movement, I thought to myself, "This is wrong." . . . One reason for the decline of the consumer movement was its failure to make any proposals to society. I really dislike the term *consumer movement*. People don't merely live in the world to "remove" and "use up." I have the feeling that the next movement—the next stage of our engagement with society—will emerge through the very denial of the notion of "consumer." In that sense I really want to end our attachment to the consumer movement.[66]

Takami proposed that, in contrast to the earlier so-called failed activism, citizens' movements feed themselves *(meshi o kueru shimin undō)*—a provocative opinion he shared with Fujita and one roundly criticized by many consumer, women's, and advocacy groups.[67] Takami saw three concrete advantages of financially self-sustaining activism. First, it linked to professionalization and specialization arguably lacking in earlier citizen protest. Accusation, struggle, and criticism alone were not enough: civic movements also needed to develop an alternative-proposal style *(daian teiji-gata)*, and this demanded a high level of professionalization, sometimes even greater than that of politicians and bureaucrats.[68] Second, self-sustenance demanded movement continuity, and the old model of ad hoc protest was simply inappropriate here.[69] And third, in order to guarantee such continuity, movements had to foster the support of nonactivists through public relations and advertising; otherwise they risked disappearing altogether or degenerating once again into antiestablishment groups.[70] For Takami, financial self-sustenance was far more than a means for movement survival: it was concrete proof that society valued such activism.[71] As he explained,

Over the past ten years I have continually restated the easily misinterpreted idea of "making a living through citizens' movements" *(shimin undō de meshi o kū)*. . . . I do not think the popular term *volunteer (borantia)* should be valorized. . . . The original meaning has disappeared as a result of too much masturbation *(masutābēshon)*. I just want citizens' movements to give up the idea that everyone has to bring their own lunch. I can't go along with such dogma. Underlying the idea of "making a living through citizens' movements" is our desire to raise societal awareness vis-à-vis the existence of so-called NPOs. . . . To put it rather crudely, company employees work for the organization; NPO activists will work for society.[72]

Taking his description of protest as masturbation to vulgar extremes, Takami claimed that in order to "create a new set of values," activists had to give up on "self-satisfaction" and "keep on fucking society" *(shakai o fakku shitsuzukeru)*—a process he explained as an "intense communication" between the movement and society.[73] As he put it in a 1986 magazine interview, "making love to society" *(shakai to mēku rabu suru)* was to replace the "masturbation" of "struggle" *(tōsō)*.[74]

Takami certainly sculpted his public message to shock, but at base it shared much with Fujita's: the absolute rejection of protest and dissent within *shimin* politics, a commitment to individual value change through self-examination and self-help, and an ambivalent set of messages about economic and political institutions: that they were the cause of all social evil but, at the same time, could be the seedbeds for a new creative style of activism that promised to change them. And, like Fujita and Daichi, Takami and his recycling movement became one of the most high-profile models of what citizens' movements should *be* and *do* and of how *shimin* should think.

Fujita and, even more so, Takami brought a decidedly hard edge to the message of the new *shimin*: movement success hinged on managerial acumen and rational decision making by self-reliant and self-assured activists. Others, such as Harima Yasuo, of the Tanpopo no Ie (Dandelion House) movement for the disabled, echoed similar sentiments but did so in a less assertive, more symbiotic tone reminiscent of 1980s New Age thinking. As a *Mainichi* newspaper journalist working on environmental issues in the early 1970s, Harima had a chance contact with a group of disabled youths in the Nara region. Thereafter, he became involved in a movement to create a facility for these youths to gather and to pursue their creative endeavors in a secure yet invigorating environment. In 1973 the group formed the Nara Tanpopo Association (Nara Tanpopo no Kai) and, in 1976, incorporated as the Tanpopo no Ie Foundation (Zaidan Hōjin Tanpopo no Ie). Later, Harima and fellow activists involved themselves in numerous groundbreaking initiatives for the disabled, especially in the realm of normalization (i.e., keeping the disabled and elderly within society and out of institutions as much as possible). Apart from the provision of physical space, the Tanpopo movement also organized various cultural initiatives to promote the artistic work of the disabled and to foster community interaction by inviting in specialists to teach as volunteers in its "Freedom School" (Jiyū Gakkō). In the late 1980s the movement also began to provide welfare services to the disabled after gaining the status of an official social welfare corporation *(shakai fukushi hōjin)*. The movement also looked abroad, establishing contacts with groups for the disabled throughout Asia.[75] Those who have visited Tanpopo no Ie—including myself—soon realize that Harima and others created a space of dignity and self-esteem for the disabled that, within limits, aims to undermine the very notion of disability altogether. The Tanpopo movement is a model of normalization and community-based care that warrants further research.

My focus here, however, is not the movement's implications for the rights of the disabled but rather the implications for citizen activism and civil society in Japan in the mid-1970s. Like Daichi and Takami's recycling movement, Tanpopo no Ie occupied an important place in discussions about civic activism at that time. Harima was a leading public advocate of the new style of activism and, like Takami, later became intimately involved in the movement for nonprofit legislation and the subsequent NPO boom. Like both Fujita and Takami, Harima was wholly dissatisfied with earlier citizen protest.

Harima's first encounter with social protest came during the 1960 Anpo struggle, which he saw as both a high point in political conscious-ness among the people and, at the same time, a losing game *(make gēmu)* for civic groups.[76] While reporting on antipollution and antide-velopment movements of the 1960s and 1970s as a newspaper journal-ist, Harima concluded that movements based on criticism *(hihan)* and accusation *(kokuhatsu)* were doomed to failure. The problem, as he saw it, lay in their tendency toward hierarchy both organizationally and ideologically. As he explained, these early citizens' movements often had an intellectual leader who saw it as his role to teach the people difficult things that they would obey with all their energy. Not only did this result in a kind of despotic rule within movements; it also opened them up to co-optation: it was often said that the key to defeat-ing a residents' movement lay in buying out the leadership. If the top lost its energy, then the movement as a whole would fall apart (an observation made also by anti-freight-line activist Miyazaki Shōgo).[77]

Conversely, Harima imagined new civic movements based on loose relations among ordinary people and focused on the proposal of practi-cal alternatives.[78] They discarded zero-sum choices such as between environmental protection *or* the security treaty, forging compromises such as environmental conservation based on an understanding of the necessity of the security treaty.[79] Such flexibility—a kind of symbiosis—marked a sharp turnaround from earlier movements, which he felt had been both tragic and angry. Indeed, Harima called his movement Tanpopo no Ie—literally, the Dandelion House—because these sturdy yet bright flowers symbolized the synthesis of nature, enjoyment, and durability possible in social activism.[80]

Harima's approach played out on numerous levels in the Tanpopo movement. Ideologically, the movement disassociated itself from the established left. After the movement was labeled "red" by both Nara City administrators and local residents in its early days, Harima promulgated three rules: first, there would be no politics or religion in the movement; second, the organization would not govern the movement; and third, membership and participation would be limited to individuals (i.e., no organizational membership).[81] Organizationally, Harima rejected hierarchy in favor of a movement in which everyone was supposedly a lead actor.[82] Invoking New Age imagery, he spoke of a shift from tree-style movements (bureaucracies and the managed society, for example) to rhizome-style movements, which were fluid, open, and difficult to pin down.[83] In these ambiguous structures, movement actors would discard the flawed notion of benevolent bureaucracy.[84] In its stead, people would stretch and bend the fibrous boundaries of their rhizomes as they helped themselves in the best traditions of bricolage and DIY (do it yourself).[85] Harima believed a bricolage approach to activism created both autonomy *(jiritsu)* and synergy *(kyōdō)* within movements, since it freed people to take responsibility.[86] Moreover, not only did a DIY mentality mean self-sufficiency; it also connected to the discovery of identity in yourself.[87]

This presentation of the movement as a loose, nonideological association of like-minded individuals clearly drew on the legacy of earlier civic activism, but its reworking of that past made the logistics of the present all the easier. By equating earlier citizen protest with ideology and failure, Harima could connect strategies of contemporary movements to common sense and success. And in terms of these self-styled indicators of success, Tanpopo was nothing short of exemplary. To raise money, Harima and associates established a birthday fund *(otanjōbi kikin),* which in two years had around two thousand people annually contributing one thousand yen on their birthdays.[88] Leaders also initiated a highly successful and novel system of ten-year, redeemable, non-interest-bearing welfare bonds *(fukushi shōken)* to give those not actively involved in the movement a way to participate.[89] Though bureaucrats were unwilling to grant social welfare corporation status to Tanpopo at the time, in mid-1976 the Nara prefectural governor granted it foundation status *(zaidan hōjin)* and provided the fledgling group rent-free land.[90] Just as Fujita and Takami showed that market principles could be successfully injected into civic movements, Harima and fellow members in the Tanpopo movement proved that *shimin* activists and government officials could indeed forge relations of symbiosis and cooperation. And, to reiterate, such new approaches and relationships in the realm of civic activism were always—and intentionally—contrasted with what had been "unsuccessful" in the past.[91]

Any discussion of progenitors among the new civic movements would not be complete without treatment of the progressive consumer cooperatives collectively calling themselves the Seikatsu Club (hereafter the SC). In this movement we see a fascinating intersection of ideas and perspectives: Gramscian notions of hegemony and civil society; criticism of Western modernity and capitalism; the melding of the *shimin* and *seikatsusha* ideas; the lionization of the politics of daily life and the housewife identity; and the proposal of an alternative daily life powered by a reconfigured capitalism of self-help. And, as in the other movements of its generation, in the Seikatsu Club we discover how a movement imagined as a solution to postwar capitalist excess and conservative hegemony came to endorse many of the same values eventually celebrated by corporate and government elites.

As I discussed in chapter 2, the SC movement can be traced back to the fallout from the Anpo struggle and various initiatives to take back democracy from the grass roots. The history of consumer cooperatives in Japan stretched back much further, of course, to the early twentieth century, when Christian evangelist Kagawa Toyohiko established a purchasing cooperative in the Kobe region in 1921. Though suppressed during the war, consumer co-ops made a triumphant return in the early postwar years, responding to grave shortages in everyday necessities.[92] But, as Muto Ichiyo notes, the SC and the other so-called daily life cooperative unions *(seikatsu kyōdō kumiai)* that were mobilized during the 1960s and 1970s represented a new phenomenon in that they spoke to issues beyond price, such as food safety and supply, individual patterns of daily life and consumption, and concerns about the environment and social welfare.[93] Moreover, these daily life co-ops drew their leadership from a generation socialized in the citizen and student protests of the 1960s. For example, the two founders of the SC in Tokyo and Kanagawa prefectures, Iwane Kunio and Yokota Katsumi, cut their activist teeth in the Anpo struggle and soon after, and the leader of the Green co-op in Kyushu, Yukioka Ryōji, entered the movement after being jailed for his involvement in the student organization Zenkyōtō.[94] So, in terms of issues and leadership, the daily life co-ops certainly broke with earlier cooperativism and, important to note, assumed a central position in the new wave of citizen activism beginning in the mid-1970s.

But beyond issues and leadership, ideology and organizational style also connected the SC movement to the new wave of citizens' movements. These two aspects owed much to their leaders' experience with the Anpo struggle, their (negative) opinions about protest, and the affluent urban housewives at whom they targeted their message. Reflecting on social activism during and after the Anpo struggle, the SC's leaders became convinced that monopoly capitalism and conservative hegemony could be overcome only through the creation of an alternative, liberated life space. Ideologically, this project for counterhegemony at the local level shared much in common with Matsushita Keiichi and the Tosei Chōsakai's project for local democracy, although it led not so much to a political movement as to a grassroots self-help project. Though their housewife constituency cared little—if at all— about grand plans for counterhegemony, they were nevertheless responsive to Iwane and Yokota's privileging of their sphere of activity, hence making an alliance possible. Both the male leadership and the female membership aspired, in the end, to the attainment of individual autonomy in an alternative realm, fiercely independent of the mainstream market, establishment politics, and the state, yet resigned to the persistence of these institutions and the need to engage with them for the purpose of self-preservation.[95]

Like Matsushita Keiichi, both Iwane and Yokota came out of the Anpo struggle with a new political intent. Iwane had found himself unintentionally drawn into the protests while working as a freelance photographer on the day student Kanba Michiko was killed in rioting. As he explained, "I decided I would throw away my camera and enter political activism."[96] In the course of the protests he also had a brief but significant encounter with the Voices of the Voiceless Association, with whom he felt an emotional resonance, because, like him, they were merely ordinary *shimin* mobilized from the bottom up.[97] In July 1960, Iwane joined the JSP in Tokyo's Setagaya Ward, assuming the position of bureau chairman for the party's Socialist Youth League, or Shaseidō (Shakaishugi Seinen Dōmei).[98] Similar to Matsushita Keiichi, Iwane became enamored with the theory of structural reform *(kōzō kaikaku)* most popularly supported briefly by the JSP heavyweight Eda Saburō.[99] Though Iwane would later sever all ties with Eda and the JSP, the idea of structural reform had a lasting impact on his approach to social activism, as it had on Matsushita, especially regarding his belief that change was best brought about gradually through incremental reform within the system of market capitalism. This, in turn, led him to the ideas of Antonio Gramsci and the project for counterhegemony within civil society. As Lam Peng-Er notes, Iwane was later joined in the SC movement by a number of communists who quit or were purged from the JCP for their heretical support of structural reform.[100]

Supported by the JSP structural reform faction, Iwane mounted an abortive campaign for election to the Setagaya council in 1963, after which—deeply in debt—he became more and more disenchanted with the JSP. Thereafter, Iwane briefly tried his hand at selling cosmetics and then, in late 1964, made the fortuitous decision to start delivering cheap milk to Setagaya housewives with the help of his wife and others.[101] Sales increased in the years after, and in 1968 Iwane was able to register the SC for official status as a lifestyle cooperative union (seikatsu kyōdō kumiai). In the previous year, adding to Iwane's run of success, his wife, Shizuko, ran successfully for the Setagaya Ward Assembly, crafting her landslide victory almost completely around the image of the smiling gubernatorial candidate, Minobe Ryōkichi.[102]

The SC's other key leader, Yokota Katsumi, a self-proclaimed "Marx Boy" at the time and subsequent founder of the movement in Kanagawa Prefecture, spent the 1960s as a labor activist in Tōkyū Railways.[103] He recalls how, at first, he and his activist colleagues had been unable to comprehend the mechanism by which local residents would, for example, support Tōkyū against laborers striking for greater railway safety.[104] Over time, however, they eventually concluded that Tōkyū had become a new postwar zaibatsu, habitually exercising its hegemony as a local monopoly (chiiki dokusentai).[105] Tōkyū signified far more than a railway and a department store: its presence in the community influenced public monies spent on facilities, shaped local cultural activities, guaranteed shopping convenience, increased land value, and contributed to a general rise in the status of local communities. The return payment for this benevolent hegemony, Yokota and his colleagues believed, was local residents' consent to Tōkyū's local monopoly.[106]

In 1964, while continuing his labor movement activities, Yokota began to help Iwane with his milk distribution movement in Tokyo and, in due course, formed a cooperative unit (a purchasing group) with fifty or so Tōkyū union activists.[107] In an attempt to break the "bond of consent" between Tōkyū and local residents—to get in behind capital (shihon no ushiro ni)—Yokota extended his cooperative purchasing model into the local community.[108] Following the lead of Iwane in Tokyo, he established the Midori Lifestyle Cooperative Union in Yokohama in May 1971, raising the necessary capital from just over a thousand subscribers.[109] Later, in 1977, the co-op changed its name to the Seikatsu Club Seikyō Kanagawa.[110] Together with the Tokyo SC, the Kanagawa SC would go on to be a leader of not only progressive postwar cooperativism but also the new civic movements.

Indeed, the SC proved to be the most thorough and successful example of civic self-help in the mid-1970s, and like their contemporaries its leaders broadcast a stringent message of constructive alternative proposal over simpleminded protest. Yokota, for example, argued that claiming power in the public sphere would come not through criticism (hihan) but through the creation of hegemony (hegemonī), since a healthy public sphere also demanded risk and responsibility on the part of citizens.[111] More stringently, Iwane Kunio proclaimed that resistance was for the weak and amounted to nothing. "Creation," he resolutely concluded, had "foresight" and was "ahead of things," and only when people "took control" would they "make their history."[112] He understood the movement's slogan "change your lifestyle" (ikikata o kaeyō) as not only a critical examination of one's life but also the production of a new way of life.[113]

Such convictions played out in a number of concrete initiatives and practices within the SC movement. Central to these has been the establishment of han, or small squads of housewife members (fewer than ten), which have collectively received and distributed their product orders from the cooperative. As observers have explained, involvement in these collective purchasing units—while definitely an education in collaboration and social responsibility—is often burdensome, because housewives essentially forgo the convenience of shopping when and how they wish.[114] Movement publications note that some 20 percent of members quit the movement when the han system began because of the extra time and commitment required.[115] SC leaders such as Yokota, however, portrayed such hardships as a lesson in self-examination, explaining collective purchasing as a process by which people break away from their passive situation as "purchasing robots" and gain relative independence from the modern market.[116] Yokota portrayed the often-trying process of receiving and dividing collective purchases as an opportunity for members to reflect on their role in the product cycle and their relationship to producers.[117] In other words, movement practice was also about creative self-examination.

Beginning with a movement to replace synthetic detergents with natural soap in the 1980s, the SC also extended its activities into the realm of local politics through its so-called proxy movement (dairinin undō), also known as Netto.[118] The first success for an SC proxy came in 1983, with Terada Etsuko's election to the Kawasaki Municipal Assembly.[119] Building on this success, fourteen Netto candidates were elected to local councils in 1987, and this number increased to twenty-six in 1991. Involvement in electoral politics and community organizing has indeed resulted in a sense of empowerment and greater gender consciousness among some female members.[120] But, at the same time, as with the politics of the movements discussed above, the SC's proxy movement is self-limiting—perhaps even conservative—in that it is not so much about fundamental systemic or political transformation as about the rigorous defense of an alternative realm of daily life. Organizationally, for example, Netto politicians are required to donate part of their salaries to the movement, and they must accept term limits or thereafter run independently—a clear message that Netto is, and will remain, a movement of political amateurs. Netto's policies also tend to revolve around issues of daily life in local communities, such as food, recycling, and the environment. As LeBlanc explains, the SC and Netto represent opportunities "to make a public space for the *housewife's* point of view."[121] But while such "housewife consciousness" may help to define the movement's platform and provide legitimacy, it also "introduces constraints on the movement."[122] Thus, while on the surface Netto may appear to represent the infiltration of the new citizens' movements into politics, on closer inspection its organization and policy platform pose no real threat to the established political order and, if anything, tend to reinforce the state's aspirations for greater citizen self-reliance at the local level, so prevalent since the early 1970s.

The SC has also expanded into the realm of welfare service provision. In 1987, for example, the SC first proposed the idea of creating a welfare co-op *(fukushi kōpu)* in reaction to government calls for privatization of so-called silver industries and reductions in public spending on welfare. According to Yokota, the shift in state policy led people to the conclusion that they could not entrust their old age to either the government or industry; they would have to take care of themselves.[123] In the 1990s, as Gelb and Estevez-Abe describe, SC members became "highly active in the social welfare service sector," influencing "the social policy arena not only in terms of policy making but in terms of policy implementation as well." In 1992 the SC established a number of elderly day care facilities after the government changed the law prohibiting co-op provision of welfare and social services.[124] Such developments may represent evidence of the new movements directly influencing public policy and perhaps even a shift in the state-society dynamic.[125] But, as I discussed earlier, we need to keep in mind that Ministry of Health and Welfare bureaucrats had long been interested in utilizing citizen volunteers for welfare provision, so it is less than astounding that groups interested in shouldering welfare, like the SC, should find sympathetic bureaucratic ears.

Though he was speaking of the Green Co-op group, Jean-Marie Bouissou's comments are instructive: members, he tells us, are "very sensitive to the dramatizing discourse which the LDP has used for years as a powerful means to reduce social security benefits 'in order to cope with the aging society.' In fact, this discourse and that of many alternative groups are complementary: when they advocate local communities taking responsibility for the aged, be it through self-support, the alternatives help the government by making up for the glaring deficiencies of the public service."[126] In fact, Yokota Katsumi even boasts of the SC's successes in providing cheap welfare through members' volunteerism. Though home helpers could earn one thousand yen an hour elsewhere, in the SC's community facilities they earned only six or seven hundred yen an hour. "Our thinking," he explained, "is that if you do something good for someone in your own neighborhood, it will come back to you sooner or later."[127] As Satō Yoshiyuki, a longtime ideologue for the Seikatsu Club movement, argues, co-op activities, unlike those of ordinary social movements aimed at toppling their self-identified enemy, are about "self-reflection on one's everyday daily life," followed by activism to change that life.[128]

All of these activities form part of the SC's attempt (or, more accurately, its *leaders'* attempt) to forge a local counterhegemony or, in more palatable language, the creation of an alternative daily life. Iwane Kunio, the movement founder, likes to present his movement as a kind of hybrid: a new social movement in civil society combined with a business possessing a strong corporate ethos and a commitment to innovation and sound management.[129] But, like Fujita and Takami, Iwane has a rather complicated take on capitalism because of his deep ambivalence toward the so-called West. On the one hand, he portrays the SC as a movement operating on principles different from the logic of capitalism (which he conflates with "modernity" and the "West"). Yet, on the other hand, the movement owes much of its success to rational business management and an ability to brand itself as an eco-friendly choice for consumers in a modern market.

Iwane portrays the SC as nothing less than a solution to the universalism of western European modernity *(seiō kindai no fuhensei)* and the notion of progress *(shinpō)*, which, he claims, was a problem not only for Marx but for the whole of modern European thought. He rejects outright, for example, an understanding of the French Revolution as a moment of liberty, equality, and fraternity that gave birth to republicanism and western European justice, universalism, and modernization.[130] On the contrary, he asserts, "that thing called European universalism was a means for the establishment of world domination *(haken)* by the core of countries shouldering so-called Western modernity." These countries "forced their values" on other civilizations, "making them obey these by force."[131] For Iwane the speed with which capitalism developed in late nineteenth-century Japan proves how the Japanese people were "completely led astray by the logic of European universalism and modernization"—almost as though Japan had no choice in the matter or as though the principles of capitalism were so foreign to the Japanese that only through a mass national delusion could capitalism have spread so fast in the country.[132]

Iwane's extreme claims aside, the interesting point is the way in which the SC's leaders have mounted their attack on capitalism not only as a system built on injustice but also, more fundamentally, as a non- (or perhaps, anti-) Japanese system intentionally created by Western civilization to spread its "hegemonic" control over the world. Iwane argues that the undercurrent of modern ethnic and religious struggles is the rejection of western European universalism and the general rethinking of the concept of progress.[133] And, until the Japanese people recognize this undercurrent, he argues, they are always at risk of accidentally taking sides with the West.[134] In the 1990s Iwane observed that when problems such as Islamic extremism and the Gulf War arose, many Japanese tended to believe that the United States was right. "It's not that I particularly support [Saddam] Hussein," Iwane explained, "but if you compare Hussein and [George H. W.] Bush, I don't believe Bush is so right."[135]

So, it is in the context of such beliefs that we need to understand Iwane's championing of a civil society set against the state. As in the vision of Oda Makoto, Tsurumi Shunsuke, and other influential citizen movement intellectuals throughout the postwar period, in Iwane's vision of the *shimin* and civil society, they emerge as opportunities for the Japanese nation to resist a state and a market long under the thumb of Western domination. Echoing such values, Yokota Katsumi has long championed the nurturing of autonomous citizens who will solve problems by themselves.[136] He suggests that the community most convenient for the state and capital to manipulate is one in which the people are divided, dependent on cash, and forced to live on handouts.[137] The alternative to this, however, is a community for citizens by citizens, kept alive by a barter economy, and capable of supporting itself even if the state were to go bankrupt.[138] Since Yokota proposed the idea of alternatives in 1984, it has come to symbolize this community of self-help liberated (if only partly) from the mainstream market and the state.[139]

And, the driving force behind this community is movement members, the totality of social and political human beings that Yokota has called *seikatsusha-shimin*—a synthetic activist identity that tells us much about the complex motivations fueling the movement. Together with the *shimin* idea, the *seikatsusha* has been a recurrent motif in new civic movements beginning in the mid-1970s. The word *seikatsusha*—even more so than *shimin*—is difficult to translate, and throughout this study I have used the somewhat-labored phrase "inhabitant of daily life." But *seikatsusha* is probably best understood for what it is *not* or what it has been imagined *against*. In one way or another, the *seikatsusha* always seems to have been juxtaposed to what is pejoratively seen as "modern" and, hence, "Westernized," whether this be the state, the intellectual, the decadent urbanite, or the rational consumer. As early as 1926 the playwright and social critic Kurata Hyakuzō used the term in an article for the *Tokyo Asahi Shimbun* titled "*Seikatsusha* and the Literati" and later in a magazine titled the *Seikatsusha*. According to Amano Masako, Kurata was deeply disturbed by the vulgar commercialization of literature by writers who had no more in mind than the pursuit of self-interest—that is, the commodification of literature. For Kurata, proper literary arts simply had to begin with the self as *seikatsusha (seikatsusha toshite no jiko)*. Faced with the chaos and profanity of the world, *seikatsusha* emerged as seekers of truth who regulated the ego *(jiko o rissuru)* and resisted profanity via a stoic set of ethical principles. Kurata's *seikatsusha* was one who transcended a daily life compromised by the carnal desires, chaos, and violations born of the commercialization in 1920s Japan.[140]

In the 1940s, the ill-fated philosopher Miki Kiyoshi also turned to the *seikatsusha* in an effort to find a subject that might reconstruct an authentic culture of daily life *(seikatsu bunka)* to dislodge the hegemonic hold of a cultural daily life *(bunka seikatsu)* defined by mass production, mass consumption, mass communication, and Westernization.[141] True daily life, Miki concluded, found meaning in more authentic practices rooted in the ancient traditions of the nation. The culture of daily life involved active transformation and refashioning by ordinary Japanese people; it belonged to them and not the elites, Miki concluded, and above all else it was something "created out of the importance people attributed to everydayness *(nichijōsei).*"[142] Around the same time, writer Nii Itaru used *seikatsusha* to denote the man in the street *(shisei no hito),* to whom he contrasted those who belonged *(kizokunin)* to the institutions of modernity—the bureaucracy and the large corporations.[143] And, as I explained in chapter 1, in the early postwar years Tsurumi Shunsuke and others contrasted the *seikatsusha* idea to intellectuals and researchers, who they believed had lost touch with the authentic daily life of the Japanese people. Economist Ōkuma Nobuyuki also toyed with the idea in a number of theoretical essays in the 1960s,[144] but lifestyle co-ops and other new civic groups of the 1970s were left to present the *seikatsusha* (along with the *shimin*) as a progressive activist identity transcendent of self-indulgent consumption and sensitive to the productive side of society.[145] Common in all of these versions was the contrast of an essentially Western modernity to a *seikatsusha* embedded in an authentic Japanese daily life—as though the two could be seamlessly distinguished or separated.

As LeBlanc incisively notes, the reemergence of the *seikatsusha* identity within the SC has meant that it is something that, though technically accessible to men, is ultimately possible only for fulltime housewives. Ironically, then, *seikatsusha* status qualifies the housewife as the guardian of something authentically Japanese but, at the same time, reinforces her delimited political subjectivity as a "bicycle citizen"—to use LeBlanc's imagery. Yokota, conversely, prefers to explain the *seikatsusha* in far more upbeat terms by marrying it to the new *shimin* of the mid-1970s. As he explains, a *shimin* is one who "exercises [his or her] various political rights," whereas a *seikatsusha* is one who "purposively *(mokutekiteki)* acts within the everyday social and economic environment." Once synthesized, the *seikatsusha-shimin* type of human takes responsibility for the totality of his or her life.[146] In the *seikatsusha-shimin* of the SC, then, we have a perfect union of political and social responsibility and a set of principles for action.[147]

Of course, the historical trajectory of both *shimin* and *seikatsusha* points to another imagination of the *seikatsusha-shimin* as an obedient, apolitical, culturally embedded, and usually gendered subjectivity, populating a civil society based on principles that are anathema to Western capitalism and are in keeping with the best Japanese traditions of creative community building. In this sense, SC leaders' formulation of the *seikatsusha-shimin* points again to some of the unintended synergies emerging among state, market, and civil society in the mid-1970s. The presentation of an alternative identity tended to complement the goals of a state intent on ever smaller government; furthermore, identifying a stratum of *seikatsusha-shimin* among Japanese housewives amounted to identifying an emerging market exploitable not only by principled and authentic activists but by any who could commodify the values and desires of that stratum. We might say the SC's leaders were pioneers in a market catering to the amorphous masses as well as to a far more diversified conglomeration of highly discerning "micromasses."[148] Moreover, in common with activists such as Fujita of Daichi, the SC's leaders—especially in their invocation of the *seikatsusha*—continued to imagine the *shimin*, daily life, and civil society as part of an authentic national imaginary liberated (at least potentially) from the logic of a state and a market captured by the apparently "pseudo"-universalism of the West.

These progenitor movements and their leaders were at the forefront of an intentional drive to promote the new proposal-style citizens' movements in the mid-1970s. They were by no means the only instances, but they are spotlighted because of the clarity of their message and, crucially, their high profile both within and beyond the activist community. Most notably, in 1986, Fujita, Takami, Harima, and others organized the much publicized trip to the islands of Okinawa to meet organic banana farmers. Setting sail on the appropriately named vessel *New Utopia* and bringing together 510 activists from 170 citizens' groups around Japan, the so-called Banana Boat Cruise stands out as one of the defining moments of the new civic groups in the 1980s. Apart from visiting banana growers, participants spent most of the cruise in workshops ranging from soil quality to education, democratic economics, a Minamata university, and in keeping with the New Age flavor, study sessions on Eastern cosmological principles.[149] Organizers also compiled and published a networking list of some thirteen hundred civic groups.[150] As figure 1 reveals, most prevalent were environmental, consumer, and citizen enterprises.

The Banana Boat Cruise was significant for three reasons. First, in practical terms, it represented one of the earliest attempts by activists from different spheres to mobilize under the banner of networking. As a postcruise publication put it, participants "came to the conclusion that if the many small civic groups in Japan pulled together, they could

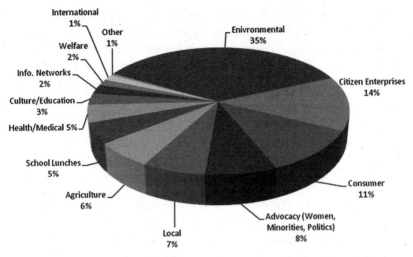

FIGURE 1. "Banana Boat" civic groups' areas of activity (multiple response). Source: Bananabōto Jikkō Iinkai, ed. *Inochi, Shizen, Kurashi: Bananabōto: Mōhitotsu no Seikatsu o Tsukuru Nettowākāzu no Funade* (Tokyo: Honnoki, 1986).

generate much more power than they had previously, and could in some way stand up to the pressure being applied by the LDP, big business, and the bureaucrats who opposed their existence."[151] Second, the cruise became a mouthpiece for influential movement intellectuals to trumpet the idea of constructive, alternative-proposal-style activism. Nowhere was the contrast between the supposed accusation *(kokuhatsu)* of the past versus the proposal *(teian)* of the present stressed more—so much so as to cause rifts among cruise participants representing movements with a range of strategies.[152] Third, the cruise sent out a strong message about the need for civic groups to be financially self-sustaining. As if to presage developments in the 1990s, Takami Yūichi contrasted volunteerism, in which activists brought their own lunch *(tebentō)*, with NPOs, which would provide lunch for participants.[153] True or not, the message of the cruise and the leading movement intellectuals was crystal clear: citizen groups needed to be financially stable, resolutely apolitical, and founded on the best traditions of self-help. Rather than contingent on resistance, accusation, or opposition to the market and the state, their success depended on engaging with these sectors—using the system to change the system.

Let me attempt, then, to draw together these streams of civic thought and activism. As Jeffrey Berry has noted, "Movements must all go somewhere from the streets or they die—and die they often do."[154] For civic groups interested in organizational continuity and specific initiatives, the proposal paradigm made good sense, especially its focus on marshaling any and all useful resources. To borrow from Berry: it was a practical method for movement intellectuals and activists to redirect activism from the "streets" (i.e., protest) into more enduring and, some might say, sophisticated forms of activism. The problem, however, lay in the meaning that movement intellectuals and their supporters attributed to this shift from the streets to a new sphere of civic activism. By demonizing earlier contentious approaches to social change, they arguably began to circumscribe the legitimate repertoire of strategies available to civic groups thereafter. Or, if not actually circumscribing some approaches, their interventions at least had the effect of making others seem more commonsensical and rational. Also of importance, many of these same movement intellectuals spearheaded initiatives in the late 1980s, first, to further professionalize the civic sector, and, second, to reform the existing legal framework for such groups. In other words, their attempts to reshape *shimin* symbolism and civic activism in their own movements eventually developed into a much wider campaign to transform Japanese civil society.

THE TOYOTA FOUNDATION, CITIZENS' ACTIVITIES, AND NETWORKING

Corporate philanthropic organizations intent on nurturing and promoting their own vision of the new civic groups and civil society came onto the scene in the early 1980s. Of these, the Toyota Foundation was by far the most active and influential, notably through its grant program for new civic groups from 1984. Set up by Toyota Motors in 1974 to celebrate forty years of auto manufacturing, the foundation originally targeted grants to academics and researchers working in three core areas: transport safety, daily life, and the natural environment; the sphere of social welfare; and the sphere of education and culture. The foundation's attention to new civic groups came later as program officers slowly became aware of innovative groups beyond academia tackling the issues of these core areas. Starting with tentative funding for collaborative research between local residents and specialists in the 1970s, the foundation gradually directed financial support toward new civic movements. As program officer Yamaoka Yoshinori explained in 1982, solving social problems did indeed require basic research and development of new technology from a bird's-eye perspective; however, there was also room for the discovery of problems and their *"kaizen"* (improvement) from a bug's-eye perspective. To this end, the foundation opened up applications for research funding to any, regardless of academic or professional qualification, conceptualizing its stance under the rubric of citizen-participation-style research activity *(shimin sanka-gata kenkyū katsudō)*.[155]

In 1984 the foundation established a special program to fund civic groups engaged in creative and pioneering activities.[156] The program had three specific objectives: to enable activists to write narrative histories of their movements, to conduct research on the relationship between philanthropic foundations and civic groups, and to fund public forums on grassroots networking.[157] Renamed and expanded in scope in 1988, the grant evolved into a powerful resource for citizens' groups engaged in social-capital-style activism.[158] In its first two decades (1984–2003) the program funded some four hundred groups in four major areas: care for the elderly and disabled, overseas and refugee support, environmental protection, and village revitalization/local community building *(muraokoshi/machizukuri)*. The majority of groups were voluntary associations, though some, such as Harima Yasuo's Tanpopo movement, had legal status as public interest corporations. Figure 2 shows proportions of funding by activity given out by the program from its inception in 1984 through 2003.[159] Generally speaking, funding conforms to broader trends among the new civic groups, with a strong focus on welfare. Noticeable, too, are grants for citizen businesses *(shimin jigyō)* such as Daichi, demonstrating the foundation's desire to promote financially self-sustaining activism.

The Citizen Activities Grant had two palpable legacies for the new civic movements: one ideational, the other organizational. Ideationally, the grant helped popularize the term *citizens' activities (shimin katsudō)*, later adopted by bureaucrats, the mass media, civic groups, and thousands of volunteer centers as the official term for new civic movements. Program officers did not invent this term, which had had a prewar life followed by a brief resurrection in the 1960s and 1970s.[160] Matsushita Keiichi, for example, used the term in the 1960s as part of his structural reform project for local democracy and political reform, as did progressive Tokyo governor Minobe Ryōkichi, who in the 1970s established the Citizen Activities Service Corner (Shimin Katsudō Sābisu Kōnā) in Tachikawa City in western Tokyo.[161] Their use of *citizens' activities* was rather unusual at the time, given the more common terms *citizens'*

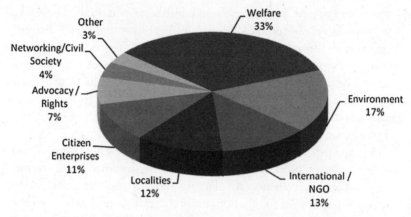

FIGURE 2. Program activities supported by the Toyota Foundation Citizens' Activities Grant, 1984–2003. Source: Toyota Foundation, *Shimin Katsudō Josei* (1986–2003), and *Kenkyūjosei (Tokutei Kadai—Shimin Katsudō no Kiroku no Sakusei)* (1984–85).

movement (shimin undō) and *residents' movement (jūmin undō)*, and, in fact, exposed the dilemma that even progressive municipal administrations faced in describing and dealing with civic activism.[162] On the one hand, *citizens' activities* certainly captured the innovative spirit of the postpollution-era movements, but, on the other, recombining *citizen* with *activities* as opposed to *movement* represented a conscious compromise on the part of bureaucrats faced with the dilemma of endorsing energies often understood as antiestablishment and destructive (i.e., "bad citizens").

Toyota Foundation officers did not know of this history when naming their grant in the 1980s, but their logic mirrored that of the Minobe administration. According to former foundation official Yamaoka Yoshinori, the foundation originally considered a number of titles for the new grant: resident activities, grassroots activities, volunteer activities, networking activities, social participation activities, citizens' movements, and citizens' activities.[163] Program officers wanted the title to speak to three issues: the active and socially transformative role of the new movements; the shared social mission of the sphere, despite a diversity of activities; and the ways the new movements transcended earlier activism.[164] As with the Minobe administration, program officers were motivated by contradictory impulses. On the one hand they wanted to associate the new movements with the tradition of the *shimin* idea, yet on the other, they felt uncomfortable with the symbolic baggage of resistance in the citizens' movement model and, hence, a desire to negate it. Echoing prominent activists, they concluded that many earlier citizens' movements had merely engaged in the rhetoric of resistance and accusation and, in a kind of bureaucratic dependency, often resorted to making demands.

Program officers also pointed to the tendency of citizens' movements to disband quietly upon reaching their objective or being defeated—a transience apparently not befitting the new movement ethos. *Citizens' activities,* conversely, projected an evolutionary enhancement: the *citizen* embodied the autonomy and solidarity of the citizens' movement tradition, and *activities* addressed the activeness, stability, and networked nature of the new movements. To be sure, *citizens' activities* helped program officers conceptualize a meaningful sphere of activity beyond the state and the market, but, as with *proposal* and *participation,* this idea also tended to undermine the contribution of earlier protest movements, not to mention question the ongoing viability of contentious social activism. As one observer later commented, *citizens' activities* represented a diluted *(dasshoku)* and neutralized *(chūwa)* vision of civic activism, which spoke as much to ideologies of harmonization as it did to any synthesis of the so-called *shimin* tradition of dissent.[165] In a sense, *citizens' activities* was a safely domesticated adaptation of the mercurial *citizens' movement,* and, crucially, it became one of the dominant symbols of the new civic groups.

As important as the Toyota Foundation's ideational interventions was its support for networking among the new civic groups. Yamaoka Yoshinori noted that before the rise of the new activism in the 1980s, Japanese civic groups were like "islands," and Harima Yasuo, a grant recipient, lamented how citizens' groups would divide up like so many "octopus traps."[166] To remedy this tendency, the foundation funded networking initiatives among citizen activists, most significantly through the Networking Study Group (Nettowākingu Kenkyūkai), established in 1984 to facilitate network building among citizens' groups. With Toyota Foundation backing, this study group developed into one of the most influential public voices advocating regulatory reform for nonprofits in the early 1990s.

Following a series of Toyota Foundation–sponsored networking seminars in the late 1980s, the Networking Study Group—now the Japan Networkers' Conference (JNC)—held the first Japan Networkers' Forum, confidently focused on "the new world opened by networking," in November 1989 in Tokyo and Osaka, with some six hundred participants. More expansively conceived than the 1986 Banana Boat Cruise, the forum brought together prominent movement intellectuals, academics, Toyota Foundation program officers, and guests from abroad, such as networking gurus Jessica Lipnack and Jeffrey Stamps from the United States.[167] For the most part, the 1989 forum was a celebration of networking with much ambiguous talk about postindustrial society, alternatives, nodes, and links. Asakura Yūko, of the JNC, for example, described a network as a "mutual connection among people as citizens (shimin)" or a "link that makes possible mutual understanding among various activities, desires, and ideals."[168] The conference booklet was no less concrete, defining networking as an alternative format (mōhitotsu no katachi) for bringing people together. Lipnack and Stamps, the honored guests, were convinced their Japanese counterparts had perfected the art of networking. As Stamps gushed in a letter written after the conference, "After two and a half of the most extraordinary weeks of our lives . . . we have returned to the U.S. with this knowledge: you have gone farther and explored more deeply the meaning of networking than any other group of people we have met."[169] For Lipnack, the explanation lay in Japan's "social structure," which had emerged quite "naturally" for "over a thousand years." Japan, with its historical "group" style of leadership based on a "system of elders," had placed great emphasis on "networked organization," and on this point it was "beating" the United States, where "individual ego" prevailed over the group.[170] Lipnack and Stamps's praise for Japanese cultural communitarianism struck a chord: Asakura Yūko even argued that networking could bring about a symbiosis (kyōsei) and harmony (chōwa) between civic groups on the one hand and government and corporate networks on the other. Indeed, through this novel tool, she opined, it would be possible to transcend these divergent streams of activity and move toward a third networking (dai-san no nettowākingu).[171]

Asakura's comments certainly capture the mellifluous tone of this Toyota Foundation–sponsored event, though it is worth mentioning a minority opinion that articulated a more critical perspective on networking and the new civic movements. Masamura Kimihiro, a Senshu University academic, for instance, questioned activists' deep-seated fears of bureaucratic co-optation and control from above and their almost religious commitment to autonomy. He advised participants, on the contrary, to be wary of ideas such as citizen-participation-style welfare, which, rather than directly controlling or co-opting civic groups, was a sophisticated device for the state to pass off its welfare responsibilities in the name of individual freedom of choice and popular involvement in public policy.[172] For the most part, however, opinions such as this were drowned out by the overwhelming rhetoric of civic group self-help, autonomy, and symbiosis at this first major networking event.

Meeting again in 1992, the JNC group was joined by a cadre of nonprofit experts from the United States, as well as by prominent volunteer groups, such as the Japan Youth Volunteer Center. At the 1992 gathering specialists from the United States spoke about the management, history, support system, and legal framework of nonprofits in their country, and Japanese experts outlined the difficulties and limitations of the regulatory framework in Japan. Others—including a representative from Keidanren's newly established Social Contribution Division—spoke about the state of corporate philanthropy and the need for a new relationship *(aratana kankei)* between corporations and citizens' groups.[173] The growing specificity of the JNC's publications in 1992 neatly encapsulates the direction of debate by the early 1990s: *NPO to wa Nanika* (What Is an NPO?) (1992); *Nihon ni okeru Kōeki Katsudō no Genjō to Kadai* (The Current Situation and Issues concerning Public-Interest Activities in Japan) (1994); and *Hieiri Dantai to Shakai Kiban* (Nonprofit Groups and Social Infrastructure) (1995).[174] Needless to say, earlier concerns about the link between rising volunteerism and state welfare retrenchment were largely absent from this ever more legalistic and technical discussion.

Emblematic of the convergence among officials and civic activists is the NIRA (National Institute for Research Advancement) report of 1994, titled *Shimin Kōeki Katsudō Kihon Seibi ni kansuru Chōsa Kenkyū* (Research Report on the Support System for Citizens' Public-Interest Activities) and compiled by a who's who of corporate philanthropists, leading activists, and state officials.[175] Interestingly, in its history of civic activism, the report devoted only a few sentences to the movements of the 1960s and 1970s, focusing instead on traditional, community-oriented civic groups and philanthropic practices, such as the Tokugawa period five-family unit *(goningumi)*, prewar Hōtokusha societies based on the teachings of Ninomiya Sontoku, postwar neighborhood associations, imperial benevolence, community hall groups *(kōminkan katsudō)*, and children's groups *(kodomokai)*. The report explicitly contrasted the serious *(majime)* movements of the 1960s with the enjoyable *(tanoshii)* activities of the 1980s.[176] Similarly, a report of the Japan Networkers' Conference around the time of the 1995 earthquake suggested that the foundation of the new wave of activism lay in its warm humanity *(atatakai ningensei)* and participants' sincere passion *(shinshi na jōnetsu)*.[177] The same report noted the spread of a new border area *(keikai ryōiki)* of issues traditionally the responsibility of the state and corporations. It suggested that, in the future, volunteer-ism by civic groups would have to shoulder a greater responsibility in these areas, especially in welfare provision and mutual assistance among citizens in local communities.[178] To be fair, activists did recognize the need to maintain a critical eye toward the state and corporations, but more often than not this position was couched in terms such as con-structive criticism *(kensetsuteki na hihan)*[179] or activism based on con-structive proposals and partnerships.[180]

As Matsubara Akira, a leading civil society advocate, later noted, by the beginning of 1995 the three key groups involved in the political movement for nonprofit legislation—politicians, bureaucrats, and civic groups—were more or less mobilized.[181] The significant point here is that the Toyota Foundation played no small part in making this move-ment possible by providing crucial institutional support for movement intellectuals championing a new era of constructive and symbiotic activism in Japan.

A CITIZEN-PARTICIPATION-STYLE CIVIL SOCIETY

To conclude, then, consider again the emergence of new civic groups in the 1970s and the implications of their ideas and activism for Japa-nese civil society. As I argued, influential movement intellectuals articu-lated a pervasive vision of civic activism centered on notions of creative, engaged, and financially sustainable activism. Lionizing constructive, alternative-proposal-style civic activism, these intellectuals contrasted the new groups with earlier protest movements, which supposedly had adopted losing strategies of opposition to and dependence on official-dom. True independence, these individuals argued, would come about only when civic groups actively and constructively engaged with the state, the market, and society in general. Institutional interventions and barriers certainly facilitated this 1970s shift in civic activism, but movement intellectuals became the catalysts of civic movement change by identifying new social needs, articulating an attractive and novel vision, and successfully organizing people into a new generation of civic movements.

The new vision of civic activism promoted by movement intellectuals benefited greatly from state and corporate support. Faced with new socioeconomic and demographic challenges beginning around the early 1970s, state officials in the Ministry of Health and Welfare and Economic Planning Agency became interested in independent volunteerism and forms of community and welfare activism. The MHW, in particular, funded various projects to nurture and promote independent volunteerism, in the process shaping elite attitudes about the significance of civic activism for Japanese society. State officials also enthusiastically adopted central elements of the *shimin* paradigm, such as autonomy, community, and self-help, fashioning these into an overarching vision of the citizen-participation-style welfare society. State support for institutionalized forms of association and volunteerism continued but was enhanced now by policies supportive of useful new civic groups. Of course, bureaucrats' vision of civil society and the new civic groups by no means perfectly matched that of civic activists. As Robert Pekkanen has carefully documented, civic group advocates and their political supporters' vision of nonprofit legislation differed from that of conservative lawmakers and bureaucrats.[182] The former group pushed successfully for a system of approval and minimal supervision, whereas the latter wanted extensive state screening and supervision similar to the existing legal regime for public-interest corporations. In other words, government officials and civic advocates disagreed on the issue of civic group autonomy. Nevertheless, such conflicts and tensions must be seen against the backdrop of state support for new civic groups in the preceding decades. Rather than evidencing how civil society has transcended the state, official involvement in volunteerism and civic activism from the 1970s onward reveals how officials at all levels of government have moved to incorporate these new civic energies within their policy programs.

Corporate actors also made consequential interventions in the 1980s with targeted funding for new civic groups and support for networking initiatives. Among the more important corporate actors was the Toyota Foundation, which promoted new civic groups under the banner of "citizens' activities." Program officers chose the term *citizens' activities* over the more common *citizens' movement* to distance their vision of the new civic groups from contentious forms of activism. The Toyota Foundation also worked to funnel its vision of citizens' activities into the political movement for nonprofit legislation during the late 1990s. Its financial and logistical support for networking events in the mid-1980s provided movement intellectuals at the forefront of the new civic movements with an influential forum to advocate the formal legal legitimization of the civic group sector—ultimately realized in 1998. Furthermore, program officers continued thereafter to shape public perceptions and understandings of the new groups, playing leading roles in the 1994 NIRA report on citizens' public-interest activities and the 1996 EPA report on citizens' activities.

In the space of a few decades, leading movement intellectuals, supported by bureaucratic and corporate elites, redefined the *shimin* idea, demonizing the recent past, which they depicted as one of accusation and protest, and lionizing the bright future, in which they envisioned creation, proposal, and symbiosis. Although they drew liberally on core elements of earlier *shimin* thought, such as self-help, participation, and community, their application of these ideas drove civic activism in new directions and into new spheres of activity. Not only did this tend to undervalue—if not demonize—the history of 1960s and 1970s protest in Japan, but also in the late 1980s it reinforced an ascendant vision of civil society as a harmonious space for social capital initiatives by largely apolitical and domesticated civic groups—what we might call a citizen-participation-style civil society. The historical irony, of course, is that the starting point for the new paradigm was movement intellectuals' fundamental critique of postwar politics and economic development. Never did they imagine that their model of alternatives would become an endorsement of the state's own communitarian vision of civil society and a mechanism for self-imposed political quietism.

The *Shimin* Idea and Civil Society

THE NEW CITIZENS

In 1992 a group of Japanese scholars published an unassuming volume on political strategy and civic autonomy in contemporary Japan.[1] Although by no means a best seller, the book is interesting historically, because it represents a conjuncture in the theory, history, and politics of civic activism in Japan at that moment. Conceptually, the authors were attempting to connect the *shimin* idea and its postwar history to the then-ascendant notion of civil society *(shimin shakai)*—a novel undertaking because, apart from a few important exceptions, the two concepts were essentially divorced in progressive discourse throughout most of the postwar period. *Shimin,* of course, had charted a history onward and upward in civic thought and activism since the mid-1950s, whereas *shimin shakai* had mostly languished on the conceptual fringes as the pejorative Marxist designation for bourgeois or capitalist society. In actuality, reform-minded Marxian economists had begun to rehabilitate the civil society idea in Japan as early as the 1940s, but not until the final decade of the twentieth century did it recombine with *shimin* in a public discourse on political and social transformation in the country.[2]

The 1992 book is also noteworthy for its intentional modification and rearticulation of the *shimin* idea as *shin-shimin,* or "new citizen." After all, if there were new citizens, then—by force of logic—there must be older, earlier, or perhaps even outdated citizens. And if this were so, what marked the difference? If the new citizen spoke to a revitalized vision of civil society in Japan, then what had earlier citizens represented, and what had become of them? Moreover, how did the old *shimin* idea connect to the new one, if at all? In this final chapter I want to think through these questions, reframing them as follows: First, how have civic thought and activism unfolded throughout the postwar period, and how might we categorize these into phases of historical development? Second, how does this history connect to the contemporary rise of civil society in Japan? And third, what is the present of the *shimin* idea, hinted at in notions such as the "new citizen"?

PHASES OF CIVIC THOUGHT AND ACTIVISM IN POSTWAR JAPAN

The accompanying table sets out the six historical phases of civic thought and activism in postwar Japan with a possible additional phase beginning around 1990. I categorize these phases as *nascent, formative, elaborative,* and *transformative,* according to the ways they broke new ground, drew upon earlier practices and ideas, affected later developments, or did any combination of these. I see cultural circle activism in the early postwar period as the nascent phase of civic activism, when movement intellectuals and others began to experiment with ideas and practices that would become important in later civic activism. With their interrogation of the intellectual and their lionization of the quotidian perspective, Tsurumi Shunsuke and others opened the way for later imaginations of the *shimin* as a progressive, grassroots expression of performative citizenship. Tsurumi and others' rehabilitation of the nation as a progressive historical vehicle also paved the way for ethnic nationalist ideas in later civic movements. With their focus on spontaneous associationalism and celebration of individual autonomy, cultural circles also anticipated many of the organizational practices of later citizens' movements, such as inclusivity and self-help. But given that activities were largely limited to academic debate and cultural pursuits, this period is best categorized as a nascent phase of activism: in it we see the early convergence but not the meeting of a number of important institutional and ideational elements, such as war remorse, the new constitutional mentality, the revival and adaptation of nonaligned activism, and the nurturing of influential citizen movement intellectuals.

The formative moment of civic activism began in the late 1950s and reached a crescendo in the Anpo struggle. In the debate on mass society

PHASES OF CIVIC ACTIVISM IN POSTWAR JAPAN

Phase	Movement	Identities	Ideational Elements
Nascent	Cultural circle activism (ca. 1945–55)	The people	• The progressive ethnic nation • Spontaneous associationalism • Ideological nonalignment
Formative	The Anpo struggle (1958–60)	*Shimin*	• Linking private life and democracy • Conscientious civic activism • Pragmatic civic activism
Elaborative	Beheiren (1965–74)	*Shimin* as Japanese and Asians	• The Pacific War and the Vietnam War • Individual aggression and victimization • Ethnic nationalism + anti-Americanism
Elaborative	Antipollution and Antidevelopment protest (ca. 1964–75)	*Shimin* as *jūmin* (local residents)	• Self-help • Local autonomy • Ideological nonalignment • Strategically targeted action
Elaborative	The movement for citizen participation (ca. 1963–75)	*Shimin as kokumin* (Japanese nationals)	• Civil rights + civic duties • Institutionalizing civic energies
Transformative	The new civic movements (ca. 1975–89)	*Shimin as seikatsusha* (inhabitants of daily life)	• Critique of free market • Constructive activism • Engagement with state and corporate actors • Promotion of community
?	The rise of civil society (ca. 1990–present)	*Shimin* as *shin-shimin* (new citizens)	• Professionalization • Institutionalization • Depoliticization • Transnationalization

during the mid-1950s, Matsushita Keiichi and others began to detach the *shimin* idea from its negative petit bourgeois connotations in Marxist theory. Indeed, they helped to rehabilitate the idea by relocating it in an enlightenment discourse on the birth of civic consciousness among Japan's incipient new middle stratum. Though Matsushita and others were initially committed to a socialist future, with the independent citizen mobilizations before, during, and after the Anpo struggle, they more or less abandoned the centrality of class for the *shimin* as a new historical actor. The civic thought and activism of the Anpo struggle was pivotal in that it crafted a language, a rudimentary praxis, and a legitimizing framework for grassroots activism thereafter. As Snow and Benford explain, "Movements that surface early in a cycle of protest are likely to function as progenitors of master frames that provide the ideational and interpretive anchoring for subsequent movements within the cycle."[3] Movement intellectuals of the Anpo struggle contributed to the formation of a master frame of civic activism in two ways. First, they used the *shimin* idea to articulate a new activist mentality that connected independent political action to private life, self-interest, and the postwar ethos of "peace and democracy." Second, in terms of modes of activism, movement intellectuals attached the *shimin* idea to two streams of collective action: one based on conscientious dissent and the other embedded in prosaic local activities. This ideational work by no means predetermined the shape of later activism, but it clearly influenced the way later movement intellectuals defined their activist identities and conceptualized their concrete activities.

I see the next three phases of civic activism as elaborative, in that they adopted, adapted, embellished, and sometimes added to the master frame articulated during the Anpo struggle. The ideational work of the late 1950s and 1960 certainly provided the language and grammar for civic activism, but, as Baud and Rutten observe, once created and proved, successful ideational frames often become "modular"—in other words, receptive to creative and dynamic recombination.[4] Movement intellectuals' use of the *shimin* idea in the Beheiren movement from 1965 evidences such modularity. On the one hand, Beheiren continued the conscientious stream of civic activism, staying loyal to decentralized and independent mobilization. On the other hand, this antiwar movement differed from civic protests during the Anpo struggle in two ways. First, the civic mobilizations of 1960 drew on the energy of a broad national movement led by students, labor groups, political parties, and other large associations, whereas the agenda of the Beheiren movement was largely defined from within. It was movement intellectuals like Oda Makoto and Tsurumi Yoshiyuki, not outsiders, who elaborated the Anpo struggle model into one of the most emblematic antiwar civic mobilizations of the postwar era. Most significant, of course, was Oda and others' linking of the *shimin* identity to a nationalist, Pan Asian, and racialized discourse on liberation from so-called U.S. imperialism. This endeavor certainly resonated with the ethnic national flavor of earlier civic discourse, but it propelled the discourse

further by linking the *shimin* idea in an overt way to third world liberation and Black Power. The result was a troubling ethnocentric, culturally
chauvinistic, and even xenophobic tenor in many of the writings and
public statements of the movement's intellectual leadership—all clothed,
of course, in the protective armor of *shimin* symbolism.

Antipollution and antidevelopment activism in the mid-1960s developed the pragmatic stream of Anpo-struggle civic activism into a theory
and praxis of localism. Movement intellectuals deeply shaped the mentality and objectives of participants in these mobilizations by shifting
attention from grand strategies, such as the overthrow of conservative
hegemony, to more parochial desires to protect the local living environment. Miyazaki Shōgo's provocative rendition of the public interest as
the sum total of private interests was the most graphic expression of
this position. But the contribution of movement intellectuals here was
not only ideological; they also elaborated a sophisticated organizational
and strategic repertoire for local activism. The groundbreaking movements in Shizuoka in the early 1960s, for instance, redirected practices
of self-help into basic scientific experimentation, targeted public lectures, and pollution-site visits. Picking up on earlier ideas of inclusivity
and political neutrality, activists also recognized that avoiding dogmatic
leftist ideology facilitated broad-based alliances and often the support
of both progressive and conservative government elites.

Thus, while the intellectuals of the Beheiren adapted the master
frame of Anpo-struggle civic activism for an overtly idealistic and conscientious set of aspirations, antipollution and antidevelopment activists reworked it to fit a remarkably instrumental agenda. In the long
run this instrumentalist approach exercised its own distinctive influence
on *shimin* activism, especially the primacy it afforded self-help. In the
1970s and even more so the 1980s, movement intellectuals' discourse
on localized community-based self-help spread not only among activists
but also among officials at all levels of government, now worried about
rising energy costs, national self-sufficiency, and servicing a rapidly
aging population.

The movement for citizen participation in the same period drew on
both the pragmatic and the idealistic aspects of the *shimin* idea. Unlike
local activists or those involved in the Beheiren movement, however,
Matsushita Keiichi, the Tosei Chōsakai, and progressive local officials
were deeply committed to the complete institutionalization of civic
energies. Only by funneling spontaneous residential movements into
formalized procedures for citizen participation, they believed, would

residents overcome their narrow local egoism, local government be reformed, and conservative hegemony finally overcome. Matsushita and his contemporaries not only brought notions of civic rights and duties, civic nationalism, and community to the center of *shimin* thought; they also adapted the *shimin* idea for the domain of public administration. This focus on citizen involvement in bureaucratic policymaking and local governance—as opposed to unsystematic and sporadic dissent—opened the way for later discourses and practices of symbiosis and collaboration between citizens' groups and the state.

New civic movements from the 1970s through the 1980s represent a transformation of the *shimin* idea. We can observe any number of renovations in these movements: notions of self-help, now expressed in terms of financial sustainability, professionalization, and the proposal of constructive alternatives; earlier ideas about civic engagement now discussed in the context of collaboration, symbiotic networking, and communitarianism; and nationalist perspectives animated by a critique of Western free-market capitalism and globalization. Most striking in this period was influential movement intellectuals' vociferous demonization and rejection of contentious activism and the accompanying communitarian rhetoric of symbiosis and collaboration. This position certainly reflected the institutional impediments activists had faced in earlier movements and was undoubtedly a strategy to escape from the "ice age" of civic activism.[5] But it was not only reactive. As an elaborated and sophisticated framework for collective action, the new paradigm adapted ideas central to civic activism throughout the postwar era; moreover, it transformed them so extensively that actors in all spheres of Japanese society began to recognize the necessity for and legitimacy of a robust—if securely domesticated—civil society. So, problematic though the new approach was, it contributed to the significant shift in Japanese civic activism, both perceptually and practically, beginning around the early 1970s.

The final and seventh phase, which I tentatively call "the rise of civil society," began in the 1990s. The reemergence of civil society first in central and eastern European social movements and later throughout the Western world helped stimulate this new phase, but so too did activists, academics, the media, and government circles' increasing attention to Japanese civic activism as an identifiable, demarcatable, and instrumentally useful sphere of social activity. The tragic earthquake of 1995 and regulatory reform in 1998 only further stimulated public discussion and interest in civil society. Of course, whether this phase is merely an elaboration on earlier phases—a consolidation of the new civic movements—or a moment of substantive transformation remains unclear. To be sure, the creation of a new category of nonprofit corporations, or NPOs, in the Civil Code has afforded many thousands of previously informal voluntary groups unheard-of social legitimacy, so the reality of fundamental institutional change cannot be denied. But just as important will be the meanings and interpretations that activists, officials, and others bring to the law and the now-legitimate idea of civil society in Japan. As chapter 5 revealed, the rise of Japanese civil society in the 1990s owed much to the relentless efforts of influential civic activists to mend broken bridges with government and corporate elites (and vice versa) and to distance civic activism from its earlier moments of contention and protest. Any perceived transformation, reimagination, or rebirth in civil society needs to be read in its historical context, unromantic though this may be. Nevertheless, while this history may bring into question claims of fundamental change, it also reminds us that civic activists have played a prominent and formative role in shaping this history too—the central thesis of this study and an issue I return to now.

MOVEMENT INTELLECTUALS AND THE RISE OF CIVIL SOCIETY IN JAPAN

Although the *shimin* idea has been circulating in political discourse for many years now, widespread public and academic attention to the notion of civil society *(shimin shakai)* is relatively recent, traceable largely to the years after 1990. One definitive moment, of course, was in January 1995, when the massive earthquake struck near Kobe City and thousands of volunteers spontaneously rushed to assist while the authorities floundered. Thereafter—and depending on one's terminological preference—Japan experienced nothing short of a rebirth, a reimagination, a burgeoning, and a revolution in its civil society. Anecdotal evidence of the rising popularity of the *shimin shakai* idea is suggestive: a simple survey of books containing the term *shimin shakai* in the National Diet Library of Japan reveals an eighteenfold increase from 1995 to 2005. The imagery of these publications is decidedly upbeat, with titles trumpeting "The Age of the Citizens' Movement," "Civil Society Transcending the State," and, more bluntly, "The Age of the Citizen."[6] As figure 3 reveals, volunteers *(borantia)*, citizens *(shimin)*, and NPOs are darlings of the print media nowadays. Other

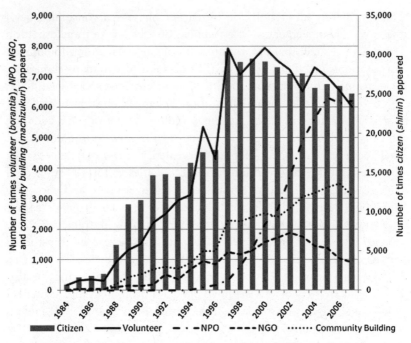

FIGURE 3. Frequency of civil society terms' appearing in articles in *Asahi Shimbun*, 1984–2007. Source: *Asahi Shimbun* database, www.asahi.com (accessed April 2008).

indicators also point to the rising prominence and legitimacy of a particular configuration of civil society: the number of registered volunteers at social welfare councils nationwide is at an all-time high (over seven million in early 2005).[7] And, perhaps most emblematic of all, in 1998 the Japanese Diet passed the groundbreaking Law to Promote Specified Nonprofit Activities (Tokutei Hieiri Katsudō Sokushin Hō). This law is important in numerous ways. Civic groups can now incorporate with less bureaucratic oversight and red tape and, once incorporated, can enjoy greater social legitimacy and the logistical benefits of formal legal status. The law promises a more robustly autonomous civil society and perhaps even a new configuration of political power in Japan.

Intellectually, the emergence of a civil society discourse has also shone a brighter light on Japan's own indigenous traditions of grassroots activism and thought (for example, the *shimin* idea). Researchers have begun to hotly debate whether postwar thinkers—Maruyama Masao, Ōtsuka Hisao, Kawashima Takeyoshi, et cetera—*did* or *did not* possess a concept of *shimin shakai*, why they might have avoided the term, and whether they were pessimistic, ambivalent, unaware, or simply did not care.[8] Even more interesting has been the newly gained prominence of a critical stream of civil society thought that developed within the Marxist tradition in Japan. In the scholarship of Uchida Yoshihiko and Hirata Kiyoaki in the 1960s, civil society scholar John Keane has discovered "phase one of the contemporary renaissance of civil society." in the world.[9] As I intimated above, until Uchida and Hirata appeared on the scene, civil society denoted nothing more than bourgeois or capitalist society and, for Japanese Marxists, was at best a transitory stage on the way to socialism. But as Andrew Barshay explains, for Uchida, civil society became "the very instrument of positive social transformation" and "could not possibly be the mere ideological reflex of bourgeois hegemony because that hegemony had never formed." Focusing on his studies of the great Scottish philosopher Adam Smith, "Uchida drew the basic notion that real *Homo economicus* was not just a cold calculator, but the individual constituent of civil society, in which market relations and the social division of labor itself must be, and in fact are, underlain by a basic human sympathy between equals who recognize the 'sanctity' of each other's good-faith efforts."[10]

Beginning with his seminal 1969 work *Shimin Shakai to Shakaishugi* (Civil Society and Socialism), Uchida's contemporary Hirata Kiyoaki attempted to reconstitute Marxism (as Matsushita Keiichi did) by injecting the concept of civil society back into socialism as an end in itself—as an objective *(mokuteki)*. According to Yamaguchi Yasushi, this project emerged from Hirata's critique of Soviet-style socialism, which he saw as a negative product of revolution in late-developing countries.[11] As Hirata explained many years later, socialism without civil society was not socialism at all; it was a crude and despotic configuration he branded as state socialism *(kokka shakaishugi)*.[12] Drawing on the thought of Antonio Gramsci, Hirata envisioned civil society as a strategic space for civic groups to create a new hegemony through the reabsorption of the state.[13] In the late 1980s, Hirata and his students began to refer to this project as a revolution *(senkai)* in civil society theory, because it effectively replaced the historicist Hegelian-Marxist characterization of civil society with a vision in which the constituents of civil society had historical agency: they made their history.[14] Hence, Hirata boldly proclaimed that civil society should be redesignated as the furnace of history *(rekishi no kamado)*—a nod to Marx and Engels's characterization of civil society in *The German Ideology*, yet a clear attempt to move beyond this.[15] Around this time, the ideas of Hirata and his students began to merge with other normative treatments of civil society else-where—in other words, with the ideas of Jean Cohen and Andrew Arato, Jürgen Habermas, John Keane, Michael Walzer, and proponents of radical democracy and new social movements, such as Ernesto Laclau and Chantal Mouffe.[16] Signaling these linkages in the late 1990s, a group of Hirata's former apprentices confidently declared the "rehabilitation of civil society theory" as a "new social paradigm."[17]

But we should keep in mind that Uchida, Hirata, and their students' theorizations on *shimin shakai*—limited as they were to complex academic debate—played essentially no intellectual role in the development of civic thought and activism I have traced in this book. Or to put it in conceptual terms: for most of the postwar era, ideas about the *shimin* and *shimin shakai* unfolded along largely separate trajectories—resonance without cross-fertilization in a sense. There are a number of interesting moments of connection, nevertheless. For example, movement intellectual Iwane Kunio of the Seikatsu Club had Hirata write the foreword to his self-congratulatory 1993 book on the movement.[18] Moreover, it was Hirata, his students, and activists such as Yokota Katsumi (from the Seikatsu Club) who led the contemporary revival of Gramscian thought in Japan.[19] And as I have shown throughout this study, individuals such as Matsushita Keiichi, Maruyama Masao, and Kuno Osamu clearly had an idea of civil society in its contemporary, liberal sense, even if they did not use the term *shimin shakai* regularly. But, at least in an overt and large-scale way, not until the 1990s was the relationship between the *shimin* idea and *shimin shakai* finally consummated in the work of Sakamoto Yoshikazu and proponents of the new citizen.

More complicated, of course, are the reasons for the recent renaissance of civil society in the country and its connections to earlier phases of civic activism. Some, for example, see Japan's emergent civil society in the context of wider global-historical processes of democratization identified by Samuel Huntington, Lester Salamon, and others.[20] Tsuji-naka Yutaka, for example, suggests that Japan has "undergone waves of democratization that have stimulated civil society organizations," giving them "greater access and acceptance in the postwar era."[21] Sakamoto Yoshikazu positions developments in Japan within the "century of the citizen," when the state and the market will be "relativized" by a universal "civil society" of mutual interdependence.[22] Romantic master narratives aside, however, there is no doubting that global processes have stimulated and shaped Japan's civil society in recent decades. Research shows how international norms supportive of active state-NGO cooperation in the 1980s pressured Japanese officials to reconsider their relationship with and support for the civic group sector.[23] As Stephen Osborne puts it, Japan—like most other countries—"is susceptible to the trends of globalization and convergence" in which nongovernment, nonprofit actors are "seen as important actors."[24]

But not all the stimuli have been external. Observers also point to the role of the state in fostering—sometimes purposively, sometimes inadvertently—the rise of civil society. On the broadest level, Robert Pekkanen argues that "the very success of the developmental state brought Japan to a new level of affluence and led to the increasing prominence of civil society organizations."[25] Paradoxically, Japan's activist state may have empowered ordinary citizens by providing them with the economic elbow room to act. Such potentialities were only aided by transformations and challenges to the extant structure of governance in the 1990s. During that decade, bureaucratic supremacy was greatly undermined by a string of scandals, including HIV-contaminated blood, bid rigging, nuclear accidents, extravagant bureaucratic expense accounts, and, perhaps most emblematic of all, the woeful government response to the 1995 earthquake.[26] Victoria Bestor describes this as a moment of awakening for Japanese, who saw the potential of "a spontaneously formed coalition" of ordinary citizens.[27] For Shaw and Goda, the stronger sense of self-governance and community solidarity generated by the earthquake "brought new dimensions to civil society in Japan."[28] Coupled with the earthquake, changes to electoral institutions in 1994 also led to "altered incentives for political actors," especially with respect to their support for civic groups and desire for regulatory reform.[29]

State impact on civil society has not all been inadvertent, of course. As Susan Pharr argues, the Japanese state "has taken an activist stance toward civic life, monitoring it, penetrating it, and seeking to steer it with a wide range of distinct policy tools targeted by group or sector."[30] Indeed, some scholars explain civil society in the context of changed government objectives after the 1973 oil shock and, specifically, the challenges of dealing with welfare costs in an ever-aging society. Herein, Japan's civic rebirth emerges less as a reaction or solution to the developmental state than, ironically, as another instance of shrewd official management of social energies. Akihiro Ogawa, for example, claims that "volunteerism institutionalized under the NPO Law serves the state . . . which pursues small government with an emphasis on market rationality"—something Nakano Toshio likens to a "civil society of mobilized volunteers."[31] Rhetorically, Yasuda Tsuneo points to the official co-optation of civic symbols such as *shimin* (citizen). Previously a marker of everything antiestablishment and antistate, *shimin*, he laments, has been narrowly recast to denote subjects who fulfill their self-responsibility and strive for self-governance in a neoliberal order.[32] Whether we agree or not, the striking expansion of independent welfare groups in recent years suggests that technologies and rationalities of responsible autonomy, marketization, and degovernmentalization provide part of the backdrop to the rise of civil society in Japan.[33] In other words, though state governance may have changed (or been forced to change) and become more sophisticated in the face of growing pressure from civic groups, the outcomes may be similar: a domesticated and largely service-oriented civil society.

Largely absent from this discourse, however, has been any systematic attempt to connect the emergence of Japanese civil society in the 1990s to the postwar history of civic thought and activism in the country.[34] There has been little room for discussion about the agency of civic actors in a narrative dominated by global transformations and powerful political and economic institutions. Of course, my point is not that such factors have been unimportant. On the contrary, this study evidences the ways political and economic institutions have intentionally and unintentionally shaped civic activism throughout the postwar period. What I argue, however, is that an overemphasis on such aspects tends to obscure the ways in which ideas and traditions of activism forged by grassroots activists over the past half century have also shaped the conceptualization and development of civil society in contemporary Japan. The *shimin* idea and its history in thought and activism is part of contemporary civil society; it shapes the way advocates imagine civil society and is, in turn, reimagined within that contemporary realm.

Throughout the study I have attempted to marry two traditionally distinct approaches: the history of ideas on the one hand and ideational theories of social movements on the other, to show how the ideas of individuals found expression in civic movements and modes of governance. Citizen movement intellectuals knit together various ideational components: war memories and remorse; reimaginations of local and national community; the symbolism of the postwar constitution; and a vision of ordinary individuals building democracy through active association. The point is not that movement intellectuals forced an agenda and identity on movement participants but that their personal histories and aspirations helped shape social interaction, identity construction, and objective setting within movements. During the early postwar years, for example, this involved the articulation of an indigenous democratic subjectivity and associationalism. During the Anpo crisis it meant defining an activist identity beyond leftist categories, an identity that spoke to middle-class aspirations for affluence, peace, and political participation. In the anti–Vietnam War movement it entailed locating the *shimin* idea in discourses on Pan Asianism, third world liberation, and the victimization of ordinary people by the United States and its client, the Japanese state. In antipollution and antidevelopment movements, it involved the articulation of a strong vision of local self-help, and for proponents of local government reform it meant promoting the full institutionalization of civic movements into the structures of modern governance. And finally, after the protest of the 1970s and a general reconsideration of high-growth economics, movement intellectuals began to rearticulate the *shimin* idea as a self-reflexive, self-responsible subject open to collaboration and engagement with traditional opponents, all in the name of fundamental social change.

As each of these phases reveals, movement intellectuals' ideas had a creative and autonomous aspect, operating as crucial intervening variables between structure and mobilization. Faced with institutional hurdles, activists did not simply retreat into their shells; the most creative and entrepreneurial of them pushed civic activism in new directions on the basis of a vision of what they believed activism could and should be. This was a vision very much grounded in reality, but it also contained a creative and personal component. As I discussed in the introduction, this enduring impact of the ideas of movement intellectuals on civic activism becomes clear only when we step back from theories (such as the new social movement theory) or master narratives that would portray the *shimin* idea and related civic movements as inherently "progressive" and "antiestablishment." By doing so we see the choices that civic actors made at crucial moments and the often troubling motivations driving their ideas and actions. Recall the ethnic nationalism pervading civic thought in the earliest days of the postwar years and in the Beheiren movement; the commitment of Matsushita Keiichi and influential activists to civic self-discipline and their rejection of "egoistic" dissent; and the logic of "proposal" that similarly rejected contentious activism in favor of movement marketization, collaboration, and an apolitical vision of the *shimin*. Troubling though they have been, such ideas influenced the development of civic activism in postwar

Japan and, hence, deserve consideration alongside institutional and macrostructural theories explaining civil society in the country. Grassroots ideas have mattered in Japanese civil society, although perhaps not as progressive master narratives might suggest.

THE *SHIMIN* IDEA TODAY

What then of the present of the *shimin* idea—the historical legacies of over a half century of civic thought and activism? Where did the ideational work of movement intellectuals arrive, and where might the *shimin* idea be headed? Although writing a history of the present is largely speculative, there is no doubt that the *shimin* idea informs recent discussions of civil society in the country. Concretely, the *shimin* idea has made possible the construction of an idea of civil society in Japan that is at once national and international. In defining civil society, Satō Yoshiyuki for example, speaks of a civic public sphere *(shiminteki kōkyōen)*, or an open social space, where "individuals liberated from communal groups express their own ideas and opinions through words and action." He calls such individuals *"shimin."* For Satō, the civic public sphere is formed by the diverse associational groups that discuss and take action on specific issues, and as an aggregation, this becomes a civil society. This new civil society *(atarashii shimin shakai)*, Satō points out, is not bourgeois civil society or capitalist society but the sphere of the daily-life world *(seikatsu sekai)* outside the market and state.[35] Another contemporary champion of civil society, Yamaoka Yoshinori, also leans heavily on powerful motifs of participation, self-responsibility, and autonomy in the *shimin* idea. A civil society, Yamaoka suggests, is a society in which "each and every citizen participates on the basis of self-responsibility *(jiko sekinin)*" and in which the aspirations of each and every citizen are realized.[36]

The most boldly confident presentation of the *shimin* and *shimin shakai*, however, belongs to the Anpo struggle veteran Sakamoto Yoshikazu and is outlined in his 1997 work *Sōtaika no Jidai* (The Age of Relativization). Here Sakamoto describes *shimin shakai* as the "public space that produces social relations founded on the mutual recognition of human dignity and equal rights." *Shimin shakai* "is not a timeless space," he tells us, "but an unending process of historical formation." "What I have in mind is not an ahistorical definition hammered together in an a priori way," but a concept that was "resurrected" and "redefined" in the "process of historical transformation produced by democratic movements and various civic movements in eastern Europe and elsewhere in the 1980s." Sakamoto is particularly enamored by the Solidarity movement in Poland and its appeal to "spontaneous solidarity," "plurality," "free communication," and "democratic participation." Ultimately, Sakamoto asserts, *shimin shakai* is not merely a set of "empirically existing social relationships" or an "analytical concept" but a "critical conceptualization" with "normative meaning." In other words, it signifies the "social relations of citizens who act to create and support a society and human relations that mutually recognize human dignity and equal rights." Sounding very much like citizen movement intellectuals of the Anpo struggle, *shimin,* in Sakamoto's definition, are the "*actually existing individuals possessed* of such a *normative consciousness.*"[37]

Of course, the connections between the *shimin* idea and *shimin shakai* extend further than the genealogy or history of ideas. Particularly significant, I believe, was the period from the mid-1970s to the present, which unfolded as a process of convergence among influential civic, state, and market actors. It was this convergence that paved the way for the contemporary imagination of *shimin shakai* as a harmonious space for social capital initiatives by largely apolitical civic groups. Movement intellectuals' unabashed remolding of *shimin* symbolism and activism beginning in the early 1970s cannot be underestimated here. By criticizing discourses of dissent and marrying the *shimin* idea to collaboration and self-reliant volunteerism, they undeniably paved the way for such a vision. But the connections stretch back even further: from its origins in discourses on the people in the early postwar era, the *shimin* idea displayed potentialities visible in the *shimin shakai* of contemporary Japan. Even during the period of high protest, activists, local politicians, and intellectuals were actively linking the *shimin* idea to notions of participation and civic contribution to the nation, so it is no coincidence that the contemporary vision and reality of *shimin shakai* should draw on and reflect this history. From this perspective, the rise of *shimin shakai* in Japan during the 1990s may be understood better as an elaboration than as an absolute transformation in the sphere of civic thought and activism—more a modulation than a metamorphosis.

Indeed, while most sing praises of the *shimin* and *shimin shakai,* some have recently begun to express doubts. Such observers refuse to accept any logical or practical connection among the absence of coercion, the display of spontaneity, and the condition of human autonomy. For them, *shimin shakai* is a space under siege, a battleground for the control of civic energies by groups with remarkably different agendas and ideological positions. And beating at the heart of such critiques is a deep suspicion of the contemporary state (admittedly, often conceptualized as monolithic) and its arguably neoliberal agenda vis-à-vis civil society. Yasuda Tsuneo, for instance, has noted the remarkable transformation in the meaning of the *shimin* idea. He argues that, with the rise of neoliberalism in the 1980s, the *shimin* idea, once signifying a position deeply critical of state-defined visions of the public interest, came to connote self-responsibility and self-regulation as the idea was coupled with ideas of volunteerism and nonprofit civic activism. As the *shimin* found a new home in the NPOs and the NGOs, Yasuda asserts, the idea of it resisting neoliberalism or neonationalism became nothing more than an "illusion." Rather than standing firm as antiestablishment symbols, terms such as *shimin* and *shimin undō* themselves became "critical sites of conflict," he argues—a battle, one supposes, between liberation and autonomy on the one hand and institutional mobilization on the other.[38]

Echoing Yasuda's pessimism, others such as Kurihara Akira have suggested that a citizen politics *(shimin seiji)* based on institutionalized NPOs has "set its own limits." He explains the inventory of these limits as follows: the preservation of capitalism; the affirmation of sustainable development; receptivity to commercialization; the formation of partnerships with the bureaucracy; the acceptance of globalization; and not saying "no" to the political system.[39] Even Takabatake Michitoshi, an original champion of the *shimin* idea, began to have fears about Japanese civil society in his later years. Reflecting on the transformation of religious, educational, and labor associations from the powerful foundation stones of civil society into co-opted interest groups *(rieki shūdan),* Takabatake wondered if NPOs and NGOs would tread the same path as they became more organized and institutionalized.[40]

Nakano Toshio has outlined what is perhaps the most vehement criticism of *shimin shakai* in a suggestively titled essay, "Borantia Dōin-gata Shimin Shakai Ron no Kansei" (The Pitfalls of a Civil Society Theory Modeled on Volunteer Mobilization).[41] Nakano takes direct aim at Sakamoto Yoshikazu and other *shimin shakai* advocates who claim that globalization has relativized *(sōtaika)* the nation-state to such an extent that we now live under postnational conditions in which global civil society reigns supreme. Nakano is not convinced by Sakamoto's claims about the century of the citizen *(shimin no seiki),* the autonomy of civil society from the state, or the contemporary autonomy of the human subject. On the contrary, Nakano argues that, rather than a simple relativization of the nation-state, what we are witnessing is a change in its function *(kinō)*. We are seeing, according to Nakano, a shift from the welfare state to the system-crisis-management state *(shisutemu kiki kanri-gata kokka)*, wherein administrations are at once small and yet constantly prepared to react in a time of crisis—be this political, military, or economic.[42] Nakano wonders whether we can make a logical jump from the recent spontaneity *(jihatsusei)* of Japanese volunteers to a glorification of such spontaneity as a manifestation of autonomous human subjectivity. He directly addresses here the tight relationship based on collaboration and cooperation among government ministries, corporations, and civic groups that I traced in chapter 5. Nakano argues that, rather than letting go, the state actually "nurtures the subject," and the subject—so nurtured—"contributes" to the system by "preparing countermeasures" for the "solution of problems." In other words, within a state-defined policy agenda, *shimin shakai* contributes through advocacy-style citizen participation. Rather than transcending the state, volunteerism becomes a clever form of mobilization extremely efficient for the reduction of costs, especially in the realm of welfare.[43]

As anthropologist Akihiro Ogawa pessimistically concludes, "The institutionalization of NPOs is a calculated reorganization of the Japanese public sphere designed to establish a small government in the postwelfare state through the transfer of social services originally delivered by the state to volunteer-driven NPOs."[44] Nakano similarly points to the circumscribed nature of volunteerism in Japan, which at base is shaped by a state-driven discourse of the public interest *(kōekisei)*.[45] Any kind of action outside this sphere *cannot* be volunteerism. Or, to put it in concrete terms, helping old people or victims of disaster is to be a legitimate *borantia,* but to be a *borantia* for the rights of minorities or to halt construction of a trash incineration facility is almost a contradiction in terms. For Nakano, any link between volunteerism and human autonomy must be premised on an investigation of what social function such action fulfills and who is vociferously lauding it.[46] Ogawa has a similarly damning assessment of the *shimin* in contemporary Japan, arguing that "today's *shimin* under the NPO structure are actually avoiding politics. NPO activities are realized in a very moderate tone, encouraging participation in collaborations . . . with the government."[47] For Ogawa, "*shimin* under the NPO system have internalized a coercive volunteer subjectivity, and they are expected to be apolitical and to collaborate with authority."[48]

To get a sense of what the *shimin* idea connotes in current-day Japan, consider the *Asahi Shimbun,* which, in February 2007, ran the final article in a fascinating two-year series on a new breed of grassroots activists it called *shin-shimin*—new citizens.[49] As in the 1992 volume mentioned at the start of the conclusion, the "new" modifier clearly distinguishes these activists from old or earlier *shimin* before the rise of the new civic movements of the 1970s and during an age of protest and accusation. At the same time, identifying contemporary activism with the *shimin* idea—even if modified by newness—also simultaneously connects it to a long and now apparently legitimate history of civic thought and activism. Most interesting is the way this idea of the new citizen tightly dovetails with recent images of an efficiently synchronized civil society in Japan, underwritten by selfless volunteerism and specified nonprofit activities. The *Asahi Shimbun* article of February 2007 contains a suggestive image here, in which three cogs—one for the state (*gyōsei,* or bureaucracy), one for the market (*kigyō,* or enterprise), and one for civil society (NPO)—all turn together like the gears of a finely made wristwatch. In this image the NPO cog, powered by new citizens and their activities, towers over the cogs of the state and the corporate sector: *shimin shakai* is big now; it is pulling its weight for the nation and the globe. To the left of the image stands a smiling, uniformed technician—wrench at the ready—hoping out loud that all the cogs will "gear together smoothly" *(umaku kamiaeba iina).* At least at this moment in Japanese history the *shimin* and *shimin shakai* appear to have become yardsticks in the determination of normality and levels of integration and, by consequence, tools for the demarcation of their illegitimate siblings—the abnormal, the anomalous, and the contentious.

But, though my reading of civil society in contemporary Japan resonates with recent critical assessments, I cannot totally agree with perspectives that afford absolute agency to the state or to some ethereal, yet inevitably malevolent, power. As I have argued throughout this study, the *shimin* idea was a historical and synthetic construction: movement intellectuals and other advocates were constantly working on it, modulating it to fit the needs of the moment. This modularity certainly left the idea open to manipulation by those who hoped to shape and domesticate civic energies, but it was also the wellspring of human agency in Japanese civic activism. So, as much as I concur with recent critiques of Japanese civil society as a largely apolitical communitarian space populated by disciplined and self-responsible *shimin*, the long history of agency-in-activism precludes any crude explanations of this present as one of power (modernist or postmodernist in construction) undermining and neutralizing human subjectivity. Movement intellectuals and other civic activists made their choices, and these choices helped shape activism and, in turn, the broader contours of Japanese civil society. As Joseph Bradley wisely observes, "It is difficult to determine whether any given 'civil society' is becoming or established."[50] The same might be said of the *shimin* idea, which, like any other "hegemonic articulation," has always had an "outside" that constantly inhibits "its full realization," leaving room for reappropriation, recombination, and transformation.[51] And it is this outside—certainly unsettling at times—that has continued and will continue to sustain the *shimin* idea as an expression of performative citizenship in contemporary Japan.

Notes

ABBREVIATIONS

AMC   *Ara Masato Chosakushū*

MMS   *Maruyama Masao Shū*

MMZ   *Maruyama Masao Zadan*

OMZ   *Oda Makoto Zenshigoto*

SBU   *Shiryō "Beheiren" Undō*

SIC   *Shimizu Ikutarō Chosakushū*

Tayori *Fukkokuban: Koe naki Koe no Kai no Tayori*

TSC   *Tsurumi Shunsuke Chosakushū*

TSS   *Tsurumi Shunsuke Shū*

TYC   *Tsurumi Yoshiyuki Chosakushū*

INTRODUCTION

Epigraph: Matsushita Keiichi, "Shimin Sanka to Sono Rekishiteki Kanōsei," in *Gendai ni Ikiru*, vol. 6: *Shimin Sanka*, ed. Matsushita Keiichi (Tokyo: Tōyō Keizai Shinpōsha, 1971), 198. All translations from the Japanese are mine, unless otherwise indicated.

1. That thinker is Maruyama Masao. The relevant essay is Maruyama Masao, "'De aru' koto to 'Suru koto,'" in Maruyama Masao, *Maruyama Masao Shū*, vol. 8 (Tokyo: Iwanami Shoten, 1996), 23–44.

2. In Joseph Bradley, "Subjects into Citizens: Societies, Civil Society, and Autocracy in Tsarist Russia," *American Historical Review* 107, no. 4 (2002),

www.historycooperative.org.libproxy1.nus.edu.sg/journals/ahr/107.4/ ah0402001094.html: paragraph 1. In this study, I understand civil society in terms of Susan Pharr's recent definition: "*Civil society consists of sustained, organized social activity that occurs in groups that are formed outside the state, the market, and the family.* Cumulatively, such activity creates a public sphere outside the state, a space in which groups and individuals engage in public discourse" (emphasis in the original). See Susan Pharr, preface to *The State of Civil Society in Japan,* ed. Frank J. Schwartz and Susan J. Pharr (Cambridge and New York: Cambridge University Press, 2003), xiii. Given this definition, the civic groups I focus on in this study by no means represent the entirety of Japanese civil society, but I argue that they have fundamentally affected its development.

3. Robert Pekkanen, for example, shows convincingly how government regulation has contributed to a civil society comprising many small groups and very few large professionalized organizations with political advocacy functions. See Robert Pekkanen, *Japan's Dual Civil Society: Members without Advocates* (Stanford, CA: Stanford University Press, 2006). Many of the essays in Schwartz and Pharr, *The State of Civil Society in Japan,* also illustrate the shaping impact of an activist state on civil society. For an application of historical institutionalism to the consumer movement, see Patricia Maclachlan, *Consumer Politics in Postwar Japan: The Institutional Boundaries of Citizen Activism* (New York: Columbia University Press, 2002).

4. Others have also recognized the role and significance of ideational and identity factors in civic movements. For example, see Maclachlan, *Consumer Politics in Postwar Japan* (78–83); also Patricia Maclachlan, "The Struggle for an Independent Consumer Society: Consumer Activism and the State's Response in Postwar Japan," in *The State of Civil Society in Japan,* ed. Schwartz and Pharr, especially 218–21 and 225–27; Patricia Maclachlan, "From Subjects to Citizens: Japan's Evolving Consumer Identity," *Japanese Studies* 24, no. 1 (2004): 115–34; Robin LeBlanc, *Bicycle Citizens: The Political World of the Housewife* (Berkeley and Los Angeles: University of California Press, 1999); and Wesley Sasaki-Uemura, *Organizing the Spontaneous: Citizen Protest in Postwar Japan* (Honolulu: University of Hawaii Press, 2001). Mary Alice Haddad shows how citizens' ideas about individual and governmental responsibility affect both rates and types of volunteerism in communities; see Haddad, *Politics and Volunteering in Japan: A Global Perspective* (Cambridge and New York: Cambridge University Press, 2007).

5. On "master frames," see the conclusion and David A. Snow and Robert D. Benford, "Master Frames and Cycles of Protest," in *Frontiers in Social Movement Theory,* ed. Aldon D. Morris and Carol McClurg Mueller (New Haven, CT, and London: Yale University Press, 1992), 133–55.

6. Claude Lévi-Strauss, *The Savage Mind* (Chicago: University of Chicago Press, 1966), 33.

7. Georges Sorel, *Reflections on Violence,* ed. Jeremy Jennings (Cambridge and New York: Cambridge University Press, 1999), 116.

8. Ibid., 115.

9. Tsurumi Shunsuke, "Kotoba no Omamoriteki Shiyōhō ni tsuite," in Tsurumi Shunsuke, *Tsurumi Shunsuke Chosakushū,* vol. 3 (Tokyo: Chikuma

Shobō, 1976), 12–25. It is important to note that Tsurumi never suggested that the *shimin* was a talisman similar to wartime slogans such as the "Greater East Asian Coprosperity Sphere." On the contrary, Tsurumi's thought represents a formative moment in the *creation* of that civic mythology.

10. Saeki Keishi, *"Shimin" to wa dare ka: Sengo Minshushugi o toinaosu* (Tokyo: PHP Kenkyūjo, 1997), 47.

11. Kurihara Akira, "New Social Movements in Present-Day Japan," *Journal of Pacific Asia* 5 (1999): 7–22.

12. Claus Offe, "New Social Movements: Challenging the Boundaries of Institutional Politics," *Social Research* 52, no. 4 (Winter 1985): 829.

13. Donatelle Della Porta and Mario Diani, eds., *Social Movements: An Introduction* (Oxford, U.K.: Blackwell Publishers, 1999), 13.

14. From an empirical-historical perspective, of course, there are also serious problems with NSM theory. Many of the so-called new aspects (tactical and ideological) of the new movements can be seen in earlier social movements. Moreover, as others have noted, by shifting attention from politics narrowly defined to the politics of identity and daily life, NSMs effectively turn their backs on the key institutions for effecting substantive change. At least at the time of this writing, many social movement scholars seem, at best, highly skeptical about the potential of the NSM perspective as a theory. For an excellent critique of the NSM approach, see Nelson A. Pichardo, "NEW SOCIAL MOVEMENTS: A Critical Review," *Annual Review of Sociology* 23 (1997): 411–30.

15. John Hoffman, *Citizenship beyond the State* (London, Thousand Oaks, CA, and New Delhi: Sage Publications, 2004), 162.

16. Ibid., 165.

17. Derek Heater, *What Is Citizenship?* (Cambridge, U.K.: Polity Press, 1999), 122.

18. Robert Pekkanen, for example, explains the shift from the protest of the 1960s and early 1970s to the social-capital-style activism thereafter in terms of an "inhospitable state and regulatory framework" (Pekkanen, *Japan's Dual Civil Society*, 159). Sheldon Garon points to the ways local governments "appropriated the language and organization of citizens' movements to reintegrate a great many civic groups into local administrations" from the 1970s (Sheldon Garon, "From Meiji to Heisei: The State and Civil Society in Japan," in *The State of Civil Society in Japan*, ed. Schwartz and Pharr, 61). Drawing on Samuel Huntington's work, Tsujinaka Yutaka sees the proliferation of Japanese civic groups (NGOs and other nonprofits) as part of the third wave of global democratization from the mid-1970s (Tsujinaka Yutaka, "From Developmentalism to Maturity: Japan's Civil Society Organizations in Comparative Perspective," in *The State of Civil Society in Japan*, ed. Schwartz and Pharr, 83–115).

19. Roland Barthes, *Mythologies*, trans. Annette Lavers (London: Jonathon Cape, 1972), 143.

20. Sheri Berman, "Review Article: Ideas, Norms, and Culture in Political Analysis," *Comparative Politics* 33, no. 2 (January 2001): 238.

21. See David A. Snow and Robert D. Benford, "Ideology, Frame Resonance, and Participant Mobilization," in *From Structure to Action: Social Movement*

Participation Across Cultures, ed. Bert Klandermans, Hanspeter Kriesi, and Sidney Tarrow (Greenwich CT: JAI Press, 1988), 197–217; and David A. Snow, E. Burke Rochford Jr., Steven K. Worden, and Robert D. Benford, "Frame Alignment Processes, Micromobilization, and Movement Participation," *American Sociological Review* 51, no. 4 (August 1986): 464–81.

22. Doug McAdam, John D. McCarthy, and Mayer N. Zald, "Introduction," in *Comparative Perspectives on Social Movements: Political Opportunities, Mobilizing Structures, and Cultural Framings,* ed. Doug McAdam, John D. McCarthy, and Mayer N. Zald (Cambridge: Cambridge University Press, 1996), 5.

23. David A. Snow and Robert D. Benford, "Framing Processes and Social Movements: An Overview and Assessment," *Annual Review of Sociology* 26 (2000): 614.

24. Ibid.

25. Snow and Benford, "Master Frames and Cycles of Protest," 136.

26. Ron Eyerman and Andrew Jamison, *Social Movements: A Cognitive Approach* (University Park, PA: Pennsylvania State University Press, 1991), 98.

27. Ibid., 115.

28. Ibid.

29. Michiel Baud and Rosanne Rutten, "Introduction," *International Review of Social History* 49 (2004): 8

30. *Shiminken* is also rendered into English as "citizenship."

31. As Vera Mackie correctly points out, men enjoyed a greater level of "subjecthood" than women, so though everyone was a subject, there was a clear hierarchy. The same could be said of Japan's colonial subjects. See Vera Mackie, *Feminism in Modern Japan: Citizenship, Embodiment, and Sexuality* (Cambridge and New York: Cambridge University Press, 2003), 5.

32. Of course, *kokumin,* as Kevin Doak has shown, is a term with a complex history and as an expression of political nationalism has been in constant tension with the state while competing with other collective imaginaries, such as the ethnic nation *(minzoku),* which lays claim to great cultural authenticity. Kevin Doak, *A History of Nationalism in Modern Japan: Placing the People* (Leiden, The Netherlands, and Boston: Brill, 2007), especially chapters 5 and 6.

33. Ellis S. Krauss and Bradford L. Simcock, "Citizens' Movements: The Growth and Impact of Environmental Protest in Japan," in *Political Opposition and Local Politics in Japan,* ed. Kurt Steiner, Ellis S. Krauss, and Scott Flanagan (Princeton, NJ: Princeton University Press, 1980), 214. Krauss and Simcock quite rightly viewed the *shimin undō* ideal as an ideational resource mobilized by individual movements to universalize their cause, bring in outside allies, and remove social-psychological barriers to participation.

34. Tsurumi Shunsuke, Ueno Chizuko, and Oguma Eiji, *Sensō ga Nokoshita Mono: Tsurumi Shunsuke ni Sengo Sedai ga Kiku* (Tokyo: Shinyōsha, 2004), 285; Takabatake Michitoshi, "'Rokujūnen Anpo' no Seishinshi," in *Sengo Nihon Seishinshi,* ed. Tetsuo Najita, Maeda Ai, and Kamishima Jirō (Tokyo: Iwanami Shoten, 1988), 74.

35. Oda was not the first to head in such a direction. See, for example, Ryoko Nakano's interesting work on Yanaihara Tadao. Ryoko Nakano, "Uncovering *Shokumin*: Yanaihara Tadao's Concept of Global Civil Society," *Social Science Japan Journal* 9, no. 2 (October 2006): 187–202.

I. BEFORE THE *SHIMIN*

1. For an earlier version of the first half of this chapter, see Simon Avenell, "From the 'People' to the 'Citizen': Tsurumi Shunsuke and the Roots of Civic Mythology in Postwar Japan," *positions: east asia cultures critique* 16, no. 3 (Winter 2008): 711–42. The same edition also contains three thoughtful and much appreciated commentaries on my article by Laura Hein, "The Art of Persuasion: Audiences and Philosophies of History," 743–51; J. Victor Koschmann, "Avenell's 'Citizen,'" 753–60; and Wesley Sasaki-Uemura, "A Rectification of Names: Response to Simon Avenell," 761–68.

2. Institute membership included some of the foremost progressive intellectuals: Hidaka Rokurō, Maruyama Masao, Kuno Osamu, Tsuru Shigeto, Tsurumi Kazuko, Tsurumi Yoshiyuki, and Takabatake Michitoshi, to name but a few.

3. In his study of the Anpo protests, George Packard accused Tsurumi and the institute of "ninjutsu." See Packard, *Protest in Tokyo: The Security Treaty Crisis of 1960* (Princeton, NJ: Princeton University Press, 1966), 275.

4. Ara Masato, "Yoko no Tsunagari," *Kindai Bungaku* 14 (October 1947): 1–11.

5. Andrew Barshay, "Postwar Social and Political Thought," in *Modern Japanese Thought*, ed. Bob Tadashi Wakabayashi (Cambridge: Cambridge University Press, 1998), 336.

6. Tsurumi Shunsuke, "Nihon Shisō no Kanōsei," in Tsurumi Shunsuke, *Tsurumi Shunsuke Chosakushū*, vol. 3 (Tokyo: Chikuma Shobō, 1975), 3–4 (hereafter *TSC*).

7. These biographical details are drawn from Lawrence Olson, *Ambivalent Moderns: Portraits of Japanese Cultural Identity* (Savage, MD: Rowman and Littlefield, 1992), 113–30; Oguma Eiji, *Minshu to Aikoku: Sengo Nashonarizumu to Kōkyōsei* (Tokyo: Shinyōsha, 2002), 717–19; Tsurumi Shunsuke, *Kitai to Kaisō*, vol. 1 (Tokyo: Shōbunsha, 1997), 10–36; Tsurumi Shunsuke, "Gyokuchū kara mita Amerika," 490–99, and "Kōkansen no Chikyū Hanshū," 499–507, in Tsurumi Shunsuke, *Tsurumi Shunsuke Shū*, vol. 11 (Tokyo: Chikuma Shobō, 2000) (hereafter *TSS*); and Tsurumi, Ueno, and Oguma, *Sensō ga Nokoshita Mono*, 23–35.

8. The economist Ōkuma Nobuyuki was another. See Ōkuma Nobuyuki, *Kokka Aku: Jinrui ni Mirai wa aru ka* (Tokyo: Ushio Shuppansha, 1971). On Tsurumi's wartime activity, see his "Sensōchū ni ita Basho," *Shisō no Kagaku* 8 (August 1959): 55–59; "Techō no naka no Doitsu to Jawa," *TSS*, vol. 11, 507–15; "Sensō no kureta Jibiki," *TSC*, vol. 5, 464–81; Olson, *Ambivalent Moderns*, 123–24; Oguma, *Minshu to Aikoku*, 719–29; Tsurumi, Ueno, and Oguma, *Sensō ga Nokoshita Mono*, 46–76.

9. Tsurumi, "Techō no naka no Doitsu to Jawa," 509.

10. Tsurumi, "Sensōchū ni ita Basho," 55.

11. Ibid.

12. Tsurumi, Ueno, and Oguma, Sensō ga Nokoshita Mono, 65.

13. Tsurumi, "Sensō no kureta Jibiki," 477; and Tsurumi, Ueno, and Oguma, Sensō ga Nokoshita Mono, 188–89.

14. Tsurumi, "Sensō no kureta Jibiki," 477–78.

15. Shisō no Kagaku Kenkyūkai, ed., Shisō no Kagaku Kaihō, vol. 1 (Tokyo: Kashiwa Shobō, 1982), 206.

16. Tsurumi, "Sensō no kureta Jibiki," 477.

17. Ibid.

18. Arai Naoyuki, Haisen Taiken to Sengo Shisō—12 nin no Kiseki (Tokyo: Ronsōsha, 1997), 3.

19. Tsurumi, Ueno, and Oguma, Sensō ga Nokoshita Mono, 125.

20. Arai, Haisen Taiken to Sengo Shisō, 3. Tsurumi goes on to say that this self-hatred continued until Bloody May Day in 1952, after which he became more and more drawn into antistate grassroots activism. (See ibid., 3 and 9.)

21. Tsurumi, Ueno, and Oguma, Sensō ga Nokoshita Mono, 139.

22. Tsurumi, "Sensō no kureta Jibiki," 464.

23. Tsurumi, "Taishū no Jidai," TSC, vol. 3, 323, quoted in Oguma, Minshu to Aikoku, 732.

24. Tsurumi, "Kotoba no Omamoriteki Shiyōhō ni tsuite," 15.

25. Ibid., 16.

26. Ibid., 19.

27. Ibid., 23–24.

28. Tsurumi, Kitai to Kaisō, vol. 2, 190. For all his skepticism of talismans, however, as far as I can discern Tsurumi never subjected the citizen (shimin) or the inhabitant of daily life (seikatsusha)—identities that have operated as talismans for a variety of groups over the past fifty years—to the same sort of scrutiny.

29. See, for instance, Yonehara Ken, Nihonteki "Kindai" e no Toi: Shisōshi toshite no Sengo Seiji (Tokyo: Shinhyōron, 1995), 107; and Oguma, Minshu to Aikoku, 730.

30. Tsurumi, "Tetsugaku no Hansei," TSC, vol. 1, 240.

31. Ibid., 239.

32. Ibid., 240.

33. Ibid., 253.

34. Oguma, Minshu to Aikoku, 730.

35. Ibid., 733.

36. Yonehara, Nihonteki "Kindai," 107; Oguma, Minshu to Aikoku, 733–34.

37. Tsurumi, "Tetsugaku no Hansei," 255.

38. Tsurumi Shunsuke, "Dogura Magura no Sekai," TSC, vol. 4, 212. Tsurumi's allusions to the base of the ethnic community were clearly influenced by Tanigawa Gan. See, for example, Tanigawa's "Sōkan Sengen: Sarani Fukaku Shūdan no Imi o" (1958), reproduced in Matsubara Shinichi, Gen'ei no Kommyūn: "Sākuru Mura" o Kenshō suru (Fukuoka: Sōgensha, 2001), 235–41.

39. Oguma, Minshu to Aikoku, 732.

40. I say prophetic because life composition would, in the 1950s, become the springboard for independent cultural circle activism.

41. Tsurumi, "Tetsugaku no Hansei," 252.

42. Ibid., 255.

43. Tsurumi juxtaposes the researcher *(kenkyūsha)* and the inhabitant of daily life *(seikatsusha)* in his later essay "Denki ni tsuite," in *Minshū no Za,* ed. Shisō no Kagaku Kenkyūkai (Tokyo: Kawade Shinsho, 1955), 11.

44. Tsurumi's wartime experience also stimulated his later research and writing on the issue of war responsibility, most notably in the group research project on intellectual recantation *(tenkō).* See *TSC,* vol. 2, 3–255, and a number of other significant essays such as "Migoto na Senryō no Owari ni" (1952), "Chishikijin no Sensō Sekinin" (1956), and "Sensō Sekinin no Mondai" (1957) all contained in *TSC,* vol. 5.

45. Tsurumi Shunsuke, "Amerika Tetsugaku," *TSS,* vol. 1, 270.

46. These essays were published in book form in 1950 under the title *Amerika Tetsugaku* (see *TSC,* vol. 1, 3–270).

47. Shimizu Ikutarō, "Nijusseiki Kenkyūjo," in Shimizu Ikutarō, *Shimizu Ikutarō Chosakushū,* vol. 14, ed. Shimizu Reiko (Tokyo: Kōdansha, 1993), 303–4 (hereafter *SIC*).

48. Reproduced in *SIC,* vol. 6, 9–135.

49. Amano Masako, *"Seikatsusha" to wa Dareka: Jiritsuteki Shiminzō no Keifu* (Tokyo: Chūkō Shinsho, 1996), 78. Andrew Barshay makes a similar point vis-à-vis the institute, noting how "the institute . . . was about practice, or application." See his essay "Postwar Social and Political Thought," 305.

50. Tsurumi, "Puragumatizumu no Kōzō," *TSC,* vol. 1, 103–4.

51. Otto is not even mentioned in Louis Menand's recent survey *Pragmatism: A Reader* (New York: Vintage Books, 1997).

52. Tsurumi, "Otto no Hito to Shisō," *TSC,* vol. 1, 71.

53. Ibid.

54. Ibid.

55. Ibid., 72.

56. Ibid., 74–75.

57. Tsurumi, "Puragumatizumu to Nihon," *TSC,* vol. 1, 171–72.

58. Tsurumi, "Puragumatizumu no Kōzō," *TSC,* vol. 1, 104–5.

59. See Shisō no Kagaku Kenkyūkai, ed., *Watashi no Tetsugaku,* 2 vols. (Tokyo: Chūō Kōronsha, 1950), for results of the questionnaire. For Tsurumi's analysis, see "Hitobito no Tetsugaku ni tsuite no Chūkan Hōkoku," *Shisō no Kagaku* 3, no. 2 (February 1948): 57–64, and 3, no. 3 (March 1948): 43–53.

60. Tsurumi, "Puragumatizumu no Kōzō," 104.

61. Harada Tōru, *Tsurumi Shunsuke to Kibō no Shakaigaku* (Tokyo: Sekai Shisōsha, 2004), 194.

62. Ibid., 188.

63. Amano Masako, "Minshū Shisō e no Hōhōteki Jikken: 'Hitobito no Tetsugaku' kara 'Minoue Sōdan' e no Sōi," in *Sengo "Keimō" Shisō no Nokoshita Mono,* ed. Yasuda Tsuneo and Amano Masako (Tokyo: Kyūzansha, 1992), 121.

64. Tsurumi Shunsuke, "Shōka no Tsuma—Kadota Ine no Seikatsu to Shisō," *TSC*, vol. 3, 76.

65. Tanigawa Gan, *Kōsakusha Sengen* (1959; repr., Tokyo: Ushio Shuppansha, 1977), 14.

66. Yoshimoto Takaaki, "Nihon no Nashonarizumu," in Yoshimoto Takaaki, *Yoshimoto Takaaki Zenchosakushū*, vol. 13 (Tokyo: Keisō Shobō, 1969), 233–34, quoted in Harada, *Tsurumi Shunsuke*, 199.

67. Tsurumi, Ueno, and Oguma, *Sensō ga Nokoshita Mono*, 163.

68. On the naming of the magazine, see ibid. 169–71; and Tsurumi, *Kitai to Kaisō*, vol. 2, 186, 197.

69. Tsurumi, *Kitai to Kaisō*, vol. 1, 57, and vol. 2, 100.

70. Cited in Harada, *Tsurumi Shunsuke*, 102. See Harada's essay for an interesting discussion of Tsurumi Shunsuke's successful use of "social capital" in building academic and activist alliances (67–111).

71. Olson, *Ambivalent Moderns*, 131.

72. Tsurumi, Ueno, and Oguma, *Sensō ga Nokoshita Mono*, 159–60.

73. The above citations are reproduced in Tsurumi Kazuko, " 'Sengo' no Naka no 'Shisō no Kagaku,' " in *Shisō no Kagaku Kaihō*, ed. Shisō no Kagaku Kenkyūkai, vol. 1, 9–10.

74. Ibid., 20.

75. Shimizu, "Nijusseiki Kenkyūjo," *SIC*, vol. 14, 307.

76. See Leslie Pincus, "A Salon for the Soul: Nakai Masakazu and the Hiroshima Culture Movement," *positions: east asia cultures critique* 10, no. 1 (Spring 2002): 173–94. On the Shomin Daigaku, see Barshay, "Postwar Social and Political Thought," 307. On the Kamakura Academia, see Shisō no Kagaku Kenkyūkai, ed., *Kyōdō Kenkyū Shūdan: Sākuru no Sengo Shisōshi* (Tokyo: Heibonsha, 1976), 95–104.

77. Shimizu Ikutarō, "Heiwa Mondai Danwakai," *SIC*, vol. 14, 314–38; Rikki Kersten, *Democracy in Postwar Japan: Maruyama Masao and the Search for Autonomy* (London and New York: Routledge, 1996), 175–86.

78. Curtis Anderson Gayle, "Progressive Representations of the Nation: Early Post-War Japan and Beyond," *Social Science Japan Journal* 4, no. 1 (2001): 1.

79. See Curtis Anderson Gayle, *Marxist History and Postwar Japanese Nationalism* (London and New York: Routledge, 2003), especially chapter 7; and Oguma, *Minshu to Aikoku*, chapter 8.

80. See *Rekishi Hyōron* 37 (June–July 1952) for discussion of *gimin* (grassroots martyrs) as well as essays on Sakura and Tanaka. *Rekishi Hyōron* 48 (September 1953) contains another article on the thought and activism of Tanaka Shōzō. Also see Oguma, *Minshu to Aikoku*, 335.

81. Ara Masato, "Minshū wa Doko ni iru," in Ara Masato, *Ara Masato Chosakushū*, vol. 1 (Tokyo: Sanichi Shobō, 1983), 103 (hereafter *AMC*).

82. On the *shutaisei* debate, see J. Victor Koschmann, *Revolution and Subjectivity in Japan* (Chicago and London: University of Chicago Press, 1996).

83. Ara Masato, "Minshū to wa Tare ka," *AMC*, vol. 1, 64.

84. Ibid., 66.

85. Ara Masato, "Minshū wa Doko ni iru," 105.

86. Ara Masato, "Shimin toshite," *Kindai Bungaku* (September 1947): 7–8.

87. Shimizu Ikutarō, "Tokumei no Shisō," *SIC*, vol. 8, 209.

88. Ibid., 212.

89. Ibid., 218.

90. Shimizu Ikutarō, "Shomin," *SIC*, vol. 8, 286.

91. Ibid., 302. The translation "our values in their desires and our method in their experiences" is Koschmann's. See his *Revolution and Subjectivity in Japan*, 219.

92. Shimizu Ikutarō, "Nihonjin," *SIC*, vol. 10, 7. For a trenchant analysis of Shimizu, see Oguma Eiji, *Shimizu Ikutarō: Aru Sengo Chishikijin no Kiseki*, Kanagawa Daigaku Hyōron Bukkuretto, no. 26 (Tokyo: Ochanomizu Shobō, 2003).

93. Shimizu Ikutarō, Miyahara Seiichi, and Ueda Shōzaburō, *Kichi no Ko: Kono Jijitsu o dō Kangaetara yoi ka* (Tokyo: Kōbunsha, 1953).

94. Tsurumi, Ueno, and Oguma, *Sensō ga Nokoshita Mono*, 199–200.

95. Oguma, *Minshu to Aikoku*, 412.

96. Ronald Dore, "The Tokyo Institute for the Science of Thought," *Far Eastern Quarterly* 13, no. 1 (1953): 34.

97. Kurata Ichirō, "Jōmin no Tetsugaku: Chōsa to Bunseki," in *Shisō no Kagaku—Me*, vol. 1, ed. Yasuda Tsuneo and Amano Masako (Tokyo: Kyūzansha, 1992), 365. Kurata's other important essay in the December 1946 edition, "Zendai Seikatsu no Riron ni tsuite," is contained in the same volume.

98. Kurata, "Jōmin no Tetsugaku," 366.

99. Shisō no Kagaku Kenkyūkai, ed., *Watashi no Tetsugaku*.

100. Dore, "The Tokyo Institute for the Science of Thought," 26.

101. Shisō no Kagaku Kenkyūkai, ed., *Gendaijin no Seitai: Aru Shakaiteki Kōsatsu* (Tokyo: Kōdansha, 1953).

102. Shisō no Kagaku Kenkyūkai, ed., *Yume to Omokage: Taishū Goraku no Kenkyū* (Tokyo: Chūō Kōronsha, 1950).

103. Tsurumi, "Oikawa Setsu," *TSC*, vol. 3, 72. This interview was conducted as part of field research led by Kawashima Takeyoshi in Machida City, just south of Tokyo (see Tsurumi Kazuko, " 'Sengo' no Naka," 23).

104. Tsurumi, "Shōka no Tsuma," 76–82.

105. Ibid., 76.

106. Watanabe Katsumi, "Shomin Retsuden: Tankōfu—Toda Ichizō no Seikatsu to Shisō," *Me* 11–12 (May 1954): 2.

107. Takeda Kiyoko, "Ningenkan no Shozai," *Shisō no Kagaku* 3 (November 1946): 115–22; and a later abridged version, "Kōjō ni mita Uso to Kaigara Ningenzō," *Me* 8 (1953): 39–41.

108. Takeda, "Ningenkan no Shozai," 118.

109. Ibid.

110. Ibid., 119.

111. Ibid.

112. Ibid.

113. Ibid. Tsurumi Kazuko argues that Takeda's Christian belief led her to the conclusion that the absence of an absolute god in Japanese religious belief

meant the inevitable absorption of horizontal relationships into the vertical power hierarchy (Tsurumi Kazuko, " 'Sengo' no Naka," 18).

114. Tsurumi Shunsuke, "Nihon no Shisō Hyakunen," *TSC*, vol. 2, 366.

115. Ibid.

116. Ibid., 368.

117. Ibid., 367.

118. Ibid., 368.

119. Ibid.

120. Tsurumi, "Denki ni tsuite," 15–16.

121. See the special edition of *Me* devoted to personal advice columns (September 1953).

122. Matsubara, *Gen'ei no Kommyūn*, 151.

123. Andrew Gordon, *The Wages of Affluence: Labor and Management in Postwar Japan* (Cambridge, MA: Harvard University Press, 1998), 97.

124. Sasaki-Uemura, *Organizing the Spontaneous*, 28.

125. Gordon, *The Wages of Affluence*, 98.

126. Amano, "Sākuru 'Shūdan no Kai,' " in *Kyōdō Kenkyū Shūdan*, ed. Shisō no Kagaku Kenkyūkai, 34.

127. Ibid.

128. Shisō no Kagaku Kenkyūkai, ed., *Kyōdō Kenkyū Shūdan*.

129. Sasaki Gen, "Kono Hon no Hōhō," in *Kyōdō Kenkyū Shūdan*, ed. Shisō no Kagaku Kenkyūkai, 22–32.

130. Ibid., 26.

131. Ōsawa Shinichirō, *Kōhō no Shisō: Arui wa Chōsei e no Shuppatsu* (Tokyo: Shakai Hyōronsha, 1971), 29.

132. Ibid.

133. Ibid., 73.

134. For more on this group, see Sasaki-Uemura, *Organizing the Spontaneous*, chapter 3; and Shiratori Kunio, *Mumei no Nihonjin: "Yamanami no Kai" no Kiroku* (Tokyo: Miraisha, 1961).

135. Pincus, "A Salon for the Soul," 175.

136. Ibid., 179.

137. Ibid., 181.

138. A distinction far clearer on paper than in practice, of course.

139. Robert A. Scalapino, *The Japanese Communist Movement, 1920–1966* (Berkeley and Los Angeles: University of California Press, 1967), 88–89.

140. Tsurumi, "Sengo Nihon no Shisō Jōkyō," *TSC*, vol. 2, 301.

141. Hidaka Rokurō, "Taishūron no Shūhen: Chishikijin to Taishū no Tairitsu ni tsuite," *Minwa* 6 (March 1959): 5.

142. Ōsawa Shinichirō, "Sākuru no Sengoshi," in *Kyōdō Kenkyū Shūdan*, ed. Shisō no Kagaku Kenkyūkai, 78.

143. See Tsurumi Kazuko, *Korekushon: Tsurumi Kazuko Mandara II—Nihonjin no Raifu Hisutorī* (Tokyo: Fujiwara Shoten, 1998), 479.

144. I use "life composition" as a composite of various terms used in Japanese, such as "daily life recording" *(seikatsu kiroku)* and "daily life composition" *(seikatsu tsuzurikata)*.

145. For more on the life composition movement, see Gerald Figal, "How to Jibunshi: Making and Marketing Self-Histories of Shōwa among the Masses in Postwar Japan," *Journal of Asian Studies* 55, no. 4 (November 1996): 902–33; Tsurumi Shunsuke, "Sengo Nihon no Shisō," in *TSC*, vol. 2, 264–77; Kuno Osamu and Tsurumi Shunsuke, *Gendai Nihon no Shisō: Sono Itsutsu no Uzu* (Tokyo: Iwanami, 1956), 71–115; and Tsurumi Kazuko, *Korekushon*, 308–643.

146. Figal, "How to Jibunshi," 907.

147. Kuno and Tsurumi, *Gendai Nihon no Shisō*, 77.

148. Ibid., *seiza*: literally, "quiet sitting."

149. Ibid., 78.

150. Ibid., 77–78.

151. Muchaku Seikyō, ed., *Yamabiko Gakkō* (Tokyo: Yuri Shuppan, 1990); Kokubun Ichitarō, *Atarashii Tsuzurikata Kyōshitsu—Zōhoban* (Tokyo: Shinhyōronsha, 1952).

152. Mari Yamamoto, *Grassroots Pacifism in Postwar Japan: The Rebirth of a Nation* (Oxon, U.K.: RoutledgeCurzon, 2004), 163.

153. Shimizu, Miyahara, and Ueda, *Kichi no Ko*.

154. Sasaki-Uemura, *Organizing the Spontaneous*, 127.

155. Ibid., 129–32.

156. For details, see Tsurumi Kazuko, *Korekushon*, 322–411, 534–52, 600–616.

157. Ibid., 331.

158. Ibid., 603.

159. Ibid., 330.

160. Ibid., 527.

161. For the collected writings of the group, see Seikatsu o Kiroku suru Kai, ed., *Bōseki Joshi Kōin Seikatsu Kirokushū*, 4 vols. (Tokyo: Nihon Tosho Sentā, 2002).

162. Tsurumi Kazuko, *Korekushon*, 539.

163. Ibid., 329.

164. Ibid., 330.

165. Ibid., 334, emphasis in original.

166. Ibid., 335–36.

167. Ibid., 339–40.

168. See Sasaki-Uemura, *Organizing the Spontaneous*, chapter 5. The formal title of the treaty in English is the Treaty of Mutual Cooperation and Security between the United States of America and Japan; and in Japanese, Nihonkoku to Amerika Gasshūkoku to no aida no Sōgō Kyōryoku oyobi Anzen Hoshō Jōyaku.

169. Ibid., 121–24; and Yamamoto, *Grassroots Pacifism*, 166.

170. Tsurumi Kazuko, *Korekushon*, 549. Sawai also acted as lead editor for the four-volume collection of writings and publications by the antipollution movement in Yokkaichi. See Kōgai o Kiroku suru Kai, ed., *"Yokkaichi Kōgai" Shimin Undō Kirokushū*, 4 vols. (Tokyo: Nihon Tosho Sentā, 2007).

171. Tsurumi Kazuko, *Korekushon*, 551.

172. Amano Masako, "Midori no Kai," in *Kyōdō Kenkyū Shūdan*, ed., Shisō no Kagaku Kenkyūkai, 200.

173. Amano Masako, *"Tsukiai" no Sengoshi: Sākuru—Nettowākingu no Hiraku Chihei* (Tokyo: Yoshikawa Hirobumi Kan, 2005), 82.

174. Amano, "Midori no Kai," 199–200.

175. Amano, *"Tsukiai,"* 83.

176. Amano, "Midori no Kai," 200.

177. Ibid.

178. Amano, *"Tsukiai,"* 84

179. Ibid.

180. Amano, "Midori no Kai," 202.

181. See ibid., 201, for the Green Pledge.

182. Amano, *"Tsukiai,"* 84.

183. Ibid.

184. Amano, "Midori no Kai," 202–3.

185. Ibid.

186. Ibid., 205.

187. Sasaki Ayao, "Sākuru Undō no Rekishitekina Imi," *Chūō Kōron* (June 1956): 255.

188. Ibid., 256.

189. Ibid.

190. Ibid.

191. Literally, "ethnic-national national culture." Ibid., 257.

192. Ōsawa, "Sākuru no Sengoshi," 68.

193. Tsurumi, "Sengo Nihon no Shisō Jōkyō," 313.

194. Ibid., 313–14.

195. Ibid., 302.

196. For a fascinating discussion of Tanigawa, see Wesley Sasaki-Uemura, "Tanigawa Gan's Politics of the Margins of Kyushu and Nagano," *positions: east asia cultures critique* 7, no. 1 (Spring 1999): 129–63.

197. Tanigawa Gan, *Genten ga Sonzai suru* (Tokyo: Gendaishichōsha, 1969), 80–81.

198. Ibid., 31.

199. The magazine, together with other interesting materials, is reprinted in full in Fuji Shuppan, ed., *Sākuru Mura,* 5 vols. (Tokyo: Fuji Shuppan, 2006).

200. Tsurumi, "Shisō no Hakkō Botai," *TSC*, vol. 3, 305–6.

201. Ōsawa, *Kōhō no Shisō,* 47.

202. Tanigawa, "Sōkan Sengen," 235.

203. Ibid., 240.

204. Ibid., 238.

205. Hidaka Rokurō, "Taishūron no Shūhen: Sākuru Mondai o megutte," *Minwa* 7 (April 1959): 3.

206. Ibid., 5.

207. Ibid.

208. Ibid., 8.

209. Ibid., 10.

210. Ibid.

2. MASS SOCIETY, ANPO, AND THE BIRTH OF THE *SHIMIN*
Epigraphs: From Koe Naki Koe no Kai, ed., *Fukkokuban: Koe naki Koe no Kai no Tayori*, vol. 1: *1960–1970* (Tokyo: Shisō no Kagakusha, 1996), 16 and 13 (hereafter *Tayori*).

1. Barshay, "Postwar Social and Political Thought," 322.
2. Ishida Takeshi, Shinohara Hajime, and Fukuda Kanichi, "Yakudō suru Shimin Seishin," *Chūō Kōron* (July 1960): 66–83.
3. Takabatake Michitoshi, "Kyojūchi Soshiki no Teian," in *Tayori*, vol. 1, 14.
4. Kuno Osamu, *Seijiteki Shimin no Fukken* (Tokyo: Ushio Shuppansha, 1975), 7–22.
5. Tsurumi Shunsuke, "Nemoto kara no Minshushugi," *Shisō no Kagaku* 19 (July 1960): 27.
6. *Tayori*, vol. 1, 30–31.
7. Krauss and Simcock, "Citizens' Movements," 192.
8. Ibid., 191.
9. Of course, it is worth reiterating that nonaligned grassroots political activism and protest had precedents, such as the circle movement, the antinuclear movement, and the Mothers' Congress. My argument, however, is that the understanding of such activism matured fundamentally with the embellishment of civic mythology in 1960.
10. J. Victor Koschmann, "Intellectuals and Politics," in *Postwar Japan as History*, ed. Andrew Gordon (Berkeley and Los Angeles: University of California Press, 1993), 406.
11. Kurihara Akira, "Shimin Seiji no Ajenda: Seimei Seiji no Hō e," *Shisō* 908 (February 2000): 7–8.
12. Tsurumi, Ueno, and Oguma, *Sensō ga Nokoshita Mono*, 285.
13. Shimizu Ikutarō, "Taishū Shakai Ron no Shōri: Anpo Kaitei Soshi Tōsō no naka de," *Shisō* 436 (October 1960): 26–45.
14. See Masamura Kimihiro, *Sengoshi*, vol. 2 (Tokyo: Chikuma Shobō, 1985), 100–101; Packard, *Protest in Tokyo*, 101–2; Tsuzuki Tsutomu, *Sengo Nihon no Chishikijin: Maruyama Masao to Sono Jidai* (Yokohama: Seori Shobō, 1995), 291–95; and Hoshino Yasuzaburō, "Keishokuhō Tōsō," in *Shōwa no Sengo Shi*, vol. 3: *Gyakuryū to Teikō*, ed. Matsuura Sōzō (Tokyo: Sekibunsha, 1976), 58–74.
15. Editorial, *Mainichi Shimbun*, October 12, 1958, reproduced in Tsuji Kiyoaki, ed., *Shiryō—Sengo Nijūnen Shi: 1 Seiji* (Tokyo: Nihon Hyōronsha, 1966), 133–34.
16. Ienaga Saburō, "Anpo Tōsō no Tenkai," in *Shōwa no Sengo Shi*, vol. 3, ed. Matsuura, 70.
17. The full statement is reproduced in Tsuji, ed., *Shiryō—Sengo Nijūnen Shi*, 133–34.
18. In Hidaka Rokurō, *1960 nen 5 gatsu 19 nichi* (Tokyo: Iwanami Shoten, 1970), 24.
19. The Japan Council against Atomic and Hydrogen Bombs.
20. Oguma notes that the JCP was allowed entry into the National Congress to Block the Security Treaty Revision because most organizations accepted that

the party had mended its ways in the wake of its "extreme left adventurism" of the early 1950s. The inclusion of the JCP did have consequences, however, causing a split in the JSP and the formation of the Democratic Socialist Party (DSP) in January 1960. Adding to the nationalistic flavor of the moment, a judge in Tokyo's District Court ruled in late March that U.S. military bases in Japan were unconstitutional—the first formal legal decision to connect the security treaty, the constitution, and the movements against U.S. military bases. The ruling was later quashed by the high court, however. See Oguma, *Minshu to Aikoku*, 503–4; and Masamura, *Sengoshi*, 107.

21. Reproduced in Tsuzuki, *Sengo Nihon no Chishikijin*, 302–4.

22. Hidaka, *1960 nen 5 gatsu 19 nichi*, 100.

23. Zen Nihon Gakusei Jichikai Sōrengō (the National Federation of Students' Self-Government Associations).

24. The anticommunist stance of the Bund had its origins in the turnaround in JCP strategy at the Sixth National Conference of the Japanese Communist Party (Rokuzenkyō), held in July 1955. Here the JCP discarded the strategy of extreme-left adventurism in favor of more mainstream political tactics—a tactical shift that left radical young party members out in the cold. It was these disaffected elements who mobilized into the Bund. For more on this, see Scalapino, *The Japanese Communist Movement*. Informative works on the student movement include Takagi Masayuki, *Zengakuren to Zenkyōtō* (Tokyo: Kōdansha, 1985); Yamanaka Akira, *Sengo Gakusei Undō Shi* (Tokyo: Gun Shuppan, 1981); Kazuko Tsurumi, "Student Movements in 1960 and 1969: Continuity and Change," in *Postwar Trends in Japan: Studies in Commemoration of Rev. Aloysius Miller, S.J.*, ed. Shunichi Takayanagi and Kimitada Miwa (Tokyo: University of Tokyo Press, 1975), 195–227; and Ellis S. Krauss, *Japanese Radicals Revisited: Student Protest in Postwar Japan* (Berkeley: University of California Press, 1974).

25. Masamura, *Sengoshi*, 135.

26. To mention but a few of these high-profile encounters: on January 16, 1960, Bund students staged an unsuccessful sit-in at Tokyo's Haneda Airport in an attempt to stop Kishi from departing for the United States, where he would sign the treaty. On April 15, 1960, over one thousand students clashed with police outside the Diet. Soon after, both the National Congress to Block the Security Treaty Revision and Sōhyō criticized the Bund, asking it to reconsider its tactics. Nevertheless, a similar riot ensued on April 26, this time with some fifty-five hundred students. In the end twenty-eight people were injured. On May 20, the day of Kishi's infamous "midnight coup d'état," Bund students infiltrated the prime minister's residence, resulting again in clashes with riot police and the injury of forty students. And then, on the evening of June 14, 1960, Bund students clashed with police outside the south gate of the Diet. By the following morning, over 180 students had been arrested and more than 1,000 injured. But, more shockingly, a young University of Tokyo student, Kanba Michiko, was found dead, apparently because of suffocation from pressure applied to the chest and stomach but perhaps also because of (intentional) pressure applied to her mouth, nose, and neck.

27. Barshay, "Postwar Social and Political Thought," 328. Oguma makes a similar observation in *Minshu to Aikoku,* 506.

28. Hidaka, *1960 nen, 5 gatsu, 19 nichi,* 100.

29. Tsuzuki Tsutomu, "Maruyama Masao ni okeru Seiji to Shimin," in *Gendai Shimin Seiji Ron,* ed. Takabatake Michitoshi (Kanagawa: Seori Shobō, 2003), 56.

30. Nihon Kokugo Daijiten Dainihan Henshū Iinkai, ed., *Nihon Kokugo Daijiten Dainihan,* vol. 6 (Tokyo: Shogakkan, 2001), 1030.

31. Ibid.

32. Michael Lewis, *Rioters and Citizens: Mass Protest in Imperial Japan* (Berkeley, Los Angeles, Oxford: University of California Press, 1990), 85.

33. Tsuzuki, "Maruyama Masao ni okeru Seiji to Shimin," 55.

34. Ibid., 56. The Kōza-ha, or Lectures Faction, of Japanese Marxism argued that Japan's mid-nineteenth-century Meiji Restoration was, from the perspective of Marxist theory, an incomplete revolution, in that the feudal aristocracy (the samurai class) was not completely eradicated but instead combined with bourgeois (capitalist) elements to produce a form of absolutism under the umbrella of imperial patronage. For adherents of this position, modern Japan never experienced a liberal moment, and hence there were no truly autonomous citizens in the country. In the context of revolutionary strategy, this implied that any movement to socialism would have to incorporate or be preceded by an expulsion of these semifeudal remnants.

35. Ibid., 55–56.

36. Hirano's and Hani's use of *shimin* might also be traced to the rise of an urban mass culture during the early twentieth century. Matsushita Keiichi, for instance, argued that with the shift to monopoly capitalism during the Taishō and early Shōwa periods an early form of mass society emerged in Japan. But this social formation did not develop into a full-blown mass society. Instead, it was absorbed by Emperor System fascism, and this made mobilization for total war possible. Only with the postwar reforms and the reemergence of monopoly capital after the Korean War did mass conditions begin to spread once again. See Matsushita Keiichi, "Taishū Shakai Ron no Konnichiteki Ichi," *Shisō* 436 (October 1960): 5.

37. Oguma, *Minshu to Aikoku,* 246.

38. Quoted ibid., 247.

39. Ibid.

40. The debate on mass society played itself out in a number of forums, but readers are directed to the following special issues: *Shisō* (November 1956), *Chūō Kōron* (May 1957), and *Shisō* (October 1960). Also see Yonehara, *Nihonteki "Kindai" e no Toi,* 129–31 and 136–39; Matsumoto Reiji, "Sengo Shimin Shakai Ron Saikō," in *Gendai Shimin Seiji Ron,* ed. Takabatake, 46–51; Tsuzuki, *Sengo Nihon no Chishikijin,* 234–46; and Sasaki-Uemura, *Organizing the Spontaneous,* 178–81.

41. Matsushita Keiichi, "Taishū Kokka no Seiritsu to Sono Mondaisei" (1956), reproduced in Matsushita Keiichi, *Sengo Seiji no Rekishi to Shisō* (Tokyo: Chikuma Shobō, 1994), 13–60. See below for more discussion of this text.

42. Quoted in Tsuzuki, *Sengo Nihon no Chishikijin*, 235.

43. For a discussion of criticisms of mass society theory at the time, see Matsushita Keiichi, "Nihon ni okeru Taishū Shakai Ron no Igi," *Chūō Kōron* (August 1957): 80–92. Shimizu's and others' negative reading of mass society was a view shared by many commentators on the phenomenon in the West too. See, for example, William Kornhauser, *The Politics of Mass Society* (Glencoe, IL: Free Press, 1959).

44. Shimizu, "Taishū Shakai Ron no Shōri," 26–45.

45. Charles Yuji Horioka, "Consuming and Saving," in *Postwar Japan as History*, ed. Gordon, 263.

46. Kenneth Pyle, *The Making of Modern Japan* (Lexington, MA: Heath, 1978), 244.

47. John Dower, "Peace and Democracy in Two Systems: External Policy and Internal Conflict," in *Postwar Japan as History*, ed. Gordon, 17. See also Simon Partner, *Assembled in Japan: Electrical Goods and the Making of the Japanese Consumer* (Berkeley: University of California Press, 1999).

48. Matsuura Sōzō, "Kokumin Seikatsu no Henka," in *Shōwa no Sengo Shi*, vol. 3: *Gyakuryū to Teikō*, ed. Matsuura Sōzō (Tokyo: Chōbunsha, 1976), 210–32.

49. Quoted ibid., 226.

50. Matsushita Keiichi, "Wasurerareta Teikōken," *Chūō Kōron* (November 1958): 44.

51. Matsushita Keiichi, "Taishū Kokka no Seiritsu to Sono Mondaisei," 15.

52. Ibid., 15.

53. Ibid., 16.

54. Ibid., 17.

55. Ibid., 36.

56. Ibid., 40.

57. Ibid., 51.

58. Ibid., 42.

59. Ibid., 48.

60. See any of the following essays by Matsushita Keiichi: "Marukushugi Riron no Nijūseikiteki Tenkan: Taishū Nashonarizumu to Seiji no Ronri," *Chūō Kōron* (March 1957): 142–57; "Shakai Minshushugi no Kiki," *Chūō Kōron* (February 1958), in Matsushita Keiichi, *Gendai Seiji no Jōken* (*Zōhanban*) (Tokyo: Chūō Kōronsha, 1969), 104–21; "Shiteki Yuibutsuron to Taishū Shakai," *Shisō* 395 (May 1957): 43–63; "Nihon ni okeru Taishū Shakairon no Igi," *Chūō Kōron* (August 1957): 80–93; and "Wasurerareta Teikōken."

61. Matsushita, "Shiteki Yuibutsuron to Taishū Shakai," 45, 60. On this point Matsushita shared a similar position to the later civil society advocate Hirata Kiyoaki. See my conclusion for more discussion of Hirata.

62. Ibid., 62. The quote here is from the English translation of the *German Ideology* in Robert C. Tucker, ed., *The Marx Engels Reader* (2nd ed.) (New York and London: W. W. Norton, 1978), 197.

63. Matsushita, "Wasurerareta Teikōken," 40.

64. Ibid., 41.

65. Here Matsushita's thought resonated closely with the subjectivity debate of the early postwar.

66. Matsushita, "Wasurerareta Teikōken," 41.

67. Ibid., 42.

68. Ibid., 43.

69. Ibid., 44.

70. Ibid., 45.

71. Ibid., 48.

72. Matsushita, "Taishū Shakai Ron no Konnichiteki Ichi," 9.

73. Matsushita Keiichi, " 'Shimin' teki Ningengata no Gendaiteki Kanōsei," *Shisō* 504 (June 1966): 16.

74. Ibid., 25.

75. Ibid., 26.

76. Ibid., 17.

77. This quote is reproduced in Matsushita, *Sengo Seiji no Rekishi to Shisō*, 504.

78. Yonehara, *Nihonteki "Kindai" e no Toi*, 129–30.

79. Katō Hidetoshi, *Chūkan Bunka* (Tokyo: Heibonsha, 1957), 4 and 8.

80. Ibid., 9.

81. Ibid., 32.

82. Ibid., 30, 32.

83. Ibid., 42.

84. Ibid., 50.

85. Ibid., 27.

86. Ibid., 203.

87. Ibid., 204.

88. Katō Hidetoshi, "Nichijō Seikatsu to Kokumin Undō," *Shisō no Kagaku* 19 (July 1960): 28–35.

89. Ibid., 30.

90. Ibid., 31.

91. Ibid., 30–31.

92. Ibid., 31.

93. Ibid., 35.

94. Maruyama expressed his dissatisfaction with the sheer ambiguity *(tagiteki)* of *shimin*, noting the wide range of possible translations: *civil, civic, burgher, citoyen,* and *bourgeoisie.* He also disliked the idea of *shiminshugi,* or civic ethos, since this implied yet another "ism" among the already divisive range of political ideologies. As he explained, the *shimin* was not something of substance *(jittai)* like the citizen on the street. Rather, it was that aspect of the people as the bearers of democracy—something shared by both organized workers and other members of the nation *(kokumin).* See Maruyama Masao and Satō Noboru, "Gendai ni okeru Kakumei no Riron," in *Maruyama Masao Zadan,* vol. 4 (Tokyo: Iwanami Shoten, 1998), 146, 149 (hereafter *MMZ*).

95. Contained in Maruyama Masao, *Thought and Behavior in Modern Japanese Politics,* ed. Ivan Morris (London, Oxford, and New York: Oxford University Press, 1969), 57–58.

96. Ibid., 58–59.

97. Ibid., 58.

98. Ibid., 59–60.

99. Oguma, *Minshu to Aikoku*, 245.

100. Ibid. Tsuzuki also notes Maruyama's lack of faith in the political activities of the "petit bourgeois strata" from the prewar years through the early 1950s. Tsuzuki, "Maruyama Masao ni okeru Seiji to Shimin," 66, 67.

101. Maruyama Masao, "Dansō," in *Maruyama Masao Shū*, vol. 6 (Tokyo: Iwanami Shoten, 1996), 147 (hereafter *MMS*). Also see Tsuzuki, "Maruyama Masao ni okeru Seiji to Shimin," 69.

102. Maruyama pointed out the traditional lack of "independence" in Japanese intermediary organizations in a late 1950s essay, "Chūsei to Hangyaku." Cited in Tsuzuki, "Maruyama Masao ni okeru Seiji to Shimin," 72.

103. Maruyama Masao, "Hachi-Jūgo to Go-Jūkyū: Nihon Minshushugi no Rekishiteki Imi," *MMS*, vol. 8, 372.

104. Maruyama and Satō, "Gendai ni okeru Kakumei no Riron," 142.

105. Ibid.

106. Ibid.

107. Ibid., 143.

108. Ibid., 145.

109. Maruyama, " 'De aru' koto to 'Suru koto,' " 38–39.

110. Maruyama Masao, "Gendai ni okeru Taido Kettei," in *MMS*, vol. 8, 314–15.

111. Maruyama Masao, Takeuchi Yoshimi, and Kaiko Takeshi, "Giji Puroguramu kara no Dakkyaku," in *MMZ*, vol. 4, 125–26.

112. Maruyama and Satō, "Gendai ni okeru Kakumei no Riron," 150. Tsuzuki Tsutomu says that Maruyama's *shimin* combined three elements: ideal or ethos *(rinen)*, his comprehension of mass society, and the experience of Anpo. Tsuzuki, "Maruyama Masao ni okeru Seiji to Shimin," 83.

113. Ibid., 150.

114. Ishida, Shinohara, and Fukuda, "Yakudō suru Shimin Seishin," 69.

115. Ibid., 71–72. Though Shinohara distinguished citizen activism after May 19, 1960 from that during the Keishokuhō dispute, he still saw connections to earlier movements. Writing in *Shisō* in September 1960, he outlined a narrative of nonaligned postwar activism beginning with the anti-nuclear-bomb signature campaign of Suginami housewives (1954), the World Conference against Atomic and Hydrogen Bombs (1955), the protest struggles against U.S. military bases at Sunagawa and elsewhere, and the Keishokuhō dispute. See Shinohara Hajime, "Taishū Undō to Mutōha Katsudōka," *Shisō* (September 1960): 36.

116. Ishida, Shinohara, and Fukuda, "Yakudō suru Shimin Seishin," 71.

117. Fukuda Kanichi, "Nihon Minshushugi no Kanōsei: Sekinin Seiji no Kakuritsu o," *Sekai* 176 (August 1960): 56–57.

118. Ishida Takeshi et al., "Genzai no Seiji Jōkyō: Nani o nasu beki ka," *Sekai* 176 (August 1960): 217.

119. Ishida, Shinohara, and Fukuda, "Yakudō suru Shimin Seishin," 81.

120. Ishida et al., "Genzai no Seiji Jōkyō," 250, 254.

121. I am using the original essay here. Kuno Osamu, "Shiminshugi no Seiritsu," in Kuno Osamu, *Kuno Osamu Shū vol. 2: Shiminshugisha toshite* (Tokyo: Iwanami Shoten, 1998), 63–79. A reedited version of the original was republished under the title "Seijiteki Shimin no Seiritsu: Hitotsu no Taiwa," in Kuno, *Seijiteki Shimin no Fukken.*

122. Kuno, "Shiminshugi no Seiritsu," 64–65.

123. Ibid., 66.

124. Ibid., 74.

125. For example, in 1959 Tsurumi said that people had the responsibility as citizens to act *(shimin toshite no kōdō no sekinin ga aru).* See Tsurumi Shunsuke, "Sensōchū ni ita Basho," 56.

126. Shinohara Hajime et al., "Soshiki to Kokumin Undō: Go-Jūkyū Igo no Undō o Chūshin ni," *Sekai* (October 1960): 38–39.

127. Tsurumi, "Nemoto kara no Minshushugi," 25.

128. Ibid., 27.

129. Ibid.

130. On the storeowner strikes, see Iwata Tōichi, "Kurīninguya mo Tachiagaru," *Sekai* (August 1960), reproduced in *Dokyumento Shōwa Shi*, vol. 7: *Anpo to Kōdō Seichō*, ed. Yamada Munemutsu (Tokyo: Heibonsha, 1975), 130–34; and Iwata Tōichi, "Shōnin no Jiko Henkaku—Keizai Shutai kara Seijiteki Shimin e," *Shisō no Kagaku* (July 1961): 41–44.

131. Hidaka, *1960 nen, 5 gatsu, 19 nichi,* 77.

132. For an excellent study on these groups, see Sasaki-Uemura, *Organizing the Spontaneous.*

133. I would note that others have pointed to such a schematization in grassroots activism. Hasegawa Koichi, for instance, distinguishes between citizens' movements *(shimin undō)* and residents' movements *(jūmin undō).* He says the former are more likely to be pedagogic and idealistic, whereas the latter focus narrowly on the welfare of local communities. For this reason, the *shimin* of citizens' movements are, in Hasegawa's words, "conscience constituents who participate from a commitment to specific values rather than direct interests." But, as Hasegawa admits, the division on the ground is not always so clear, especially when, for example, nonresidents of an area join in support of a movement: is this a *shimin* or a *jūmin* movement? Distinctions aside, however, my approach is to accept the difference in objectives, approach, and ethos of such categories of movements and to tease out the intellectual *implications* of these movements for later civic activism. The purpose of this is to show not only linkages over time but, more important, the unintended outcomes of earlier praxis. See Koichi Hasegawa, *Constructing Civil Society in Japan: Voices of Environmental Movements* (Melbourne, Australia: Trans Pacific Press, 2004), 39–42.

134. On this group, see ibid., 121–24.

135. As we will see in chapter 4, stretching from around the mid-1960s to the mid-1970s, a number of Marxist scholars also left their theoretical and ethical mark on the pragmatic stream of activism. Though I deal with the issue in later chapters, I would also note that Matsushita's vision of local government and citizen participation did not always sit well with local activists. Beginning

in the mid-1960s, for example, activists in Yokohama came into direct conflict with a prefectural administration deeply influenced by Matsushita's ideas on local government-resident relations.

136. Of course, it is worth noting that my typology here does not (nor is it intended to) capture the sheer diversity of civic groups. For example, contemporary NPOs are but one part of a complex civic sector (although they occupy a more and more prominent and dominant place). Nevertheless, I think the typology is useful in clarifying the historical trajectory of this important stream of activism.

137. *Tayori*, vol. 2, 242.

138. *Tayori*, vol. 1, 5.

139. Ibid.

140. Ide Busaburō, *Anpo Tōsō* (Tokyo: Sanichi Shobō, 1960), 156.

141. *Tayori*, vol. 2, 405.

142. *Tayori*, vol. 2, 414. The song is reproduced on p. 415.

143. Kobayashi Tomi, " 'Koe naki Koe' no Kōshin," *Shisō no Kagaku* (July 1960), reproduced in *Dokyumento Shōwa Shi*, ed. Yamada, 127.

144. *Asahi Jyānaru* (July 3, 1960). See *Tayori*, vol. 2, 408.

145. *Tayori*, vol. 1, 8.

146. *Tayori*, vol. 2, 406–7.

147. The report on this meeting is contained in *Tayori*, issue no. 5 (October 1960), in *Tayori*, vol. 1, 43–46.

148. As I explain below, the Voices' role as a citizen movement liaison center soon shifted to another group of activists and intellectuals led by the proponent of local government reform and citizen participation Matsushita Keiichi and his Tosei Chōsakai colleagues. This proved to be an important baton pass from a core of activists committed to conscientious dissent to a group more interested in the pragmatics of civic activism.

149. Activists coined the term *"minikomi"* (minicommunications) to distinguish their movement newsletters from the *masukomi* (mass communications), implicitly recognizing the rise of the institutions of mass society. For more on the history of *minikomi*, see Maruyama Hisashi, *Minikomi no Dōjidaishi* (Tokyo: Heibonsha, 1985); and Maruyama Hisashi, *Rōkaru Nettowāku no Jidai: Minikomi to Chiiki to Shimin Undō* (Tokyo: Nichigai Asoshiētsu, 1997).

150. *Tayori*, issue no. 5 (October 1960), in *Tayori*, vol. 1, 46–8.

151. *Tayori*, issue no. 6 (November 1960), in *Tayori*, vol. 1, 49–52.

152. *Tayori*, vol. 1, 55.

153. See *Tayori*, issues no. 11 (June 1961): 87–94, 13 (August 1961): 103–10, 14 (September 1961): 111–18, and 15 (November 1961): 127–34, all in *Tayori*, vol. 1; Seibōhō o Sekitomeru Kai (Seibōhō Hantai Shimin Kaigi), "Seibōhō o Sekitomeyō: Shimin wa Seibōhō ni Hantai suru," in *Tayori*, vol. 1, 119–26; and Fuchibe Tomohiro, "Beheiren Undō Kenkyū Josetsu—Shimin Undō no Tōjō to Tenkai," master's thesis, Graduate School of Literature, Waseda University, 1999, 18.

154. *Tayori*, vol. 1, 7.

155. *Tayori*, vol. 1, 66. For Takabatake's early position on residential organizations, see his article "Kyojūchi Soshiki no Teian," 14–15. This is rather

ironic, because by the 1970s he would be lamenting how easily such residential movements fit "into the establishment view of postwar democracy." For Takabatake, going local had made such groups "less ideological and more concerned with material demands." He pointed out, "So far has the movement degenerated over the past decade" that many of the new movements were "being transformed into subcontract organs of the government." See Takabatake Michitoshi, "Citizens' Movements: Organizing the Spontaneous," in *Authority and the Individual in Japan: Citizen Protest in Historical Perspective*, ed. J. Victor Koschmann (Tokyo: University of Tokyo Press, 1978), 191.

156. *Tayori*, vol. 1, 41–42.

157. Ibid., 81.

158. This discussion is reproduced in *Tayori*, vol. 1, 263–70.

159. *Tayori*, vol. 2, 464–65.

160. Useful sources here include: *Tayori*, vol. 1; Narumi Masayasu, *Sengo Jichitai Kaikakushi* (Tokyo: Nihon Hyōronsha, 1982), 171–76; Narumi Masayasu, "Shimin Soshiki no Ichinenkan—Chiiki ni okeru Ningen no Sōzō," *Shisō no Kagaku* (July 1961): 48–55; Hidaka, *1960 nen, 5 gatsu, 19 nichi*, 81–84; Tosei Chōsakai, ed., "Chiiki Katsudō no Tebiki," contained in Shiryō: Kakushin Jichitai Kankō Iinkai, ed., *Shiryō: Kakushin Jichitai* (Tokyo: Nihon Hyōronsha, 1990), 19–25; Fujita Hiroshi, "Anpo Tōsō no Taiken to Kyōkun," *Shisō no Kagaku* (June 1963): 11–13; and the Tosei Chōsakai magazine *Tosei* (March 10, 1961): 56–61. Also see Matsushita Keiichi, "Chiiki Minshushugi no Kadai to Tenbō," *Shisō* 443 (May 1961): 23 n. 1 for more sources.

161. On the Tosei Chōsakai, see Matsushita, *Sengo Seiji no Rekishi to Shisō*, 512–13; Michiba Chikanobu, "Sen Kyūhyaku Rokujū Nendai ni okeru 'Chiki' no Hakken to 'Kōkyōsei' no Saiteigi: Miketsu no Aporia o megutte," *Gendai Shisō* 31, no. 6 (May 2002): 100; and Fuchibe, "Beheiren Undō Kenkyū Josetsu," 11–13.

162. In Tokyo: the Suginami Association, the Koganei Citizens' Association for the Protection of Peace and Democracy, the Higashi Fushimi Danchi Association to Oppose Anpo, the Shakujii Citizens' Association, the Central Nerima Citizens' Association, the Eastern Nerima Citizens' Association, the Ōta Ward Association to Protect Democracy, the Musashino Line Citizens' Association, the Ōizumi Association for the Defense of Peace and Daily Life, the Mitaka Association, and the Hibarigaoka Association to Protect Democracy. Outside Tokyo: the Kōrigaoka Cultural Conference (Osaka) and Matsudo City Association to Protect Democracy (Chiba).

163. Matsushita, however, purposely refused public service in local or national government, but his colleague Narumi Masayasu became the head of policymaking in the administration of progressive Yokohama JSP mayor Asukata Ichio beginning in 1963, while others accepted positions as special secretaries *(tokubetsu hisho)* in the progressive Minobe administration of Tokyo and the Shimano administration in Sendai. As we will see, in an ironic twist, by the mid-1960s Mayor Asukata and his adviser Narumi would find themselves in a fierce battle with a local residents' movement opposing construction of a new freight line through the outskirts of Yokohama.

164. Matsushita, "Chiiki Minshushugi no Kadai to Tenbō," 513.

165. Ibid., 519.
166. Ibid., 522–23 nn. 9 and 13.
167. Matsushita, *Sengo Seiji no Rekishi to Shisō*, 498.
168. Matsushita, "Chiiki Minshushugi no Kadai to Tenbō," 532–23.
169. *Tayori*, vol. 1, 70.
170. The four groups were the Central Nerima Citizens' Association, the Eastern Nerima Citizens' Association, the Ōizumi Association, and the Shakujii Citizens' Association.
171. Narumi, "Shimin Soshiki no Ichinenkan," 52. Narumi's article also contains reports on other similar groups in Tokyo.
172. Ibid., 50.
173. Ibid., 51–52.
174. Fuchibe, "Beheiren Undō Kenkyū Josetsu," 10.
175. Tosei Chōsakai, *Daitoshi ni okeru Chiiki Seiji no Kōzō* (Tokyo: Tosei Chōsakai, 1961).
176. Narumi, "Shimin Soshiki no Ichinenkan," 52–53.
177. *Tayori*, vol. 1, 75.
178. Ibid.
179. Narumi, "Shimin Soshiki no Ichinenkan," 53.
180. Hosaka Masayasu, *Rokujūnen Anpo Tōsō* (Tokyo: Kōdansha, 1986), 138. For the statement see Tsuji, ed., *Shiryō*, 154.
181. Narumi, "Shimin Soshiki no Ichinenkan," 54.
182. Ibid.
183. *Tayori*, vol. 1, 15.
184. Narumi, "Shimin Soshiki no Ichinenkan," 48.
185. Ibid.
186. Ibid.

3. BEHEIREN AND THE ASIAN *SHIMIN*

Epigraphs: "Betonamu ni Heiwa o!" Shimin Rengō, ed., *Shiryō "Beheiren" Undō*, vol. 1 (Tokyo: Kawade Shobō Shinsha, 1974), 5, 6 (hereafter *SBU*).

1. Amano, *"Seikatsusha" to wa Dareka*, 170. The original name of the movement was the Alliance of Citizens' and Cultural Organizations for "Peace in Vietnam!" ("Betonamu ni Heiwa o!" Shimin—Bunka Dantai Rengō). In October 1966, this was changed to the Citizens' Alliance for "Peace in Vietnam!" ("Betonamu ni Heiwa o!" Shimin Rengō) to stress the importance of individual action. In its English-language pamphlets and publications, Beheiren often used the name Beheiren: Japan "Peace for Vietnam" Committee. See Beheiren: "Betonamu ni Heiwa o!" Shimin Rengō, ed., *"Beheiren Nyūsu" Gappon Shukusatsuban* (Tokyo: self-published, 1974), 32.
2. *SBU*, vol. 1, 39.
3. Oda was responsible for the full name; Takabatake, for the abbreviation.
4. On the origins of the movement, see Tsurumi Shunsuke, "Hitotsu no Hajimari—Aruiwa, Beheiren Izen," in *SBU*, vol. 1, xi–xii.
5. Masamura, *Sengoshi*, vol. 2, 300.

6. There are a wealth of sources in Japanese on the specifics of Beheiren activism. Readers are directed to the following key collections of source materials: Beheiren, ed., *"Beheiren Nyūsu";* and *SBU,* vols. 1–3. The Center for Education and Research in Cooperative Human Relations (Kyōsei Shakai Kyōiku Kenkyū Sentā), at Saitama University, houses the largest collection of primary source materials on the movement donated by the former secretary general Yoshikawa Yūichi. See www.kyousei.saitama-u.ac.jp/top/. Much useful information on the movement is also available at www.jca.apc.org/beheiren/, Beheiren's official homepage. The Takazawa Collection at the University of Hawaii also houses some source materials from the Beheiren movement. See www.takazawa.hawaii.edu/. In English, see Thomas Havens, *Fire across the Sea: The Vietnam War and Japan 1965–1975* (Princeton, NJ: Princeton University Press, 1987); and Simon Avenell, "Core Activists, Ideas, and the Development of Citizen Activism in Postwar Japan," PhD diss., University of California, Berkeley, 2003.

7. Both the *Asahi* and *Mainichi* newspapers reported on activists with "white balloons" and "flower bouquets" at the first march in 1965 (*SBU,* vol. 1, 10). As new and more radical elements entered the movement in the late 1960s, Beheiren's secretary general Yoshikawa Yūichi called on Beheiren members to maintain a "spirit of play" in their activism (*SBU,* vol. 2, 97). Paradoxically for one who had helped initiate the new style of activism in the postwar era, Yoshikawa began to express frustration in the 1990s with young Gulf War protesters who preferred terms such as *peace festival* over *antiwar demonstration.* See Yoshikawa Yūichi, "Demo to Parēdo to Pīsu Wōku: Iraku Hansen Undō to Kongo no Mondaiten," *Ronza* 106 (March 2004), 88–93.

8. Kuno, *Seijiteki Shimin no Fukken,* 157. By the same token, Kuno also admitted there was an intellectual top-heaviness in Beheiren that produced a gap between the mobilizers and the mobilized (ibid., 159).

9. Iida Momo, "Shimin Minshushugi Undō no Ronri to Shinri," in *Shimin Undō to wa Nanika,* ed. Oda Makoto (Tokyo: Tokuma Shoten, 1968), 18.

10. Takabatake, "Citizens' Movements," 196.

11. Takabatake Michitoshi, *Jiyū to Poritiku: Shakaigaku no Tenkai* (Tokyo: Chikuma Shobō, 1976), 66–67.

12. Ibid., 119. I would note, however, that Takabatake, like Kuno, also expressed some reservations with Beheiren. Individual autonomy, he realized, did not make for a strongly united movement. Moreover, as the movement expanded, Takabatake, echoing Kuno Osamu, saw a split between the regulars, activists, and leaders and the rest of the citizen masses, who tended to participate for a short time and then leave (Ibid., 120–21).

13. Amano, *"Seikatsusha" to wa Dareka,* 170, 174, 175.

14. Amano is referring here, of course, to the thought of Ōtsuka Hisao and his Weberian-inspired vision of the strongly ascetic modern man. See Ōtsuka Hisao, "Robinson Kurūsō no Ningen Ruikei," in *Gendai Nihon Shisō Taikei,* vol. 34: *Kindaishugi,* ed. Hidaka Rokurō (Tokyo: Chikuma Shobō, 1964), 99–106.

15. Hayden White, *Metahistory: The Historical Imagination in Nineteenth-Century Europe* (Baltimore, MD: Johns Hopkins University Press, 1973), 5.

16. On regional Beheiren movements, see www.jca.apc.org/beheiren/grouplist.html. Also see Hirai Kazuomi, "Sengo Shakai Undō no naka no Beheiren: Beheiren Undō no Chiikiteki Tenkai o Chūshin ni," *Hōsei Kenkyū* 71, no. 4 (March 2005): 723–55.

17. In a recent study of Oda Makoto, Roman Rosenbaum correctly characterizes Beheiren's strategy as one of "peaceful civil disobedience." Of course, we need to balance this aspect against Beheiren's open support for the armed struggle of the North Vietnamese and the Vietcong. See Roman Rosenbaum, "Defamiliarising the Postwar: The Enigma of Oda Makoto," *Japanese Studies* 25, no. 2 (September 2005): 149. Discussions of Beheiren in the context of postwar pacifism *(heiwashugi)* and the peace movement *(heiwa undō)* are common. See, for example, Wada Susumu, "Heiwa Undō to Heiwa Ishiki," in *Gendai Nihon Shakai Ron: Sengoshi kara Genzai o Yomu 30 shō*, ed. Watanabe Osamu (Tokyo: Rōdōjunpōsha, 1996), 570–91; and Michiba Chikanobu, *Senryō to Heiwa: Sengo to iu Keiken* (Tokyo: Seidosha, 2005), part 2, chapter 4, where he deals with Beheiren under the rubric of the "postwar experience of 'antiwar and peace'" *("hansen heiwa" no sengo taiken)*.

18. Oda Makoto, *Gimu toshite no Tabi* (Tokyo: Iwanami Shinsho, 1974), 166.

19. Lawrence Beer puts it best: "Pure pacifism requires, in all circumstances, that a person or community turn the other cheek and refrain from hostile reaction, based on faith in human goodness and disciplined conviction in the face of provocation, or on a belief that, on balance, violent response is counterproductive according to some other cost-benefit calculus. Only peaceful resistance to evil violence is permissible. That does not describe the official or popular pacifism of Japan, although some Japanese believe that Japan should not respond militarily even to an invasion, so horrible is war." Lawrence W. Beer, "The Constitution of Japan: 'Pacifism' and Mass Media Freedom," in *Law in Japan: A Turning Point*, ed. Daniel H. Foote (Seattle and London: University of Washington Press, 2007), 258.

20. Oda, *Gimu toshite no Tabi*, 167.

21. At the time, Oda and Kaikō made a pact not to criticize each other publicly, and Kaikō promised not to criticize Beheiren. See Kuno Osamu, *Shimin toshite Tetsugakusha toshite*, with Takabatake Michitoshi (Tokyo: Mainichi Shimbunsha, 1995), 280. For a masterful treatment of Kaiko's ambivalence and nihilism over the Vietnam conflict, see Irena Powell, "Japanese Writer in Vietnam: The Two Wars of Kaiko Ken (1931–1989)," *Modern Asian Studies* 32, no. 1 (February 1998): 219–44.

22. *SBU*, vol. 1, 22–23, emphasis added.

23. Oda Makoto, "Ima Nani o Nasu beki ka," in *Oda Makoto Zenshigoto*, vol. 9 (Tokyo: Kawade Shobō Shinsha, 1970), 305 (hereafter *OMZ*).

24. This statement was part of an invitation to participate in the so-called U.S.–Japan Citizens' Conference in August 1966 (*SBU*, vol. 1, 120).

25. Ibid.

26. Others have noticed such tendencies too. Though only in passing, Hirata Keiko notes that Beheiren was a movement about "pan-Asianism (opposition to Western colonialism in Asia)" and "nationalism (hostility to the U.S. use of

Japanese soil for the prosecution of the war and the U.S.–Japan Security Treaty that allowed the U.S. military station *[sic]* in Japan)." See Hirata Keiko, *Civil Society in Japan: The Growing Role of NGOs in Tokyo's Aid and Development Policy* (New York: Palgrave, 2002), 17. Oguma Eiji also recognizes Oda Makoto's nationalism and affinity with third worldism, especially in the late 1950s. See Oguma, *Minshu to Aikoku*, 761, 763–67.

27. Tsurumi, "Hitotsu no Hajimari," xii.

28. A poll taken by the *Asahi Shimbun* in August 1965 revealed these reasons. See "The Asahi Poll on Vietnam," *Japan Quarterly* 12, no. 4 (October–December 1965): 463–66.

29. A letter from "N" in Kyoto. See Beheiren, ed., *"Beheiren Nyūsu,"* 2.

30. On the dynamics of the postwar peace movement in Japan, see James J. Orr, *The Victim as Hero: Ideologies of Peace and National Identity in Postwar Japan* (Honolulu: University of Hawaii Press, 2001); and Yamamoto, *Grassroots Pacifism in Postwar Japan.*

31. Oda Makoto, "Heiwa e no Gutaiteki Teigen: Nichibei Shimin Kaigi de no Bōtō Enzetsu," in *SBU*, vol. 1, 107.

32. Oda Makoto, "Nanshi no Shisō," in *OMZ*, vol. 8, 15.

33. Ibid.

34. Oda was referring, of course, to the debate on modernity (or *overcoming modernity*) conducted among influential Japanese intellectuals shortly after the outbreak of the war, as well as to the philosopher Kōyama Iwao's 1942 book on the philosophy of world history. See Tetsuo Najita and H. D. Harootunian, "Japanese Revolt against the West: Political and Cultural Criticism in the Twentieth Century," in *The Cambridge History of Japan*, vol. 6: *The Twentieth Century*, ed. Peter Duus (Cambridge and New York: Cambridge University Press, 1989), chapter 14, 758–68; and Kōyama Iwao, *Sekaishi no Tetsugaku* (Tokyo: Iwanami Shoten, 1942).

35. Ibid., 13–14.

36. Ibid., 16.

37. Oguma, *Minshu to Aikoku*, 763.

38. Oda, "Nanshi no Shisō," 14.

39. Powell, "Japanese Writer in Vietnam," 240.

40. Quoted ibid., 241.

41. Beheiren ran full-page advertisements in the *New York Times* (November 16, 1965) and the *Washington Post* (April 3, 1967). See *SBU*, vol. 1, 58, for the *New York Times* advertisement that begins "America's best friends in Asia are the 100 million people of Japan."

42. Tsurumi Shunsuke, "Shiminteki Fufukujū no Kokusaiteki Rentai: 'Hansen to Henkaku ni kansuru Kokusai Kaigi' deno Hōkoku," in *SBU*, vol. 1, 404.

43. Ibid., 405.

44. Oda was referring to Kishi Nobusuke, who was prime minister at the time. See *OMZ*, vol. 6, 241.

45. Oda, *Gimu toshite no Tabi*, 64–66.

46. Kaiko Takeshi writing in the *Asahi Jyānaru*, September 19, 1965, reproduced in *SBU*, vol. 1, 48–49.

47. Tsurumi Yoshiyuki, "Atarashii Sekai to Shisō no Yōsei: Nichibei Shimin Kaigi no Imi," in Tsurumi Yoshiyuki, *Tsurumi Yoshiyuki Chosakushū*, vol. 2: *Beheiren*, ed. Yoshikawa Yūichi (Tokyo: Misuzu Shobō, 2002), 38 (hereafter TYC).

48. Ibid., 39.

49. Tsurumi, "Shiminteki Fufukujū no Kokusaiteki Rentai," 405.

50. Oda had originally invited the antiwar activist-historian-lawyer Staughton Lynd, who was unable to come. See Tsurumi Shunsuke, *Tsurumi Shunsuke Chosakushū*, vol. 5 (Tokyo: Chikuma Shobō, 1976), 97 (hereafter TSC).

51. E-mail correspondence with Howard Zinn, April 29, 2001.

52. Oda Makoto, "Genri toshite no Minshushugi no Fukken," OMZ, vol. 10, 16.

53. Oda Makoto and Tsurumi Shunsuke, eds., *Hansen to Henkaku: Teikō to Heiwa e no Teigen* (Tokyo: Gakukei Shobō, 1969), 14.

54. That being said, Oda vehemently asserted that Beheiren was "homegrown" and no imitation of social movements in the West. He preferred to see the link as an antiwar "chain" among global activists. See Oda Makoto, *"Beheiren": Kaikoroku denai Kaiko* (Tokyo: Daisan Shokan, 1995), 252, 254, 255.

55. See "Tokushū: Watashi wa Heiwa no tame ni Nani o suru no ka— 'Betonamu ni Heiwa o! Nichibei Shimin Kaigi,'" *Bungei* (October 1966): 245.

56. The wording in the original draft was: "The struggle to oppose American aggression in Vietnam is not merely a struggle to oppose the United States of America; rather we must remember to struggle against the inhumanity and cruelty that is within all of us." See ibid., 253.

57. Ibid., 257.

58. Ibid., 239.

59. Oda Makoto, "Heiwa no Rinri to Ronri" and "Heiwa o Tsukuru: Sono Genri to Kōdō—Hitotsu no Sengen," in OMZ, vol. 9, 85–131; and Oda, "Heiwa e no Gutaiteki Teigen," 104–19.

60. Beheiren, ed., *"Beheiren Nyūsu,"* 25.

61. Oda, "Heiwa no Rinri to Ronri," 91–92.

62. Ibid., 94.

63. Oda Makoto, "Ningen: Aru Kojinteki Kōsatsu," in OMZ, vol. 9, 25.

64. Oda, "Heiwa no Rinri to Ronri," 104.

65. For such an approach, see Rosenbaum, "Defamiliarising the Postwar," esp. 147–49.

66. Tsurumi, Ueno, and Oguma, *Sensō ga Nokoshita Mono*, 136.

67. Rosenbaum, "Defamiliarising the Postwar," 145–46.

68. Oda, *"Beheiren,"* 33.

69. See ibid., 34. Oda was probably referring to Edward Seidensticker, who published a book titled *Japan* with the editors of Time-Life Books in 1961. Oda also used his 1966 tour with Howard Zinn and Ralph Featherstone to attack Seidensticker and the Asian Studies establishment in the United States, saying that such individuals denigrated not only Japan but also the whole of Asia and Africa. (See SBU, vol. 1, 78.) Lest we think that race was on the minds of only the Japanese, consider Seidensticker's comments on the Japanese: "The

great British student of Japan, Basil Hall Chamberlain, offered this description of the Japanese half a century ago: 'Compared with the people of European race, the average Japanese has a long body, short legs, a large skull with a tendency to pronathism (projecting jaws), a flat nose, coarse hair, scanty eyelashes, puffy eyelids, a sallow complexion, and a low stature.' Except for the sallowness and shortness, which improved nutrition is now changing, this description is still generally accurate. It of course overlooks the fact that Japanese faces are often very good-looking, and frequently likeable and engaging. Though not as given to laughter as the Koreans and Chinese, the Japanese are likely to impress one as a sunny people. The Japanese smile is a complex one, possibly containing sadness and uncertainty, but its pleasantness is still enough to obscure the frequently bad teeth." And elsewhere: "Bereft of their clothes, they are frequently to be distinguished by a tendency toward hairiness, revealing mixture with a people distant from the Koreans (one such people, the Ainu of northern Japan, survives precariously)." See Edward Seidensticker, *Japan*, with the editors of TIME-LIFE Books, Life World Library series (New York: TIME-LIFE International, 1961), 14.

70. Oda, *Gimu toshite no Tabi*, 17.
71. Ibid., 55.
72. Oda Makoto, "Raishawā Kyōju no Nihon Ninshiki," *OMZ*, vol. 7, 169. Oda did, however, see hope in the new generation of young Asian researchers who only ever knew a post-colonial world. For them, the third world was even a role model in Oda's opinion. Oda, *Gimu toshite no Tabi*, 19–20.
73. Oda, "Nandemo Mite Yarō," *OMZ*, vol. 6, 237.
74. Ibid.
75. Ibid., 238.
76. Ibid.
77. Ibid.
78. Ibid.
79. Oda, *"Beheiren,"* 33.
80. Oda, "Nandemo Mite Yarō," 34.
81. Ibid.
82. *SBU*, vol. 3, 304.
83. Oda, "Nandemo Mite Yarō," 108.
84. Ibid., 34.
85. Ibid., 108.
86. Oda himself uses the English *sick* here. Oda, "Nandemo Mite Yarō," 109. For Kojève's commentary, see Alexandre Kojève, *Introduction to the Reading of Hegel* (Ithaca, NY, and London: Cornell University Press, 1991), 159–62. Interestingly, Kojève saw in Japanese civilization a different end of history, defined not by a return to animality and nature but by a "snobbery" of "formalized values." Kojève explained that "post-historical Man must continue to *detach* 'form' from 'content,' doing so no longer in order actively to transform the latter, but so that he may *oppose* himself as a pure 'form' to himself and to others taken as 'content' of any sort" (ibid., 162).
87. Tsurumi Yoshiyuki, "Atarashii Rentai no Shisō: Kokka Kenryoku no Kanata ni," in *TYC*, vol. 2, 58.

88. Ibid., 60.

89. Tsurumi Yoshiyuki, "Beikoku Nyū Refuto to no Taiwa," in *TYC*, vol. 2, 112–13. Tsurumi Yoshiyuki also discussed the activism and ideas of Carmichael in another article, "Kāmaikeru: Burakku Pawā no Teishōsha," *Asahi Jyānaru* (October 20, 1968): 52–56.

90. Tsurumi Yoshiyuki, "Beikoku Nyū Refuto to no Taiwa," 117.

91. Ibid., 118.

92. Ibid.

93. *TSC*, vol. 5, 99–100.

94. Oda, "Nandemo Mite Yarō," 68.

95. Ibid., 69, 72.

96. Ibid., 74.

97. Ibid., 77.

98. Ibid.

99. Ibid., 69.

100. Ibid., 71.

101. Ibid., 69.

102. Ibid., 70.

103. Ibid., 73.

104. Quoted in Oda Makoto, "Ningen no naka no rekishi," in *OMZ*, vol. 10, 212. Oda quotes directly from the translated *Autobiography of Malcolm X*. I use the original here. See Malcolm X, *The Autobiography of Malcolm X*, with Alex Haley (New York: Grove Press, 1965), 175.

105. Oda, *Gimu toshite no Tabi*, 73.

106. Ibid., 74.

107. Ibid., 76.

108. Ibid., 77.

109. Oda, "Ningen no naka no rekishi," 221.

110. Oda, "Nandemo Mite Yarō," 224.

111. Oda, *Gimu toshite no Tabi*, 47.

112. Oda, "Nandemo Mite Yarō," 226. Here, Oda's thought came very close to that of Tsurumi Shunsuke and also the enigmatic poet Tanigawa Gan, who, as we saw, in the 1950s spoke of a descent to the primeval base of the Asian ethnic commune.

113. Oda, "Nandemo Mite Yarō," 241–42.

114. Oda, "Ningen no naka no rekishi," 213.

115. Ibid., 214.

116. Ibid.

117. In a seeming turnaround, in the mid-1990s Oda grumbled that the "Restoration" was a "revolution" and should rightly be known as such. Oda Makoto, *"Beheiren,"* 411.

118. Oda, "Ningen no naka no rekishi," 217.

119. Ibid., 225.

120. Ibid., 224.

121. Ibid., 224–25.

122. Ibid., 225.

123. In this context it is worth noting Oda's wholly misguided lionization of dictator Kim Il Sung and the North Korean communist regime. See Oda Makoto, *Watashi to Chōsen* (Tokyo: Chikuma Shobō, 1977); and Oda Makoto, *"Kitachōsen" no Hitobito* (Tokyo: Ushio Shuppansha, 1978).

124. Oda, "Ningen no naka no rekishi," 227–28.

125. Ibid., 228.

126. Yoshikawa Yūichi, "Shōsetsu 'Hiemono' Hihan o Keiki to suru Tōron ni tsuite: Undō e no Seisanshugiteki Hihan o yameyō," in *"Beheiren Nyūsu,"* ed. Beheiren, 448.

127. Oda, "Ningen no naka no rekishi," 229.

128. Havens, *Fire across the* Sea, 141–45.

129. A wealth of materials exists on the deserters and Beheiren-JATEC support. *Dassōhei Tsūshin* and *Jatekku Tsūshin,* the official newsletters for citizen groups supporting the deserters, are reprinted in Beheiren, ed., *"Beheiren Nyūsu."* Also see Sekiya Shigeru and Sakamoto Yoshie, eds., *Tonari ni Dassōhei ga ita Jidai: Jatekku, Aru Shimin Undō no Kiroku* (Tokyo: Shisō no Kagakusha, 1998); and Anai Fumihiko, *Beheiren to Dassō Beihei* (Tokyo: Bungei Shunjū, 2000). In English, see Havens, *Fire across the Sea,* 141–45.

130. See John M. Barrilla, Richard D. Bailey, Michael A. Lindner, and Craig W. Anderson, "Wareware wa Naze Kono Kyo ni Deta no ka: Dassōhei Yonshi no Seimeibun (Zenbun)," in *"Beheiren Nyūsu,"* ed. Beheiren, 94-96; and Havens, *Fire across the Sea,* 141–42.

131. Statements by the four deserters can be found in Beheiren, ed., *"Beheiren Nyūsu,"* 94–96.

132. Oda, "Ningen: Aru Kojinteki Kōsatsu," 14.

133. On the Ōmura facility, see Tessa Morris-Suzuki, "Invisible Immigrants: Undocumented Migration and Border Controls in Postwar Japan," *Journal of Japanese Studies* 32, no. 1 (Winter 2006), 119–53.

134. For more on the Kim Jin Suh, see Avenell, "Core Activists, Ideas, and the Development of Citizen Activism in Postwar Japan," 158–74.

135. Oda, "Ningen: Aru Kojinteki Kōsatsu," 15.

136. Tsurumi Shunsuke, "Kintōki ni totte Nihon wa dōiu Kuni ka," *TSC,* vol. 5, 109, 110.

137. Oda Makoto, "Watashi no naka no Nihonjin: 'Watashi no Nihon' to 'Karera no Nihon,'" in *OMZ,* vol. 10, 141.

138. Ibid., 142.

139. Oda, *Gimu toshite no Tabi,* 192–93.

140. Tsurumi Yoshiyuki, "Nihon Kokumin toshite no Dannen: 'Kokka' no Kokufuku o Ika ni Heiwa Undō e Kesshū suru ka," in *TYC,* vol. 2, 83–98.

141. Ibid., 83.

142. Ibid., 90.

143. Ibid., 83.

144. Tsurumi Yoshiyuki, "Watashi no Sōkenron: Isshiron toshite no Shōsū Iken," in *TYC,* vol. 2, 141.

145. Tsurumi Yoshiyuki, "Nihon Kokumin toshite no Dannen," 93.

146. Ibid.

147. Ibid., 95.

148. Oda, "Nanshi no Shisō," 25.

149. Ibid.

150. Ibid., 26.

151. Ibid., 30.

152. Tsurumi Yoshiyuki, "Betonamu Sensō to Nihon Tokuju Sono hoka no Mondai," in *Beheiren Nyūsu,* ed. Beheiren, 16.

153. Wada Haruki, "Saa, Koko de Sensō Kikai o tomeyō," *Asahi Jyānaru* (July 5, 1971), reproduced in *SBU,* vol. 3, 46–53; Wada Haruki, "'Haena Kigyō' to Wareware—Sonī to Toyota no Minami Betonamu Shinshitsu ni Kōgi shite," *Asahi Jyānaru* (January 14, 1972), also reproduced in *SBU,* vol. 3, 163–72.

154. See "Sony and Those Smart Bombs: An Honest Mistake?" *Ampo: A Report from the Japanese New Left* 15 (December 1972): 28–29.

155. Ibid., 29.

156. Ibid.

157. Muto Ichiyo, "Sengo Kōki e no Ikō—Sengogata 'Heiwa to Minshushugi' no Hōkai Igo," *Tenbō* (September 1967): 87.

158. Ibid.

159. Ibid., 88.

160. Muto Ichiyo, "Beheiren Undō no Shisō: Sengo Minshushugi no Yukue ni yosete," *Shisō no Kagaku* (January 1968): 19.

161. Oda Makoto, "Watashi wa Shi ga Kowai," in Oda Makoto, *Nani o Watashitachi wa Hajimete iru no ka* (Tokyo: Sanichi Shobō, 1970), 157.

162. Muto, "Beheiren Undō no Shisō," 20.

163. Ibid.

164. Moriyama Yūichi, "Watashitachi wa Korekara . . . ," *Noroshi* (June 1, 1971): 2.

4. RESIDENTS INTO CITIZENS

1. Jeffrey Broadbent, *Environmental Politics in Japan: Networks of Power and Protest* (Cambridge and New York: Cambridge University Press, 1998), 97.

2. In practice, of course, the debate over approach was never so tidy. Proponents on all sides mixed their terminology, sometimes using *shimin* and other times using *jūmin*. Nevertheless, in terms of the crux of the debate itself—what should be the basic motivation for citizen activism, identity, and political engagement?—I think a clear delineation of the three perspectives is instructive.

3. Hoshino Shigeo, Nishioka Akio, and Nakajima Isamu, "Numazu, Mishima, Shimizu (nishi ittchō) Sekiyu Konbinato Hantai Tōsō to Fuji-shi o Meguru Jūmin Tōsō," in *Kōza Gendai Nihon no Toshi Mondai,* vol. 8: *Toshi Mondai to Jūmin Undō,* ed. Miyamoto Kenichi and Endō Akira (Kyoto and Tokyo: Chōbunsha, 1971), 72–209; Ui Jun, "Kōgai Genron II," in *Gappon Kōgai Genron,* ed. Ui Jun (Tokyo: Aki Shobō, 1990), 135–66; Iijima Nobuko, *Kaiteiban Kankyō Mondai to Higaisha Undō* (Tokyo: Gakubunsha, 1993),

209–12; Iijima Nobuko, *Kankyō Mondai no Shakaishi* (Tokyo: Yūhikaku, 2000), 151–54; Matsubara Haruo, ed., *Kōgai to Chiki Shakai: Seikatsu to Jūmin Undō no Shakaigaku* (Tokyo: Nihon Keizai Shimbunsha, 1971), 211–21; Margaret McKean, *Environmental Protest and Citizen Politics in Japan* (Berkeley and Los Angeles: University of California Press, 1981), 28–32; Jack Lewis, "Civic Protest in Mishima: Citizens' Movements and the Politics of the Environment in Contemporary Japan," in *Political Opposition and Local Politics in Japan*, ed. Kurt Steiner, Ellis S. Krauss, and Scott Flanagan (Princeton, NJ: Princeton University Press, 1980), 274–313; Norie Huddle and Michael Reich, *Island of Dreams: Environmental Crisis in Japan* (Rochester, VT: Schenkman Books, 1987), 256–70.

4. For discussion of the tactics and organization of the Shizuoka movements, see Iijima, *Kaiteiban Kankyō Mondai*, 211; Iijima, *Kankyō Mondai no Shakaishi*, 152–53; and Huddle and Reich, *Island of Dreams*, 258–63.

5. Iijima, *Kaiteiban Kankyō Mondai*, 212–14.

6. Shōji Hikaru and Miyamoto Kenichi, *Nihon no Kōgai* (Tokyo: Iwanami Shoten, 1975), 220–21.

7. Miyamoto Kenichi, "Jūmin Undō no Riron to Rekishi," in *Kōza Gendai Nihon no Toshi Mondai*, vol. 8, 59.

8. For details, see Yokoyama Keiji, "Kono Wakitatsu Teikō no Nami," *Asahi Jyānaru* (April 23, 1971): 41–62.

9. See "Tokushū Minikomi '71: Honryū suru Chikasui," *Asahi Jyānaru* (March 26, 1971): 4–60; Jūmin Toshokan, ed., *Minikomi Sōmokuroku* (Tokyo: Heibonsha, 1992); Maruyama, *Minikomi no Dōjidaishi*; and Maruyama, *Rōkaru Nettowāku no Jidai*. The Center for Education and Research in Cooperative Human Relations also houses a massive collection of *minikomi*. Go to www.kyousei.saitama-u.ac.jp/top/.

10. Shōji Hikaru and Miyamoto Kenichi, *Osorubeki Kōgai* (Tokyo: Iwanami Shoten, 1964).

11. Matsubara, ed., *Kōgai to Chiki Shakai*, 77. Fuji City was famously known as a "pollution department store" for its *hedoro* (sludge) pollution. See Ui, "Kōgai Genron II," 166–67.

12. Yokoyama, "Kono Wakitatsu Teikō no Nami," 41.

13. Irokawa Daikichi, "The Survival Struggle of the Japanese Community," in *Authority and the Individual in Japan: Citizen Protest in Historical Perspective*, ed. J. Victor Koschmann (Tokyo: University of Tokyo Press, 1978), 282.

14. Taketsugu Tsurutani, "A New Era of Japanese Politics: Tokyo's Gubernatorial Election," *Asian Survey* 12, no. 5 (1972): 443.

15. Matsushita, "Shimin Sanka to Sono Rekishiteki Kanōsei," 195.

16. Ibid., 194.

17. Narumi, *Sengo Jichitai Kaikakushi*, 179.

18. Ibid., 179.

19. Ibid., 183.

20. Miyamoto, "Jūmin Undō no Riron to Rekishi," 56–57.

21. Endō Akira, "Jūmin Undō no Kadai to Tenbō," in *Kōza Gendai Nihon no Toshi Mondai*, vol. 8, 398.

22. Ibid., 450; Shōji and Miyamoto, *Osorubeki Kōgai*, 168.

290 I Notes to Pages 155–159

23. Shōji and Miyamoto, Osorubeki Kōgai, 140.

24. Ui Jun, "Kōgai Genron I," in Gappon Kōgai Genron, ed. Ui, 25–26.

25. Kawana Hideyuki, Dokyumento Nihon no Kōgai Dai-5kan Sōgōkaihatsu (Tokyo: Ryokufu, 1990), 33.

26. Ibid., 38.

27. Masamura, Sengoshi, 201.

28. Miyamoto, "Jūmin Undō no Riron to Rekishi," 58.

29. Kawana, Dokyumento Nihon no Kōgai, 59.

30. Ibid., 57–59. Of course, the government did not abandon comprehensive planning, and rural communities by no means abandoned efforts to attract industry. Economic development may have caused pollution, but, as everyone recognized, it also improved standards of living. Hence, the broad popularity of later plans such as the Satō administration's Zensō of 1969 and, even more so, Tanaka Kakuei's best-selling 1972 work, Nihon Rettō Kaizō Ron (A Plan for Remodeling the Japanese Archipelago) (Tokyo: Nikkan Kōgyō Shimbunsha, 1972). See Huddle and Reich, Island of Dreams, 237–38.

31. Masamura, Sengoshi, 253.

32. Ibid., 254; Broadbent, Environmental Politics in Japan, 118.

33. Masamura, Sengoshi, 257; Broadbent, Environmental Politics in Japan, 120.

34. McKean, Environmental Protest, 42–79; Masamura, Sengoshi, 246–57; Julian Gresser, Koichiro Fujikura, and Akio Morishima, Environmental Law in Japan (London and Cambridge, MA: MIT Press, 1981), 29–30.

35. McKean, Environmental Protest, 67, 69, 78.

36. Hasegawa, Constructing Civil Society in Japan, 45.

37. On the Fuji movement, see Ui, "Kōgai Genron II," 166–86; Matsubara, ed., Kōgai to Chiki Shakai, 221–43; and Kōda Toshihiko, Waga Sonzai no Teiten kara: Fuji Kōgai to Watashi (Tokyo: Sōdosha, 2005).

38. Asahi Jyānaru Henshūbu, Sanrizuka (Tokyo: Sanichi Shobō, 1981); Kitahara Kōji, Daichi no Ran Narita Tōsō: Sanrizuka Hantai Dōmei Jimukyokuchō no 30 nen (Tokyo: Ochanomizu Shobō, 1996); David E. Apter and Nagayo Sawa, Against the State: Politics and Social Protest in Japan (Cambridge, MA: Harvard University Press, 1984).

39. On environmental rights, see McKean, Environmental Protest, 2, 4; Matsubara Haruo and Nitagai Kamon, eds., Jūmin Undō no Riron: Undō no Tenkai Katei to Tenbō (Tokyo: Gakuyō Shobō, 1976), 237, 364–65; Matsushita Ryūichi, Buzen Kankyō Saiban (Tokyo: Nihon Hyōronsha, 1980). Pages 19–20 in Matsushita have an excellent list of publications on the legal issues under discussion at the time.

40. Michiba Chikanobu suggests a similar schematization with respect to the discovery of locality, identifying a local government group (Matsushita Keiichi, etc.) and a jūmin group (Miyazaki Shōgo, etc.). See Michiba, "Sen Kyūhyaku Rokujū Nendai," 97. Nakamura Kiichi also identifies a "class faction" (kaikyū-ha), a "citizen faction" (shimin-ha), and a "resident faction" (jūmin-ha). See Nakamura Kiichi, "Jūmin Undō no Kanken: 'Shiron' e no Josetsu," in Jūmin Undō "Shiron": Jissensha kara mita Jichi no Shisō, ed.

Nakamura Kiichi (Tokyo: Sōdosha, 2005), 11–52 (this is a reprint of the original 1976 version).

41. Miyamoto, "Jūmin Undō no Riron to Rekishi," 2.

42. Endō, "Jūmin Undō no Kadai to Tenbō," 462.

43. Miyamoto, "Jūmin Undō no Riron to Rekishi," 63.

44. Ibid., 62.

45. Endō, "Jūmin Undō no Kadai to Tenbō," 459.

46. Miyamoto, "Jūmin Undō no Riron to Rekishi," 7.

47. Shōji and Miyamoto, Osorubeki Kōgai, 198; Shōji and Miyamoto, Nihon no Kōgai, 232.

48. Endō, "Jūmin Undō no Kadai to Tenbō," 477.

49. Ibid.

50. Ibid.

51. Ibid., 479.

52. Ui Jun, "Joshō: Jishu Kōza no Jūgonen," in Kōgai Jishu Kōza 15 nen, ed. Ui Jun (Tokyo: Aki Shobō, 1991), 9.

53. Ibid., 16.

54. Ibid., 31.

55. Ibid., 10.

56. Ibid., 11, 36.

57. Ui Jun, Kōgai Genron Hokan II: Kōgai Jūmin Undō (Tokyo: Aki Shobō, 1974), 57.

58. Ui, "Joshō," 36.

59. Ibid., 11.

60. Ui Jun, "Gappon Maegaki," in Gappon Kōgai Genron, ed. Ui, 9.

61. Ibid., 9–10.

62. Ibid., 10.

63. Ibid., 10.

64. Ibid., 10.

65. Ui Jun, "Kōgai Genron III," in Gappon Kōgai Genron, ed. Ui, 217.

66. Ibid.

67. Ibid., 218.

68. Ibid., 219.

69. Ui, "Gappon Maegaki," 10.

70. Ui, Kōgai Genron Hokan II, 48.

71. Ibid., 20.

72. Ibid., 47.

73. Ibid., 49.

74. Ibid., 49–50.

75. Ibid., 56.

76. Quoted in Yasuda Tsuneo, "Gendaishi ni okeru Jichi to Kōkyōsei ni kansuru Oboegaki: Yokohama Shinkamotsusen Hantai Undō no 'Keiken' o Tōshite," Hōgaku Shinpō 109, no. 1–2 (2002): 362. It is also worth noting that while Asukata pursued a "conciliatory" approach to the problem he also used his political allies in the assembly and local associations to convince landowners to sell their properties, many of whom eventually did so (ibid., 359).

77. On the freight line movement, see Miyazaki Shōgo, *Ima, Kōkyōsei o Utsu: "Dokyumento" Yokohama Shinkamotsusen Hantai Undō* (Tokyo: Shinsensha, 1975); Miyazaki Shōgo, "Yokohama Hōshiki no Mondaiten," in *Kōgai Jishu Kōza 15 nen,* ed. Ui, 180–90; Miyazaki Shōgo, "'Kōkyōsei' to wa Nanika," in *Jūmin Undō "Shiron,"* ed. Nakamura, 53–76; Yasuda, "Gendaishi ni okeru Jichi," 356–70; and Michiba, "Sen Kyūhyaku Rokujū Nendai," 109–25.

78. Miyazaki, "'Kōkyōsei' to wa Nanika," 60.

79. Miyazaki, *Ima, Kōkyōsei o Utsu,* 75.

80. Miyazaki, "'Kōkyōsei' to wa Nanika," 63; Michiba, "Sen Kyūhyaku Rokujū Nendai," 119; Miyazaki, *Ima, Kōkyōsei o Utsu,* 129.

81. Miyazaki, "'Kōkyōsei' to wa Nanika," 64.

82. Miyazaki, *Ima, Kōkyōsei o Utsu,* 167.

83. Ibid., 104.

84. Ibid., 103.

85. Ibid., 107.

86. Ibid., 137.

87. Ibid., 145.

88. Ibid., 78.

89. Ibid., 117.

90. Ibid., 148–49.

91. Ibid., 139.

92. Ibid.

93. Ibid., 139.

94. Frantz Fanon, *The Wretched of the Earth* (New York: Grove Press, 1963), 200–201.

95. Ibid., 247; Miyazaki, *Ima, Kōkyōsei o Utsu,* 157. In Japanese, Fanon's "national consciousness" is rendered as *minzoku ishiki* (ethnic national consciousness); "nationalism," as *minzokushugi* (ethnic nationalism); and "international dimension," as *fuhensei no kiso* (the foundation of universalism).

96. Fanon, *The Wretched of the Earth,* 247–48.

97. Miyazaki, *Ima, Kōkyōsei o Utsu,* 157.

98. Quoted in Tsurumi, "Nihon no Shisō Hyakunen," 367.

99. Michiba, "Sen Kyūhyaku Rokujū Nendai," 123.

100. Tomura Issaku, *Waga Jūjika: Sanrizuka* (Tokyo: Kyōbunkan, 1974); Tomura Issaku, *No ni Tatsu: Watashi no Sanrizuka Tōsōshi* (Tokyo: Sanichi Shobō, 1974); Tomura Issaku, *Tatakai ni Ikiru: Sanrizuka Tōsō* (Tokyo: Aki Shobō, 1970).

101. Quoted in Nakamura, "Jūmin Undō no Kanken," 31.

102. Matsushita Ryūichi, *Matsushita Ryūichi Sono Shigoto: Kurayami no Shisō,* vol. 12 (Tokyo: Kawade Shobō Shinsha, 1999), 29.

103. The essay is reproduced ibid., 139–42.

104. Matsushita Ryūichi, "Buzen Karyoku to Tatakau Sakka," in *Kōgai Jishu Kōza 15 nen,* ed. Ui, 372–95. For discussion of Matsushita's *minikomi,* see Maruyama, *Minikomi no Dōjidaishi,* 255–58. Copies of the *minikomi* are held at the Center for Education and Research in Cooperative Human Relations, www.kyousei.saitama-u.ac.jp/top/.

105. Yasuda, "Gendaishi ni okeru Jichi," 368.

106. Michiba, "Sen Kyūhyaku Rokujū Nendai," 123.

107. Shinohara Hajime, "Shimin Undō no Dessan," *Shimin* 2 (May 1971): 20.

108. Ibid.

109. Quoted in Nakamura, "Jūmin Undō no Kanken," 19.

110. Shinohara, "Shimin Undō no Dessan," 20.

111. Shinohara Hajime, *Nihon no Seiji Fūdo* (Tokyo: Iwanami Shoten, 1968), 192.

112. Ibid., 194.

113. Matsubara and Nitagai, eds., *Jūmin Undō no Riron*, 207.

114. Ibid., 369.

115. Ibid., 207.

116. Ibid., 369.

117. Ibid., 369–70.

118. Ibid., 370.

119. Ibid., 370–71.

120. Ibid., 371.

121. Ibid.

122. Ibid., 374.

123. Ibid., 373.

124. Ibid.

125. Ibid., 381.

126. Narumi, *Sengo Jichitai Kaikakushi*, 189.

127. Ibid.

128. Narumi Masayasu, *Toshi Henkaku no Shisō to Hōhō* (Tokyo: Renga Shobō, 1972), 12.

129. Ibid.

130. Ibid., 13.

131. Ibid., 12.

132. Ibid., 13.

133. Ibid.

134. Ibid.

135. Ibid., 13–14.

136. Ibid., 14.

137. Ibid., 15.

138. Ibid., 15–16.

139. Matsushita, " 'Shimin' teki Ningengata no Gendaiteki Kanōsei," 17.

140. For statistics on the progressive administrations, see Shiryō: Kakushin Jichitai Kankō Iinkai, ed., *Shiryō: Kakushin Jichitai* (Tokyo: Nihon Hyōronsha, 1990), 549–72; and Narumi, *Sengo Jichitai Kaikakushi*, 170, 188.

141. Matsushita, *Sengo Seiji no Rekishi to Shisō*, 515.

142. Alan Rix, "Tokyo's Governor Minobe and Progressive Local Politics in Japan," *Asian Survey* 15, no. 6 (June 1975): 530.

143. Michiba, "Sen Kyūhyaku Rokujū Nendai," 116.

144. Ibid., 117.

145. Narumi, *Toshi Henkaku*, 62.

146. Ibid., 63.

147. Ibid., 64.

148. Michiba, "Sen Kyūhyaku Rokujū Nendai," 100.

149. Ibid.

150. Matsushita Keiichi, "Jichitai ni okeru Kakushin Seiji Shidō," in *Jichitai Kaikaku no Rironteki Tenbō*, ed. Asukata Ichio (Tokyo: Nihon Hyōronsha, 1965), 69–70.

151. Ibid., 62.

152. Ibid., 63.

153. Ibid.

154. Asukata Ichio, "Shimin ni yoru Jichitai-zukuri no Kōsō," in *Gendai ni Ikiru*, vol. 6: *Shimin Sanka*, ed. Matsushita, 165.

155. Ibid.

156. Michiba, "Sen Kyūhyaku Rokujū Nendai," 117.

157. Ibid.

158. Matsushita, "Shimin Sanka to Sono Rekishiteki Kanōsei," 233.

159. Ibid., 225.

160. Shiryō: Kakushin Jichitai Kankō Iinkai, ed., *Shiryō: Kakushin Jichitai*, 227.

161. Ibid.

162. Ibid. See also Honda Kaichirō, *Katsudōya Shichō Funsenki: Tokyo Chōfushi ni nezuku Kakushin Shisei* (Tokyo: Shakai Shinpō, 1968).

163. Shiryō: Kakushin Jichitai Kankō Iinkai, ed., *Shiryō: Kakushin Jichitai*, 228.

164. See ibid., 228–31. For a brief case study on *shimin sanka* in Musashino, see Matsushita Keiichi, *Shinseijikō* (Tokyo: Asahi Shimbunsha, 1977), 81–92.

165. Shiryō: Kakushin Jichitai Kankō Iinkai, ed., *Shiryō: Kakushin Jichitai*, 231.

166. Ibid., 232.

167. Ibid., 233.

168. Ibid., 233, 234, 235.

169. Narumi, *Toshi Henkaku*, 61.

170. Asukata, "Shimin ni yoru Jichitai-zukuri no Kōsō," 160.

171. Michiba, "Sen Kyūhyaku Rokujū Nendai," 114.

172. Ibid.

173. Miyazaki, "Yokohama Hōshiki no Mondaiten," 189.

174. Ibid., 188.

175. Ibid., 189.

176. Shiryō: Kakushin Jichitai Kankō Iinkai, ed., *Shiryō: Kakushin Jichitai*, 226.

177. Narumi Masayasu, *Chihō Bunken no Shisō: Jichitai Kaikaku no Kiseki to Tenbō* (Tokyo: Gakuyō Shobō, 1994), 94.

178. Matsushita, *Shinseijikō*, 62.

179. Tōkyōto Kikaku Chōseikyoku Chōseibu, ed., *Hiroba to Aozora no Tōkyō Kōsō* (Tokyo: Tokyo Metropolitan Government, 1971).

180. Yonehara, *Nihonteki "Kindai" e no Toi*, 141.

181. Matsushita Keiichi, *Toshi Seisaku o Kangaeru* (Tokyo: Iwanami Shoten, 1971), 111.

182. Komori Takeshi, *Toshizukuri: Toshi Mondai no Genjitsu to Mirai* (Tokyo: Kawade Shobō Shinsha, 1965); Narumi, *Sengo Jichitai Kaikakushi,* 222.

183. Narumi, *Sengo Jichitai Kaikakushi,* 222–23.

184. Matsushita Keiichi, *Shibiru Minimamu no Shisō* (Tokyo: Tokyo Daigaku Shuppankai, 1971), 273; Matsushita, *Toshi Seisaku o Kangaeru,* 108; Matsushita Keiichi, "Shibiru Minimamu to Toshi Seisaku," in *Iwanami Kōza Gendai Toshi Seisaku,* vol. 5: *Shibiru Minimamu,* ed. Matsushita Keiichi (Tokyo: Iwanami Shoten, 1973), 3–5.

185. Matsushita, *Toshi Seisaku o Kangaeru,* 114–15.

186. Ibid., 120–21; Narumi, *Chihō Bunken no Shisō,* 82.

187. Narumi, *Sengo Jichitai Kaikakushi,* 222; Narumi, *Chihō Bunken no Shisō,* 77–78.

188. Narumi, *Sengo Jichitai Kaikakushi,* 222.

189. Ibid., 223. Other examples of civil minimums in municipal policymaking include Aomori City's Sōgō Keikaku (Comprehensive Plan); Musashino City's Chōki Keikaku (Long-Term Plan); and Asahikawa City's Shibiru Minimamu Kenkyūkai (Civil Minimum Research Group). See Narumi, *Chihō Bunken no Shisō,* 78–80.

190. Narumi, *Chihō Bunken no Shisō,* 81.

191. Matsushita, *Toshi Seisaku o Kangaeru,* 133, 145.

192. Yonehara, *Nihonteki "Kindai" e no Toi,* 141.

193. Matsushita, *Toshi Seisaku o Kangaeru,* 166.

194. Matsushita, "Shibiru Minimamu to Toshi Seisaku," 19.

195. Ibid., 20.

196. Narumi, *Chihō Bunken no Shisō,* 161.

197. Matsushita, *Shinseijikō,* 63.

198. Matsushita, "Shimin Sanka to Sono Rekishiteki Kanōsei," 230.

199. Miyazaki, "'Kōkyōsei' to wa Nanika," 68.

200. Ibid., 68–69.

201. Shinohara Hajime, "Shimin Sanka no Seido to Undō," in *Iwanami Kōza Gendai Toshi Seisaku,* vol. 2: *Shimin Sanka,* ed. Itō Mitsuharu, Shinohara Hajime, Matsushita Keiichi, and Miyamoto Kenichi (Tokyo: Iwanami Shoten, 1973), 4.

202. Ibid.

203. Quoted in Michiba, "Sen Kyūhyaku Rokujū Nendai," 124.

204. Narumi, *Chihō Bunken no Shisō,* 101.

205. Ibid., 102.

206. Matsushita Keiichi, *Toshigata Shakai no Jichi* (Tokyo: Nihon Hyōronsha, 1987), 89–90.

207. Ibid., 107.

208. Ibid., 175–76.

209. Broadbent, *Environmental Politics in Japan,* 110.

210. See Frank Upham, *Law and Social Change in Postwar Japan* (Cambridge, MA: Harvard University Press, 1987), especially chapter 2; and Miranda

A. Schreurs, *Environmental Politics in Japan, Germany, and the United States* (Cambridge and New York: Cambridge University Press, 2002), 73, 89.

211. Nakamura Kiichi, "Nijūhachi-nen-me no 'Atogaki,'" in *Jūmin Undō "Shiron,"* ed. Nakamura, 249–53.

212. Ibid., 252.

213. For example, the 1997 *Kōsei Hakusho (White Paper on Welfare)* of what was then the Ministry of Welfare (Kōseishō) discussed the promotion of wide-ranging citizen participation *(habahiroi shimin sanka no sokushin)* as an important device for nurturing human resources to shoulder the burden of an aging society. Kōseisho, *Kōsei Hakusho,* 1997. Available at www.hakusyo .mhlw.go.jp/wp/index.htm (accessed March 13, 2007); see part 1, chapter 4.

5. SHIMIN, NEW CIVIC MOVEMENTS, AND THE POLITICS OF PROPOSAL

Epigraph: Kokumin Seikatsu Shingikai Sōgō Kikaku Bukai Dai 4 Kai NPO Hōjin Seido Kentō Iinkai, *Giji Yōshi* (March 20, 2006), 2, accessible at http:// www5.cao.go.jp/seikatsu/shingikai/kikaku/20th/npo/index.html (accessed May 24, 2007).

1. For an earlier, abridged version of this chapter, see Simon Avenell, "Civil Society and the New Civic Movements in Contemporary Japan: Convergence, Collaboration, and Transformation," *Journal of Japanese Studies* 35, no. 2 (Summer 2009): 247–83.

2. *Fuyu no jidai:* literally, "winter period." See, for example, Maruyama, *Minikomi no Dōjidaishi,* 61.

3. Shinohara Hajime and Wada Akiko, eds., *Kawasaki Shimin Akademī Sōsho 3 Kōdo Seichō no Hikari to Kage: Seiji to Bungaku no Mado o tōshite* (Kawasaki: Kawasaki Shōgai Gakushū Shinkō Jigyōdan, Kawasaki Shimin Akademī Shuppanbu, 2003), 94.

4. See McKean, *Environmental Protest,* 21–22; and Upham, *Law and Social Change in Japan,* 56–57.

5. Toyota Zaidan, *Jiritsu to Kyōsei o Mezashite: "Kusa no Ne" Katsudō no Kadai to Tenbō* (Tokyo: Toyota Zaidan, 1992), 25–26.

6. Garon, "From Meiji to Heisei"; Sheldon Garon, *Molding Japanese Minds: The State in Everyday Life* (Princeton, NJ: Princeton University Press, 1997); Susan Pharr, "Conclusion: Targeting by an Activist State: Japan as a Civil Society Model," in *The State of Civil Society,* ed. Schwartz and Pharr, 36.

7. Robert Pekkanen, "Japan's New Politics: The Case of the NPO Law," *Journal of Japanese Studies* 26, no. 1 (Winter 2000): 113.

8. Sasaki-Uemura, *Organizing the Spontaneous;* Havens, *Fire across the Sea;* McKean, *Environmental Protest;* Daniel P. Aldrich, *Site Fights: Divisive Facilities and Civil Society in Japan and the West* (Ithaca, NY: Cornell University Press, 2008).

9. Garon, "From Meiji to Heisei," 61.

10. John Creighton Campbell, *How Policies Change: The Japanese Government and the Aging Society* (Princeton, NJ: Princeton University Press, 1992), especially chapter 7.

11. Murakami Kimiko, "Shakai Fukushi Jigyō no Seido Kaikaku," in *Nihon Shakai Hoshō no Rekishi*, ed. Yokoyama Kazuhiko and Tada Hidenori (Tokyo: Gakubunsha, 1991), 374; Jiyūminshutō, *Nihongata Fukushi Shakai* (Tokyo: Jiyūminshutō Kōhōiinkai Shuppankyoku, 1979); Kōyama Kenichi, *Eikokubyō no Kyōkun* (Kyoto: PHP Kenkyūjo, 1978).

12. Campbell, *How Policies Change*, 217, 252; Gregory J. Kasza, *One World of Welfare: Japan in Comparative Perspective* (Ithaca, NY, and London: Cornell University Press, 2006), 110.

13. Garon, *Molding Japanese Minds*, 223.

14. Kōroki Hiroshi, "Borantia no Rekishi kara Kangaeru," *Kikan Mado* 20 (Summer 1994): 106.

15. Keizai Kikakuchō Kokumin Seikatsukyoku, *Borantia Katsudō no Jittai: Chōsa Kekka to Dantai Meibō* (Tokyo: Kokuritsu Insatsukyoku, 1981), 36.

16. Zenkoku Shakai Fukushi Kyōgikai Kyūjūnen Tsūshi Hensan Iinkai, *Zenkoku Shakai Fukushi Kyōgikai Kyūjūnen Tsūshi: Jizen kara Fukushi e* (Tokyo: Zenkoku Shakai Fukushi Kyōgikai, 2003), 327.

17. Borantia Hakusho 1999 Henshū Iinkai, ed., *Borantia Hakusho 1999: Watashitachi ga Tsukuru Atarashii "Kōkyō"* (Tokyo: Shadan Hōjin Nihon Seinen Hōshi Kyōkai, JYVA, 1999), 13.

18. Borantia Hakusho Henshū Iinkai, ed., *Borantia Hakusho 1990 nenban: Borantia no Nyū Wēbu o Saguru* (Tokyo: Shadan Hōjin Nihon Seinen Hōshi Kyōkai, JYVA, 1990), 92.

19. Zenkoku Shakai Fukushi Kyōgikai, *Borantia Katsudō o Ikusei suru tame ni: Borantia Ikusei Kihon Yōkō* (Tokyo: Zenkoku Shakai Fukushi Kyōgikai, 1973), 2.

20. Ibid., 7–8, 17.

21. Kōseisho, *Kōseihakusho Shōwa 59 nenban* (1984), chapter 1, section 1.4, "Fukushi no Yakuwari Buntan to Borantia Katsudō," www.hakusyo .mhlw.go.jp/wp/index.htm (accessed February 27, 2008).

22. Chūō Shakai Fukushi Shingikai Chiiki Fukushi Senmon Bunkakai, *Borantia Katsudō no Chūchōtekina Shinkō Hōsaku ni tsuite: Chūō Shakai Fukushi Shingikai Chiiki Fukushi Senmon Bunkakai Iken Gushin* (Tokyo: Kōseishō Shakai-Engokyoku, 1993), 3.

23. Ibid., 5, 11.

24. Borantia Hakusho 1999 Henshū Iinkai, ed., *Borantia Hakusho 1999*, 148–49.

25. Kokumin Seikatsu Shingikai Chōsabukai Komyuniti Mondai Shōiinkai, ed., *Komyuniti: Seikatsu no Ba ni okeru Ningensei no Kaifuku* (Tokyo: Ōkurashō Insatsukyoku, 1969).

26. Keizai Kikakuchō Kokumin Seikatsu Kyoku, ed., *Jishuteki Shakai Sanka Katsudō no Igi to Yakuwari: Katsuryoku to Rentai o Motomete* (Tokyo: Ōkurashō Insatsukyoku, 1983), 1.

27. Ibid., 3, 55.

28. Keizai Kikakuchō Kokumin Seikatsu Kyoku, ed., *Jikaku to Sekinin no aru Shakai e* (Tokyo: Ōkurashō Insatsu Kyoku, 1994), preface, 1, 2.

29. Ibid., 11.

30. Ibid., 5.

298 | Notes to Pages 205–210

31. Ibid., 12.

32. Ibid., 18–20.

33. Ibid., 15.

34. Yokoyama, "Kono Wakitatsu Teikō no Nami," 41; "Seikatsu Teian-gata Shimin Undō no Atarashii Nami," *Asahi Jyānaru* (August 1, 1986): 16.

35. "Seikatsu Teian-gata Shimin Undō," *Asahi Jyānaru*, 16.

36. Ibid.

37. Fujita Kazuyoshi and Komatsu Kōichi, *Inochi to Kurashi o Mamoru Kabushiki Gaisha: Nettowākingugata no aru Seikatsusha Undō* (Tokyo: Gakuyō Shobō, 1992), 52–53.

38. Harima Yasuo, *Chi En Shakai no Nettowākingu* (Tokyo: Kashiwa Shobō, 1986), 16–17.

39. Bananabōto Jikkō Iinkai, ed., *Inochi, Shizen, Kurashi—Banana Bōto: Mōhitotsu no Seikatsu o Tsukuru Nettowākāzu no Funade* (Tokyo: Honnoki, 1986), 16.

40. Watanabe Gen, *Dokokade Nanika ga hajimatteiru!? Suimenkade Ugomeku Mōhitotsu no Shakai Keisei e no Kokoromi* (Tokyo: Toyota Zaidan, 1988).

41. Ibid.

42. For example, Bananabōto Jikkō Iinkai, ed,. *Inochi, Shizen, Kurashi*; NGO Katsudō Suishin Sentā, ed., *NGO Dairekutorī: Kokusai Kaihatsu Kyōryoku ni Tazusawaru Minkan Kōeki Dantai* (Tokyo: NGO Katsudō Suishin Sentā, 1988); Yasōsha: "80 nendai" Henshūbu, ed., *Mō hitotsu no Nihon Chizu* (Nara: Yasōsha, 1985); and Hisada Megumi, ed., *Onna no Nettowākingu: Onna no Gurūpu Zenkoku Gaido* (Tokyo: Gakuyō Shobō, 1987).

43. For data showing the increase in NGOs, see Yamauchi Naoto, ed., *NPO Dētabukku* (Tokyo: Yuhikaku, 1999), 142–43; Yamaoka Yoshinori, ed., *NPO Kiso Kōza*, vol. 2: *Shimin Katsudō no Genzai* (Tokyo: Gyōsei, 1998), 79.

44. Kim Reimann, "Building Global Civil Society from the Outside In? Japanese International Development NGOs, the State, and International Norms," in *The State of Civil Society in Japan*, ed. Schwartz and Pharr, 298–315. Two pioneering international NGOs active in the 1970s were Shapla Neer: the Citizens' Committee in Japan for Overseas Support (est. 1972). See www.shaplaneer.org; Shapura Nīru Katsudō Kiroku Henshūbu, *Shapura Nīru no Atsui Kaze* (Tokyo: Mekon, 1989); Shapura Nīru Katsudō Kiroku Henshūbu, *Shapura Nīru no Atsui Kaze Dainibu* (Tokyo: Mekon, 1992); and PARC: the Pacific Asia Resource Center (est. 1973) (www.parc-jp.org).

45. As of September 2006, 271 corporate and 1,026 individual members were in the club. Kōroki, "Borantia no Rekishi kara Kangaeru," 107.

46. This report is available at the Japan Management Association's home page: www.jma.or.jp/keikakusin/1990/proposal/90shiminshugikeiei.html (accessed May 8, 2007).

47. Snow and Benford suggest that movements appearing early "are likely to function as progenitors of master frames that provide the ideational and interpretive anchoring for subsequent movements in the cycle." See Snow and Benford, "Master Frames and Cycles of Protest," 144.

48. Fujita and Komatsu, *Inochi to Kurashi o Mamoru Kabushiki Gaisha*, 2–3.

49. Ibid., 80.

50. Ibid., 53.

51. Ibid.

52. On agrarian nationalism, see Thomas Havens, *Farm and Nation in Modern Japan: Agrarian Nationalism, 1870–1940* (Princeton, NJ: Princeton University Press, 1974).

53. Fujita and Komatsu, *Inochi to Kurashi o Mamoru Kabushiki Gaisha*, 54.

54. Ibid., 22.

55. Ibid., 165.

56. Fujita Kazuyoshi, "Yūki Nōgyō Undō no Atarashii Nagare o Tsukuru tame ni," *Daichi* 37 (May 10, 1981): 1.

57. Fujita and Komatsu, *Inochi to Kurashi o Mamoru Kabushiki Gaisha*, 53.

58. Ibid., 208.

59. Ibid., 4.

60. Ibid. In 1987 the movement also joined with consumer organizations to oppose U.S. pressure for the liberalization of rice imports (see ibid., 172–73).

61. Ibid., 84.

62. Ibid.

63. "Shirīzu Seishun: Ikirukoto, Moerukoto (Dai-3-kai)," *Gekkan Big Tomorrow* 74 (August 1986): 103; Takami Yūichi, *Deru Kui ni Naru: NGO de Meshi o Kū* (Tokyo: Tsukiji Shokan, 1998), 19–20.

64. Bananabōto Jikkō Iinkai, ed., *Inochi, Shizen, Kurashi*, 15.

65. Takami, *Deru Kui ni Naru*, 15, 16; Takami Yūichi, "NPO no Kanōsei," *Nihon Saiken e no Shinario: Gurōbaru Sutandādo e no Daigyakuten*, ed. Ōmae Kenichi and Isshinjuku (Tokyo: Daiyamondosha, 1998), 154.

66. The Chinese characters for *remove (kesu)* and *use up (tsuiyasu)* combine to form the character compound meaning "consume" *(shōhi)*. Bananabōto Jikkō Iinkai, ed., *Inochi, Shizen, Kurashi*, 16–17.

67. Takami, *Deru Kui ni Naru*, 27; Takami, "NPO no Kanōsei," 156.

68. Takami, *Deru Kui ni Naru*, 28.

69. Ibid., 29.

70. Ibid.

71. Ibid., 30.

72. Takami carried this same sentiment into his campaign for an NPO law in the mid-1990s, while he was a member of the House of Representatives. Instead of an NPO law, Takami originally wanted an NGO law (non-government organization), because the latter would allow civil society organizations to pursue profits and "make a living." For the original quote see Bananabōto Jikkō Iinkai, ed., *Inochi, Shizen, Kurashi*, 34–35.

73. Takami, *Deru Kui ni Naru*, 31.

74. "Shirīzu Seishun," *Gekkan Big Tomorrow*, 103.

75. See the movement's home page: http://popo.or.jp/index.php (accessed May 18, 2007).

76. Harima Yasuo, *NPO to Borantia no Sōzōteki na Kankei: Ningen ga Kōfuku ni naru tame ni wa, NPO wa ikanaru Sonzai dearu beki ka,* Ōmi Nettowāku Sentā Bukkuretto, no. 8 (Ōtsu City: Ōmi Bunka Shinkō Zaidan, 1999), 6.

77. Ibid., 13.

78. Harima, *Chi En Shakai no Nettowākingu,* 17.

79. Ibid.

80. Ibid., 12.

81. Ibid., 117.

82. Tanpopo no Undō o Kiroku suru Kai, *Tanpopo no Undō 16 nen no Kiroku: Hana ni nare Kaze ni nare—Nettowākingu no Kiseki* (Nara: Zaidan Hōjin Tanpopo no Ie, 1990), 32.

83. Harima, *Chi En Shakai no Nettowākingu,* 17–18.

84. Tanpopo no Undō o Kiroku suru Kai, *Tanpopo no Undō 16 nen no Kiroku,* 33.

85. Harima, *NPO to Borantia no Sōzōteki na Kankei,* 12.

86. Harima uses the English translation *synergy* for the Japanese *kyōdō,* which is, literally, "cooperative work" or "collaboration" (ibid.).

87. Ibid.

88. Ibid., 10.

89. Harima, *Chi En Shakai no Nettowākingu,* 118; Tanpopo no Undō o Kiroku suru Kai, *Tanpopo no Undō 16 nen no Kiroku,* 115.

90. Tanpopo no Undō o Kiroku suru Kai, *Tanpopo no Undō 16 nen no Kiroku,* 107, 114.

91. Ibid., 33.

92. For background on the consumer cooperative movement, see Okutani Matsuji, *Nihon Seikatsu Kyōdō Kumiai Shi,* revised and expanded ed. (Tokyo: Minshūsha, 1973); Yamamoto Osamu (aka "Aki"), *Nihon Seikatsu Kyōdō Kumiai Undō Shi* (Tokyo: Nihon Hyōronsha, 1982); Nomura Hidekazu, ed., *Seikyō: 21 Seiki e no Chōsen Nihongata Moderu no Jikken* (Tokyo: Ōtsuki Shoten, 1992), 21–39; Iwadare Hiroshi, "Consumer Cooperatives in the Spotlight," *Japan Quarterly* (October–December 1991): 429–35; and Maclachlan, *Consumer Politics in Postwar Japan,* 67–71.

93. Muto Ichiyo, "The Alternative Livelihood Movement," *AMPO: Japan-Asia Quarterly Review* 24, no. 2 (1993): 4–5.

94. Ibid., 5–6.

95. Yokota candidly acknowledged that the alternative market became possible only because of the primacy of the mainstream market. Indeed, he noted that as much as the former attempted to transcend the latter (to become a "rebellious child"), it was also the latter's offspring. Yokota Katsumi, *Orutanatibu Shimin Shakai Sengen: Mōhitotsu no "Shakai" Shugi* (Tokyo: Gendai no Rironsha, 1989), 78.

96. Iwane Kunio, *Seikatsu Kurabu to tomo ni: Iwane Kunio Hanseifu* (Tokyo: Seikatsu Kurabu Seikatsu Kyōdō Kumiai, 1978), 56.

97. Ibid., 55.

98. Ibid., 68; and Yokota Katsumi, *Oroka na Kuni no, Shinayaka Shimin* (Tokyo: Honnoki, 2002), 31.

99. Iwane, *Seikatsu Kurabu to tomo ni*, 65.

100. Lam Peng-Er, *Green Politics in Japan* (London and New York: Routledge, 1999), 101.

101. There are competing narratives of the early days of the SC, some putting far more emphasis on the role of Iwane's wife, Shizuko, for example. Such narratives substitute Iwane's "masculine" project for "counterhegemony" with the struggle of a group of Japanese housewives for self-realization and empowerment. Intellectually, of course, both narratives are mutually supportive. See, for example, Seikatsu Kurabu Seikatsu Kyōdō Kumiai, ed., *Shufu no Seikyō-zukuri: 10 man no Shufu, 10 nen no Taiken* (Tokyo: Sanichi Shobō, 1978).

102. Iwane, *Seikatsu Kurabu to tomo ni*, 63.

103. Yokota, *Oroka na Kuni no*, 35.

104. Yokota, *Orutanatibu Shimin Shakai Sengen*, 36–37.

105. Ibid., 37.

106. Yokota, *Oroka na Kuni no*, 41.

107. Ibid., 36.

108. Ibid., 42.

109. Ibid., 50.

110. Ibid., 61.

111. Yokota, *Orutanatibu Shimin Shakai Sengen*, 124.

112. Iwane Kunio, *Atarashii Shakai Undō no Shihan Seiki: Seikatsu Kurabu, Dairinin Undō* (Tokyo: Kyōdō Tosho Sābisu, 1993), 31.

113. Ibid., 37.

114. LeBlanc, *Bicycle Citizens*, 134–35.

115. Seikatsu Kurabu Seikatsu Kyōdō Kumiai, ed., *Shufu no Seikyō-zukuri*, 113–14. Not that members rely completely on the SC for their needs: in the 1980s, movement statistics indicate that members spent only 10–20 percent of their monthly food budget on SC goods (Yokota, *Orutanatibu Shimin Shakai Sengen*, 84).

116. Yokota, *Orutanatibu Shimin Shakai Sengen*, 60, 64.

117. Ibid., 72.

118. The term *proxy* is used to stress how SC's elected politicians are merely representatives for other members rather than distinguished leaders.

119. Yokota, *Oroka na Kuni no*, 122.

120. Joyce Gelb and Margarita Estevez-Abe, "Political Women in Japan: A Case Study of the *Seikatsusha* Network Movement," *Social Science Japan Journal* 1, no. 2 (1998): 263.

121. LeBlanc, *Bicycle Citizens*, 127.

122. Ibid., 126.

123. Yokota, *Orutanatibu Shimin Shakai Sengen*, 23.

124. Gelb and Estevez-Abe, "Political Women in Japan," 276.

125. Mikiko Eto suggests that these groups forced the state to change from below. See Mikiko Eto, "Women's Leverage on Social Policymaking in Japan," *PS: Political Science and Politics* 34, no. 2 (June 2001): 241–46; and Mikiko Eto, "Women's Movements in Japan: The Intersection between Everyday Life and Politics," *Japan Forum* 17, no. 3 (2005): 311–33.

126. Jean-Marie Bouissou, "Ambiguous Revival: A Study of Some 'New Civic Movements' in Japan," *Pacific Review* 13, no. 3 (2000): 345.

127. Maggie Kinser-Saiki, ed., *Japanese Working for a Better World: Grassroots Voices and Access Guide to Citizens' Groups in Japan* (San Francisco: Honnoki USA, 1992), 118.

128. Satō Yoshiyuki, Amano Masako, and Nasu Hisashi, *Joseitachi no Seikatsusha Undō: Seikatsu Kurabu o Sasaeru Hitobito* (Tokyo: Marujusha, 1995), 4.

129. Iwane, *Atarashii Shakai Undō no Shihan Seiki*, 127.

130. Ibid., 91.

131. Ibid.

132. Ibid., 92–93.

133. Ibid., 119.

134. Ibid., 120.

135. Ibid.

136. Yokota Katsumi, "Raiburīna Shōhisha Undō no Tenkai," in *Raiburī Poritikusu: Seikatsu Shutai no Atarashii Seiji Sutairu o Motomete,* ed. Shinohara Hajime (Tokyo: Sōgō Rōdō Kenkyūjo, 1985), 183.

137. Ibid., 188.

138. Ibid.

139. Yokota, *Oroka na Kuni no,* 64.

140. Amano, *"Seikatsusha" to wa Dareka,* 20.

141. Satō, Amano, and Nasu, *Joseitachi no Seikatsusha Undō,* 22–23.

142. Miki's words here are drawn from ibid., 23.

143. Ibid., 26.

144. See Ōkuma Nobuyuki, *Seimei Saiseisan no Riron: Ningen Chūshin no Shisō,* 2 vols. (Tōyō Keizai Shinpōsha, 1974–75).

145. See Patricia Maclachlan's *Consumer Politics in Postwar Japan,* 80–83; and her "From Subjects to Citizens." Apart from Amano's 1996 work on the *seikatsusha,* also see Miyagi Kenichi, "Seikatsusha no Tanjō," *Gendai no Riron* 211 (March 1985): 60–69; Dentsū Māketingukyoku and Dentsū Sōken, *Senryakuteki Seikatsusha: Korekara no Shijō o Tsukuru Shinshūdan Pawā* (Tokyo: Purejidentosha, 1990); Saigusa Saeko, *Seikatsusha Hassō: Jittai to Nīzu o Saguru 15 hen* (Tokyo: Jitsugyō no Nihonsha, 1994); and Katayama Mataichirō, *Gendai Seikatsusha Shiron: Ruikeika to Tenkai* (Tokyo: Hakutō Shobō, 2000).

146. Yokota, *Orutanatibu Shimin Shakai Sengen,* 94.

147. Satō, Amano, and Nasu, *Joseitachi no Seikatsusha Undō,* 19.

148. On postwar mass society, see Marilyn Ivy, "Formations of Mass Culture," in *Postwar Japan as History,* ed. Andrew Gordon (Berkeley and Los Angeles: University of California Press, 1993), 239–58.

149. Bananaboat Network, *Bananabōto: Shimin Undō o Tsunagi Hirogeru Ba* (Tokyo: Honnoki, 1987), 22–24.

150. See Bananabōto Jikkō Iinkai, ed., *Inochi, Shizen, Kurashi,* 162–226, for the original in Japanese and Kinser-Saiki, ed., *Japanese Working for a Better World,* 126–83, for the abridged English-language version.

151. Kinser-Saiki, ed., *Japanese Working for a Better World,* introduction.

152. Conflict also arose between the "internationalists" and the "domestic group" over foreign produce imports. Bananaboat Network, *Bananabōto*, 4–5.

153. Ibid.

154. Jeffrey M. Berry, *The New Liberalism: The Rising Power of Citizens' Groups* (Washington DC: Brookings Institution Press, 1999), 28.

155. Yamaoka Yoshinori, *Kenkyū Katsudō e no Shimin Sanka to Minkan Zaidan no Yakuwari* (Tokyo: Toyota Zaidan, 1982).

156. Originally, in 1984, the program was titled Documenting Citizen Activities Aiming for a New Human Society (Atarashii Ningen Shakai o mezashita Shimin Katsudō no Kiroku no Sakusei).

157. Yamaoka Yoshinori, *Shimin Katsudō no Taiken o Kyōyū no Zaisan ni* (Tokyo: Toyota Zaidan, 1987). For a summary of the foundation's findings and a list of the books published, see Toyota Zaidan, ed., *Jiritsu to Kyōsei o Mezashite*.

158. In its first five years the program funded most of the important progenitor movements discussed earlier. Toyota Zaidan, ed., *Jiritsu to Kyōsei o Mezashite*.

159. Around sixteen groups were funded yearly until 1998. Thereafter this climbed to around thirty.

160. Nakamura Yōichi, " 'Shimin Katsudō' no Tōjō to Tenkai," in *Nihon no NPO 2000,* ed. Nakamura Yōichi and Nihon NPO Sentā (Tokyo: Nihon Hyōronsha, 1999), 32–34.

161. Matsushita, *Sengo Seiji no Rekishi to Shisō,* 191, 192, 199.

162. Nakamura, " 'Shimin Katsudō' no Tōjō to Tenkai," 33–34.

163. Yamaoka Yoshinori, *Shimin Katsudō no Igi to Yakuwari,* Ōmi Nettowāku Senta Bukkuretto, no. 2 (Ōtsu City: Ōmi Bunka Shinkō Zaidan, 1998), 6.

164. Yamaoka was also using the terms *nonprofit activities (hieiri katsudō)* and *the third sector (daisan sekutā)* as early as 1987 (for example, as in Yamaoka, *Shimin Katsudō no Taiken o Kyōyū no Zaisan ni). Shimin katsudō* appears in Yamaoka's 1982 report *Kenkyū Katsudō e no Shimin Sanka.*

165. Yamaoka, *Shimin Katsudō no Taiken o Kyōyū no Zaisan ni,* 34. Interestingly, the term *shimin katsudō* also appears in EPA public opinion surveys at around the same time. For example, a question on free time in a 1972 EPA survey of women listed "citizen activities and voluntary activities *(hōshi katsudō)*" as one option. See *Fujin ni kansuru Yoron Chōsa—Josei Taishō* (1972), http://www8.cao.go.jp/survey/s47/index-s47.html (accessed May 5, 2008).

166. Yamaoka, *Shimin Katsudō no Igi to Yakuwari,* 6.

167. Nihon Nettowākazu Kaigi, ed., *Nettowākingu ga Hiraku Atarashii Sekai: Dai Ikkai Nihon Nettowākazu Kaigi yori* (Tokyo: Nihon Nettowākazu Kaigi, 1990), 2. For Jessica Lipnack and Jeffrey Stamps's writings on networking, see their books *Networking: The First Report and Directory* (Garden City, NY: Doubleday, 1982); *The Networking Book: People Connecting with People* (New York and London: Routledge and Kegan Paul, 1986); and, in Japanese, *Nettowākingu,* trans. Masamura Kimihiro and Shakai Kaihatsu Tōkei Kenkyūjo (Tokyo: Purejidentosha, 1984).

168. Ibid., 1.

169. Reproduced in Japan Networkers' Conference, ed., *ABSTRACT of the Report of the First Networkers' Conference* (Tokyo: Japan Networkers' Conference, 1990), 57.

170. Nihon Nettowākāzu Kaigi, ed., *Nettowākingu ga Hiraku Atarashii Sekai*, 30.

171. Ibid., 68.

172. Ibid., 92.

173. Nihon Nettowākazu Kaigi, ed., *Nettowākingu o Katachi ni! Dai 2 kai Nettowākāzu Fōramu Hōkokusho* (Tokyo: Nihon Nettowākāzu Kaigi, 1993), 3.

174. Nihon Nettowākāzu Kaigi, ed., *NPO to wa Nanika: Sono Rikai no tame ni*—Understanding Nonprofit Organizations (Tokyo: Nihon Nettowākāzu Kaigi, 1992); Nihon Nettowākāzu Kaigi, ed., *Nihon ni okeru Kōeki Katsudō no Genjō to Kadai* (Tokyo: Nihon Nettowākāzu Kaigi, 1994); Nihon Nettowākāzu Kaigi, ed., *Hieiri Dantai to Shakaiteki Kiban: Borantarī Katsudō Suishin no tame no Shikumizukuri ni kansuru Chōsa Kenkyū Hōkokusho—Designing a Nonprofit Support Infrastructure* (Tokyo: Nihon Nettowākāzu Kaigi, 1995).

175. Members of the report drafting committee came from private sector foundations such as the Toyota Foundation and the Keidanren and from voluntary organizations such as the YMCA, the EPA, and Tokyo University. Sōgō Kenkyū Kaihatsu Kikō (NIRA), *Shimin Kōeki Katsudō Kihon Seibi ni kansuru Chōsa Kenkyū* (Tokyo: Sōgō Kenkyū Kaihatasu Kikō, 1994).

176. Ibid., 6–13.

177. Nihon Nettowākāzu Kaigi, ed., *Hieiri Dantai to Shakaiteki Kiban*, 20.

178. Ibid.

179. Nihon Nettowākāzu Kaigi, ed., *Nihon ni okeru Kōeki Katsudō no Genjō to Kadai*, 5.

180. Nihon Nettowākāzu Kaigi, *Hieiri Dantai to Shakaiteki Kiban*, 20–21.

181. Matsubara Akira, "NPO Hō ni itaru Haikei to Rippō Katei," in *Nihon NPO 2000*, ed. Nakamura and Nihon NPO Sentā, 55.

182. Pekkanen, "Japan's New Politics," 111–48.

CONCLUSION

1. Yamaguchi Yasushi, Takarada Zen, Shindō Eiichi, and Sumizawa Hiroki, eds., *Shimin Jiritsu no Seiji Senryaku: Korekara no Nihon o dō Kangaeruka* (Tokyo: Asahi Shimbunsha, 1992).

2. There is very little work in English on the intellectual history of civil society in Japan, even though it is a history worth telling. The one exception is Andrew Barshay's important essay "Capitalism and Civil Society in Postwar Japan: Perspectives from Intellectual History," in *The State of Civil Society in Japan*, ed. Frank J. Schwartz and Susan J. Pharr (Cambridge and New York: Cambridge University Press, 2003), 63–80. I think a strong case can be made that the contemporary global revival of civil society idea *began* in Japan and, moreover, that Japanese intellectuals broke ground, first, by articulating an

affirmative idea of civil society within and beyond Marxism and, second, by connecting the civil society idea to post-Marxist strategies informed by Gramscian theory. I defer this fascinating and important discussion until another occasion.

3. Snow and Benford, "Master Frames and Cycles of Protest," 144.

4. Baud and Rutten, "Introduction," 2.

5. Pekkanen, *Japan's Dual Civil Society.*

6. Uemura Shinsaku, *Shimin Undō no Jidai desu* (Tokyo: Daisan Shokan, 2001); Saitō Hideharu, *Kokka o Koeru Shimin Shakai: Dōin no Seiki kara Nomado no Seiki e* (Tokyo: Gendai Kikaku Shitsu, 1998); Imai Hiromichi, ed., *"Shimin" no Jidai: Hō to Seiji kara no Sekkin* (Tokyo: Hokkaido Daigaku Tosho Kankōkai, 1998).

7. Zenkoku Borantia Katsudō Shinkō Sentā, *Borantia Katsudō Nenpō 2005 nen (Gaiyō)* (May 1, 2007), available at http://www3.shakyo.or.jp/cdvc/shiryo/joho1_v.asp (accessed May 4, 2007).

8. For discussion of Maruyama and Civil Society, see Ishida Takeshi and Kang Sangjung, *Maruyama Masao to Shimin Shakai* (Yokohama: Seori Shobō, 1997); Tsuzuki, "Maruyama Masao ni okeru Seiji to Shimin"; Hiraishi Naoaki, "Maruyama Masao no 'Shimin Shakai Ron,'" in *Maruyama Masao Ron—Shutaiteki Sakui, Fashizumu, Shimin Shakai,* ed. Kobayashi Masaya (Tokyo: Tokyo Daigaku Shuppan Kai, 2003), 176–90; Barshay, "Capitalism and Civil Society in Postwar Japan," 79–80; and Fumio Iida, "Liberalism and the Moral Effects of Civil Society: The Case of Postwar Japan," in *Gurōbaruka Jidai ni okeru Shimin Shakai Ron no Tenkai: Ōshū, Hokubei, Nihon no Hikaku Kenkyū,* ed. Chiba Shin, Monbushō Kagaku Kenkyūhi Joseikin Kenkyū Seika Hōkokusho, 1998–2000, 72–105.

9. John Keane, *Civil Society: Old Images, New Visions* (Cambridge, U.K.: Polity Press, 1998), 13.

10. Barshay, "Capitalism and Civil Society in Postwar Japan," 68–69.

11. Yamaguchi Yasushi, *Shimin Shakai Ron: Rekishiteki Isan to Shintenkai* (Tokyo: Yuhikaku, 2004), 12.

12. Hirata Kiyoaki, "Gendai Shimin Shakai to Kigyō Kokka," in *Gendai Shimin Shakai to Kigyō Kokka,* ed. Hirata Kiyoaki et al. (Tokyo: Ochanomizu Shobō, 1994), 3.

13. Ibid., 26.

14. See Hirata Kiyoaki, Yamada Toshio, and Yagi Kiichirō, *Gendai Shimin Shakai no Senkai* (Kyoto: Shōwadō, 1987).

15. Quoted in Yamaguchi, *Shimin Shakai Ron,* 107.

16. For example, see Jean L. Cohen and Andrew Arato, *Civil Society and Political Theory* (Cambridge, MA: MIT Press, 1992); Keane, *Civil Society;* Jürgen Habermas, *The Structural Transformation of the Public Sphere: An Inquiry into a Category of Bourgeois Society,* trans. Thomas Burger (Cambridge, MA: MIT Press, 1989); Michael Walzer, "The Civil Society Argument," in *Dimensions of Radical Democracy: Pluralism, Citizenship, Community,* ed. Chantal Mouffe (London: Verso, 1992); Ernesto LaClau and Chantal Mouffe, *Hegemony and Socialist Strategy: Toward a Radical Democratic Politics* (New York: Verso, 1985). For essays by Mouffe translated into Japanese, see *Shisō*

867 (September 1996) and 924 (May 2001). Volume 867 also contains essays by Habermas and Walzer.

17. Yagi Kiichirō, Yamada Toshio, Senga Shigeyoshi, and Nozawa Toshi-haru, *Fukken suru Shimin Shakai Ron: Atarashii Soshietaru Paradaimu* (Tokyo: Nihon Hyōronsha, 1998).

18. Iwane, *Atarashii Shakai Undō no Shihan Seiki*, 1–5.

19. See Yokota and Hirata's essays on Gramsci in Forum 90's, ed., *Guramushi no Shisō Kūkan: Guramushi no Shinseiki-Seitan 101 nen Kinen Ronshū* (Tokyo: Bunryū, 1992).

20. Samuel P. Huntington, *The Third Wave: Democratization in the Late Twentieth Century* (Norman: University of Oklahoma Press, 1991); Lester M. Salamon, "The Rise of the Nonprofit Sector," *Foreign Affairs* 73, no. 4 (July–August 1994): 109–22.

21. Yutaka Tsujinaka, "From Developmentalism to Maturity: Japan's Civil Society Organizations in Comparative Perspective," in *The State of Civil Society*, ed. Schwartz and Pharr, 83–115.

22. Sakamoto Yoshikazu, *Sōtaika no Jidai* (Tokyo: Iwanami Shoten, 1997), 3, 51.

23. Reimann, "Building Global Civil Society from the Outside In?" 301–4.

24. Stephen P. Osborne, "The Voluntary and Non-Profit Sector in Japan: Emerging Roles and Organizational Challenges in a Changing Society," in Stephen P. Osborne, ed., *The Voluntary and Non-Profit Sector in Japan: The Challenge of Change* (London and New York: RoutledgeCurzon, 2003), 11.

25. Robert Pekkanen, "After the Developmental State: Civil Society in Japan," *Journal of East Asian Studies* 4 (2004): 363, 375.

26. Iokibe Makoto, "Japan's Civil Society: An Historical Overview," in *Deciding the Public Good: Governance and Civil Society in Japan*, ed. Yamamoto Tadashi (Tokyo: Japan Center for International Exchange, 1999), 92.

27. Victoria Lyon Bestor, "Reimaging Civil Society in Japan," *Washington-Japan Journal*, special issue (Spring 1999): 6–7.

28. Rajib Shaw and Katsuichirō Goda, "From Disaster to Sustainable Civil Society: The Kobe Experience," *Disasters* 28, no. 1 (2004): 20.

29. Pekkanen, *Japan's Dual Civil Society*, 134.

30. Susan Pharr, "Conclusion: Targeting by an Activist State: Japan as a Civil Society Model," 325.

31. Akihiro Ogawa, "Invited by the State: Institutionalizing Volunteer Subjectivity in Contemporary Japan," *Asian Anthropology* 3 (2004): 93; Nakano Toshio, "Borantia Dōin-gata Shimin Shakai Ron no Kansei," *Gendai Shisō* 27, no. 5 (1999): 72–93.

32. Yasuda, "Gendaishi ni okeru Jichi to Kōkyōsei ni kansuru Oboegaki," 354.

33. John Morrison, "The Government-Voluntary Sector Compacts: Governance, Governmentality, and Civil Society," *Journal of Law and Society* 27, no. 1 (March 2000): 119.

34. There are exceptions. See Yamamoto Tadashi, "Emergence of Japan's Civil Society and Its Future Challenges," in *Deciding the Public Good*, ed. Yamamoto, 97–124. Though Robert Pekkanen emphasizes the 1990s, he rec-

ognizes earlier civic lobbying and activism (Robert Pekkanen, "The Politics of Regulating the Non-Profit Sector," in *Voluntary and Non-Profit Sector in Japan*, ed. Osborne, 70). Hasegawa and colleagues discuss a rising "social expectation" for civil society in the 1990s (Koichi Hasegawa, Chika Shinohara, and Jeffrey P. Broadbent, "The Effects of 'Social Expectation' on the Development of Civil Society in Japan," *Journal of Civil Society* 3, no. 28 [September 2007]: 179–203).

35. Satō Yoshiyuki, *NPO to Shimin Shakai* (Tokyo: Yuhikaku, 2002), 149–50.

36. Yamaoka Yoshinori, *Jidai ga Ugoku Toki: Shakai no Henkaku to NPO no Kanōsei* (Tokyo: Gyōsei, 1999), 95.

37. Sakamoto, *Sōtaika no Jidai*, 42–43, emphasis in original.

38. Yasuda, "Gendaishi ni okeru Jichi to Kōkyōsei ni kansuru Oboegaki," 354.

39. Kurihara, "Shimin Seiji no Ajenda," 12.

40. Takabatake Michitoshi, "'Shimin Shakai' to wa Nanika," in *Gendai Shimin Seiji Ron*, ed. Takabatake Michitoshi (Yokohama: Seori Shobō, 2003), 32.

41. Nakano Toshio, "Borantia Dōin-gata Shimin Shakai Ron no Kansei," *Gendai Shisō* 27, no. 5 (1999): 72–93.

42. Ibid., 73.

43. Ibid., 76.

44. Akihiro Ogawa, *The Failure of Civil Society? The Third Sector and the State in Contemporary Japan* (Albany: State University of New York Press, 2009), 174.

45. Nakano, "Borantia Dōin-gata Shimin Shakai Ron no Kansei," 87.

46. Ibid., 76.

47. Ogawa, *The Failure of Civil Society?* 159.

48. Ibid., 21.

49. "Shinshimin ga Shakai o Ninau," *Asahi Shimbun*, Saturday, February 24, 2007, be Report section, b3.

50. Joseph Bradley, "Subjects into Citizens: Societies, Civil Society, and Autocracy in Tsarist Russia," *American Historical Review* 107, no. 4 (2002): paragraph 2, available at www.historycooperative.org (accessed July 21, 2007).

51. I draw here on Laclau and Mouffe's discussion of "pluralist democracy." Laclau and Mouffe, *Hegemony and Socialist Strategy*, xviii.

Bibliography

Aldrich, Daniel P. *Site Fights: Divisive Facilities and Civil Society in Japan and the West.* Ithaca, NY: Cornell University Press, 2008.

Amano Masako. "Midori no Kai." In *Kyōdō Kenkyū Shūdan: Sākuru no Sengo Shisōshi,* ed. Shisō no Kagaku Kenkyūkai, 199–207. Tokyo: Heibonsha, 1976.

———. "Minshū Shisō e no Hōhōteki Jikken: 'Hitobito no Tetsugaku' kara 'Minoue Sōdan' e no Sōi." In *Sengo "Keimō" Shisō no Nokoshita Mono,"* ed. Yasuda Tsuneo and Amano Masako, 107–29. Tokyo: Kyūzansha, 1992.

———. "Sākuru 'Shūdan no Kai.'" In *Kyōdō Kenkyū Shūdan: Sākuru no Sengo Shisōshi,* ed. Shisō no Kagaku Kenkyūkai, 33–44. Tokyo: Heibonsha, 1976.

———. "Seikatsusha" to wa Dareka: Jiritsuteki Shiminzō no Keifu.* Tokyo: Chūkō Shinsho, 1996.

———. "Tsukiai" no Sengoshi: Sākuru—Nettowākingu no Hiraku Chihei.* Tokyo: Yoshikawa Hirobumi Kan, 2005.

Anai Fumihiko. *Beheiren to Dassō Beihei.* Tokyo: Bungei Shunjū, 2000.

Apter, David E., and Nagayo Sawa. *Against the State: Politics and Social Protest in Japan.* Cambridge, MA: Harvard University Press, 1984.

Ara Masato. "Minshū to wa Tare ka." In Ara Masato, *Ara Masato Chosakushū,* vol. 1, 36–67. Tokyo: Sanichi Shobō, 1983.

———. "Minshū wa Doko ni iru." In Ara Masato, *Ara Masato Chosakushū,* vol. 1, 103–14. Tokyo: Sanichi Shobō, 1983.

———. "Shimin toshite." *Kindai Bungaku* (September 1947): 7–8.

———. "Yoko no Tsunagari." *Kindai Bungaku* 14 (October 1947): 1–11.

Arai Naoyuki. *Haisen Taiken to Sengo Shisō—12 nin no Kiseki.* Tokyo: Ronsōsha, 1997.

Asahi Jyānaru Henshūbu. *Sanrizuka.* Tokyo: Sanichi Shobō, 1981.

"The Asahi Poll on Vietnam." *Japan Quarterly* 12, no. 4 (October–December 1965): 463–66.

Asukata Ichio. "Shimin ni yoru Jichitai-zukuri no Kōsō." In *Gendai ni Ikiru*, vol. 6: *Shimin Sanka*, ed. Matsushita Keiichi, 153–72. Tokyo: Tōyō Keizai Shinpōsha, 1971.

———, ed. *Jichitai Kaikaku no Rironteki Tenbō*. Tokyo: Nihon Hyōronsha, 1965.

Avenell, Simon. "Civil Society and the New Civic Movements in Contemporary Japan: Convergence, Collaboration, and Transformation," *Journal of Japanese Studies* 35, no. 2 (Summer 2009): 247–83.

———. "Core Activists, Ideas, and the Development of Citizen Activism in Postwar Japan." PhD diss., University of California, Berkeley, 2003.

———. "From the 'People' to the 'Citizen': Tsurumi Shunsuke and the Roots of Civic Mythology in Postwar Japan." *positions: east asia cultures critique* 16, no. 3 (Winter 2008): 711–42.

———. "Regional Egoism as the Public Good: Residents' Movements in 1960s and 1970s Japan." *Japan Forum* 18, no. 1 (2006): 89–113.

Bananaboat Network. *Bananabōto: Shimin Undō o Tsunagi Hirogeru Ba.* Tokyo: Honnoki, 1987.

Bananabōto Jikkō Iinkai, ed. *Inochi, Shizen, Kurashi—Banana Bōto: Mōhitotsu no Seikatsu o Tsukuru Nettowākāzu no Funade*. Tokyo: Honnoki, 1986.

Barrilla, John M., Richard D. Bailey, Michael A. Lindner, and Craig W. Anderson. "Wareware wa Naze Kono Kyo ni Deta no ka: Dassōhei Yonshi no Seimeibun (Zenbun)." In *"Beheiren Nyūsu" Gappon Shukusatsuban*, ed. Beheiren: "Betonamu ni Heiwa o!" Shimin Rengō, 94–96. Tokyo: self-published, 1974.

Barshay, Andrew. "Capitalism and Civil Society in Postwar Japan: Perspectives from Intellectual History." In *The State of Civil Society in Japan*, ed. Frank J. Schwartz a 1 Susan J. Pharr, 63–80. Cambridge and New York: Cambridge University Press, 2003.

———. "Postwar Social and Political Thought." In *Modern Japanese Thought*, ed. Bob Tadashi Wakabayashi, 273–355. Cambridge: Cambridge University Press, 1998.

Barthes, Roland. *Mythologies*. Translated by Annette Lavers. London: Jonathon Cape, 1972.

Baud, Michiel, and Rosanne Rutten. "Introduction." *International Review of Social History* 49 (2004): 1–14.

Beer, Lawrence W. "The Constitution of Japan: 'Pacifism' and Mass Media Freedom." In *Law in Japan: A Turning Point*, ed. Daniel H. Foote, 257–75. Seattle and London: University of Washington Press, 2007.

Beheiren: "Betonamu ni Heiwa o!" Shimin Rengō, ed. *"Beheiren Nyūsu" Gappon Shukusatsuban*. Tokyo: self-published, 1974.

Berman, Sheri. "Review Article: Ideas, Norms, and Culture in Political Analysis." *Comparative Politics* 33, no. 2 (January 2001): 231–50.

Berry, Jeffrey M. *The New Liberalism: The Rising Power of Citizens' Groups*. Washington DC: Brookings Institution Press, 1999.

Bestor, Victoria Lyon. "Reimaging Civil Society in Japan." *Washington-Japan Journal*, special issue (Spring 1999): 1–10.

"Betonamu ni Heiwa o!" Shimin Rengō, ed. *Shiryō "Beheiren" Undō*, 3 vols. Tokyo: Kawade Shobō Shinsha, 1974.

Borantia Hakusho Henshū Iinkai, ed. *Borantia Hakusho 1990 nenban: Borantia no Nyū Wēbu o Saguru*. Tokyo: Shadan Hōjin Nihon Seinen Hōshi Kyōkai (JYVA), 1990.

Borantia Hakusho 1999 Henshū Iinkai, ed. *Borantia Hakusho 1999: Watashitachi ga Tsukuru Atarashii "Kōkyō."* Tokyo: Shadan Hōjin Nihon Seinen Hōshi Kyōkai (JYVA), 1999.

Bouissou, Jean-Marie. "Ambiguous Revival: A Study of Some 'New Civic Movements' in Japan." *Pacific Review* 13, no. 3 (2000): 335–66.

Bradley, Joseph. "Subjects into Citizens: Societies, Civil Society, and Autocracy in Tsarist Russia." *American Historical Review* 107, no. 4 (2002), www.historycooperative.org (accessed July 21, 2007).

Broadbent, Jeffrey. *Environmental Politics in Japan: Networks of Power and Protest*. Cambridge and New York: Cambridge University Press, 1998.

Campbell, John Creighton. *How Policies Change: The Japanese Government and the Aging Society*. Princeton, NJ: Princeton University Press, 1992.

Chūō Shakai Fukushi Shingikai Chiiki Fukushi Senmon Bunkakai. *Borantia Katsudō no Chūchōtekina Shinkō Hōsaku ni tsuite: Chūō Shakai Fukushi Shingikai Chiiki Fukushi Senmon Bunkakai Iken Gushin*. Tokyo: Kōseishō Shakai-Engokyoku, 1993.

Cohen, Jean L., and Andrew Arato. *Civil Society and Political Theory*. Cambridge, MA: MIT Press, 1992.

Deguchi, Masayuki. "A Comparative View of Civil Society." *Washington-Japan Journal*, special issue (Spring 1999): 11–20.

Della Porta, Donatelle, and Mario Diani, eds. *Social Movements: An Introduction*. Oxford, U.K.: Blackwell Publishers, 1999.

Dentsū Māketingukyoku and Dentsū Sōken. *Senryakuteki Seikatsusha: Korekara no Shijō o Tsukuru Shinshūdan Pawā*. Tokyo: Purejidentosha, 1990.

Doak, Kevin. *A History of Nationalism in Modern Japan: Placing the People*. Leiden, The Netherlands, and Boston: Brill, 2007.

Dore, Ronald. "The Tokyo Institute for the Science of Thought." *Far Eastern Quarterly* 13, no. 1 (1953): 23–36.

Dower, John. "Peace and Democracy in Two Systems: External Policy and Internal Conflict." In *Postwar Japan as History*, ed. Andrew Gordon, 3–33. Berkeley and Los Angeles: University of California Press, 1993.

Endō, Akira. "Jūmin Undō no Kadai to Tenbō." In *Kōza Gendai Nihon no Toshi Mondai vol. 8: Toshi Mondai to Jūmin Undō*, ed. Miyamoto Kenichi and Endō Akira, 396–480. Kyoto and Tokyo: Chōbunsha, 1971.

Eto, Mikiko. "Women's Leverage on Social Policymaking in Japan." *PS: Political Science and Politics* 34, no. 2 (June 2001): 241–46.

———. "Women's Movements in Japan: The Intersection between Everyday Life and Politics." *Japan Forum* 17, no. 3 (2005): 311–33.

Eyerman, Ron, and Andrew Jamison. *Social Movements: A Cognitive Approach*. University Park, PA: Pennsylvania State University Press, 1991.

Fanon, Frantz. *The Wretched of the Earth.* New York: Grove Press, 1963.

Figal, Gerald. "How to Jibunshi: Making and Marketing Self-Histories of Shōwa among the Masses in Postwar Japan." *Journal of Asian Studies* 55, no. 4 (November 1996): 902–33.

Forum 90's, ed. *Guramushi no Shisō Kūkan: Guramushi no Shinseiki-Seitan 101 nen Kinen Ronshū.* Tokyo: Bunryū, 1992.

Fuchibe Tomohiro. "Beheiren Undō Kenkyū Josetsu—Shimin Undō no Tōjō to Tenkai." Master's thesis, Graduate School of Literature, Waseda University, 1999.

Fujin ni kansuru Yoron Chōsa—Josei Taishō (1972). http://www8.cao.go.jp/survey/s47/index-s47.html (accessed May 5, 2008).

Fuji Shuppan, ed. *Sākuru Mura.* 5 vols. Tokyo: Fuji Shuppan, 2006.

Fujita Hiroshi. "Anpo Tōsō no Taiken to Kyōkun." *Shisō no Kagaku* (June 1963): 11–13.

Fujita Kazuyoshi. "Yūki Nōgyō Undō no Atarashii Nagare o Tsukuru tame ni." *Daichi* 37 (May 10, 1981): 1.

Fujita Kazuyoshi and Komatsu Kōichi. *Inochi to Kurashi o Mamoru Kabushiki Gaisha: Nettowākingugata no aru Seikatsusha Undō.* Tokyo: Gakuyō Shobō, 1992.

Fujita Shōzō. "Taishū Sūhaishugi Hihan no Hihan." *Minwa* 5 (February 1959): 2–8.

Fukuda Kanichi. "Nihon Minshushugi no Kanōsei: Sekinin Seiji no Kakuritsu o." *Sekai* 176 (August 1960): 42–58.

Garon, Sheldon. "From Meiji to Heisei: The State and Civil Society in Japan." In *The State of Civil Society in Japan,* ed. Frank J. Schwartz and Susan J. Pharr, 42–62. Cambridge and New York: Cambridge University Press, 2003.

———. *Molding Japanese Minds: The State in Everyday Life.* Princeton, NJ: Princeton University Press, 1997.

Gayle, Curtis Anderson. *Marxist History and Postwar Japanese Nationalism.* London and New York: Routledge, 2003.

———. "Progressive Representations of the Nation: Early Post-War Japan and Beyond." *Social Science Japan Journal* 4, no. 1 (2001): 1–19.

Gelb, Joyce, and Margarita Estervez-Abe. "Political Women in Japan: A Case Study of the *Seikatsusha* Network Movement." *Social Science Japan Journal* 1, no. 2 (1998): 263–79.

Gordon, Andrew. *The Wages of Affluence: Labor and Management in Postwar Japan.* Cambridge, MA: Harvard University Press, 1998.

Gresser, Julian, Koichiro Fujikura, and Akio Morishima. *Environmental Law in Japan.* London and Cambridge, MA: MIT Press, 1981.

Habermas, Jürgen. *The Structural Transformation of the Public Sphere: An Inquiry into a Category of Bourgeois Society.* Translated by Thomas Burger. Cambridge, MA: MIT Press, 1989.

Haddad, Mary Alice. *Politics and Volunteering in Japan: A Global Perspective.* Cambridge and New York: Cambridge University Press, 2007.

Harada Tōru. *Tsurumi Shunsuke to Kibō no Shakaigaku.* Tokyo: Sekai Shisōsha, 2004.

Harima Yasuo. *Chi En Shakai no Nettowākingu.* Tokyo: Kashiwa Shobō, 1986.

———. *NPO to Borantia no Sōzōteki na Kankei: Ningen ga Kōfuku ni naru tame ni wa, NPO wa ikanaru Sonzai dearu beki ka.* Ōmi Nettowāku Sentā Bukkuretto, no. 8. Ōtsu City: Ōmi Bunka Shinkō Zaidan, 1999.

Hasegawa, Koichi. *Constructing Civil Society in Japan: Voices of Environmental Movements.* Melbourne, Australia: Trans Pacific Press, 2004.

Hasegawa, Koichi, Chika Shinohara, and Jeffrey P. Broadbent. "The Effects of 'Social Expectation' on the Development of Civil Society in Japan." *Journal of Civil Society* 3, no. 28 (September 2007): 179–203.

Havens, Thomas R. H. *Farm and Nation in Modern Japan: Agrarian Nationalism, 1870–1940.* Princeton, NJ: Princeton University Press, 1974.

———. *Fire across the Sea: The Vietnam War and Japan 1965–1975.* Princeton, NJ: Princeton University Press, 1987.

Hayase Noboru. "Kawarihajimeta Borantia: 'Tadashisa Shikō' kara 'Tanoshisa Shikō' e." *Kikan Mado* 20 (Summer 1994): 18–25.

Heater, Derek. *What Is Citizenship?* Cambridge, U.K.: Polity Press, 1999.

Hein, Laura. "The Art of Persuasion: Audiences and Philosophies of History." *positions: east asia cultures critique* 16, no. 3 (Winter 2008): 743–51.

Hidaka Rokurō. "Gogatsu Hatsuka kara Rokugatsu Jūkunichi made: 'Minshushugi Yōgo Tōsō' no Mondaiten." *Shisō* 433 (July 1960): 129–36.

———. *1960 nen 5 gatsu 19 nichi.* Tokyo: Iwanami Shoten, 1970.

———. "Shimin to Shimin Undō." In *Iwanami Kōza Gendai Toshi Seisaku 2: Shimin Sanka,* ed. Shinohara Hajime, 39–60. Tokyo: Iwanami Shoten, 1973.

———. "Taishūron no Shūhen: Chishikijin to Taishū no Tairitsu ni tsuite." *Minwa* 6 (March 1959): 2–10.

———. "Taishūron no Shūhen: Sākuru Mondai o megutte." *Minwa* 7 (April 1959): 2–11.

Hirai Kazuomi. "Sengo Shakai Undō no naka no Beheiren: Beheiren Undō no Chiikiteki Tenkai o Chūshin ni." *Hōsei Kenkyū* 71, no. 4 (March 2005): 723–55.

Hiraishi Naoaki. "Maruyama Masao no 'Shimin Shakai Ron.'" In *Maruyama Masao Ron—Shutaiteki Sakui, Fashizumu, Shimin Shakai,* ed. Kobayashi Masaya, 176–90. Tokyo: Tokyo Daigaku Shuppan Kai, 2003.

Hirata, Keiko. *Civil Society in Japan: The Growing Role of NGOs in Tokyo's Aid and Development Policy.* New York: Palgrave, 2002.

Hirata Kiyoaki. "Gendai Shimin Shakai to Kigyō Kokka." In *Gendai Shimin Shakai to Kigyō Kokka,* ed. Hirata Kiyoaki, Yamada Toshio, Katō Tetsurō, Kurosawa Nobuaki, and Itō Masazumi, 3–46. Tokyo: Ochanomizu Shobō, 1994.

———. *Shimin Shakai to Shakaishugi.* Tokyo: Iwanami Shoten, 1969.

Hirata Kiyoaki, Yamada Toshio, and Yagi Kiichirō. *Gendai Shimin Shakai no Senkai.* Kyoto: Shōwadō, 1987.

Hisada Megumi, ed. *Onna no Nettowākingu: Onna no Gurūpu Zenkoku Gaido.* Tokyo: Gakuyō Shobō, 1987.

Hoffman, John. *Citizenship beyond the State.* London, Thousand Oaks, CA, and New Delhi: Sage Publications, 2004.

Honda Kaichirō. *Katsudōya Shichō Funsenki: Tokyo Chōfushi ni nezuku Kakushin Shisei.* Tokyo: Shakai Shinpō, 1968.

Honma Masaaki, Ueno Chizuko, and Takarazuka NPO Sentā, eds. *NPO no Kanōsei: Atarashii Shimin Katsudō.* Kamogawa Bukkuretto, no. 115. Kyoto: Kamogawa Shuppan, 1998.

Horioka, Charles Yuji. "Consuming and Saving." In *Postwar Japan as History,* ed. Andrew Gordon, 259–92. Berkeley and Los Angeles: University of California Press, 1993.

Hosaka Masayasu. *Rokujūnen Anpo Tōsō.* Tokyo: Kōdansha, 1986.

Hoshino Shigeo, Nishioka Akio, and Nakajima Isamu. "Numazu, Mishima, Shimizu (nishi ittchō) Sekiyu Konbinato Hantai Tosō to Fuji-shi o Meguru Jūmin Tōsō." In *Kōza Gendai Nihon no Toshi Mondai,* vol. 8: *Toshi Mondai to Jūmin Undō,* ed. Miyamoto Kenichi and Endō Akira, 72–209. Kyoto and Tokyo: Chōbunsha, 1971.

Hoshino Yasuzaburō. "Keishokuhō Tōsō." In *Shōwa no Sengo Shi,* vol. 3: *Gyakuryū to Teikō,* ed. Matsuura Sōzō, 58–74. Tokyo: Sekibunsha, 1976.

Huddle, Norie, and Michael Reich. *Island of Dreams: Environmental Crisis in Japan.* Rochester, VT: Schenkman Books, 1987.

Huntington, Samuel P. *The Third Wave: Democratization in the Late Twentieth Century.* Norman: University of Oklahoma Press, 1991.

Ide Busaburō. *Anpo Tōsō.* Tokyo: Sanichi Shobō, 1960.

Ienaga Saburō. "Anpo Tōsō no Tenkai." In *Shōwashi no Sengo Shi,* vol. 3: *Gyakuryū to Teikō,* ed. Matsuura Sōzō. Tokyo: Sekibunsha, 1976.

Iida, Fumio. "Liberalism and the Moral Effects of Civil Society: The Case of Postwar Japan." In *Gurōbaruka Jidai ni okeru Shimin Shakai Ron no Tenkai: Ōshū, Hokubei, Nihon no Hikaku Kenkyū,* ed. Chiba Shin, 72–105. Monbusho Kagaku Kenkyūhi Joseikin Kenkyū Seika Hōkokusho, 1998–2000.

Iida Momo. "Shimin Minshushugi Undō no Ronri to Shinri." In *Shimin Undō to wa Nanika,* ed. Oda Makoto. Tokyo: Tokuma Shoten, 1968.

Iijima Nobuko. *Kaiteiban Kankyō Mondai to Higaisha Undō.* Tokyo: Gakubunsha, 1993.

———. *Kankyō Mondai no Shakaishi.* Tokyo: Yūhikaku, 2000.

Imai Hiromichi, ed. *"Shimin" no Jidai: Hō to Seiji kara no Sekkin.* Tokyo: Hokkaido Daigaku Tosho Kankōkai, 1998.

Iokibe Makoto. "Japan's Civil Society: An Historical Overview." In *Deciding the Public Good: Governance and Civil Society in Japan,* ed. Yamamoto Tadashi. Tokyo: Japan Center for International Exchange, 1999.

Irokawa Daikichi. "The Survival Struggle of the Japanese Community." In *Authority and the Individual in Japan: Citizen Protest in Historical Perspective,* ed. J. Victor Koschmann, 250–82. Tokyo: University of Tokyo Press, 1978.

Ishida Takeshi and Kang Sangjung. *Maruyama Masao to Shimin Shakai.* Yokohama: Seori Shobō, 1997.

Ishida Takeshi, Sakamoto Yoshikazu, Shinohara Hajime, Sumiya Mikio, Taguchi Fukuji, Hidaka Rokurō, Fujita Shōzō, and Maruyama Masao.

"Genzai no Seiji Jōkyō: Nani o nasu beki ka." *Sekai* 176 (August 1960): 217–59.

Ishida Takeshi, Shinohara Hajime, and Fukuda Kanichi. "Yakudō suru Shimin Seishin." *Chūō Kōron* (July 1960): 66–83.

Ishimoda Sho. *Rekishi to Minzoku no Hakken: Rekishi no Kadai to Hōhō.* Tokyo: Tokyo Daigaku Shuppankai, 1952.

Ivy, Marilyn. "Formations of Mass Culture." In *Postwar Japan as History,* ed. Andrew Gordon, 239–58. Berkeley and Los Angeles: University of California Press, 1993.

Iwadare Hiroshi. "Consumer Cooperatives in the Spotlight." *Japan Quarterly* (October–December 1991): 429–35.

Iwane Kunio. *Atarashii Shakai Undō no Shihan Seiki: Seikatsu Kurabu, Dairinin Undō.* Tokyo: Kyōdō Tosho Sābisu, 1993.

———. *Seikatsu Kurabu to tomo ni: Iwane Kunio Hanseifu.* Tokyo: Seikatsu Kurabu Seikatsu Kyōdō Kumiai, 1978.

Iwata Tōichi. "Kurīninguya mo Tachiagaru." In *Dokyumento Shōwa Shi,* vol. 7: *Anpo to Kōdō Seichō,* ed. Yamada Munemutsu, 130–34. Tokyo: Heibonsha, 1975.

———. "Shōnin no Jiko Henkaku—Keizai Shutai kara Seijiteki Shimin e." *Shisō no Kagaku* (July 1961): 41–47.

Jain, Purnendra. "Green Politics and Citizen Power in Japan: The Zushi Movement." *Asian Survey* 31, no. 6 (June 1991): 559–75.

Japan Networkers' Conference, ed. ABSTRACT *of the Report of the First Networkers' Conference.* Tokyo: Japan Network rs' Conference, 1990.

Jiyūminshutō. *Nihongata Fukushi Shakai.* Tokyo: Jiyūminshutō Kōhōiinkai Shuppankyoku, 1979.

Jūmin Toshokan, ed. *Minikomi Sōmokuroku.* Tokyo: Heibonsha, 1992.

Kaikō Takeshi. *Kagayakeru Yami.* Tokyo: Shinchōsha, 1968. Translated by Cecilia Segawa Seigle as *Into a Black Sun* (Tokyo and New York: Kodansha International, 1980).

Kaneko Ikuyō. *Borantia: Mōhitotsu no Jōhō Shakai.* Tokyo: Iwanami Shoten, 1992.

———. *Nettowākingu e no Shōtai.* Tokyo: Chūkō Shinsho, 1986.

Kashiwagi Hiroshi. *Amerika no NPO Shisutemu: Hieiri Soshiki no Genjō to Unei.* Tokyo: Nihon Taiheiyō Shiryō Nettowāku, 1992.

Kasza, Gregory J. *One World of Welfare: Japan in Comparative Perspective.* Ithaca, NY, and London: Cornell University Press, 2006.

Katayama Mataichirō. *Gendai Seikatsusha Shiron: Ruikeika to Tenkai.* Tokyo: Hakutō Shobō, 2000.

Katō Hidetoshi. *Chūkan Bunka.* Tokyo: Heibonsha, 1957.

———. "Nichijō Seikatsu to Kokumin Undō." *Shisō no Kagaku* 19 (July 1960): 28–35.

Kawana Hideyuki. *Dokyumento Nihon no Kōgai Dai-5kan Sōgōkaihatsu.* Tokyo: Ryokufu, 1990.

Keane, John. *Civil Society: Old Images, New Visions.* Cambridge, U.K.: Polity Press, 1998.

Keizai Kikakuchō Kokumin Seikatsu Kyoku. *Borantia Katsudō no Jittai: Chōsa Kekka to Dantai Meibō.* Tokyo: Kokuritsu Insatsukyoku, 1981.

———. *Jishuteki Shakai Sanka Katsudō no Igi to Yakuwari: Katsuryoku to Rentai o motomete.* Tokyo: Ōkurashō Insatsukyoku, 1983.

———. *Shimin Katsudō Dantai no Rīdā no tame ni.* Tokyo: Ōkurashō Insatsukyoku, 1997.

———. *Shimin Katsudō Repōto: Shimin Katsudō Dantai Kihon Chōsa Hōkokusho.* Tokyo: Ōkurashō Insatsukyoku, 1997.

———. *Shimin no Me de mita Shimin Katsudō: Kojin kara mita Shimin Katsudō ni kansuru Chōsa Hōkokusho.* Tokyo: Ōkurashō Insatsukyoku, 1997.

———, ed. *Jikaku to Sekinin no aru Shakai e.* Tokyo: Ōkurashō Insatsu Kyoku, 1994.

Keizai Kikakuchō Sōgō Keikakukyoku, ed. *2010 nen e no Sentaku Shirīzu 1: 2010 nen e no Sentaku.* Tokyo: Ōkurashō Insatsukyoku, 1991.

Kersten, Rikki. *Democracy in Postwar Japan: Maruyama Masao and the Search for Autonomy.* London and New York: Routledge, 1996.

Kingston, Jeffrey. *Japan's Quiet Transformation: Social Change and Civil Society in the Twenty-first Century.* Oxon, U.K., and New York: Routledge-Curzon, 2004.

Kinser-Saiki, Maggie, ed. *Japanese Working for a Better World: Grassroots Voices and Access Guide to Citizens' Groups in Japan.* San Francisco: Honnoki USA, 1992.

Kitahara Kōji. *Daichi no Ran Narita Tōsō: Sanrizuka Hantai Dōmei Jimukyokuchō no 30 nen.* Tokyo: Ochanomizu Shobō, 1996.

Kobayashi Tomi. "'Koe naki Koe' no Kōshin." In *Dokyumento Shōwa Shi,* vol. 7: *Anpo to Kōdō Seichō,* ed. Yamada Munemutsu, 126–30. Tokyo: Heibonsha, 1975.

Kōda Toshihiko. *Waga Sonzai no Teiten kara: Fuji Kōgai to Watashi.* Tokyo: Sōdosha, 2005.

Koe Naki Koe no Kai, ed., *Fukkokuban: Koe naki Koe no Tayori,* vol. 1: *1960–1970,* and vol. 2: *1970–1995.* Tokyo: Shisō no Kagakusha, 1996.

Kōgai o Kiroku suru Kai, ed. *"Yokkaichi Kōgai" Shimin Undō Kirokushū.* 4 vols. Tokyo: Nihon Tosho Sentā, 2007.

Kojève, Alexandre. *Introduction to the Reading of Hegel.* Ithaca, NY, and London: Cornell University Press, 1991.

Kokubun Ichitarō. *Atarashii Tsuzurikata Kyōshitsu—Zōhoban.* Tokyo: Shinhyōronsha, 1952.

Kokumin Seikatsu Shingikai Chōsabukai Komyuniti Mondai Shōiinkai, ed. *Komyuniti: Seikatsu no Ba ni okeru Ningensei no Kaifuku.* Tokyo: Ōkurashō Insatsukyoku, 1969.

Kokumin Seikatsu Shingikai Sōgō Kikaku Bukai Dai 4 Kai NPO Hōjin Seido Kentō Iinkai. *Giji Yōshi* (March 20, 2006). http://www5.cao.go.jp/seikatsu/shingikai/kikaku/20th/npo/index.html (accessed May 24, 2007).

Komori Takeshi. *Toshizukuri: Toshi Mondai no Genjitsu to Mirai.* Tokyo: Kawade Shobō Shinsha, 1965.

Kornhauser, William. *The Politics of Mass Society.* Glencoe, IL: Free Press, 1959.

Kōroki Hiroshi. "Borantia no Rekishi kara Kangaeru." *Kikan Mado* 20 (Summer 1994): 104–16.

Koschmann, J. Victor. "Avenell's 'Citizen.' " *positions: east asia cultures critique* 16, no. 3 (Winter 2008): 753–60.

———. "Intellectuals and Politics." In *Postwar Japan as History,* ed. Andrew Gordon, 395–423. Berkeley and Los Angeles: University of California Press, 1993.

———. *Revolution and Subjectivity in Japan.* Chicago and London: University of Chicago Press, 1996.

Kōseisho, *Kōseihakusho Shōwa 59 nenban.* (1984). Chapter 1, section 1.4, "Fukushi no Yakuwari Buntan to Borantia Katsudō." www.hakusyo.mhlw .go.jp/wp/index.htm (accessed February 27, 2008).

Kōyama Iwao. *Sekaishi no Tetsugaku.* Tokyo: Iwanami Shoten, 1942.

Kōyama Kenichi. *Eikokubyō no Kyōkun.* Kyoto: PHP Kenkyūjo, 1978.

Krauss, Ellis S. *Japanese Radicals Revisited: Student Protest in Postwar Japan.* Berkeley: University of California Press, 1974.

Krauss, Ellis S., and Bradford L. Simcock. "Citizens' Movements: The Growth and Impact of Environmental Protest in Japan." In *Political Opposition and Local Politics in Japan,* ed. Kurt Steiner, Ellis S. Krauss, and Scott Flanagan, 187–227. Princeton, NJ: Princeton University Press, 1980.

Kuno Osamu. *Seijiteki Shimin no Fukken.* Tokyo: Ushio Shuppansha, 1975.

———. "Seikatsu-Shimin no Genri o Uchitateyō: Shimin ni totte no Endaka Fukyō." *Ekonomisuto* (November 10, 1978): 30–38.

———. "Shiminshugi no Seiritsu." In Kuno Osamu, *Kuno Osamu Shū* vol. 2: *Shiminshugisha toshite,* ed. Sataka Makoto, 63–79. Tokyo: Iwanami Shoten, 1998.

———. *Shimin toshite Tetsugakusha toshite.* With Takabatake Michitoshi. Tokyo: Mainichi Shimbunsha, 1995.

Kuno Osamu and Tsurumi Shunsuke. *Gendai Nihon no Shisō: Sono Itsutsu no Uzu.* Tokyo: Iwanami, 1956.

Kurata Ichirō. "Jōmin no Tetsugaku: Chōsa to Bunseki." In *Shisō no Kagaku— Me,* vol. 1, ed. Yasuda Tsuneo and Amano Masako, 362–70. Tokyo: Kyūzansha, 1992.

———. "Zendai Seikatsu no Riron ni tsuite." In *Shisō no Kagaku—Me,* vol. 1, ed. Yasuda Tsuneo and Amano Masako. Tokyo: Kyūzansha, 1992.

Kurihara, Akira. "New Social Movements in Present-Day Japan." *Journal of Pacific Asia* 5 (1999): 7–22.

———. "Shimin Seiji no Ajenda: Seimei Seiji no Hō e." *Shisō* 908 (February 2000): 5–14.

LaClau, Ernesto, and Chantal Mouffe. *Hegemony and Socialist Strategy: Toward a Radical Democratic Politics.* New York: Verso, 1985.

Lam, Peng-Er. *Green Politics in Japan.* London and New York: Routledge, 1999.

LeBlanc, Robin. *Bicycle Citizens: The Political World of the Housewife.* Berkeley and Los Angeles: University of California Press, 1999.

Lévi-Strauss, Claude. *The Savage Mind.* Chicago: University of Chicago Press, 1966.

Lewis, Jack. "Civic Protest in Mishima: Citizens' Movements and the Politics of the Environment in Contemporary Japan." In *Political Opposition and Local Politics in Japan*, ed. Kurt Steiner, Ellis S. Krauss, and Scott Flanagan, 274–313. Princeton, NJ: Princeton University Press, 1980.

Lewis, Michael. *Rioters and Citizens: Mass Protest in Imperial Japan*. Berkeley and Los Angeles: University of California Press, 1990.

Lipnack, Jessica, and Jeffrey Stamps. *Nettowākingu*. Translated by Masamura Kimihiro and Shakai Kaihatsu Tōkei Kenkyūjo. Tokyo: Purejidentosha, 1984.

———. *Networking: The First Report and Directory*. Garden City, NY: Doubleday, 1982.

———. *The Networking Book: People Connecting with People*. New York and London: Routledge and Kegan Paul, 1986.

Mackie, Vera. *Feminism in Modern Japan: Citizenship, Embodiment, and Sexuality*. Cambridge and New York: Cambridge University Press, 2003.

Maclachlan, Patricia L. *Consumer Politics in Postwar Japan: The Institutional Boundaries of Citizen Activism*. New York: Columbia University Press, 2002.

———. "From Subjects to Citizens: Japan's Evolving Consumer Identity." *Japanese Studies* 24, no. 1 (2004): 115–34.

———. "The Struggle for an Independent Consumer Society: Consumer Activism and the State's Response in Postwar Japan." In *The State of Civil Society in Japan*, ed. Frank J. Schwartz and Susan J. Pharr, 214–32. Cambridge and New York: Cambridge University Press, 2003.

Malcolm X. *The Autobiography of Malcolm X*. With Alex Haley. New York: Grove Press, 1965.

Maruyama Hisashi. *Minikomi no Dōjidaishi*. Tokyo: Heibonsha, 1985.

———. *Rōkaru Nettowāku no Jidai: Minikomi to Chiiki to Shimin Undō*. Tokyo: Nichigai Asoshiētsu, 1997.

Maruyama Masao. "Anpo Tōsō no Kyōkun to Kongo no Taishū Tōsō." In *Maruyama Masao Shū*, vol. 8, 325–39. Tokyo: Iwanami Shoten, 1996.

———. "Dansō." In *Maruyama Masao Shū*, vol. 6, 143–57. Tokyo: Iwanami Shoten, 1996.

———. "'De aru' koto to 'Suru koto.'" In Maruyama Masao, *Maruyama Masao Shū*, vol. 8, 23–44. Tokyo: Iwanami Shoten, 1996.

———. "*Fukusho no Setsu*." In *Maruyama Masao Shū*, vol. 8, 351–58. Tokyo: Iwanami Shoten, 1996.

———. "Gendai ni okeru Taido Kettei." In *Maruyama Masao Shū*, vol. 8, 301–17. Tokyo: Iwanami Shoten, 1996.

———. "Hachi-Jūgo to Go-Jūkyū: Nihon Minshushugi no Rekishiteki Imi." In *Maruyama Masao Shū*, vol. 8, 359–77. Tokyo: Iwanami Shoten, 1996.

———. "*Sentaku no Toki*." In *Maruyama Masao Shū*, vol. 8, 347–50. Tokyo: Iwanami Shoten, 1996.

———. *Thought and Behavior in Modern Japanese Politics*. Edited by Ivan Morris. London, Oxford, and New York: Oxford University Press, 1969.

Maruyama Masao and Satō Noboru. "Gendai ni okeru Kakumei no Riron." In *Maruyama Masao Zadan*, vol. 4, 127–74. Tokyo: Iwanami Shoten, 1998.

Maruyama Masao, Takeuchi Yoshimi, and Kaiko Takeshi. "Giji Puroguramu kara no Dakkyaku." In *Maruyama Masao Zadan,* vol. 4, 108–26. Tokyo: Iwanami Shoten, 1998.

Maruya Saiichi. *Singular Rebellion.* Translated by Dennis Keene. Tokyo and New York: Kodansha International, 1990.

———. *Tatta Hitori no Hanran.* 2 vols. Tokyo: Kōdansha, 1982.

Masamura Kimihiro. *Sengoshi,* vol. 2. Tokyo: Chikuma Shobō, 1985.

Matsubara Akira. "NPO Hō ni itaru Haikei to Rippō Katei." In *Nihon no NPO 2000,* ed. Nakamura Yōichi and Nihon NPO Sentā, 51–63. Tokyo: Nihon Hyōronsha, 1999.

Matsubara Haruo, ed. *Kōgai to Chiki Shakai: Seikatsu to Jūmin Undō no Shakaigaku.* Tokyo: Nihon Keizai Shimbunsha, 1971.

Matsubara Haruo and Nitagai Kamon, eds. *Jūmin Undō no Riron: Undō no Tenkai Katei to Tenbō.* Tokyo: Gakuyō Shobō, 1976.

Matsubara Shinichi. *Gen'ei no Kommyūn: "Sākuru Mura" o Kenshō suru.* Fukuoka: Sōgensha, 2001.

Matsumoto Reiji. "Sengo Shimin Shakai Ron Saikō." In *Gendai Shimin Seiji Ron,* ed. Takabatake Michitoshi, 46–51. Yokohama: Seori Shobō, 2003.

Matsushita Keiichi. "Chiiki Minshushugi no Kadai to Tenbō." *Shisō* 443 (May 1961): 1–38.

———. "Jichitai ni okeru Kakushin Seiji Shidō." In *Jichitai Kaikaku no Rironteki Tenbō,* ed. Asukata Ichio, 59–80. Tokyo: Nihon Hyōronsha, 1965.

———. "Marukushugi Riron no Nijūseikiteki Tenkan: Taishū Nashonarizumu to Seiji no Ronri." *Chūō Kōron* (March 1957): 142–57.

———. "Nihon ni okeru Taishū Shakai Ron no Igi." *Chūō Kōron* (August 1957): 80–92.

———. *Sengo Seiji no Rekishi to Shisō.* Tokyo: Chikuma Shobō, 1994.

———. "Shakai Minshushugi no Kiki." In Matsushita Keiichi, *Gendai Seiji no Jōken (Zōhanban),* 104–21. Tokyo: Chūō Kōronsha, 1969.

———. *Shibiru Minimamu no Shisō.* Tokyo: Tokyo Daigaku Shuppankai, 1971.

———. "Shibiru Minimamu to Toshi Seisaku." In *Iwanami Kōza Gendai Toshi Seisaku,* vol. 5: *Shibiru Minimamu,* ed. Matsushita Keiichi, 3–28. Tokyo: Iwanami Shoten, 1973.

———. "Shimin Sanka to Sono Rekishiteki Kanōsei." In *Gendai ni Ikiru,* vol. 6: *Shimin Sanka,* ed. Matsushita Keiichi, 173–243. Tokyo: Tōyō Keizai Shinpōsha, 1971.

———. *Shimin Seiji Ron no Keisei.* Tokyo: Iwanami Shoten, 1959.

———. "'Shimin' teki Ningengata no Gendaiteki Kanōsei." *Shisō* 504 (June 1966): 16–30.

———. *Shinseijikō.* Tokyo: Asahi Shimbunsha, 1977.

———. "Shiteki Yuibutsuron to Taishū Shakai." *Shisō* 395 (May 1957): 43–63.

———. "Taishū Kokka no Seiritsu to Sono Mondaisei" (1956). Reproduced in Matsushita Keiichi, *Sengo Seiji no Rekishi to Shisō,* 13–60. Tokyo: Chikuma Shobō, 1994.

———. "Taishū Shakai Ron no Konnichiteki Ichi." *Shisō* 436 (October 1960): 1–15.

————. *Toshigata Shakai no Jichi.* Tokyo: Nihon Hyōronsha, 1987.

————. *Toshi Seisaku o Kangaeru.* Tokyo: Iwanami Shoten, 1971.

————. "Wasurerareta Teikōken." *Chūō Kōron* (November 1958): 38–49.

Matsushita Ryūichi. *Buzen Kankyō Saiban.* Tokyo: Nihon Hyōronsha, 1980.

————. "Buzen Karyoku to Tatakau Sakka." In *Kōgai Jishu Kōza 15 nen*, ed. Ui Jun, 372–95. Tokyo: Aki Shobō, 1991.

————. *Matsushita Ryūichi Sono Shigoto: Kurayami no Shisō*, vol. 12. Tokyo: Kawade Shobō Shinsha, 1999.

Matsuura Sōzō. "Kokumin Seikatsu no Henka." In *Shōwa no Sengo Shi*, vol. 3: *Gyakuryū to Teikō*, ed. Matsuura Sōzō, 210–32. Tokyo: Chōbunsha, 1976.

McKean, Margaret. *Environmental Protest and Citizen Politics in Japan.* Berkeley and Los Angeles: University of California Press, 1981.

Mega Fumiko. "Borantia Katsudō: Kore made to Kore kara." In *Nihon no NPO 2000*, ed. Nakamura Yōichi and Nihon NPO Sentā, 40–50. Tokyo: Nihon Hyōronsha, 1999.

Menand, Louis. *Pragmatism: A Reader.* New York: Vintage Books, 1997.

Michiba Chikanobu. "Sen Kyūhyaku Rokujū Nendai ni okeru 'Chiki' no Hakken to 'Kōkyōsei' no Saiteigi: Miketsu no Aporia o megutte." *Gendai Shisō* 31, no. 6 (May 2002): 97–130.

————. *Senryō to Heiwa: Sengo to iu Keiken.* Tokyo: Seidosha, 2005.

Miyagi Kenichi. "Seikatsusha no Tanjō." *Gendai no Riron* 211 (March 1985): 60–69.

Miyamoto Kenichi. "Jūmin Undō no Riron to Rekishi." In *Kōza Gendai Nihon no Toshi Mondai*, vol. 8: *Toshi Mondai to Jūmin Undō*, ed. Miyamoto Kenichi and Endō Akira, 2–69. Kyoto and Tokyo: Chōbunsha, 1971.

Miyazaki Shōgo. *Ima, Kōkyōsei o Utsu: "Dokyumento" Yokohama Shinka-motsusen Hantai Undō.* Tokyo: Shinsensha, 1975.

————. "'Kōkyōsei' to wa Nanika." In *Jūmin Undō "Shiron": Jissensha kara mita Jichi no Shisō*, ed. Nakamura Kiichi, 53–76. Tokyo: Sōdosha, 2005.

————. "Yokohama Hōshiki no Mondaiten." In *Kōgai Jishu Kōza 15 nen*, ed. Ui Jun, 180–90. Tokyo: Aki Shobō, 1991.

Mori Mototaka. *Zushi no Shimin Undō: Ikego Beigun Jūtaku Kensetsu Hantai Undō to Minshushugi no Kenkyū.* Tokyo: Ochanomizu Shobō, 1996.

Moriyama Yūichi. "Watashitachi wa Korekara. . . ." *Noroshi* (June 1, 1971): 2.

Morris, Aldon D., and Carol McClurg Mueller. "Preface." In *Frontiers in Social Movement Theory*, ed. Aldon D. Morris and Carol McClurg Mueller, ix–x. New Haven, CT, and London: Yale University Press, 1992.

Morrison, John. "The Government-Voluntary Sector Compacts: Governance, Governmentality, and Civil Society." *Journal of Law and Society* 27, no. 1 (March 2000): 98–132.

Morris-Suzuki, Tessa. *Beyond Computopia: Information, Automation and Democracy in Japan.* London and New York: Kegan Paul International, 1988.

———. "Invisible Immigrants: Undocumented Migration and Border Controls in Postwar Japan." *Journal of Japanese Studies* 32, no. 1 (Winter 2006): 119–53.

Mouffe, Chantal. *The Return of the Political.* London and New York: Verso, 1993.

Muchaku Seikyō, ed. *Yamabiko Gakkō.* Tokyo: Yuri Shuppan, 1990.

Murakami Kimiko. "Shakai Fukushi Jigyō no Seido Kaikaku." In *Nihon Shakai Hoshō no Rekishi,* ed. Yokoyama Kazuhiko and Tada Hidenori, 358–79. Tokyo: Gakubunsha, 1991.

Muto, Ichiyo. "The Alternative Livelihood Movement." *AMPO: Japan-Asia Quarterly Review* 24, no. 2 (1993): 4–10.

———. "Beheiren Undō no Shisō: Sengo Minshushugi no Yukue ni yosete." *Shisō no Kagaku* (January 1968): 11–21.

———. "Jūmin Undō no Kanken: 'Shiron' e no Josetsu." In *Jūmin Undō "Shiron": Jissensha kara mita Jichi no Shisō,* ed. Nakamura Kiichi, 11–52. Tokyo: Sōdosha, 2005.

———. "Nijūhachi-nen-me no 'Atogaki.'" In *Jūmin Undō "Shiron": Jissensha kara mita Jichi no Shisō,* ed. Nakamura Kiichi, 249–53. Tokyo: Sōdosha, 2005.

———. "Sengo Kōki e no Ikō—Sengogata 'Heiwa to Minshushugi' no Hōkai Igo." *Tenbō* (September 1967): 84–93.

Najita, Tetsuo, and H.D. Harootunian. "Japanese Revolt against the West: Political and Cultural Criticism in the Twentieth Century." In *The Cambridge History of Japan,* vol. 6: *The Twentieth Century,* ed. Peter Duus, 711–74. Cambridge and New York: Cambridge University Press, 1989.

Nakamura Yōichi. "'Shimin Katsudō' no Tōjō to Tenkai." In *Nihon no NPO 2000,* ed. Nakamura Yōichi and Nihon NPO Sentā, 31–39. Tokyo: Nihon Hyōronsha, 1999.

Nakamura Yōichi and Nihon NPO Sentā, eds. *Nihon no NPO 2000.* Tokyo: Nihon Hyōronsha, 1999.

Nakano, Lynne. *Community Volunteers in Japan: Everyday Stories of Social Change.* London and New York: RoutledgeCurzon, 2005.

Nakano, Ryoko. "Uncovering *Shokumin:* Yanaihara Tadao's Concept of Global Civil Society." *Social Science Japan Journal* 9, no. 2 (October 2006): 187–202.

Nakano Toshio. "Borantia Dōin-gata Shimin Shakai Ron no Kansei." *Gendai Shisō* 27, no. 5 (1999): 72–93.

Narumi Masayasu. *Chihō Bunken no Shisō: Jichitai Kaikaku no Kiseki to Tenbō.* Tokyo: Gakuyō Shobō, 1994.

———. *Chihō Jichi o Miru Me.* Tokyo: Yūhikaku, 1991.

———. *Sengo Jichitai Kaikakushi.* Tokyo: Nihon Hyōronsha, 1982.

———. "Shimin Soshiki no Ichinenkan—Chiiki ni okeru Ningen no Sōzō." *Shisō no Kagaku* (July 1961): 48–55.

———. *Toshi Henkaku no Shisō to Hōhō.* Tokyo: Renga Shobō, 1972.

NGO Katsudō Suishin Sentā, ed. *NGO Dairekutorī: Kokusai Kaihatsu Kyōryoku ni Tazusawaru Minkan Kōeki Dantai.* Tokyo: NGO Katsudō Suishin Sentā, 1988.

Nihon Kokugo Daijiten Dainihan Henshū Iinkai, ed. *Nihon Kokugo Daijiten Dainihan*, vol. 6. Tokyo: Shogakkan, 2001.

Nihon Nettowākāzu Kaigi, ed. *Hieiri Dantai to Shakaiteki Kiban: Borantarī Katsudō Suishin no tame no Shikumizukuri ni kansuru Chōsa Kenkyū Hōkokusho—Designing a Nonprofit Support Infrastructure.* Tokyo: Nihon Nettowākāzu Kaigi, 1995.

———. *Nettowākingu ga Hiraku Atarashi Sekai: Dai Ikkai Nihon Nettowākāzu Kaigi yori.* Tokyo: Nihon Nettowākāzu Kaigi, 1990.

———. *Nettowākingu o Katachi ni! Dai 2 kai Nettowākāzu Fōramu Hōkokusho.* Tokyo: Nihon Nettowākāzu Kaigi, 1993.

———. *Nihon ni okeru Kōeki Katsudō no Genjō to Kadai.* Tokyo: Nihon Nettowākāzu Kaigi, 1994.

———. *NPO to wa Nanika: Sono Rikai no tame ni—Understanding Nonprofit Organizations.* Tokyo: Nihon Nettowākāzu Kaigi, 1992.

———. *Shimin Katsudō Hōseido ni kansuru Kokusai Fōramu—ABSTRACT of the Report of International Forum on Establishing a Legal Framework Supporting Citizens' Activities.* Tokyo: Nihon Nettowākāzu Kaigi, 1996.

Nomura Hidekazu, ed. *Seikyō: 21 Seiki e no Chōsen Nihongata Moderu no Jikken.* Tokyo: Ōtsuki Shoten, 1992.

Nord, Phillip. "Introduction." In *Civil Society before Democracy: Lessons from Nineteenth Century Europe,* ed. Nancy Bermeo and Phillip Nord, xiii–xxxiii. Lanham, MD: Rowman and Littlefield, 2000.

Oda Makoto. *"Beheiren": Kaikoroku denai Kaiko.* Tokyo: Daisan Shokan, 1995.

———. "Genri toshite no Minshushugi no Fukken." In *Oda Makoto Zenshigoto,* vol. 10, 13–40. Tokyo: Kawade Shobō Shinsha, 1971.

———. *Gimu toshite no Tabi.* Tokyo: Iwanami Shinsho, 1974.

———. "Heiwa e no Gutaiteki Teigen: Nichibei Shimin Kaigi de no Bōtō Enzetsu." In *Shiryō "Beheiren" Undō,* vol. 1, ed. Betonamu ni Heiwa o! Shimin Rengō, 104–18. Tokyo: Kawade Shobō Shinsha, 1974.

———. "Heiwa no Rinri to Ronri." In *Oda Makoto Zenshigoto,* vol. 9, 85–113. Tokyo: Kawade Shobō Shinsha, 1970.

———. "Heiwa o Tsukuru: Sono Genri to Kōdō—Hitotsu no Sengen." In *Oda Makoto Zenshigoto,* vol. 9, 113–31. Tokyo: Kawade Shobō Shinsha, 1970.

———. "Ima Nani o Nasu beki ka." In *Oda Makoto Zenshigoto,* vol. 9, 305–6. Tokyo: Kawade Shobō Shinsha, 1970.

———. *"Kitachōsen" no Hitobito.* Tokyo: Ushio Shuppansha, 1978.

———. "Nandemo Mite Yarō." In *Oda Makoto Zenshigoto,* vol. 6, 5–254. Tokyo: Kawade Shobō Shinsha, 1971.

———. "Nanshi no Shisō." In *Oda Makoto Zenshigoto,* vol. 8, 13–31. Tokyo: Kawade Shobō Shinsha, 1970.

———. "Ningen: Aru Kojinteki Kōsatsu." In *Oda Makoto Zenshigoto,* vol. 9, 13–42. Tokyo: Kawade Shobō Shinsha, 1970.

———. "Ningen no naka no rekishi." In *Oda Makoto Zenshigoto,* vol. 10, 211–38. Tokyo: Kawade Shobō Shinsha, 1971.

———. "Raishawā Kyōju no Nihon Ninshiki." In *Oda Makoto Zenshigoto,* vol. 7, 168–9. Tokyo: Kawade Shobō Shinsha, 1970.

———. "Watashi no naka no Nihonjin: 'Watashi no Nihon' to 'Karera no Nihon.'" In *Oda Makoto Zenshigoto,* vol. 10, 140–42. Tokyo: Kawade Shobō Shinsha, 1971.

———. *Watashi to Chōsen.* Tokyo: Chikuma Shobō, 1977.

———. "Watashi wa Shi ga Kowai." In Oda Makoto, *Nani o Watashitachi wa Hajimete iru no ka,* 156–64. Tokyo: Sanichi Shobō, 1970.

Oda Makoto and Tsurumi Shunsuke, eds. *Hansen to Henkaku: Teikō to Heiwa e no Teigen.* Tokyo: Gakukei Shobō, 1969.

Offe, Claus. "Challenging the Boundaries of Institutional Politics: Social Movements since the 1960s." In *Changing the Boundaries of the Political,* ed. Charles S. Maier, 63–105. Cambridge: Cambridge University Press, 1987.

———. "New Social Movements: Challenging the Boundaries of Institutional Politics." *Social Research* 52, no. 4 (Winter 1985): 829.

Ogawa, Akihiro. *The Failure of Civil Society? The Third Sector and the State in Contemporary Japan.* Albany: State University of New York Press, 2009.

———. "Invited by the State: Institutionalizing Volunteer Subjectivity in Contemporary Japan." *Asian Anthropology* 3 (2004): 71–96.

Oguma Eiji. *Minshu to Aikoku: Sengo Nashonarizumu to Kōkyōsei.* Tokyo: Shinyōsha, 2002.

———. *Shimizu Ikutarō: Aru Sengo Chishikijin no Kiseki.* Kanagawa Daigaku Hyōron Bukkuretto, no. 26. Tokyo: Ochanomizu Shobō, 2003.

Okabe Kazuaki. *Pasokon Shimin Nettowāku.* Tokyo: Gijutsu to Ningen, 1986.

———. *Shakai ga Sodateru Shimin Undō—Amerika no NPO Seido.* Tokyo: Nihon Shakaitō Kikanshikyoku, 1993.

Okamoto Eiichi, ed. *Borantia—NPO Yōgo Jiten.* Tokyo: Chūō Hōki Shuppan, 2004.

Ōkuma Nobuyuki. *Kokka Aku: Jinrui ni Mirai wa aru ka.* Tokyo: Ushio Shuppansha, 1971.

———. *Seimei Saiseisan no Riron: Ningen Chūshin no Shisō,* 2 vols. Tokyo: Tōyō Keizai Shinpōsha, 1974–75.

Okutani Matsuji. *Nihon Seikatsu Kyōdō Kumiai Shi.* Revised and expanded ed. Tokyo: Minshūsha, 1973.

Olson, Lawrence. *Ambivalent Moderns: Portraits of Japanese Cultural Identity.* Savage, MD: Rowman and Littlefield, 1992.

Orr, James J. *The Victim as Hero: Ideologies of Peace and National Identity in Postwar Japan.* Honolulu: University of Hawaii Press, 2001.

Ōsawa Shinichirō. *Kōhō no Shisō: Arui wa Chōsei e no Shuppatsu.* Tokyo: Shakai Hyōronsha, 1971.

———. "Sākuru no Sengoshi." In *Kyōdō Kenkyū Shūdan: Sākuru no Sengo Shisōshi,* ed. Shisō no Kagaku Kenkyūkai, 68–92. Tokyo: Heibonsha, 1976.

Osborne, Stephen P. "The Voluntary and Non-Profit Sector in Japan: Emerging Roles and Organizational Challenges in a Changing Society." In *The Voluntary and Non-Profit Sector in Japan: The Challenge of Change,* ed. Stephen P. Osborne, 7–22. London and New York: RoutledgeCurzon, 2003.

Ōtsuka Hisao. "Robinson Kurūsō no Ningen Ruikei." In *Gendai Nihon Shisō Taikei,* vol. 34: *Kindaishugi,* ed. Hidaka Rokurō, 99–106. Tokyo: Chikuma Shobō, 1964.

Packard, George R. *Protest in Tokyo: The Security Treaty Crisis of 1960.* Princeton, NJ: Princeton University Press, 1966.

Partner, Simon. *Assembled in Japan: Electrical Goods and the Making of the Japanese Consumer.* Berkeley: University of California Press, 1999.

Pekkanen, Robert. "After the Developmental State: Civil Society in Japan," *Journal of East Asian Studies* 4 (2004): 363–88.

———. *Japan's Dual Civil Society: Members without Advocates.* Stanford, CA: Stanford University Press, 2006.

———. "Japan's New Politics: The Case of the NPO Law." *Journal of Japanese Studies* 26, no. 1 (Winter 2000): 111–48.

———. "The Politics of Regulating the Non-Profit Sector." In *The Voluntary and Non-Profit Sector in Japan: The Challenge of Change,* ed. Stephen P. Osborne, 53–75. London and New York: RoutledgeCurzon, 2003.

Pharr, Susan J. "Conclusion: Targeting by an Activist State: Japan as a Civil Society Model." In *The State of Civil Society,* ed. Frank J. Schwartz and Susan J. Pharr, 313–36. Cambridge and New York: Cambridge University Press, 2003.

———. Preface. In *The State of Civil Society in Japan,* ed. Frank J. Schwartz and Susan J. Pharr, xiii–xviii. Cambridge and New York: Cambridge University Press, 2003.

Pichardo, Nelson A. "NEW SOCIAL MOVEMENTS: A Critical Review." *Annual Review of Sociology* 23 (1997): 411–30.

Pincus, Leslie. "A Salon For the Soul: Nakai Masakazu and the Hiroshima Culture Movement." *positions: east asia cultures critique* 10, no. 1 (Spring 2002): 173–94.

Powell, Irena. "Japanese Writer in Vietnam: The Two Wars of Kaiko Ken (1931–1989)." *Modern Asian Studies* 32, no. 1 (February 1998): 219–44.

Pyle, Kenneth. *The Making of Modern Japan.* Lexington, MA: Heath, 1978.

Reimann, Kim. "Building Global Civil Society from the Outside In? Japanese International Development NGOs, the State, and International Norms." In *The State of Civil Society in Japan,* ed. Frank J. Schwartz and Susan J. Pharr, 298–315. Cambridge: Cambridge University Press, 2003.

Rix, Alan. "Tokyo's Governor Minobe and Progressive Local Politics in Japan." *Asian Survey* 15, no. 6 (June 1975): 530–42.

Rosenbaum, Roman. "Defamiliarising the Postwar: The Enigma of Oda Makoto." *Japanese Studies* 25, no. 2 (September 2005): 141–58.

Ruoff, Kenneth. "Mr. Tomino Goes to City Hall: Grass-Roots Democracy in Zushi City Japan." *Bulletin of Concerned Asian Scholars* 25, no. 2 (April–June 1993): 22–32.

Saeki Keishi. *"Shimin" to wa dare ka: Sengo Minshushugi o toinaosu.* Tokyo: PHP Kenkyūjo, 1997.

Saigusa Saeko. *Seikatsusha Hassō: Jittai to Nīzu o Saguru 15 hen.* Tokyo: Jitsugyō no Nihonsha, 1994.

Saitō Hideharu. *Kokka o Koeru Shimin Shakai: Dōin no Seiki kara Nomado no Seiki e.* Tokyo: Gendai Kikaku Shitsu, 1998.

Sakamoto Yoshikazu. *Sōtaika no Jidai.* Tokyo: Iwanami Shoten, 1997.

Salamon, Lester M. "The Rise of the Nonprofit Sector." *Foreign Affairs* 73, no. 4 (July–August 1994): 109–22.

Sasaki Ayao. "Sākuru Undō no Rekishitekina Imi." *Chūō Kōron* (June 1956): 248–57.

Sasaki Gen. "Kono Hon no Hōhō." In *Kyōdō Kenkyū Shūdan: Sākuru no Sengo Shisōshi*, ed. Shisō no Kagaku Kenkyūkai, 22–32. Tokyo: Heibonsha, 1976.

Sasaki-Uemura, Wesley. *Organizing the Spontaneous: Citizen Protest in Postwar Japan*. Honolulu: University of Hawaii Press, 2001.

———. "A Rectification of Names: Response to Simon Avenell." *positions: east asia cultures critique* 16, no. 3 (Winter 2008): 761–68.

———. "Tanigawa Gan's Politics of the Margins of Kyushu and Nagano." *positions: east asia cultures critique* 7, no. 1 (Spring 1999): 129–63.

Satō Yoshiyuki. *NPO to Shimin Shakai*. Tokyo: Yuhikaku, 2002.

Satō Yoshiyuki, Amano Masako, and Nasu Hisashi. *Joseitachi no Seikatsusha Undō: Seikatsu Kurabu o Sasaeru Hitobito*. Tokyo: Marujusha, 1995.

Scalapino, Robert A. *The Japanese Communist Movement, 1920–1966*. Berkeley and Los Angeles: University of California Press, 1967.

Schreurs, Miranda A. *Environmental Politics in Japan, Germany, and the United States*. Cambridge and New York: Cambridge University Press, 2002.

Schwartz, Frank J., and Susan J. Pharr, eds. *The State of Civil Society in Japan*. Cambridge and New York: Cambridge University Press, 2003.

Seibōhō o Sekitomeru Kai (Seibōhō Hantai Shimin Kaigi). "Seibōhō o Sekitomeyō: Shimin wa Seibōhō ni Hantai suru." In *Fukkokuban: Koe naki Koe no Tayori*, vol. 1: *1960–1970*, ed. Koe Naki Koe no Kai, 119–26. Tokyo: Shisō no Kagakusha, 1996.

Seidensticker, Edward. *Japan*. With the editors of TIME-LIFE Books. Life World Library series. New York: TIME-LIFE International, 1961.

Seikatsu Kurabu Seikatsu Kyōdō Kumiai, ed. *Shufu no Seikyō-zukuri: 10 man no Shufu, 10 nen no Taiken*. Tokyo: Sanichi Shobō, 1978.

Seikatsu o Kiroku suru Kai, ed. *Bōseki Joshi Kōin Seikatsu Kirokushū*, 4 vols. Tokyo: Nihon Tosho Sentā, 2002.

"Seikatsu Teian-gata Shimin Undō no Atarashii Nami." *Asahi Jyānaru* (August 1, 1986): 16–21.

Sekiya Shigeru, and Sakamoto Yoshie, eds. *Tonari ni Dassōhei ga ita Jidai: Jatekku, Aru Shimin Undō no Kiroku*. Tokyo: Shisō no Kagakusha, 1998.

Shakai Kaihatsu Tōkei Kenkyūjo. *Shakai Sanka Katsudō no Jittai to Kadai ni Kansuru Chōsa Hōkokusho*. Tokyo: Shakai Kaihatsu Tōkei Kenkyūjo, 1984.

Shapura Nīru Katsudō Kiroku Henshūbu. *Shapura Nīru no Atsui Kaze*. Tokyo: Mekon, 1989.

———. *Shapura Nīru no Atsui Kaze Dainibu*. Tokyo: Mekon, 1992.

Shaw, Rajib, and Katsuichirō Goda. "From Disaster to Sustainable Civil Society: The Kobe Experience." *Disasters* 28, no. 1 (2004): 16–40.

Shimizu Ikutarō. "Anpo Tōsō Ichinengo no Shisō: Seiji no naka no Chishikijin." In Shimizu Ikutarō, *Shimizu Ikutarō Chosakushū*, vol. 10, ed. Shimizu Reiko, 189–208. Tokyo: Kōdansha, 1992.

———. "Anpo Tōsō no 'Fukō na Shuyaku': Anpo Tōsō wa Naze Zasetsu shitaka—Shishōsetsufū no Sōkatsu." In Shimizu Ikutarō, *Shimizu Ikutarō Chosakushū*, vol. 10, ed. Shimizu Reiko, 133–53. Tokyo: Kōdansha, 1992.

———. "Heiwa Mondai Danwakai." In Shimizu Ikutarō, *Shimizu Ikutarō Chosakushū*, vol. 14, ed. Shimizu Reiko, 314–38. Tokyo: Kōdansha, 1993.

———. "Nihonjin." In Shimizu Ikutarō, *Shimizu Ikutarō Chosakushū*, vol. 10, ed. Shimizu Reiko, 5–27. Tokyo: Kōdansha, 1992.

———. "Nijusseiki Kenkyūjo." In Shimizu Ikutarō, *Shimizu Ikutarō Chosakushū*, vol. 14, ed. Shimizu Reiko, 297–313. Tokyo: Kōdansha, 1993.

———. *Shakai Shinrigaku.* Tokyo: Iwanami Shoten, 1951.

———. "Shomin." In Shimizu Ikutarō, *Shimizu Ikutarō Chosakushū*, vol. 8, ed. Shimizu Reiko, 285–302. Tokyo: Kōdansha, 1992.

———. "Taishū Shakai Ron no Shōri: Anpo Kaitei Soshi Tōsō no naka de." *Shisō* 436 (October 1960): 26–45.

———. "Tokumei no Shisō." In Shimizu Ikutarō, *Shimizu Ikutarō Chosakushū*, vol. 8, ed. Shimizu Reiko, 199–218. Tokyo: Kōdansha, 1992.

Shimizu Ikutarō, Miyahara Seiichi, and Ueda Shōzaburō. *Kichi no Ko: Kono Jijitsu o dō Kangaetara yoi ka.* Tokyo: Kōbunsha, 1953.

Shinohara Hajime. *Nihon no Seiji Fūdo.* Tokyo: Iwanami Shoten, 1968.

———. *Shimin no Seijigaku.* Tokyo: Iwanami Shoten, 2004.

———. "Shimin Sanka no Seido to Undō." In *Iwanami Kōza Gendai Toshi Seisaku*, vol. 2: *Shimin Sanka,* ed. Itō Mitsuharu, Shinohara Hajime, Matsushita Keiichi, and Miyamoto Kenichi, 3–38. Tokyo: Iwanami Shoten, 1973.

———. "Shimin Undō no Dessan." *Shimin* 2 (May 1971): 14–23.

———. "Taishū Undō to Mutōha Katsudōka." *Shisō* (September 1960): 30–39.

Shinohara Hajime, Shimizu Shinzō, Tsurumi Shunsuke, Minami Hiroshi, and Fukuda Kanichi. "Soshiki to Kokumin Undō: Go-Jūkyū Igo no Undō o Chūshin ni." *Sekai* (October 1960): 35–60.

Shinohara Hajime and Wada Akiko, eds. *Kawasaki Shimin Akademī Sōsho 3 Kōdo Seichō no Hikari to Kage: Seiji to Bungaku no Mado o tōshite.* Kawasaki: Kawasaki Shōgai Gakushū Shinkō Jigyōdan, Kawasaki Shimin Akademī Shuppanbu, 2003.

"Shinshimin ga Shakai o Ninau." *Asahi Shimbun,* February 24, 2007, be Report section, b3.

Shiratori Kunio. *Mumei no Nihonjin: "Yamanami no Kai" no Kiroku.* Tokyo: Miraisha, 1961.

"Shirīzu Seishun: Ikirukoto, Moerukoto (Dai-3-kai)." *Gekkan Big Tomorrow* 74 (August 1986): 101–4.

Shiryō: Kakushin Jichitai Kankō Iinkai, ed. *Shiryō: Kakushin Jichitai.* Tokyo: Nihon Hyōronsha, 1990.

Shisō no Kagaku Kenkyūkai, ed. *Gendaijin no Seitai: Aru Shakaiteki Kōsatsu.* Tokyo: Kōdansha, 1953.

———. *Kyōdō Kenkyū Shūdan: Sākuru no Sengo Shisōshi.* Tokyo: Heibonsha, 1976.

———. *Shisō no Kagaku Kaihō,* vol. 1. Tokyo: Kashiwa Shobō, 1982.

————. *Watashi no Tetsugaku.* 2 vols. Tokyo: Chūō Kōronsha, 1950.
————. *Yume to Omokage: Taishū Goraku no Kenkyū.* Tokyo: Chūō Kōronsha, 1950.
Shōji Hikaru and Miyamoto Kenichi. *Nihon no Kōgai.* Tokyo: Iwanami Shoten, 1975.
————. *Osorubeki Kōgai.* Tokyo: Iwanami Shoten, 1964.
Snow, David A., and Robert D. Benford. "Framing Processes and Social Movements: An Overview and Assessment." *Annual Review of Sociology* 26 (2000): 611–39.
————. "Ideology, Frame Resonance, and Participant Mobilization." In *From Structure to Action: Social Movement Participation across Cultures,* ed. Bert Klandermans, Hanspeter Kriesi, and Sidney Tarrow, 197–217. Greenwich CT: JAI Press, 1988.
————. "Master Frames and Cycles of Protest." In *Frontiers in Social Movement Theory,* ed. Aldon D. Morris and Carol McClurg Mueller, 133–55. New Haven, CT, and London: Yale University Press, 1992.
Snow, David A., E. Burke Rochford Jr., Steven K. Worden, and Robert D. Benford. "Frame Alignment Processes, Micromobilization, and Movement Participation." *American Sociological Review* 51, no. 4 (August 1986): 464–81.
Sōgō Kenkyū Kaihatsu Kikō (NIRA). *Shimin Kōeki Katsudō Kihon Seibi ni kansuru Chōsa Kenkyū.* Tokyo: Sōgō Kenkyū Kaihatasu Kikō, 1994.
"Sony and Those Smart Bombs: An Honest Mistake?" *Ampo: A Report from the Japanese New Left* 15 (December 1972): 28–29.
Sorel, Georges. *Reflections on Violence.* Edited by Jeremy Jennings. Cambridge and New York: Cambridge University Press, 1999.
Suda Harumi. *Seisaku Teian-gata Shimin Undō no Susume.* Tokyo: Shakai Shinpō, 1993.
Swidler, Ann. "Culture in Action: Symbols and Strategies." *American Sociological Review* 51, no. 2 (April 1986): 273–86.
Takabatake Michitoshi. "Citizens' Movements: Organizing the Spontaneous." In *Authority and the Individual in Japan: Citizen Protest in Historical Perspective,* ed. J. Victor Koschmann, 189–99. Tokyo: University of Tokyo Press, 1978.
————. *Jiyū to Poritiku: Shakaigaku no Tenkai.* Tokyo: Chikuma Shobō, 1976.
————. "Kyojūchi Soshiki no Teian." In *Fukkokuban: Koe naki Koe no Tayori,* vol. 1: *1960–1970,* ed. Koe Naki Koe no Kai, 14–15. Tokyo: Shisō no Kagakusha, 1996.
————. "Nihon Shimin Undō no Shisō." In *Jiyū to Poritiku: Shakai Kagaku no Tenkai,* by Takabatake Michitoshi, 99–128. Tokyo: Chikuma Shobō, 1976.
————. " 'Rokujūnen Anpo' no Seishinshi." In *Sengo Nihon Seishinshi,* ed. Tetsuo Najita, Maeda Ai, and Kamishima Jirō, 70–91. Tokyo: Iwanami Shoten, 1988.
————. " 'Shimin Shakai' to wa Nanika." In *Gendai Shimin Seiji Ron,* ed. Takabatake Michitoshi, 3–33. Yokohama: Seori Shobō, 2003.

Takada Akihiko. "Gendai Shimin Shakai ni okeru Shimin Undō no Henyō: Nettowākingu no Dōnyū kara 'Shimin Katsudō'—NPO e." In *Gendai Shimin Shakai to Aidentiti: 21 Seiki no Shimin Shakai to Kyōdōsei—Riron to Tenbō*, ed. Aoi Kazuo, Takahashi Akira, and Jōji Kōkichi, 160–85. Tokyo: Azusa Shuppansha, 1998.

Takagi Masayuki. *Zengakuren to Zenkyōtō*. Tokyo: Kōdansha, 1985.

Takami Yūichi. *Deru Kui ni Naru: NGO de Meshi o Kū*. Tokyo: Tsukiji Shokan, 1998.

———. "NPO no Kanōsei." In *Nihon Saiken e no Shinario: Gurōbaru Sutandādo e no Daigyakuten*, ed. Ōmae Kenichi and Isshinjuku, 154–64. Tokyo: Daiyamondosha, 1998.

Takeda Kiyoko. "Kōjō ni mita Uso to Kaigara Ningenzō." *Me* 8 (1953): 39–41.

———. "Ningenkan no Shozai." *Shisō no Kagaku* 3 (November 1946): 115–22.

Takemura Kenichi and Nettowākingu Kenkyūkai. *Nettowākingu no Kiseki: Jinmyaku o Hirogeru, Nōryoku o Hikidasu*. Tokyo: Kōbunsha, 1985.

Takeuchi Yoshimi. "Tatakai no tame no Yotsu no Jōken." *Shisō no Kagaku* 19 (July 1960): 17–19.

Tanaka Kakuei. *Nihon Rettō Kaizō Ron*. Tokyo: Nikkan Kōgyō Shimbunsha, 1972.

Tanigawa Gan. *Genten ga Sonzai suru*. Tokyo: Gendaishichōsha, 1969.

———. *Kōsakusha Sengen*. 1959; repr., Tokyo: Ushio Shuppansha, 1977.

———. "Sōkan Sengen: Sarani Fukaku Shūdan no Imi o." In Matsubara Shinichi, *Gen'ei no Kommyūn: "Sākuru Mura" o Kenshō suru*, 235–41. Fukuoka: Sōgensha, 2001.

Tanpopo no Undō o Kiroku suru Kai. *Tanpopo no Undō 16 nen no Kiroku: Hana ni nare Kaze ni nare—Nettowākingu no Kiseki*. Nara: Zaidan Hōjin Tanpopo no Ie, 1990.

"Tokushū: Watashi wa Heiwa no tame ni Nani o suru no ka—'Betonamu ni Heiwa o! Nichibei Shimin Kaigi.'" *Bungei* (October 1966): 205–305.

"Tokushū Minikomi '71: Honryū suru Chikasui." *Asahi Jyānaru* (March 26, 1971): 4–60.

Tōkyōto Kikaku Chōseikyoku Chōseibu, ed. *Hiroba to Aozora no Tōkyō Kōsō*. Tokyo: Tokyo Metropolitan Government, 1971.

Tomino Kiichirō, Terasawa Haruo, and Satō Shōichirō. *Zushi, Mitake kara no Messeiji*. Tokyo: Akebi Shobō, 1989.

Tomura Issaku. *No ni Tatsu: Watashi no Sanrizuka Tōsōshi*. Tokyo: Sanichi Shobō, 1974.

———. *Tatakai ni Ikiru: Sanrizuka Tōsō*. Tokyo: Aki Shobō, 1970.

———. *Waga Jūjika: Sanrizuka*. Tokyo: Kyōbunkan, 1974.

Tosei Chōsakai. *Daitoshi ni okeru Chiiki Seiji no Kōzō*. Tokyo: Tosei Chōsakai, 1961.

———, ed. "Chiiki Katsudō no Tebiki." In *Shiryō: Kakushin Jichitai*, ed. Shiryō: Kakushin Jichitai Kankō Iinkai, 19–25. Tokyo: Nihon Hyōronsha, 1990.

Toyota Zaidan. *Jiritsu to Kyōsei o Mezashite: "Kusa no Ne" Katsudō no Kadai to Tenbō*. Tokyo: Toyota Zaidan, 1992.

Tsujii Takashi. *Yūtopia no Shōmetsu*. Tokyo: Shūeisha, 2000.

Tsuji Kiyoaki, ed. *Shiryō—Sengo Nijūnen Shi: 1 Seiji*. Tokyo: Nihon Hyōronsha, 1966.

Tsujinaka Yutaka. "From Developmentalism to Maturity: Japan's Civil Society Organizations in Comparative Perspective." In *The State of Civil Society in Japan*, ed. Frank J. Schwartz and Susan J. Pharr, 83–115. Cambridge and New York: Cambridge University Press, 2003.

Tsuru Shigeto. "Shimin Jichi no Atarashii Dankai." *Shimin* 16 (September, 1973): 9–23.

Tsurumi Kazuko. *Korekushon: Tsurumi Kazuko Mandara II—Nihonjin no Raifu Hisutorī*. Tokyo: Fujiwara Shoten, 1998.

———. "Puragumatizumu no Rekishi Riron: Kojin Rekishisei ni tsuite." *Shisō* 320 (February 1951): 102–15.

———. " 'Sengo' no Naka no 'Shisō no Kagaku.' " In *Shisō no Kagaku Kaihō*, vol. 1, ed. Shisō no Kagaku Kenkyūkai, 9–20. Tokyo: Kashiwa Shobō, 1982.

———. "Student Movements in 1960 and 1969: Continuity and Change." In *Postwar Trends in Japan: Studies in Commemoration of Rev. Aloysius Miller, S.J.*, ed. Shunichi Takayanagi and Kimitada Miwa, 195–227. Tokyo: University of Tokyo Press, 1975.

Tsurumi Shunsuke. "Amerika Tetsugaku." In Tsurumi Shunsuke, *Tsurumi Shunsuke Shū*, vol. 1: *Amerika Tetsugaku*, 3–270. Tokyo: Chikuma Shobō, 1991.

———. "Chishikijin no Sensō Sekinin." In Tsurumi Shunsuke, *Tsurumi Shunsuke Chosakushū*, vol. 5, 9–16. Tokyo: Chikuma Shobō, 1976.

———. "Denki ni tsuite." In *Minshū no Za*, ed. Shisō no Kagaku Kenkyūkai, 3–17. Tokyo: Kawade Shinsho, 1955.

———. "Dogura Magura no Sekai." In Tsurumi Shunsuke, *Tsurumi Shunsuke Chosakushū*, vol. 4, 206–14. Tokyo: Chikuma Shobō, 1975.

———. "Gyokuchū kara mita Amerika." In Tsurumi Shunsuke, *Tsurumi Shunsuke Shū*, vol. 11, 490–99. Tokyo: Chikuma Shobō, 2000.

———. "Hitobito no Tetsugaku ni tsuite no Chūkan Hōkoku." *Shisō no Kagaku* 3, no. 2 (February 1948): 57–64; and 3, no. 3 (March 1948): 43–53.

———. "Hitotsu no Hajimari—Aruiwa, Beheiren Izen." In *Shiryō "Beheiren" Undō*, vol. 1, ed. Betonamu ni Heiwa o! Shimin Rengō, xi–xii. Tokyo: Kawade Shobō Shinsha, 1974.

———. "Kintōki ni totte Nihon wa dōiu Kuni ka." In Tsurumi Shunsuke, *Tsurumi Shunsuke Chosakushū*, vol. 5, 109–10. Tokyo: Chikuma Shobō, 1976.

———. *Kitai to Kaisō*, 2 vols. Tokyo: Shōbunsha, 1997.

———. "Kōkansen no Chikyū Hanshū," In Tsurumi Shunsuke, *Tsurumi Shunsuke Shū*, vol. 11, 499–507. Tokyo: Chikuma Shobō, 2000.

———. "Kotoba no Omamoriteki Shiyōhō ni tsuite." In Tsurumi Shunsuke, *Tsurumi Shunsuke Chosakushū*, vol. 3, 12–25. Tokyo: Chikuma Shobō, 1976.

———. "Migoto na Senryō no Owari ni." In Tsurumi Shunsuke, *Tsurumi Shunsuke Chosakushū*, vol. 5, 7–8. Tokyo: Chikuma Shobō, 1976.

———. "Naze Sākuru o Kenkyū suru ka." In *Kyōdō Kenkyū Shūdan: Sākuru no Sengo Shisōshi*, ed. Shisō no Kagaku Kenkyūkai, 7–18. Tokyo: Heibonsha, 1976.

———. "Nemoto kara no Minshushugi." *Shisō no Kagaku* 19 (July 1960): 20–27.

———. "Nihon no Shisō Hyakunen." In Tsurumi Shunsuke, *Tsurumi Shunsuke Chosakushū*, vol. 2, 363–74. Tokyo: Chikuma Shobō, 1975.

———. "Nihon Shisō no Kanōsei." In Tsurumi Shunsuke, *Tsurumi Shunsuke Chosakushū*, vol. 3, 3–11. Tokyo: Chikuma Shobō, 1975.

———. "Oikawa Setsu." In Tsurumi Shunsuke, *Tsurumi Shunsuke Chosakushū*, vol. 3, 72–75. Tokyo: Chikuma Shobō, 1976.

———. "Otto no Hito to Shisō." In Tsurumi Shunsuke, *Tsurumi Shunsuke Chosakushū*, vol. 1, 70–82. Tokyo: Chikuma Shobō, 1975.

———. "Puragumatizumu no Kōzō." In Tsurumi Shunsuke, *Tsurumi Shunsuke Chosakushū*, vol. 1, 96–106. Tokyo: Chikuma Shobō, 1975.

———. "Puragumatizumu to Nihon." In Tsurumi Shunsuke, *Tsurumi Shunsuke Chosakushū*, vol. 1, 164–77. Tokyo: Chikuma Shobō, 1975.

———. "Sengo Nihon no Shisō." In Tsurumi Shunsuke, *Tsurumi Shunsuke Chosakushū*, vol. 2, 256–90. Tokyo: Chikuma Shobō, 1975.

———. "Sengo Nihon no Shisō Jōkyō." In Tsurumi Shunsuke, *Tsurumi Shunsuke Chosakushū*, vol. 2, 291–314. Tokyo: Chikuma Shobō, 1975.

———. "Sengo no Tsugi no Jidai ga Miushinatta Mono: Kasuya Kazuki shi ni Kotaeru." In Tsurumi Shunsuke, *Tsurumi Shunsuke Shū*, vol. 9: *Hōhō toshite no Anakizumu*, 3–24. Tokyo: Chikuma Shobō, 1991.

———. "Sensōchū ni ita Basho." *Shisō no Kagaku* 8 (August 1959): 55–59.

———. "Sensō no kureta Jibiki." In Tsurumi Shunsuke, *Tsurumi Shunsuke Chosakushū*, vol. 5, 464–81. Tokyo: Chikuma Shobō, 1976.

———. "Sensō Sekinin no Mondai." In Tsurumi Shunsuke, *Tsurumi Shunsuke Chosakushū*, vol. 5, 35–44. Tokyo: Chikuma Shobō, 1976.

———. "Shiminteki Fufukujū no Kokusaiteki Rentai: 'Hansen to Henkaku ni kansuru Kokusai Kaigi' deno Hōkoku." In *Shiryō "Beheiren" Undō*, vol. 1, ed. Betonamu ni Heiwa o! Shimin Rengō, 399–407. Tokyo: Kawade Shobō Shinsha, 1974.

———. "Shisō no Hakkō Botai." In Tsurumi Shunsuke, *Tsurumi Shunsuke Chosakushū*, vol. 3, 300–310. Tokyo: Chikuma Shobō, 1976.

———. "Shōka no Tsuma—Kadota Ine no Seikatsu to Shisō." In Tsurumi Shunsuke, *Tsurumi Shunsuke Chosakushū*, vol. 3, 76–82. Tokyo: Chikuma Shobō, 1976.

———. "Taishū no Jidai." In Tsurumi Shunsuke, *Tsurumi Shunsuke Chosakushū*, vol. 3, 321–33. Tokyo: Chikuma Shobō, 1975.

———. "Techō no naka no Doitsu to Jawa." In Tsurumi Shunsuke, *Tsurumi Shunsuke Shū*, vol. 11, 507–15. Tokyo: Chikuma Shobō, 2000.

———. "Tetsugaku no Hansei." In Tsurumi Shunsuke, *Tsurumi Shunsuke Chosakushū*, vol. 1, 237–62. Tokyo: Chikuma Shobō, 1975.

———. *Tsurumi Shunsuke Chosakushū*, vol. 5. Tokyo: Chikuma Shobō, 1976.

Tsurumi Shunsuke, Ueno Chizuko, and Oguma Eiji. *Sensō ga Nokoshita Mono: Tsurumi Shunsuke ni sengo Sedai ga Kiku*. Tokyo: Shinyōsha, 2004.

Tsurumi Yoshiyuki. "Atarashii Rentai no Shisō : Kokka Kenryoku no Kanata ni." In Tsurumi Yoshiyuki, *Tsurumi Yoshiyuki Chosakushū*, vol. 2: *Beheiren*, ed. Yoshikawa Yūichi, 51–62. Tokyo: Misuzu Shobō, 2002.

———. "Atarashii Sekai to Shisō no Yōsei: Nichibei Shimin Kaigi no Imi." In Tsurumi Yoshiyuki, *Tsurumi Yoshiyuki Chosakushū*, vol. 2: *Beheiren*, ed. Yoshikawa Yūichi, 27–40. Tokyo: Misuzu Shobō, 2002.

———. "Beheiren." *Japan Quarterly* 16, no. 4 (October–December 1969): 444–48.

———. "Beikoku Nyū Refuto to no Taiwa." In Tsurumi Yoshiyuki, *Tsurumi Yoshiyuki Chosakushū*, vol. 2: *Beheiren*, ed. Yoshikawa Yūichi, 105–28. Tokyo: Misuzu Shobō, 2002.

———. "Betonamu Sensō to Nihon Tokuju Sono hoka no Mondai." In *"Beheiren Nyūsu" Gappon Shukusatsuban*, ed. Beheiren: "Betonamu ni Heiwa o!" Shimin Rengō, 16. Tokyo: self-published, 1974.

———. "Kāmaikeru: Burakku Pawā no Teishōsha." *Asahi Jyānaru* (October 20, 1968): 52–56.

———. "Nihon Kokumin toshite no Dannen: 'Kokka' no Kokufuku o Ika ni Heiwa Undō e Kesshū suru ka." In Tsurumi Yoshiyuki, *Tsurumi Yoshiyuki Chosakushū*, vol. 2: *Beheiren*, ed. Yoshikawa Yūichi, 83–98. Tokyo: Misuzu Shobō, 2002.

———. "Watashi no Sōkenron: Isshiron toshite no Shōsū Iken." In Tsurumi Yoshiyuki, *Tsurumi Yoshiyuki Chosakushū*, vol. 2: *Beheiren*, ed. Yoshikawa Yūichi, 141–43. Tokyo : Misuzu Shobō, 2002.

Tsurutani, Taketsugu. "A New Era of Japanese Politics: Tokyo's Gubernatorial Election." *Asian Survey* 12, no. 5 (1972): 429–43.

Tsuzuki Tsutomu. "Maruyama Masao ni okeru Seiji to Shimin." In *Gendai Shimin Seiji Ron*, ed. Takabatake Michitoshi, 55–86. Yokohama: Seori Shobō, 2003.

———. *Sengo Nihon no Chishikijin: Maruyama Masao to Sono Jidai*. Yokohama: Seori Shobō, 1995.

Tucker, Robert C., ed. *The Marx Engels Reader*. New York and London: W. W. Norton, 1978.

Uemura Shinsaku. *Shimin Undō no Jidai desu*. Tokyo: Daisan Shokan, 2001.

Ui Jun. "Gappon Maegaki." In *Gappon Kōgai Genron*, ed. Ui Jun, 1–16. Tokyo: Aki Shobō, 1990.

———. "Joshō: Jishu Kōza no Jūgonen." In *Kōgai Jishu Kōza 15 nen*, ed. Ui Jun, 1–84. Tokyo: Aki Shobō, 1991.

———. "Kōgai Genron I, II, and III." In *Gappon Kōgai Genron*, ed. Ui Jun. Tokyo: Aki Shobō, 1990.

———. *Kōgai Genron Hokan II: Kōgai Jūmin Undō*. Tokyo: Aki Shobō, 1974.

———, ed. *Gappon Kōgai Genron*. Tokyo: Aki Shobō, 1990.

———. *Kōgai Jishu Kōza 15 nen*. Tokyo: Aki Shobō, 1991.

Upham, Frank. *Law and Social Change in Postwar Japan*. Cambridge, MA: Harvard University Press, 1987.

Wada Haruki. " 'Haena Kigyō' to Wareware—Soni to Toyota no Minami Betonamu Shinshitsu ni Kōgi shite." In *Shiryō "Beheiren" Undō*, vol. 3, ed. Betonamu ni Heiwa o! Shimin Rengō, 163–72. Tokyo: Kawade Shobō Shinsha, 1974.

————. "Saa, Koko de Sensō Kikai o tomeyō." In *Shiryō "Beheiren" Undō*, vol. 3, ed. Betonamu ni Heiwa o! Shimin Rengō, 46–53. Tokyo: Kawade Shobō Shinsha, 1974.

Wada Susumu. "Heiwa Undō to Heiwa Ishiki." In *Gendai Nihon Shakai Ron: Sengoshi kara Genzai o Yomu 30 shō*, ed. Watanabe Osamu, 570–91. Tokyo: Rōdōjunpōsha, 1996.

Walzer, Michael. "The Civil Society Argument." In *Dimensions of Radical Democracy: Pluralism, Citizenship, Community*, ed. Chantal Mouffe. London: Verso, 1992.

Watanabe Gen. "Borantia to Shakai Henkaku." In *Shimin Katsudō no Jidai: Atarashii Watashi ga Atarashii Shakai o Tsukuru*, ed. Toyonaka Kokusai Kōryū Kyōkai, 14–24. Osaka: Toyonaka Kokusai Kōryū Kyōkai, 1995.

————. *Dokokade Nanika ga hajimatteiru!? Suimenkade Ugomeku Mōhitotsu no Shakai Keisei e no Kokoromi*. Tokyo: Toyota Zaidan, 1988.

Watanabe Katsumi. "Shomin Retsuden: Tankōfu—Toda Ichizō no Seikatsu to Shisō." *Me* 11–12 (May 1954): 2–8, 17.

White, Hayden. *Metahistory: The Historical Imagination in Nineteenth-Century Europe*. Baltimore, MD: Johns Hopkins University Press, 1973.

Yagi Kiichirō, Yamada Toshio, Senga Shigeyoshi, and Nozawa Toshiharu. *Fukken suru Shimin Shakai Ron: Atarashii Soshietaru Paradaimu*. Tokyo: Nihon Hyōronsha, 1998.

Yamagishi Hideo, ed. *Amerika no NPO: Nihon Shakai e no Messēji*. Tokyo: Daiichi Shorin, 2000.

Yamaguchi Yasushi. *Shimin Shakai Ron: Rekishiteki Isan to Shintenkai*. Tokyo: Yuhikaku, 2004.

Yamaguchi Yasushi, Takarada Zen, Shindō Eiichi, and Sumizawa Hiroki, eds. *Shimin Jiritsu no Seiji Senryaku: Korekara no Nihon o dō Kangaeruka*. Tokyo: Asahi Shimbunsha, 1992.

Yamamoto, Mari. *Grassroots Pacifism in Postwar Japan: The Rebirth of a Nation*. Oxon, U.K.: RoutledgeCurzon, 2004.

Yamamoto Osamu (aka Aki). *Nihon Seikatsu Kyōdō Kumiai Undō Shi*. Tokyo: Nihon Hyōronsha, 1982.

Yamamoto Tadashi. "Emergence of Japan's Civil Society and Its Future Challenges." In *Deciding the Public Good: Governance and Civil Society in Japan*, ed. Yamamoto Tadashi, 97–124. Tokyo: Japan Center for International Exchange, 1999.

Yamanaka Akira. *Sengo Gakusei Undō Shi*. Tokyo: Gun Shuppan, 1981.

Yamaoka Yoshinori. *Jidai ga Ugoku Toki: Shakai no Henkaku to NPO no Kanōsei*. Tokyo: Gyōsei, 1999.

————. *Kenkyū Katsudō e no Shimin Sanka to Minkan Zaidan no Yakuwari*. Tokyo: Toyota Zaidan, 1982.

————. *Shimin Katsudō no Igi to Yakuwari*. Ōmi Nettowāku Sentā Bukkuretto, no. 2. Ōtsu City: Ōmi Bunka Shinkō Zaidan, 1998.

————. *Shimin Katsudō no Taiken o Kyōyū no Zaisan ni*. Tokyo: Toyota Zaidan, 1987.

————, ed. *NPO Kiso Kōza*, vol. 2: *Shimin Katsudō no Genzai*. Tokyo: Gyōsei, 1998.

Yamauchi Naoto, ed. *NPO Dētabukku*. Tokyo: Yuhikaku, 1999.
———. *NPO no Jidai*. Osaka: Osaka Daigaku Shuppankai, 2002.
Yasōsha: "80 nendai" Henshūbu, ed. *Mō hitotsu no Nihon Chizu*. Nara: Yasōsha, 1985.
Yasuda Tsuneo. "Gendaishi ni okeru Jichi to Kōkyōsei ni kansuru Oboegaki: Yokohama Shinkamotsusen Hantai Undō no 'Keiken' o Tōshite." *Hōgaku Shinpō* 109, no. 1–2 (2002): 353–76.
Yokota Katsumi. *Oroka na Kuni no, Shinayaka Shimin*. Tokyo: Honnoki, 2002.
———. *Orutanatibu Shimin Shakai Sengen: Mōhitotsu no "Shakai" Shugi*. Tokyo: Gendai no Rironsha, 1989.
———. "Raiburīna Shōhisha Undō no Tenkai." In *Raiburī Poritikusu: Seikatsu Shutai no Atarashii Seiji Sutairu o Motomete*, ed. Shinohara Hajime, 171–88. Tokyo: Sōgō Rōdō Kenkyūjo, 1985.
Yokoyama Keiji. "Kono Wakitatsu Teikō no Nami." *Asahi Jyānaru* (April 23, 1971): 41–62.
Yonehara Ken. *Nihonteki "Kindai" e no Toi: Shisōshi toshite no Sengo Seiji*. Tokyo: Shinhyōron, 1995.
Yoshikawa Yūichi. "Demo to Parēdo to Pīsu Wōku: Iraku Hansen Undō to Kongo no Mondaiten." *Ronza* 106 (March 2004): 88–93.
———. "Shōsetsu 'Hiemono' Hihan o Keiki to suru Tōron ni tsuite: Undō e no Seisanshugiteki Hihan o yameyō." In *"Beheiren Nyūsu" Gappon Shukusatsuban*, ed. Beheiren: "Betonamu ni Heiwa o!" Shimin Rengō, 448. Tokyo: self-published, 1974.
Yoshimoto Takaaki. "Gisei no Shūen." In *Minshushugi no Shinwa*, ed. Tanigawa Gan, Yoshimoto Takaaki, Haniya Yutaka, Morimoto Kazuo, Umemoto Katsumi, and Kuroda Kenichi, 69–76. Tokyo: Gendai Shinchōsha, 1975.
———. "Nihon no Nashonarizumu." In *Yoshimoto Takaaki, Yoshimoto Takaaki Zenchosakushū*, vol. 13, 186–239. Tokyo: Keisō Shobō, 1969.
Zenkoku Borantia Katsudō Shinkō Sentā. *Borantia Katsudō Nenpō 2005 nen (Gaiyō)* (May 1, 2007). http://www3.shakyo.or.jp/cdvc/shiryo/joho1_v.asp (accessed May 4, 2007).
Zenkoku Shakai Fukushi Kyōgokai. *Borantia Katsudō o Ikusei suru tame ni: Borantia Ikusei Kihon Yōkō*. Tokyo: Zenkoku Shakai Fukushi Kyōgikai, 1973.
Zenkoku Shakai Fukushi Kyōgikai Kyūjūnen Tsūshi Hensan Iinkai. *Zenkoku Shakai Fukushi Kyōgikai Kyūjūnen Tsūshi: Jizen kara Fukushi e*. Tokyo: Zenkoku Shakai Fukushi Kyōgikai, 2003.

Index

"Abandoning Japanese Nationality"
(Nihon Kokumin toshite no Dannen)
(Tsurumi Yoshiyuki), 140–41
Actions for Peace in Vietnam, 120
activist tactics and strategies: adoption of
constructive strategies, 16, 197; direct
action, 11, 69–70; for pragmatic/local
activism, 16, 101, 102, 150, 160–61,
164–65, 243; Shizuoka Konbinato
opposition, 152, 243; violent tactics,
69–70, 158; Voices of the Voiceless
newsletter articles on, 96. *See also*
cooperation; litigation; *specific groups
and issues*
affluence, 65, 71, 171–72. *See also* daily
life *entries*; economic growth and
development; mass society; middle
stratum
agency. *See* subjectivity
The Age of Relativization (Sōtaika no Jidai)
(Sakamoto), 252–53
aging society problem, 200, 204, 205,
223–24, 249
agriculture: Daichi's pesticide
activism, 210–13. *See also* organic
farming
Alliance to Protect the Constitution,
68
Allied Occupation, 20, 48
alternative-proposal activism *(teian-gata).*
See constructive activism

Amano Masako: on Association for
Groups, 46; on Beheiren, 108, 281n14;
on Kurata, 226; on Terashima,
55, 56; on Tsurumi Shunsuke, 31,
33, 34
American Annex of the Pacific Association,
34–35
American Philosophy (Amerika
Tetsugaku) (Tsurumi Shunsuke), 33,
129
American pragmatism, in Tsurumi's
thought, 30–34, 129
Americans: Beheiren activists' encounters
with, 115–16, 125–31; Fukuzawa on
Native Americans, 133. *See also* anti-
Americanism; black activism; black
Americans; U.S. *entries*
"Anonymous Thought" (Tokumei no
Shisō) (Shimizu), 38
Anpo struggle, 20, 241*table;* antecedents,
66–68, 80; daily life conservatism in,
13, 65, 66, 105, 145; established left
in, 68, 91, 271–72n20; failure of, 9,
14, 63, 65, 70–71, 97, 98–99; groups
involved in, 68–70, 90–91; ideology,
13, 65, 241*table,* 251; key intellectuals
and their responses, 90–92, 97–98, 242;
overviews, 62–64, 66–71, 240–42;
shimin rhetoric in, 3, 14, 67, 68,
93–94. See also *specific groups and
thinkers*

346 | Index

magazines, 54, 81; advice columns, 44–45;
Tanigawa's circle magazines, 59. See
also *specific titles*
Malcolm X, 111, 132, 133, 134
Maoist thought: Hidaka's cultural circle
critique, 60–61; Terashima's interest in,
55
Mao Zedong, circle groups' study of, 49
marketization, 5, 147, 194, 214, 218, 250,
251
market relations, 18, 192, 194, 196, 197,
198, 205–6; alternative market spaces,
220, 300n95. See also capitalism; cooperation; corporate philanthropy;
monopoly capitalism
Marubeni, 144
Maruyama Masahiro, 64
Maruyama Masao, 21, 26, 35, 36, 66,
183, 248; and Anpo struggle, 68; mass
society theorizing, 74, 83–87; at 1966
Japan-U.S. peace conference, 119;
shimin thought, 82, 83–84, 87, 275n94,
276n112
Marx, Karl, 78, 247
Marxist rhetoric, Beheiren's avoidance of,
108
Marxist theory and perspectives, 34, 277–
78n135; "civil society" in, 20, 72–73,
78, 80, 239, 247–48; class-faction view
of residents' movements, 150, 159–62,
173, 192–93; cultural circles and, 13,
23, 45–46; IST and, 35, 37–38; mass
society theory and, 76–78, 180; *shimin*
in, 10, 20, 37–38, 68, 72–74, 161, 241;
structural reform theory, 181–82,
220–21. See also class; established left
Masaki Hiroshi, 171–72
Masamura Kimihiro, 234–35
mass communications: vs. minicommunications, 278n149. See also mass media
mass culture: in Katō's thought, 81–82;
seikatsu as alternative to, 220,
226–27
the masses *(taishū)*, 23, 38, 45, 48, 53, 64,
76; in Kuno, 88–89; in Maruyama,
85–86; in Tsurumi Shunsuke, 29, 32,
36
mass line *(taishū rosen)*, 49, 60
mass media: civil society terms in, 245–46,
246*fig.;* "Hitotoki" column, 51, 53; in
Katō's thought, 81–82; personal advice
columns, 44–45. See also magazines
mass society theory and debate, 13–14, 66,
71; economic growth/consumerism in,

65, 74–75; impact of urbanization,
154–55; Katō, 74, 81–83; Kuno, 88–89;
Maruyama, 74, 83–87; Matsushita,
13–14, 71, 74, 75–81, 85, 180,
273n36; *shimin* and, 13–14, 74, 80–81,
82–83, 87–90, 105, 240–42; Shimizu,
74
materialism, 13, 23–24, 78. See also consumerism; daily life *entries*
Matsubara Akira, 236
Matsushita Keiichi, 66, 279n163; and
Anpo struggle's legacies, 92, 100–101;
citizen participation advocacy, 151,
178, 181–83, 191, 277–78n135; citizens' activities discourse, 231; on civil
minimums, 187–88, 189, 191; civil
society theorizing, 17, 78, 80–81, 176,
177–78, 248; criticism of Minobe's
dialogue meetings, 187; ideological
evolution, 104–5, 191; and institutionalization of citizen participation,
189–90, 194, 243; mass society theorizing, 13–14, 71, 74, 75–81, 85, 100–
101, 180, 273n36; performative view
of citizenship, 1; pragmatic activism
advocacy, 92, 100, 104–5, 148; on
structural reform theory, 181–82; views
of residents' movements, 150, 154, 176,
177–78, 191. See also Tosei Chōsakai
Matsushita Ryūichi, 163, 171–72
Matsuura Sōzō, 75
McAdam, Doug, 7
McCarthy, John D., 7
McKean, Margaret, 157
Mead, George Herbert, 30
meaningless death, in Oda's thought,
112–14, 121–22, 123
media. See magazines; mass media; newsletters; *specific publications*
meetings of ten thousand citizens (Yoko-
hama), 182, 185–86
Meiji intellectuals and activists, 72, 133;
Tanaka, 42–43, 50, 157, 161, 171
Meiji restoration, 43, 72, 123, 134,
273n34, 286n117
Melucci, Alberto, 5
Men of Culture Discussion Group on the
Anpo Problem (Anpo Mondai Bunkajin
Kondankai), 68
MHW (Ministry of Health and Welfare),
202, 203–4
Michelangelo (Hani), 73
Michiba Chikanobu, 179, 183, 186,
290–91n40

TEXT
10/13 Sabon

DISPLAY
Sabon

COMPOSITOR
Toppan Best-set Premedia Limited

INDEXER
Thérèse Shere

PRINTER AND BINDER
Maple-Vail Book Manufacturing Group